Broadcasting, Voice, and Accountability
A Public Interest Approach to Policy, Law, and Regulation

Steve Buckley • *Kreszentia Duer*
Toby Mendel • *Seán Ó Siochrú*

with
Monroe E. Price • *Mark Raboy*

The University of Michigan Press
Ann Arbor

© 2008 The International Bank for Reconstruction and
Development/The World Bank
1818 H Street, NW
Washington, DC 20433
All rights reserved
Published in the United States of America by
The University of Michigan Press
Manufactured in the United States of America

⊗ Printed on acid-free paper

2011   2010   2009   2008   4   3   2   1

A CIP catalog record for this book is available from the British Library.

Library of Congress Cataloging-in-Publication data

Broadcasting, voice, and accountability : a public interest approach
    to policy, law, and regulation / Steve Buckley ... [et al.].
      p.   cm.
    Hardcover edition published by the World Bank, Washington, D. C.
    Papers specially commissioned by the Center for Global Communication
    Studies [CGCS] at the Annenberg School for Communication, University of
    Pennsylvania after the conference on Media, Voice, and Development, held
    at Cherkley Court in Surrey (UK) on July 12, 2006, organized by McGill
    [University] and Annenberg in partnership with the Beaverbrook
    Foundation.
      Includes bibliographical references and index.
      ISBN-13: 978-0-472-03272-3 (pbk. : alk. paper)
      ISBN-10: 0-472-03272-0 (pbk. : alk. paper)
      1. Broadcasting. 2. Freedom of speech. 3. Broadcasting policy.
    I. Buckley, Steve, 1960 Jan. 24–

    HE8689.4.B753   2007
    384.54—dc22   2007039149

Foreword

The World Bank has long recognized the role that media play in development. It has done so through advocating the importance of an independent press; providing training for journalists; and offering technical and financial assistance to commercial media organizations through its private sector arm, the International Finance Corporation (IFC). At present, there is an intention to broaden the focus to include broadcast media. With this guide the World Bank Institute seeks to support the development of an independent and diverse broadcasting sector that can contribute to the public interest.

Of paramount importance is the policy, legal, and regulatory framework that influences the shape, content, and social impacts of the broadcasting sector as a whole. This is the subject matter of the current guide. It includes not only protection of basic freedoms of expression, but also issues such as the structure and functioning of regulatory bodies, management of the radio-frequency spectrum, and licensing requirements that enable broadcasting diversity. Good practices from a wide range of countries are included. The enabling environment for broadcasting has significant consequences for governance and accountability: It can enable people in the developing world to become informed and empowered, or not.

Radio broadcasting can be very accessible, even for illiterate and semiliterate people in remote locations. It can influence people's understanding of their context, interests, and view of themselves. In the many places where listening to the radio is a group activity, its content easily provokes comments and discussion. Often issues that previously could not be discussed become permissible as people refer to what they have heard. The social impacts can be pervasive and profound.

Broadcasting also provides platforms for publicly airing concerns, raising questions with experts on the air, and solving problems. Community radio programs, for example, often involve the whole listening audience in discussing matters important to them, in their local languages. This in turn strengthens people's ability and confidence in framing and analyzing issues, engaging in informed debate, and pressing local officials for actions. This process helps people to identify and grasp opportunities, address collective problems, and resist manipulation. It also strengthens people's resolve to make their government accountable and strengthens their outspokenness against abuses. From Ghana to Indonesia, groups have gone "on the air" and named officials who have stolen public funds or not delivered a long-promised road—and they have seen an active response. Such public condemnation makes officials change their calculus of their prerogatives and their responsibilities.

Broadcasting is a potent vehicle for scaling up and embedding civic engagement in the life of poor constituencies in developing countries—and in the expectations of government officials.

Freedom of information and expression and a robust mix of broadcasting ownership and uses—commonly referred to as commercial, public service, and community broadcasting—are critically important to develop and sustain an informed, engaged society. With this book, we show that improving the enabling environment for the broadcasting sector is important development terrain, where country-specific analysis and assistance are long overdue.

Rakesh Nangia
Acting Vice President, World Bank Institute, 2001–2007

Acknowledgments

Broadcasting, Voice, and Accountability: A Public Interest Approach to Policy, Law, and Regulation has been under discussion and development since 2003. It is an outgrowth of the World Bank Institute's program supporting Civic Engagement, Empowerment, and Respect for Diversity (CEERD), including Voice and Media Development. Over time, it has also benefited from collaboration with experts in fields of governance and accountability in developing countries, development communications, and telecommunications policy. Government officials and nongovernmental stakeholders have used iterative drafts to support their analyses of broadcasting policy and regulation in a number of developing countries and to inform their reform proposals.

In the first instance, the project received financial support from the Office of the World Bank President, James D. Wolfensohn (1995–2005). Since then, it has received grants from the World Bank–Netherlands Partnership Program, the Canadian International Development Agency (CIDA), and the Beaverbrook Foundation.

Kreszentia Duer, New Business Development Leader at the World Bank Institute and manager of the CEERD Program, initiated the guide project in an effort to promote the integration of media and broadcasting policy into the development field. From the outset the guide has been structured to present good practices from around the world in a coherent policy landscape that could significantly improve governance, communications access, and opportunities for disadvantaged peoples. To this end, Duer formed and led the team; shaped the guide's relevance to development issues, policy, and practice; and guided the project to completion. At several stages she invited peer reviews to ensure that the guide would reflect a collective perspective of senior specialists in diverse parts of the World Bank and among a broad range of international experts.

Steve Buckley, President of the World Association of Community Radio Broadcasters, and Toby Mendel, Law Programme Director of Article 19, built on extensive work they and others have done in the field to research and write much of the substance of Parts II and III of this guide. Without their efforts, and Steve Buckley's commitment to this project from the outset, the guide would not have been possible. Seán Ó Siochrú, founder of and spokesperson for the Campaign for Communication Rights in the Information Society and a Director of NEXUS Research, heroically produced the final edited version of the text, with considerable new material in Part I. Craig Hammer (CEERD Program, The World Bank) authored the guide's bibliographical annex and greatly facilitated the publication of this guide.

The project's expert advisers, Professors Monroe E. Price (Director of the Center for Global Communication Studies [CGCS] at the Annenberg School for Communication, University of Pennsylvania) and Marc Raboy (Beaverbrook Chair in Ethics, Media and Communications at McGill University), came on board in April 2006. The Bank contracted CGCS to act as consultant in bringing the project to fruition. Susan Abbott, Senior Research Coordinator at CGCS, was indispensable in steering the consultancy process. The project also gained valuable assistance from Sylvie Beauvais and Libby Morgan at the CGCS. The advice and consultation provided by the Annenberg School and McGill provided the World Bank Institute (WBI) and the guide's authors with creative input and critical reflection necessary to bring the guide to completion.

This guide benefited greatly from four stages of internal and external peer reviews and roundtable discussions. These occurred, first, at the early stages of conception; second, at a conference to review the full manuscript at Cherkley Court in the United Kingdom, which was followed by submission of expert papers from participants; third, at the World Bank's formal peer review and decision meeting on the economic and sector work manuscript; and fourth, at the external peer review requested by the publisher. We would like to acknowledge those involved, as follows.

Peer reviewers from within and outside the World Bank contributed thoughtful and helpful comments at the very early stages of the guide's conception. Our thanks go to Tim Carrington (Senior Communications Officer, Africa Region, The World Bank), Linn Hammergren (Senior Public Sector Management Specialist, Poverty Reduction and Economic Management, The World Bank), Gary Reid (Lead Public Sector Management Specialist, Poverty Reduction and Economic Management, The World Bank), Rick Stapenhurst (Senior Public Sector Management Specialist, Poverty Reduction and Economic Management Division, The World Bank Institute), William Ascher (Donald C. McKenna Professor of Government and Economics, Claremont McKenna College), Peter Erichs (Development Cooperation

Program Officer, Media and Culture Division, Swedish International Development Cooperation Agency), Damien Loreti (Professor of Social Sciences, the University of Buenos Aires), Tunde Oladunjoye Fagbhunlu (Barrister and Executive Director, Center for Media Education and Networking, Nigeria), Gloria Sánchez (Consultant, France), Somkiat Tangkitvanich (Research Director, Thailand Development Research Institute), Giles Tanner (General Manager, Australian Broadcasting Authority), Sahr Kpundeh (Senior Public Sector Specialist, The World Bank Institute), Rick Messick (Senior Public Sector Reform Specialist, Public Sector Reform and Governance Department, The World Bank), and Guenter Heidenhof (Lead Public Sector Specialist, Africa Public Sector Reform and Capacity, The World Bank). Thanks also to Loty Salazar (Information Officer, Operations Solutions, The World Bank) and Isabelle Bleas (Senior Operations Officer, Sector and Thematic Programs, The World Bank Institute) for their support.

A key moment in structuring and deepening the manuscript was the conference on Media, Voice and Development held at Cherkley Court in Surrey (UK) on July 12, 2006. Organized by McGill and Annenberg in partnership with the Beaverbrook Foundation, this conference brought together twenty international experts to discuss and provide feedback on a preliminary version of the guide. We thank the Beaverbrook Foundation for generously hosting the conference, as well as Dean Christopher Manfredi (McGill Faculty of Arts) and Camilla Leigh (McGill Development Office) for their support. In addition, we thank the following people for their contributions at the workshop: Mavic Cabrera-Balleza (Senior Program Associate, International Women's Tribune Centre); Peter de Costa (Consultant, London); Stuti Khemani (Economist, Development Research Group, World Bank); Elizabeth McCall (Civil Society and Access to Information Policy Adviser, Oslo Governance Centre, United Nations Development Programme); Lumko Mtimde (Chief Executive Officer, Media Diversity and Development Agency of South Africa); Jamal Eddine Naji (UNESCO Chair in Public and Community Communication, Institut, Supérieur de l'information et dela Communication, Morocco); Paikiasothy Saravanamuttu (Executive Director, the Center for Policy Alternatives, Sri Lanka); Diana Senghor (Director, the Panos Institute of West Africa); James Deane (Head, Policy Development, BBC World Service Trust and former Managing Director of the Communication for Social Change Consortium); and Karin Wahl-Jorgensen (Senior Lecturer, Journalism Studies, Cardiff University).

Based on the feedback received at the Cherkley conference, CGCS commissioned a number of focused papers on a range of topics from academic specialists, policy experts, and nongovernmental organizations active in the sphere of media and development. Their contributions have informed the guide and improved it immeasurably. In addition, we would like to thank the following for their advice, input, and recommendations: Dieter Zinnbauer, Lumko Mtimde, Damian Loreti, Stefaan Verhulst, Elizabeth McCall, Pippa Norris, Birgitte Jallov, Alfonso Gumucio Dagron, Mavic Cabrera-Balleza, Sally Burch, Ammu Joseph, Kandji Katira, Jamal Eddine Naji, Tarlach McGonagle, Kate Coyer, Mark Whitehouse, Drusilla Meneker, Ivan Sigal, Diane Senghor and her team at Panos West Africa, Patrick Butler, Luis Botello and ICFJ, Karin Wilkins, Jan Servaes and Folker Hanusch, Arne Hintz and Stefania Milan, Paul Falzone and Antonio Lambino, David Page and William Crawley, Sawsan Zaidah, Uwe Hasebrink, Nick Couldry, and Ruth Teer-Tomaselli (UNESCO Chair in Communication for Southern Africa, Culture, Communication and Media Studies, University of KwaZulu-Natal). Gustavo Gomez (Legal Director, AMARC Latin America) also provides invaluable insights on the community broadcasting section of the manuscript, which were reflected in subsequent drafts.

With the benefit of their input, the authors revised the manuscript and prepared it for the World Bank's formal peer review in Washington, DC, on January 29, 2007. The peer review process was thorough and engaged and marked a watershed as the first time senior specialists from all key departments in the World Bank collaborated to shape how the Bank should approach media and broadcasting policy reform as a mainstream development issue. This enabled the publication to reflect a collective perspective. In addition to the book's authors and advisers, the following people attended the meeting and deserve special thanks for their thoughtful comments: Michele de Nevers, Chair (Director, Sector and Thematic Programs, The World Bank Institute), Stuti Khemani, Gareth Locksley (Senior Telecommunications Specialist, Policy Division, IBRD Telecommunications and Information, The World Bank), Adesinaola Odugbemi and Paolo Mefalopulos (Senior Communications Officers, Development Communication, the World Bank), Rick Messick, and Mark Nelson (Senior Operations Officer, Sector and Thematic Programs, The World Bank Institute). Michele de Nevers provided excellent stewardship of this peer review process. The written comments of the forenamed reviewers, as well as those of Roumeen Islam

(Manager, Poverty Reduction and Economic Management, The World Bank Institute), Sahr Kpundeh, and Guenter Heidenhof, were of great assistance in shaping the final manuscript.

Finally, the publisher commissioned an external peer review of the approved manuscript that resulted from the World Bank's internal peer review. Our special thanks go to the two formal external peer reviewers of the final manuscript, Professor Ruth Teer-Tomaselli and James Deane. These two reviewers authorized the Press to reveal their identities after the reviews were completed in order to provide further feedback. Their helpful comments and critical reflections were invaluable. The guide's publication team would also like to thank Bruce Girard (Founder, Agencia Informativa Púlsar and former Researcher at the Delft University of Technology) for his reviews and contributions to the final manuscript.

We would also like to note our appreciation to the University of Michigan Press, in particular, Phil Pochoda (Director, University of Michigan Press) and Alison Mackeen (Acquiring Editor, University of Michigan Press), for their collaboration and their interest in publishing this guide with the World Bank and including it in the series The New Media World. The publication of this book by The World Bank and the University of Michigan Press enables us to reach both the broad international development community and expert-practitioners in the communications field, who will be important in helping to interpret and shape media policy as a significant development concern.

Contents

Introduction

In the foothills of the Himalayas, 100 kilometers north of the birthplace of the Buddha, is the Nepali village of Madanpokhara. It is a long walk from the nearest road. A dirt track winds up the hillside and into the village, passing homes and small outbuildings, temples and teahouses, workshops and stores. Beyond the village center a narrow path leads through the woods to the hilltop, where a white brick building sits close to a tall red mast. This is the home of Radio Madanpokhara. Inside is a simple radio studio, powered by solar batteries and a backup generator. A team of local producers, broadcasting in Nepali and other local languages, mobilize community participation in programming that is informative and educational as well as entertaining. Radio Madanpokhara broadcasts across a rural agricultural community in which few people have access to electricity or a telephone. Yet almost every household now has a radio receiver, and the radio, with its network of listener clubs and district correspondents, has become the principal means of local communication and discussion of local development. According to an independent listener survey,[1] Radio Madanpokhara, on the air since April 2000, contributes to improved agricultural techniques and a reduction in social discrimination, raises awareness of the rights of women, and improves access to news and information. It is also a voice for peace, dialogue, and democracy in the face of conflict and political turmoil.

Radio Madanpokhara is just one of thousands of broadcast services worldwide whose contribution to development is both measurable and significant and whose emergence has been a product of political reform

---

[1]Guragain, *Prospects for Promoting Equality, Development and Social Justice through FM Radio* (Kathmandu: MS Nepal—Danish Association for International Co-operation, 2005).

and of democratic social change. This guide, *Broadcasting, Voice, and Accountability: A Public Interest Approach to Policy, Law, and Regulation*, was written to illuminate the issues and their impact on civic society such as this. The growth of media, giving a voice to excluded people in most countries and in all regions of the world, and the media's emerging influence in the global struggle against poverty and social injustice, stimulated the production of this guide. A free, independent, and pluralistic media environment, offering the means and incentives for the widest participation, can have a profound influence on people's opportunities to access information and services, to understand and be able to exercise their rights, to participate in decisions that affect their lives, and to hold to account those in positions of power and responsibility. This is reflected in a growing recognition, in the context of international development, of the central importance of effective and inclusive communications systems.

The broadcast media, radio and television, have a unique and particular role to play both in enhancing governance and accountability and in giving voice to poor and marginalized communities. In addition to traditional means of expression, "voice" in this context means the capacity, opportunity, and resources of diverse segments of society to signal government as to their needs and their perception of the quality of governance, to have their views represented in mainstream media, and to develop their own media. Broadcast media, as we argue later, are especially relevant and accessible to remote communities, cultural and linguistic minorities, the very poor and illiterate people. Policies, laws, regulations, and other public actions that govern the broadcast media are central to their ability to play that role, and they form the main focus of this guide.

The guide maps out a public interest approach to fostering free, independent, and pluralistic broadcast media. Its objective is to provide guidance on how to design a policy, legal, and regulatory framework that can contribute to the achievement of public interest goals such as transparency of government and accountability to the people, enhanced quality of and participation in public debate, and increased opportunities for marginalized groups to develop and articulate their views. The guide draws from the experiences of a wide range of countries in all regions of the world and is illustrated extensively by country-level examples of policies, laws, and regulations.

The guide is intended as a tool for media reform particularly in developing and transitional democracies. At the same time, it should be useful anywhere people aspire to a deeper democracy. Building democracy is a process, often long-term, and promoting free, pluralistic, and independent media should be a central part of it. It should not be left until after the legal system has been transformed or democratic attitudes are in place; rather, it should be part and parcel of efforts to reform the social and institutional system and to build democracy in all of its aspects. As such, while the guide may not be immediately applicable in dictatorships or war zones,[2] it can help inform strategies in countries—such as those in transition or recovering from conflict—where democratic foundations are being set in place.

The guide adopts a normative approach—it is about good practice—but two further observations should be made concerning its application. The first is that the media and communications environment is dynamic, almost everywhere undergoing rapid change. The second is that vast disparities exist not only in the state of media development but also in the pace of change, and these disparities exist both between countries and between different groups of people within countries. Thus the tools themselves do not and cannot offer a "one-size-fits-all" solution and must be regularly reviewed to respond to a changing environment.

Part I offers an overview of the rationale for a public interest approach and its role in enhancing governance, development, and "voice." The focus on broadcasting is explained and justified on the basis of its reach and its enduring importance in people's lives. The different broadcasting sectors are described, along with their main trends and characteristics. Part I then turns to a regional review of broadcasting characteristics and trends and concludes by summarizing the evidence for an emerging paradigm in broadcasting policy and regulation.

The good practice guidelines are set out in Parts II and III. These are not designed to be read end-to-end but to be consulted selectively for issues of interest. To facilitate this navigation, good practices are organized under clear headings that identify and describe features of the policy, legal, and regulatory environment that are critically important for media development in the public interest. While recognizing that reform necessarily involves social, political, and institutional processes of change that take time and require adaptation to

---

[2]For further discussion on this point see Putzel and van der Zwan, *Why Templates for Media Development Do Not Work in Crisis States* (London: Crisis States Research Centre, LSE, 2005).

local circumstances and interests, these topics provide a framework that can help guide evaluations of the status quo and provide options for reforms.

Part II examines the general enabling environment for media and communications, including standards of freedom of expression and access to information, the use and misuse of defamation law, and general content rules that apply to all media, including print media and journalists.

Part III is dedicated specifically to broadcasting, including the role of regulatory bodies, broadcast content rules, the distinctive sectors commonly referred to as public service, community nonprofit, and commercial private sector broadcasting, as well as the regulation of broadcast spectrum and channels.

After short introductions to Part II and to Part III, each chapter is prefaced by a good practice checklist. The elements of good practice are elaborated and explained in the narrative and supported by country examples that illustrate their implementation. These chapters form the core of this guide and offer a tool kit for those involved in analysis, advocacy, and policy making for media and communications reform.

The final section of the guide presents a research agenda that is intended to address the lack of relevant and systematic data and information on broadcasting encountered during the process of researching and compiling this guide. It concludes by presenting some options and practical opportunities for development assistance to support a more coherent approach to reforming broadcasting in the public interest.

PART I

Governance, Broadcasting, and Development

1 Governance, Development, and Media

The primary purpose of this guide is to describe an enabling environment for a public interest approach to media, and specifically broadcasting. Special attention is devoted to how media can enhance accountability in governance and contribute to development and *voice*, particularly for those who are disadvantaged in society.

This chapter defines a public interest approach to media and describes its relationship to governance, accountability, and development. It explores how such an approach can contribute to good governance, to development, and to wider social and cultural goals. It presents some of the key media characteristics underpinning the public interest approach, as well as a reflection on the wider environmental factors that are conducive to this, and a final comment on the normative underpinnings of the guide.

In the Public Interest

The concept of *the public interest* in the media stretches back at least to the origins of radio broadcasting in the early twentieth century, with various usages coming into and falling out of favor. An official report produced in Canada, a country still intensely concerned with the public interest in broadcasting policy, quotes several sources to underline the difficulty of defining the public interest:

> The idea of the public interest in media is not new. It changes over time and when viewed from different perspectives. Defining it is thus not straightforward.

In broadcasting, a wide array of definitions of the public interest have been used, ranging from this classic 1960 statement from CBS executive Frank Stanton: "A program in which a large part of the audience is interested is by that very fact. . . in the public interest" (cited in Friendly, p. 291),[1] to this rather more elaborate example from Australian regulator Gareth Grainger: "The public interest is that interest which governments, parliaments and administrators in democratically governed nations at least must accept and reflect in laws, policies, decisions and actions in ensuring peace, order, stability, security of person, property, environment and human rights for the overall welfare of the society and nation who, through constitution and election, allow the individual citizen to renew and reflect their agreement and consent to be governed and administered" (1999 Spry Memorial Lecture, p. 9). Grainger then goes on: "After eighty years of broadcasting, the original public interest issues which were seen to be implicit in the use of the broadcasting spectrum remain largely unchanged though our way of expressing them may require some restatement." (p. 43)[2]

Thus, ensuring that media can sustain a primary focus on serving the public interest is by no means straightforward; governments and broadcasters have been grappling with it for decades. For, excepting only the most totalitarian states, the space of the media—the technological mediation of communication between people—is occupied by competing sets of interests, none of which unambiguously pursues the widest public interest but each of which at times lays claim to it.

> In the context of competing interests of different stakeholders, a public interest approach aims to ensure that the welfare of the public as a whole is kept to the fore in the formulation and implementation of legal policy, and regulatory environment for the media.

In broad terms, governments and political parties, private commercial entities, and groups in civil society each relate to media in different ways, seeing opportunities and threats to their own objectives. Media institutions themselves, no matter how large or small, inevitably

---

[1]Fred. W. Friendly, *Due to Circumstances Beyond Our Control* (New York: Random House, 1967), 291.

[2]*Our Cultural Sovereignty. The Second Century of Canadian Broadcasting* (Canada, House of Commons, Standing Committee on Canadian Heritage Report, 2003), 518, available at: *http://friends.ca/News/Friends_News/archives/articles06110311.asp* [source cited for Spry Memorial Lecture, available at: *http://www.fas.umontreal.ca*].

generate internal and external dynamics and interests of their own. Each of society's stakeholders has different general objectives and is endowed with different types and levels of resources. Left to their own devices, the media landscape can meet many public objectives but not, perhaps, the ones most critical to a society at a particular time. In addition to the general ongoing need for an informed public, special circumstances can arise surrounding conflict, economic development, moments of democratic crisis, and growth. Each of these provides justifications for policy and regulation in the wider public interest.

The goal of regulation in the public interest and of a specifically public interest approach to media is to tread a path that mediates among these interests, encouraging and offering incentives and, where necessary, imposing obligations and constraints on each group, while evading capture by any specific interests. There is some irony in the fact that those necessarily charged with the primary role of pursuing a public interest approach to media—governments—are also among those with the strongest incentive to skew it toward their own ends. Even with the best of intentions, success in negotiating this balancing act is not at all certain. Given what is at stake for society, however, attempts to get it right merit very considerable effort.

Feintuck attempts to gain an overview of a public interest approach and its associated values,[3] and to "define a theoretical and institutional framework both for a meaningful discourse regarding these values and for consideration of policies which are effective in asserting." He identifies a recurring theme among all sectors:

> The common thread underlying the public interest claims in relation to media regulation can best be described as feeding into the broader constitutional endeavour of effective citizen participation. *Effective participation can be equated with informed participation, and this in turn requires a diverse range of views to be in circulation and accessible to as wide a range of the population as possible in order to allow for comparison and triangulation.*[4] (emphasis added)

---

[3]Mike Feintuck and Mike Varney, *Media Regulation, Public Interest and the Law*, 2nd ed. (Edinburgh University Press, 2006), 6.
[4]Mike Feintuck, "Regulating the Media Revolution: In Search of the Public Interest" *JILT* (1997): 3.

The guide builds on this notion of effective citizenship as central to a public interest approach to media. We deploy the concept explicitly to mark the capacity of media to enhance social, economic, and political development through improving governance and accountability to the public; building an informed and engaged citizenry; enhancing the inclusion of marginalized groups; and fostering a culture and identity of tolerance, diversity, and creativity.

The need to revisit and reevaluate the concept of the public interest in broadcasting to suit the present circumstances and needs is a theme of this guide. Drawing on our working definition presented earlier, we focus in on the potential of the media in two broad areas: First, we look at the contribution that media can make to good governance and accountability to the people, and its more indirect relationship to the development process. Second, beyond governance, we consider the tradition and practice of the deployment of media directly toward development objectives, as well as the growing influence that media have in broader cultural evolution and change.

> The public interest approach to media as deployed here focuses especially on its potential contribution to governance, to development, and to culture and identity.

The public interest cannot be treated as a static, unambiguous concept, even as the notion of *the public* evolves, as media themselves change sometimes with great speed, and the development needs and circumstances of society change. But these key facets of a public interest approach to media—its potential impact on governance, on development, and on culture—are enduring.

Media and Governance

Enhancing the prospects for good governance in a development context has become a key goal for governments, nongovernment actors, and international organizations in recent years. Although the use of the term *governance* may vary, there is general agreement that it extends beyond the operations of governments to embrace a broad range of social institutions and necessarily includes consideration of citizens and citizenship. Before embarking on a quest to understand the relationship between media and these desiderata, it is worth pausing to consider the concept of "good governance" itself.

The World Bank defines governance as:

> . . . the traditions and institutions by which authority in a country is exercised for the common good. This includes (i) the process by which those in authority are selected, monitored and replaced, (ii) the capacity of the government to effectively manage its resources and implement sound policies, and (iii) the respect of citizens and the state for the institutions that govern economic and social interactions among them.[5]

The United Nations Development Program (UNDP) emphasizes the articulation of people's interests:

> Governance is the system of values, policies and institutions by which a society manages its economic, political and social affairs through interactions within and among the state, civil society and private sector. It is the way a society organizes itself to make and implement decisions—achieving mutual understanding, agreement and action. It comprises the mechanisms and processes for citizens and groups to articulate their interests, mediate their differences and exercise their legal rights and obligations . . . [6]

> Good governance is about both outcomes and processes that are participatory, transparent, accountable, and efficient and encompass all major groups in society.

Good governance, according to UNDP, is about processes as well as outcomes; processes that are participatory, transparent, accountable, and efficient, and that involve the private sector and civil society as well as the state.[7] Good governance is also important for development, and considerable empirical evidence now points in that direction.

A study by Kaufmann[8] demonstrates not only a high degree of correlation between six governance indicators[9] and widely used

---

[5]World Bank, *Governance Matters 2007*, at *http://info.worldbank.org/governance/wgi2007/*.
[6]UNDP Strategy Note on Governance for Human Development, 2004.
[7]UNDP, *Management & Governance Network (MAGNET)* (UNDP, 1998).
[8]D. Kaufmann, *Governance Redux: The Empirical Challenge* (Washington, DC: World Bank Institute, 2003).
[9]These are: voice and external accountability, political stability and lack of violence, government effectiveness, lack of regulatory burden, rule of law, and control of corruption.

development indicators, such as per capita income,[10] but also that there is a positive causal effect of good governance on development outcomes. The study argues that poor public governance "has become a central binding constraint to growth and development today in many settings" and concludes:

> . . . a country that significantly improves key governance dimensions such as the rule of law, corruption, the regulatory regime, and voice and democratic accountability can expect in the long run a dramatic increase on its per capita incomes and in other social dimensions.[11]

Data presented suggest that growth dividends may be as high as 400 percent for a single standard deviation improvement in governance, a highly significant result.[12]

> The evidence is that good governance also contributes significantly to development.

It thus comes as no surprise that the potential role of the media in improving governance and accountability has become an area of interest to the international development community.

That media can in a general sense promote good governance is not a new idea. Amartya Sen, the Nobel Prize winning economist, has argued consistently and forcefully since the early 1980s that no substantial famine has ever occurred in any independent country with a democratic form of government and a relatively free press.[13] In an article published to mark World Press Freedom Day 2004, Sen draws on his famine research in India:

> The Bengal famine of 1943, which I witnessed as a child, was made viable not only by the lack of democracy in colonial India, but also by severe restrictions on the Indian press, which isolated even the Parliament in Britain from the misery in British India. The disaster received serious attention only after Ian Stephens, the courageous editor of the *Statesman* of

---

[10]Kaufmann, 12, table 2, available at: *http://www.worldbank.org/wbi/governance/pdf/ govredux.pdf/*.

[11]Ibid., 25.

[12]Ibid., 26.

[13]See, for example, Amartya Sen, *Poverty and Famines: An Essay on Entitlement and Deprivation* (Oxford: Clarendon Press, 1981) and Amartya Sen, *Development as Freedom* (New York: Anchor Books, 2000).

Calcutta (then British owned) decided to break ranks by publishing graphic accounts and stinging editorials on October
14 and 16, 1943. This was immediately followed by stirs in the
governing circles in British India and by heated Parliamentary discussions in Westminster. This, in turn, was followed
by the beginning—at long last—of public relief arrangements. The famine ended then, but by this time it had already
killed millions.[14]

Both UNDP and the World Bank include media among the institutions and mechanisms that can contribute to good governance, in the
above definitions and elsewhere. Media can fulfill several critical
tasks in the context of governance and reform, overlapping with and
reinforcing other factors such as access to information and freedom of
expression. Pippa Norris, when director of the UNDP's Democratic
Governance Group, summed up three key roles for the media in contributing to democratization and good governance: as a *watchdog over
the powerful*, promoting accountability, transparency and public
scrutiny; as a *civic forum* for political debate, facilitating informed
electoral choices and actions; and as an *agenda-setter* for policy makers, strengthening government responsiveness for instance to social
problems and to exclusion.[15]

Media can achieve such an impact, in the right circumstance,
through their direct and indirect influence on a number of key parameters of governance: curbing corruption and improving accountability and transparency, enhancing informed participation in the
political processes, and facilitating and reinforcing more equitable
and inclusive policies and actions.

Though there has been little systematic evaluation, a wealth of individual cases point to the role of the media in exposing corruption,
recognized as a key constraint to development.

In Peru, investigations critical of then-president Alberto Fujimori
were first brought to light by the print media. Investigations exposed

---

[14]Amartya Sen, "What's the Point of Press Freedom?" (Paris: World Association of Newspapers, 2004).
[15]Pippa Norris, *A Virtuous Circle* (Cambridge: Cambridge University Press, 2000). Cited in
Pippa Norris, *The Role of the Free Press in Promoting Democratisation, Good Governance and
Human Development* (paper delivered at UNESCO World Press Freedom Day conference
in Colombo, Sri Lanka, May 1–2, 2006), 4.

a pattern of wrongdoing and corruption involving death squads, the military, and links between drug barons and political elites. These were followed, spectacularly, in 2000, by the broadcast over cable television of videos secretly taped by Peru's head of security, showing votes being bought with bribes. Fujimori resigned immediately after the broadcast.[16] In Sierra Leone, the series *Mr. Owl*, reporting on local police corruption, was carried on private radio stations KISS-FM, in Bo, and SKY-FM, in Freetown.[17] The coverage resulted in wage increases for the police and the establishment of a police community affairs department. The transparency of Ghana's 2000 election results was due in part to the efforts of the country's many private radio stations. Staff monitored the polls, and their reports of irregularities, alongside those of citizens, were broadcast, making it difficult to rig voting and enhancing the credibility of the results.[18] In Bangladesh, since the restoration of democracy in 1991, the media have played a central role in exposing corruption in the financial and banking system, in building permissions granted by corrupt officials, in widespread arsenic contamination, and in numerous other areas.[19]

> Examples abound of media exposing corruption and vote rigging . . .

The issue is also one of accountability. Media enhance the accountability of government and other powerful actors through uncovering and publicizing the chain of logic, decisions, and events that lead to specific outcomes, especially outcomes that run counter to the public interest. The identification of those responsible and the processes involved inherently increases accountability, and the anticipation of such identification can contribute to more responsible decision making and a positive outcome for the public interest.

> . . . improving accountability by opening decision making to view and identifying those involved . . .

[16]UNDP, *Human Development Report 2002: Deepening Democracy in a Fragmented World*, 76.
[17]See *Sierra Leone: Using radio to fight corruption*, available at: *http://www .developingradiopartners.org/caseStudies/sierraLeone.html.*
[18]UNDP, *Human Development Report 2002: Deepening Democracy in a Fragmented World*, 76.
[19]Mahfuz Anam, "The Media and Development in Bangladesh," Ch. 15 in *The Right to Tell: The Role of Mass Media in Economic Development* (WBI Development Series, 2002).

> . . . allowing people to articulate dissatisfaction and thereby enhance public services.

Transparency, however, has pervasive consequences. As Nobel Laureate and former chief economist at the World Bank Joseph Stiglitz argues, "openness is an essential part of public governance."[20] Using Hirschman's argument on "exit" and "voice"[21] he makes the point that governments benefit when citizens exercise voice. Especially where people cannot signal dissatisfaction through exit (unlike in competitive goods markets, the government holds a monopoly in public services), it is through informed discussion and interaction on the policies being pursued—voice—that dissatisfaction can be articulated and effective governance exercised. Full transparency is critical to this. Furthermore, information asymmetries in government and between it and the public lead to inefficiencies and poor management decisions.

Transparency, Stiglitz notes, depends on a number of factors, such as freedom of information legislation and public information institutions "designed to ferret out information for the benefit of the public . . . The press is among the most important of these informational institutions."[22]

Apart from their role in public accountability and transparency, the media can also play a critical part in the democratic processes at the heart of good governance. One of the outcomes of this is "agenda setting" in the form of strengthening government responsiveness, but it goes well beyond it. Media can provide the means by which people can speak out and participate in political debate, creating a crucial space in which public deliberation on matters of concern can take place. This provides opportunities for people to articulate their concerns and ideas to one another and to government, a role that is particularly important for poor and marginalized groups. Media thus has the potential to foster a "civic forum" or, as described by philosopher and sociologist Jürgen Habermas, a "public sphere": "a network for communicating information and points of view"[23] in which issues affecting the society and community can be explored openly and rigorously and "filtered and synthesized in such a way that they coalesce into . . . public opinions."[24]

---

[20]Joseph Stiglitz, "Transparency in Government," Ch. 2 in *The Right to Tell: The Role of Mass Media in Economic Development* (WBI Development Series, 2002), 31.
[21]A. O. Hirschman, *Exit, Voice and Loyalty: Responses Top Decline in Firms Organisations, and States* (Cambridge, MA: Harvard University Press, 1970).
[22]Stiglitz, 40.
[23]Jürgen Habermas, *Between Facts and Norms* (Cambridge, MA: MIT Press, 1996), 360.
[24]Ibid.

Thus media have the potential not simply to influence government agendas, but to reinforce the overall capacity of society to constitute political discussion and debate, and to enhance the participation of people, including marginalized groups, in the process of governance. This impact may occur in small ways—the radio stations in Sierra Leone mentioned earlier carried a voter education series called *Democracy Now* that resulted in higher voter turnout in their listening areas than in other parts of the country.[25] But over time and in the right circumstances, the media can also help to build the practices and culture of democracy and good governance within society as a whole.

Media beyond Governance

Beyond governance, media are implicated in several dynamics that can combine and intersect to reinforce development and overall social well-being in different ways. Particularly relevant is the role of media in the long tradition of communication for development, and the growing influence that media have in value formation, and cultural evolution and change.

Media have long been regarded by those in the field of communication for development as tools that can be deployed to promote developmental change, but they were for the most part considered independently of media policy and regulation processes. Thinking about how media can be used, and to what specific ends, has nevertheless shifted significantly over the years. In the early days, many in the field understood media mainly as a top-down tool for the dissemination of information. The challenge was to convey development "messages" on diverse subjects such as health awareness, disease prevention, agricultural practice, water management, or environmental responsibility. Recently, the emphasis has shifted to the empowering potential of media as a bottom-up means for promoting participation in society and political life, especially in marginalized communities.

> Media are also tools for development, and can be used to empower marginalized groups through bottom-up participation.

---

[25]See *Sierra Leone: Using radio to fight corruption*, available at: *http://www .developingradiopartners.org/caseStudies/sierraLeone.html.*

From this perspective citizens require not only access to information but also the ability to consult, respond, and engage with leaders and opinion makers—to have *voice*. Citizens need access to the means of communication and voice in order, also, to be able to speak with one another, to discuss their conditions and aspirations, and to develop the capacity for engagement and for action to improve access to services and rights under the law. The approach values local knowledge, it respects local cultures, and it puts people in control of the means and content of communication processes.[26]

The groundbreaking study *Voices of the Poor*[27] set out to listen to poor people's own voices on the experience of poverty. It took as its starting point a recognition that poor people's own views have rarely been part of the policy debate. The study noted that poor men and women are acutely aware of not having their voices heard, of their lack of information, and of their lack of contacts to access information. The study reports how poor people across the world discuss how this puts them at a disadvantage in dealings with public agencies, nongovernmental organizations (NGOs), employers, and traders. The results of the study have informed new thinking on empowerment and participatory approaches precisely by showing how inclusion, access to voice, and access to information can promote social cohesion and trust, enable informed citizen action, and improve the effectiveness of development.[28]

Communication for social change is a process of public and private dialogue through which people determine who they are, what they need, and what they want in order to improve their lives. It has at its heart the assumption that affected people understand their realities better than any "experts" from outside their society and that they can become the drivers of their own change.[29]

Evidence of the effectiveness of these approaches comes primarily from qualitative analysis, including ethnographic studies,

---

[26]Alfonso Gumucio-Dagron, *Roots and Relevance: Introduction to the CFSC Anthology*, in Alfonso Gumucio-Dagron and T. Tufte, eds., *Communication for Social Change Anthology: Historical and Contemporary Readings* (New Jersey: Communication for Social Change Consortium, 2006).

[27]Deepa Narayan, Robert Chambers, Meera Kaul Shah, and Patti Petesch, *Voices of the Poor: Crying Out for Change* (New York: World Bank/Oxford University Press, 2000).

[28]Deepa Narayan, *Empowerment and Poverty Reduction: A Sourcebook* (Washington, DC: World Bank, 2000).

[29]Ibid.

participatory evaluation, and other research methods that are conducive to more process-oriented than output-oriented approaches. A number of studies in the field have drawn particular attention to the role that local and community-based media can play in empowering and enabling the participation of people and communities facing exclusion and marginalization. The Rockefeller Foundation report *Making Waves: Stories of Participatory Communication for Social Change*[30] compiled 50 case studies and draws extensively on stories of community radio and television projects to provide a vivid account of people and communities appropriating media as means of empowerment, self-reliance, and mobilization for development and social change. It provides a wealth of evidence of the positive impact of community-based media on people's real lives. The report concludes that the communication for social change model has two critical implications for participation in development that are related to issues of power and of identity:

> Case studies show that participatory approaches to media can empower communities by strengthening internal democratic processes and, especially for marginalized groups, can enhance self-esteem, protect cultural values, and facilitate the integration of new elements.

An issue of power. The democratization of communication cuts through the issue of power. Participatory approaches contribute to putting decision making into the hands of the people. It also consolidates the capability of communities to confront their own ideas about development with development planners and technical staff. Within the community itself, it favors the strengthening of an internal democratic process.

An issue of identity. Especially in communities that have been marginalized, repressed, or simply neglected for decades, participatory communication contributes to . . . cultural pride and self-esteem. It reinforces the social tissue through the strengthening of local and indigenous forms of organization. It protects tradition and cultural values, while facilitating the integration of new elements.

---

[30] Alfonso Gumucio-Dagron, *Making Waves: Stories of Participatory Communication for Social Change* (New York: Rockefeller Foundation, 2001).

A second area of particular relevance is the increasingly important role that media play in the development and evolution of cultural forms, identity, and diversity. Beyond the idea of disseminating information, entertainment, or even education, media's deeper cultural role has been the subject of considerable interest and study. A high-level European Commission report concluded:

> The role of the media goes much further than simply providing information about events and issues in our societies or allowing citizens and groups to present their arguments and points of view: communication media also play a formative role in society. That is, they are largely responsible for forming (not just informing) the concepts, belief systems and even the languages—visual and symbolic as well as verbal—which citizens use to make sense of and interpret the world in which they live. Consequently, the role of communication media extends to influencing who we think we are and where we believe we fit in (or not) in our world: in other words, the media also play a major role in forming our cultural identity.[31]

The impact on the individual of extensive viewing of television may even exceed that of his or her immediate context. A leading international expert on the effects of television, George Gerbner, argued that heavy media consumers begin to articulate a view of the world directly derived from that of the media, even if the media world to which they are exposed is somewhat removed from the realities of their own daily lives.[32]

> Beyond the individual, media can influence shared beliefs and the group identity of society, and whether it will be, for instance, open, tolerant and creative.

The influence of the media does not remain only, or even primarily, at the level of the individual. Communications scholar James Carey points to the "ritual" effect of

---

[31]European Commission, *Report from the High Level Group on Audiovisual Policy*, chaired by Commissioner Marcelino Oreja (Brussels: European Commission, 1998) 4–5.

[32]George Gerbner, "Living with Television: The Dynamics of the Culturation Process," in J. Bryant and D. Zillman, eds., *Perspectives on Media Effects* (Hillside, NJ: Lawrence Erlbaum, 1986), 17–40.

the media's ability to sustain beliefs and relationships among those it reaches. In his view:

> . . . communication is linked to such terms as sharing, participation, association, fellowship and the possession of a common faith . . . A ritual view is not directed towards the extension of messages in space, but the maintenance of society in time; not the act of imparting information but the representation of shared beliefs.[33]

Such shared beliefs are central to the nature of culture in a given society, whether it is open and tolerant, and whether it encourages creativity and diversity. In developing countries, a role for media has sometimes been articulated as that of "nation building," creating a common sense of identity, and contributing to a consensus on the type of nation that is being strived after. A cultural frame emphasizes also the contribution of diversity and a commitment to pluralism[34] and to ensuring that all cultures are respected equally and are represented in media. Such an approach is particularly relevant to media in countries with large communities of marginalized groups and indigenous peoples and where traditional structures and belief systems are undergoing rapid change and evolution.

Key Features of Communication and Media

A public interest approach to media policy focuses on strengthening media's contribution to good governance and accountability, to participatory communication for development, and to cultural pluralism and social agency. These policy objectives can reinforce each other. Enhanced accountability and governance can help engender an environment for more participatory media, and thus give voice to marginalized

> Reaping the benefits of a public interest approach to media requires, at least, the presence of a number of key features of the media environment.

---

[33]James W. Carey, "A Cultural Approach to Communication," in J. W. Carey, *Communication as Culture. Essays on Media and Society* (Boston: Unwin Hyman, 1989), 18.

[34]The Report of the World Commission on Culture and Development, *Our Creative Diversity* (UNESCO 1995) puts forward the notion of "cultural freedom" as the "right of a group of people to follow or adopt a way of life of their choice. . . the condition for individual freedom to flourish," 25–26.

communities. Greater voice in turn enables a more informed and active citizenry, thereby enriching the governance process. Cultural tolerance and pluralism are reinforced by a commitment to diversity of media content, and informed participation encourages more equitable and inclusive policies.

Yet a positive relationship between media, governance, and development is by no means inevitable. Beneficial impacts can be realized only with the presence, at least in significant part, of a distinct set of media characteristics set within a supportive enabling environment, including, but not limited to, polices, laws, and regulations. Among the most important of these are, at a general level: freedom of expression and ready access to information and, relating more specifically to media, independence from vested interests; a wide diversity of media ownership and content; a broad reach within society; and a sustainable resource base. This guide expands upon this essentially simple theme.

Respect for the right to freedom of expression in society is fundamental to the capacity of media to deliver on governance and development, and a free press is a touchstone of democracy and good governance. With good reason: constraints on investigating and reporting on matters of public interest can severely compromise almost every aspect of media performance and impede its ability to sustain and promote good governance.

> First key feature: Respect for the right to freedom of expression is a primary need.

Freedom does not, however, imply absolute license. Every country imposes some limitations on what may be published or broadcast. It is nowhere considered legitimate to spread malicious lies attacking someone's reputation, and most countries ban incitement to hatred, for example, on the basis of race or ethnic origin. An appropriate balance between the various competing rights and interests is vital to protecting media freedom, and unduly restrictive laws can seriously inhibit the ability of the media to service the public interest.

Second, ready and timely access to information of public interest, from both public and private sources, is critical to the effective operation of media in relation to its various roles in governance.

> Second key feature: Ready and timely access to information of public interest is essential.

Accountability of those in power relies heavily on being able to source and retrieve information concerning decision-making processes; but efficiency of public decision making is enhanced when the basis of such decisions is open to public scrutiny and debate. Information flows through media can also improve resource allocation and are invaluable to the efficient operation of markets.[35]

Third, there is often a mix of media and media types in society (and this is increasingly the case), with various media performing various functions. As a whole, media must be independent, able to pursue their activities free from undue influence of special interest groups. Media function best when this variety is in full blossom: public service, commercial,

> Third key feature: Media independence is vital.

community, and others. Where media are wholly controlled by government or by powerful commercial interests, their overall capacity to contribute to a democratic political space is compromised.

The absence of media independence has a predictable impact on the media's ability to deliver accountability: at a minimum, the watchdog role fails in relation to the controlling owner. When the controlling owner is the government, the implications will by definition be serious. Too close a relationship to government will also pose serious problems in terms of the ability of the media to facilitate participation and to contribute to the empowerment of citizens. Participation depends on the ability to ventilate criticism of government publicly through the media, and this will without doubt be impeded by government control. When media are controlled by an oligarchy of private players the result may well be similar. Although some owners do not interfere editorially, ownership always implies a degree of actual or potential control and can be an important obstacle to pluralism and diversity. A common way to tackle this is to introduce measures to limit concentration of ownership.

Fourth, media content must reflect, even enhance and stimulate, the diversity of views in society. Media diversity

> Fourth key feature: Media must reflect and enhance the full diversity of views in society.

---

[35]World Bank, *World Development Report 2002: Building Institutions for Markets* (2002), 189.

requires a wide range of content that serves the needs and interests of different audiences and purposes. Media content should address the interests not only of urban elites, but also of the urban and rural poor, minorities, and other marginalized groups. It should reflect the different cultures, belief systems, and aspirations of minorities as well as majorities and do so in a nonpartisan manner.

Similarly, promoting accountability is premised on the idea of a media sector that, as a whole, focuses on the full spectrum of issues of public concern, including coverage of a wide range of views and of actors, not just officials but also other powerful social actors.

Fifth, effective media must achieve broad reach into society, being available and accessible to all economic, social, and cultural groups and over the widest territorial area. Factors that differentially affect the reach of various media can include high rates of illiteracy, a multiplicity of languages and numerous indigenous peoples, remoteness from urban areas, difficulty of terrain, poor transport and telecommunication networks, the cost of media equipment, including receiver sets, and the absence of electricity. Ensuring diverse media are accessible to those on the margins, socially, culturally, economically, and geographically, can be a major challenge but is nevertheless essential if the entire population, or very close to it, is to be included and given voice.

> Fifth key feature: All groups in society must be physically able to access and use the media.

Finally, a sustainable resource base is critical to effective media. An adequate and sustainable financial base is vital to fulfilling many of the media's functions, such as the more resource intensive activities of investigative reporting and current affairs.

> Finally, a sustainable economic and institutional base is required.

Some sources of funding carry inherent risks: the possibility of withholding public funding gives leverage to governments to influence media; whereas advertisers may use their ability to switch to other outlets to gain more favorable coverage. Insufficient resources exacerbate dependence on funding sources, whether public or private, and increase the risk of partisan influence or of external or self-censorship. Media in developing countries, with limited access to investment and revenues, can find it especially difficult to balance the needs of economic viability, independence, and diversity.

Sustainability, however, goes beyond economic considerations to include social and institutional dimensions.[36] Social sustainability refers to relations between a broadcaster and the community or audience it serves, including its credibility in the eyes of that community. The consequences of a loss of audience support on a commercial broadcaster can be directly measurable in terms of revenue. Public service and community broadcasters have specific obligations to the communities or audiences they serve, and their loss of social support, measured in audience share or public attitudes, can seriously impact on their sustainability, including their ability to justify access to public funding and other resources.

Institutional sustainability refers to the structural relations that drive the operation of a broadcaster. Transparent and effective governance of a public broadcaster, for example, is central to its credibility and its ongoing ability to operate. For community broadcasters, participation by and accountability to their community are important conditions of success. Similarly, commercial broadcasters also need efficient and effective management structures to achieve their business objectives.

The Wider Environment

These key features are enmeshed in broader processes of political and institutional development. Laws and related policies can be the equivalent of wallpaper—decorative but hardly a reliable indicator of what is actually happening beneath the surface. In too many states media policies are affirmed in an expansive moment but implementation does not live up to the stated aspirations.

> The wider environment is also important to engendering conditions conducive to a public interest approach to media.

A key factor is a culture of respect for, and general adherence to, the rule of law. This requires an effective judiciary. Without an enforcing arm to maintain the protections of the law, attempts to implement a positive legal and regulatory environment could even prove to be futile.

---

[36]Alfonso Gumicio-Dagron, *The Lucky Cloverleaf: Four Facets of Communication for Development and Sustainable Social Change* (commissioned for this study), 15–17.

The rule of law embraces a number of principles, including the existence of a developed hierarchical framework of laws with the constitution at the pinnacle, broad respect for these laws and their application in a nondiscriminatory manner, a separation of executive functions and judicial functions, and respect for and action on judicial decisions.

> The absence of the rule of law can render media legislation and policy irrelevant.

Many examples illustrate how the absence of the rule of law can thwart the achievement of public interest goals in the media environment. A study in 2000 by the International Bar Association, for example, highlighted serious problems with judicial independence in Malaysia in political cases, in contrast to good respect for the rule of law in business cases.[37] As a result, laws on defamation and sedition, along with regulatory controls over the media, were abused to silence criticism of government and to prevent the exposure of corruption and other wrongdoing.

In Zimbabwe, the supreme court has struck down laws restricting freedom of expression as unconstitutional on a number of occasions, breaking a government monopoly on providing telecommunications services,[38] striking down a prohibition on publishing false news,[39] and ruling out the government broadcasting monopoly.[40] In some cases, for instance the ending of its broadcasting monopoly, the government has simply refused to implement those decisions.

The absence of the rule of law thus greatly increases the risk of regulatory failure, irrespective of the quality of the regulatory regime, by potentially undermining its independence and thwarting

---

[37]See *Justice in Jeopardy: Malaysia in 2000* (London: Human Rights Institute, International Bar Association, 2000), available at: *http://archive.ibanet.org/general/Find Documents.asp.*

[38]*Retrofit (Pvt) Ltd v. Posts and Telecommunications Corporation and Anor*, 4 LRC (1996): 513.

[39]*Chavunduka and Choto v. Minister of Home Affairs and Attorney-General*, Judgment No. S.C. 36/2000 (May 22, 2000).

[40]*Capital Radio (Pvt) Ltd v. Minister of Information, Posts and Telecommunications*, 22 Judgment No. S.C. 99/2000 (September 2000).

its actions. Furthermore, a legal system that allows corruption, once exposed by the media, to continue with impunity greatly limits the extent to which such media can effect change.

A number of other factors are also important to a healthy media, including associated institutional support. Robust and effective professional associations can significantly reinforce media efforts to remain independent and enable the emergence of effective self-regulatory institutions to complement government regulation with media codes and standards. Trade unions can strengthen the hand of journalists and other media workers in producing unbiased, high quality content and defend the practice of impartial journalism against sectional interests. Training organizations can build the capacity and professionalism of media workers. A formal press is hollow in the absence of creative talent, disposed toward exercising its skills, and the means to educate and train them to a high standard.

The absence of material needs for a free press, including such basics as newsprint or the availability of broadcast channels of distribution, can have a serious effect on society as a whole. In the case of newspapers and magazines, creating a fair and open system of newsstands and other means of delivery is essential. Media monitoring and market research organizations can facilitate the growth of advertising. And government can create appropriate incentives through tax policies, incentives, and other means.

> The capacity to satisfy material needs, such as newsprint, the availability of distribution channels and outlets, and effective advertising markets, is important.

Finally, the impact of good quality media policy and law depends ultimately on how well such laws and policies are implemented in practice, and this guide principally focuses on legal and policy frameworks rather than on the role of government, judiciary, civil society, and other actors in ensuring effective implementation. Such a focus on implementation, however, is critical and should be a major concern for users of this guide.

All of these factors matter, and governments can take measures to establish or reinforce them. In Parts II and III reference is made to these at appropriate places.

Normative Underpinnings and an Emerging International Consensus

> The values that underlie the approach of this guide include:

This guide focuses on the relationship between broadcasting and the public interest. It is specifically concerned with how policy frameworks can most effectively enable media to hold authorities to account in the public interest, provide fora for informed and inclusive public debate, and help underpin effective governance. In short, it is focused on the relationship between broadcasting and society.

This guide takes an analytical approach to these issues, seeking to enable policy makers and other users to adapt the analyses and examples highlighted here to their own specific contexts. However, as its title suggests, the authors adopt normative perspectives, and it

> . . . the critical role of the media in democratic practices . . .

might be useful to explicitly articulate the underlying values. Much of the guidance provided is rooted in international law and acknowledged—and sometimes codified—good practice, but some of it emerges

from the authors' own experience and assessment, and that experience itself is rooted in a set of specific values.

First, the guide argues for and is located within a framework of democratic governance, where the role of the media is a critical part of the checks and balances that enable democratic systems to function in the interests of their people. This approach argues that democracy can be neither effective nor sustainable without a vibrant media capable of acting in the public interest.

> . . . a human rights framework . . .

Second, it is located within a framework of human rights, where the rights of the individual are fundamental not simply because they are useful to society (e.g., in providing a check on government), but because they are inherently valuable and worth upholding.

> . . . in lieu of policy prescriptions, an array of norms, standards, and experiences that can be adapted to different situations.

Third, it argues that the systems of government that regulate the role of the media within a society will and should be adapted to the contexts of such a society, and that this guide is not designed to provide a universal set of policy prescriptions. Instead, it provides a set of examples, norms, and standards that make up a public interest approach to media policy and regulation and that can be applied and adapted in various contexts.

Fourth, the authors acknowledge that much of the debate on the role of the media in governance is not principally technical, but political, in nature. It is focused on who in society can have their voices heard in public and political debate, and who can exert communicative power in society. People living in poverty face huge challenges in

> The idea that communication is a right that does not stop at freedom of expression also emerged during the 1970s and early 1980s and resonates today.

having their voices heard and the authors believe that building effective public interest media is a critical component in enabling democratic and peaceful development that advances the interests of people living in poverty.

Many concerns regarding media raised in this guide are long standing, and the history of debate on them has not always been a happy one. Although this guide focuses on national level policy and regulatory frameworks, debate at a national level is influenced, both historically and currently, by debate at an international level. Issues of excessive government influence; of media acting for narrow commercial—rather than the public—interest; of concentration of media ownership; of lack of diversity and plurality of media; of lack of reach or content of media related to people living in poverty: all these and others highlighted in this guide have a long history of debate and argument, much of it highly polarized.

Even relatively recent history has seen very different approaches to understanding the effects of media on development processes. As broadcast media went through a wave of internationalization during the 1960s and 1970s, various disputes and differences emerged, sometimes from significantly different value perspectives. The issue of direct satellite broadcasting of signals across borders became a major issue in the late 1960s and early 1970s, and provoked cultural, commercial, and political concerns among many developing countries, though the consequence was the virtually open skies of today. The most heated debate occurred in the late 1970s and early 1980s and concerned what was called the New World Information and Communication Order (NWICO);

it resulted in a special commission being established by UNESCO to consider global problems relating to communication.[41]

Many in the developing world, and elsewhere, believed that building a post-colonial world required a reconsideration of global dynamics and structures—even global governance of communication—to ensure, among other matters, "more justice, more equity, more reciprocity in information exchange . . .".[42] Proponents of market solutions, including major commercial media interests and the U.S. government, virulently opposed many of the regulatory implications of NWICO, arguing that they violated basic free speech interests. Distorted by the politics of the cold war, genuine debate was reduced to rancorous argument, and the bitter aftertaste continues even today. So intense was the feeling, that the United States and the United Kingdom withdrew from UNESCO over the issues (and only recently have returned).

One strand in this debate, in some respects an attempt to bridge the gap between the sides, focused on the idea of communication as a right. Initially raised in the early 1970s, the argument is that in the context of the massive growth in modes and technologies of communication, a right to communicate should be established to deepen freedom of expression and lead to more intensive, respectful, and interactive dialogue between people and groups in society. More recently, the idea of a right to communicate—or, less formally, of communication rights—had some influence on media debates at the World Summit on the Information Society.[43]

Several factors suggest that international debates over the role of media in development can become more constructive than they have in the past. The cold war is over and international power dynamics are more complex and multifaceted as a result. Democracy is more firmly rooted in many countries than it was in the 1980s, and the

---

[41]*International Commission for the Study of Communication Problems* delivered its report *Many Voices, One World,* to, and was endorsed by, the 1980 UNESCO General Assembly.
[42]Preface to the *Many Voices, One World,* President of the Commission, Sean MacBride (UNESCO, Paris, 1980), xviii.
[43]Rainer Kuhlen, "Why Are Communication Rights So Controversial?" In Heinrich Böll Foundation, ed., *Visions in process. World Summit on the Information Society* Geneva 2003–Tunis 2005 (2004). Also in *World Association for Christian Communication (WACC) publications 2004/3,* available at: *http://wacc.dev.visionwt.com/wacc/our_work/thinking/communication_rights/why_are_communication_rights_so_controversial.*

importance of media in development is more universally acknowledged than it has been in the past. Perhaps above all, nearly all actors (at least outside of government) argue that freedom of expression is a fundamental and nonnegotiable foundation stone for all debate in this area, and that much of the debate on public interest approaches to media must focus on enabling people living in poverty to realize and exercise their rights to freedom of expression, rights that are impossible to exercise without the creation of platforms through which they can communicate.[44]

---

[44]A meeting held at the Rockefeller Foundation's Bellagio Centre in 2003 brought together a group of media actors with highly diverse views and backgrounds to assess the degree of consensus on issues regarding media freedom and poverty. The resultant statement suggests agreement on many key issues. See Bellagio Statement on Media, Freedom and Poverty, available at: *http://www.panos.org.uk/global/Rprojectdetails.asp?ProjectID= 1033&ID= 1002&RProjectID=1058.*

2 | Broadcasting Sectors and Types

Although much of the good practice discussed in Part II of this guide is relevant to all media, the overall focus of the guide is primarily on the traditional broadcast media (i.e., radio and television). In an era in which ever more attention, not least in the media, is devoted to new media, including the multiple forms generated by the Internet, and in which the print media continue to confound premature predictions of their demise, this deserves an explanation. The rationale is both substantive and practical.

Factors that influenced the decision to limit the scope of the guide in this way are outlined in this chapter and serve as an introduction to the subsequent sections in which the main types of broadcasting and their dynamics and interrelationships are described.

A Focus on Broadcasting

Broadcasting retains a position of enormous influence over social, cultural, and political life in nearly all parts of the world for a number of reasons.

Table 2.1 compares Internet and telephone access with television (including home satellite) and radio.

This guide focuses on broadcasting because . . .

. . . radio and television are the media with the greatest reach, especially among poor people . . .

Although it might reasonably be concluded that high income people can obtain much of their information and media over the Internet, this is certainly not the case in lower and lower middle income groups. Here radio and television (only a small proportion watch home satellite) are the primary media outlets. Given that communal viewing and listening

TABLE 2.1 Total per 100 Population of: Internet Subscribers; Telephony Subscribers; Television Sets; TV Home Satellite as a % of Total Televisions; and Radio Sets

	Internet: 2004	Phones (Fixed + Mobile): 2004	Television Sets: Latest Figures	% TVs with Home Satellite: Latest Figures	Radio Sets: Latest Figures
Low income	2	7	8	3	16
Lower middle income	8	44	32	12	37
Upper middle income	16	69	37	9	48
High income	53	131	74	22	74

Source: ITU *World Telecommunication Development Report* 2006, Table 1, 19. (Radio figures calculated by weighting the *radios per 100 population* by population.)

are far more common in poor countries than in wealthy ones, the actual proportion of the population that consumes radio and television is likely to be considerably higher than the proportion that owns a set. Furthermore, radio and television coverage in 2002 (i.e., the population living in areas that can receive a signal) was 96 percent and 83 percent respectively.[1]

Directly comparable figures for print media and Internet are unavailable. However, Table 2.2 suggests that, with a few exceptions, especially in countries in transition, newspaper circulation is well below the figures for radio.

A recent comprehensive survey of television in twenty European countries, all but four being transition countries, concluded the following:[2]

> . . . broadcasting retains a lead over newspapers in terms of circulation . . .

. . . despite the rapid expansion of the Internet, television has maintained its massive appeal to viewers worldwide. Over the past ten years, television-watching has been on the rise, and in 2003 the average viewing time in Europe was more than three hours a day

> . . . television viewing is rising, and is the main, and most influential, source of information in many regions. . . .

---

[1]ITU, *World Telecommunication Development Report* (Geneva, 2003).
[2]The countries included were: Albania, Bosnia & Herzegovina, Bulgaria, Croatia, Czech Republic, Estonia, France, Germany, Hungary, Italy, Latvia, Lithuania, Poland, Republic of Macedonia, Romania, Serbia, Slovakia, Slovenia, Turkey, and United Kingdom. Viewing data was unavailable for the first two.

TABLE 2.2 Newspaper circulation per 100 population (most recent figures) *World Press Trends*, WAN, 2004

Countries in Transition		Latin America	
Bulgaria	47	Ecuador	14
Ukraine	27	Costa Rica	11
Slovenia	21	El Salvador	6
Estonia	20	Argentina	6
Czech Republic	19	Brazil	5
Latvia	18	Dominican Republic	4
Hungary	18	Colombia	4
Serbia-Montenegro	16	Uruguay	1
Croatia	14	**Asia**	
Belarus	13	Malaysia	18
Poland	13	China	9
Slovakia	12	Pakistan	8
Macedonia	10	India	4
Romania	7	Sri Lanka	4
Bosnia & Herzegovina	3	Indonesia	3
Sub-Saharan Africa		Mongolia	2
South Africa	4	**North Africa**	
Zambia	1	Egypt	4
Uganda	0.6	Tunisia	3
Tanzania	0.3	Morocco	2

Figures are rounded to nearest unit.

. . . the average viewing time for adults increased. . . in CEE [Central and Eastern Europe] from 208 minutes in 2000 to 228 minutes in 2003.[3]

> . . . radio in Africa remains the most important of all media, especially in rural areas where most people live . . .

Furthermore, "although in some countries overall trust in the media has declined in recent years, all country reports in this research confirm that television is still the main source of information for the population . . ."[4] and is "widely considered to be the most influential medium in forming public opinion."[5]

A study covering twenty countries in Africa found that, in contrast to transition countries:

> radio dominates the mass media spectrum . . . Television is less widely available, especially in rural areas. Newspapers remain concentrated in urban centres with varying growth patterns across the countries. In the new media sectors, the

[3]Open Society Institute, *Television across Europe: Regulation, Policy and Independence,* vol. 1, (2005), 39.
[4]Ibid., 40.
[5]Ibid., 21.

adoption of mobile telephony has been the most spectacular, far exceeding uptake of the Internet.[6]

The dominance of broadcasting is not surprising: Broadcasting—particularly radio broadcasting—is low cost, easy to use, and readily accessible.

It is also the case that broadcasts do not privilege the literate. This accessibility is a considerable asset, given that adult illiteracy is 38 percent in low-income countries, where 37 percent of the world's population live, and of course the incidence is much higher among the poorest in these countries.[7] Further, broadcasting can most easily speak to marginalized cultural groups in their own languages.

Radio is particularly accessible in financial terms. A cheap radio receiver today costs only two or three dollars and, for many of the world's poorest people, it is the only source of news and information

> . . . radio does not privilege the literate, and is low cost, easy to use, and readily accessible.

beyond word-of-mouth communication. It does not require electricity, or even batteries in the case of wind-up models. Significantly, in terms of its potential for widespread small-scale use, and the potential for community participation, a radio station can be established for as little as US$1,000 and has very low running costs.

Where broadcasting is not only informative but also participatory, it can help to build capacities that contribute to a healthy governance environment, cultivating collaborative leadership capabilities, self-confidence, and collective engagement. The audience, including those who are otherwise marginalized and without voice, can contribute to setting the agenda, express themselves, influence their community or society, and call for government action. A critical mass of such programming promotes an effective two-way flow of information between the government and the people that serves not only to promote better-designed policies and more-effective implementation of projects but also to highlight flawed development initiatives, wrongdoing, or government policies or programs that can harm the poor.

> Where broadcasting is participative, it can promote the two-way flow of information between people and government, and can be a building block for deliberative democracy.

---

[6]African Media Development Initiative (AMDI), Research Summary Report (BBC World Service Trust, 2006), 13.

[7]World Bank, *World Development Report 2007: Development and the Next Generation* (2007), table 1.

Community-based and some public service broadcasters, in particular, tend to be highly participatory and to encourage immediate feedback and discussion over the airwaves. They can enable communities to develop and sustain the knowledge, aptitude, and critical-thinking skills for the broad-based citizen engagement that is fundamental for participatory development. As such, they are a building block for a culture of deliberative democracy.

In short, the vigor and reach of the broadcasting sector are particularly important in the context of developing countries, where the bulk of the population may be illiterate or semiliterate, and where large numbers of people may be isolated from news, information, and public discourse.[8] Newspapers are often accessible only to the educated elite and available only in large towns and cities. The Internet, even when available, lacks the capacity and flexibility of broadcasting, especially radio, to accommodate cultural and linguistic diversity.[9]

Overall, broadcasting retains a central role in social, cultural, and political life, especially in those sections of the world and among those communities that can benefit most from enhanced governance and development.

In practical terms, some unique features of broadcasting, as compared to other media, have influenced the decision to focus on broadcasting.

However, a practical consideration also influences the scope of this guide. For a variety of reasons, including the use of radio spectrum, which is a scarce public resource, and the distinctive characteristics of broadcasting (what have been described as its pervasiveness, invasiveness, publicness and influence),[10] the nature and form of broadcast media regulation are distinct and differ significantly from those of print media and the Internet. Although there is undoubtedly a need for a good practice guide to the enabling environment for other media, the unique impact and scope of broadcasting and its distinctive policy and regulatory characteristics and requirements merit a dedicated guide.

---

[8]See, for example, World Bank *World Development Report 2000/2001: Attacking Poverty* (2000), 4.

[9]See, for example, Carter Eltzroth and Charles Kenny, *Broadcasting and Development: Options for the World Bank* (World Bank Group, October 2003), 3–4.

[10]Damien Tambini and Stefaan Verhulst, "The Transition to Digital and Content Regulation," in D. Tambini, ed., *Communication Reform* (London: Institute for Public Policy Research, 2000).

Basic Broadcasting Types

Broadcasting, both radio and television, can be defined across a range of overlapping models of ownership and control, from state-controlled to public service broadcasters, to private commercial ownership at global to local levels, to nonprofit and community ownership. Each is governed by different dynamics and embodies a different set of interests, but the configuration in any given country is the result generally of a unique, sometimes lengthy and complex, historical evolution. No two regimes are identical and the concept of an "ideal" model of broadcasting fails when confronted with the diversity of different national contexts. No single size fits all.

Even twenty-five years ago, national broadcasting systems could be classified according to the prevailing political systems in each of the countries concerned. Most European countries had a single monopoly broadcaster—although operating according to very different sets of principles in the West (public service) and in the East (state control). In Africa and most of Asia, too, national broadcasting was strictly government owned and operated. At the other extreme, the American free enterprise model of broadcasting was operational in most of the Americas (with notable exceptions). The number of countries with "mixed" systems was small,

> Unlike even a few decades ago, there now exists a wide variety of broadcasting models in terms of ownership and control.

and included the United Kingdom, Japan, Australia, Canada, and Finland. Where it existed, community broadcasting was a strictly local, marginalized phenomenon with few links to the mainstream. Global television barely existed.[11]

Since then the broadcasting world has changed utterly, as professor of ethics, media, and communication Marc Raboy has written, marked by three sets of parallel developments:

1. The explosion in channel capacity and disappearance of audiovisual and telecommunication borders made possible by new technologies and digital convergence;

---

[11]Marc Raboy, "The World Situation of Public Service Broadcasting: Overview and Analysis," Ch. 1, *Public Service Broadcasting: Cultural and Educational Dimensions* (UNESCO, 1997).

> Several factors have broken down the regionally distinctive models of the past, including the growth in channel capacity, the elimination in effect of borders, and the decline of the state-controlled model coupled with the growth of the market model.

2. The disintegration of the state-controlled broadcasting model with the collapse of the socialist bloc and the move toward democratization in various parts of the world; and

3. The upsurge in market-based broadcasting and the introduction of mixed broadcasting systems in the countries with former public service monopolies.

Far from being distinct from one another, these phenomena are in a complex interrelationship with respect to the emergence of new forms of broadcasting, locally, nationally, and internationally. The outcome is a far more variegated system of broadcasting, and one that is still in a dynamic process of change driven by global forces of market development, technological change, and the forging of a globalized culture. Thus a typology of national models of broadcasting today has to make room for a larger number of variants and combinations.

Four basic types of broadcasting (some with subtypes) coexist in different variations and combinations in any given country; broadcasters directly controlled by government, public service broadcasters, commercial broadcasters, and community broadcasters.

> Four basic models of broadcasting now exist, but in various combinations in any given country.

The following brief overview describes the dynamics of each.

Government Control of Broadcasting

Direct monopoly government ownership and control of broadcasting continues to exist in a number of developing countries, such as Belarus, Zimbabwe, Turkmenistan, China, and Myanmar (Burma). However, it is now widely agreed that a state monopoly on broadcasting can seriously compromise the potential for broadcasters to serve as a reliable source of impartial information and diverse perspectives, and to play a positive role in governance and development.[12] Even in a nonmonopoly

---

[12]World Bank, *World Development Report 2002: Building Institution for Markets* (2002), 183–188.

situation, direct state control is always open to potential government manipulation. The reliability of news and information on government-controlled broadcasters is often in doubt since they have a particular point of view and interest to protect. The lack of trust in government-controlled news and information can result in a cynical, rather than an engaged, public.

Although the government's control over content may purport to be a means of ensuring it serves development priorities, it does not empower citizens or promote effective and equitable participation, or accountability. As a result, benefits of broad-based participation—such as improved policy design and implementation, and greater ownership over development initiatives—are unlikely to be realized. For the same reasons, inequities or ineffective-

> Direct control of broadcasting is widely considered to be against the public interest, biased toward the government view, lacking in participation, and inhibiting both development and democracy. This model is thus given no further consideration here.

ness in development will rarely be identified or resolved, particularly when these result from specific government biases, as opposed to oversights. Even more seriously handicapped when they are subject to government control is broadcasters' ability to promote democracy and good governance, to expose corruption, and to hold leaders to account.

For these reasons, this guide is not aimed at those governments seeking to maintain ownership and control of broadcasting, and this particular model will not be considered further as this is a guide to good practice. There is, however, a growing impetus in many countries across several regions to transform hitherto government-controlled broadcasters into public service broadcasters (see the following).

Public Service Broadcasting

Public service broadcasters, at their best, are independent of government and commercial interests and are dedicated solely to serving the public interest. In most cases they remain in some form of public ownership but operate under a statute that explicitly confirms their editorial independence

> Public service broadcasting must be independent of government and commercial interests, aiming solely to serve the public interest.

from the government of the day and establishes governance arrangements that are intended to assure it. In Western Europe, until the emergence of commercial broadcasting in the last third of the twentieth century, monopoly public broadcasting was the predominant broadcasting model. The principle of ensuring editorial independence and public service objectives is more or less embedded today in the broadcast systems of many of the member states of the European Union, together with Norway, Switzerland, Canada, Japan, South Korea, New Zealand, and Australia, and it has been increasingly used as the model for reform of state broadcasting in Africa, Asia, and Eastern Europe.

In contrast to the approach in Europe, broadcasting in the United States and most of Latin America has been dominated by commercial broadcasters. Public service broadcasting did not emerge in the United States until the late 1960s, and then in a very different form from that in Europe. The 800 public radio stations and 350 public television stations in the United States are owned mostly by universities, nonprofit organizations, and local or state governments. The bulk of their funds are from listener and viewer donations and corporate sponsorships, but the sector also receives a substantial annual grant from Congress.[13] In Latin America, publicly owned broadcasters have historically been weak and underfunded, and some have undergone partial or full privatization rather than reform toward the public service broadcasting model.

> Public broadcasters can enhance governance and development by achieving national reach, providing quality programs and journalism, articulating the diversity of views, and promoting broad public debate.

In countries where public service broadcasters are established and well resourced, such as the United Kingdom, Japan, Germany, the Netherlands, the Nordic countries, and Australia, they often attract large audiences and are a key driver in maintaining program quality and promoting technical innovation across the broadcasting sector.

Where public broadcasters are independent and have a clear mandate, they can make a significant contribution to good governance and accountability, broadcasting diversity, and the ability of the broadcasting sector as a whole to play

---

[13]In 2007 this will be $400 million, of which $263 million is for direct distribution to radio and TV stations and $105 million for syndicated program production.

a positive role in society and development. Depending on the specific mandate of the broadcaster in question, they may do this by, among other things, ensuring full national reach for their broadcasts; providing quality programs, including investigative journalism and informational and educational programming; articulating the views and interests of all sectors and groups in society; and promoting broad social debate about matters of public importance.

One institutional approach, characterized by the British Broadcasting Corporation (BBC) in the United Kingdom and the Japan Broadcasting Corporation (NHK) in Japan, is to establish a large national public broadcaster, under unified editorial control. Other approaches have been adopted, for example in France, where a number of distinct public broadcasting services are run by different public institutions and operate under different governance models. In Germany, the public broadcasting system operates on a regional basis, with some shared programming constituting a basic national service. In the Netherlands, different national program-making companies share the same broadcast infrastructure and are complemented by separate regional and local services.

Commercial Private Sector Broadcasting

Liberalization of the broadcasting environment, understood as opening up to greater private sector participation, has been the overwhelming trend in broadcasting policy worldwide despite the continuing reluctance of many governments to cede control of this key national resource. This has been driven by political change, commercial opportunity, and technological development. Recent liberalization efforts in many countries have focused initially on opening up the airwaves to allow for the licensing of commercial broadcasters, but they have not always considered other users and in particular the potential interest in and usage by nongovernmental and community-based organizations.

> Commercial private sector broadcasting is the dominant trend, driven in part by new technologies, and its growth has in many countries enhanced the range and diversity of content.

In parallel to liberalization, and in part driving it, technological developments, such as cable, satellite, and the Internet, and the emergence of more efficient digital production and distribution technologies, are vastly increasing the number of channels that can be delivered to consumers. These developments have been marked by intense competition for position, as poorly performing publicly owned and older commercial broadcasters face the risk of extinction while new services capture mass audiences.

Together, liberalization and technological developments have led to an explosion of commercial broadcasting in a growing number of countries in Africa, Asia, and Eastern Europe. The ending of state broadcasting monopolies and the introduction of choice and competition have brought significant benefits for audiences both by increasing the range and diversity of programming and by enabling greater responsiveness to audience demand and interest.

> Some commercial broadcasters have produced quality news and reporting, sometimes mandated by regulation. Bottom-line pressure to generate profits can lead to a focus on low-cost programs, satisfying advertisers, and targeting wealthier viewers and subscribers. The potential to fulfill the public interest can thus be constrained.

Commercial broadcasters can play an important role in promoting the public interest through their program services. There are examples from diverse countries of commercial broadcasters, including at local level, that have distinguished themselves with news coverage and investigative reporting that informs the public and sheds light on important inadequacies or malfeasance in government. Some commercial broadcasters see their public information role as paramount, and contribute greatly to developing public awareness in a regional or global audience. In many countries, regulatory mechanisms mandate, in exchange for access to the publicly owned airwaves, minimum levels of news broadcasting, public service announcements, guaranteed access to political candidates under equal-time rules, and other public interest-oriented programming.

At the same time, commercial broadcasters, by the very nature of their for-profit business, are often constrained in the degree to which they can contribute to wider public goals, including good governance. Broadcasters face pressures to improve bottom-line results by reducing costs and maximizing audience. This generally promotes a focus on cheaply produced popular or imported entertainment formats and mass-marketed programs, and minimal investment in specialist or more costly public interest program content. Market forces tend to prevent commercial broadcasters from rigorously serving the public interest through in-depth news, analysis, and information. There is a tendency to target primarily those with spending power in order to deliver consumers to advertisers or attract paying subscribers. The prevailing trend among private broadcasters is to view their news coverage as a commodity, with no greater priority than the rest of their programming, and this has in turn led to an unwillingness to allocate significant resources to produce in-depth news reporting and analysis. These tendencies, which are a product of the market and regulatory environment in which commercial broadcasters operate, have constrained the potential role of commercial broadcasting in promoting equitable and sustainable development.

Community Nonprofit Broadcasting

Since the late 1940s, a new form of broadcasting has emerged that is today known as community broadcasting. Independent of the government, having social objectives, and not run for profit, community broadcasters have been established by civil society groups and organizations in all regions and most of the countries of the world.

Community broadcasting has developed in response to the needs of grassroots social movements and community-based organizations to find an accessible and affordable means to express their own issues, concerns, cultures, and languages, and to create an alternative to the national broadcaster and the growth of commercial media.

> Community nonprofit broadcasting has a special development role to play for those facing poverty and exclusion, is highly participative, and can offer an avenue into influencing policy.

It is this bottom-up rationale that sets community broadcasting apart from its local commercial counterpart. Its relationship to the community is different in terms of its mandate from the community, which requires ongoing renewal; in terms of its governance and the need for transparency and participation; and, also, in terms of economic sustainability. For while community broadcasters can on the one hand draw from the community for funding, they must on the other hand be more wary of pressures from commercial advertising and public funding. Furthermore, community broadcasting has an important transformative role through the empowering activities that occur in the very process of mobilizing participation.

Local and community-based media have become recognized as having a particular role to play for people and communities facing poverty, exclusion, and marginalization, and by giving voice to these communities can contribute to governance through wider and better-informed participation.[14] They can assist in providing access to information and can stimulate debate, including in local and vernacular languages. They can reinforce traditional forms of communication, such as storytelling, group discussion, and theater, and they can enable grassroots participation in policy making and democracy. Using technologies that are appropriate and affordable, they can reach out to the most remote communities and to people from all walks of life.

A recent major report, involving seventeen countries in Africa, found widespread support among media stakeholders for initiatives to support community media, pointing to:

> the role of community media in advancing development objectives; community media success in giving a voice to communities; and, the sector's ability to empower and skill communities who participate in supporting activities generated by such media.[15]

> Community broadcasters can improve local dialogue, enhance capacities, and be an effective conduit for information in all directions. Radio is especially effective and sometimes viable even for very poor communities.

Community broadcasters often develop their programs through community consultations in focus groups and interviews. Their programming includes phone-in and write-in question-and-answer programs, regular programs on particular themes, roundtable discussions, community reporting on events and issues, broadcasts of local government meetings, and development-oriented information programs. The stations perform an important public service for poor constituencies, eliciting their views and concerns, enabling them to raise issues and problems that might otherwise be taboo, and encouraging them to speak out, both among themselves and to local government.

At its best, community broadcasting has improved the internal dialogue, problem solving, and self-organization of the people it

---

[14]See, for example, *Declaration of the Ninth United Nations Roundtable on Communications for Development* (Rome: Food and Agriculture Organisation, 2004).
[15]AMDI Research Summary Report (BBC World Service Trust, 2006), 94.

serves, and given people the self-confidence to talk directly to local officials to get action. From a developmental perspective, community radio, in particular, has been a highly effective medium. Not only do the participatory programs on community radio profoundly improve poor and marginalized people's ability to articulate issues needing attention, but they also encourage hitherto isolated people to reach out for information and advice when they need it, for example, by getting experts (such as a nurse or an agricultural extension worker) in the area to volunteer their time, sometimes on a weekly basis, and to give advice on the air. When programs include sensitive topics, such as domestic violence, child abuse, or alcoholism, they open up a space for families and neighbors to discuss the programs and their views on the topic. Experience shows that this kind of discussion can have significant impacts on people's behavior, and on their ability to cooperate and deal with social problems that have, in some cases, been corroding their communities.

Opening the Range of Broadcasting Types

The consideration of four relatively distinct types of broadcasting, just described, is not intended to suggest that they each operate in a discreet domain, motivated by a unique set of values and principles and seeking different target groups, but rather is intended to highlight the different values, principles, and outcomes that can motivate the provision of broadcasting services. There is considerable scope for deliberation among stakeholders, including policy makers, regulators, the media, and the wider public, regarding the balance and mix appropriate to different circumstances, and the extent to which regulation can be designed so that the broadcasting system as a whole can achieve public interest goals. Part of the objective of policy, and of the regulator, is to deploy measures that steer the motivations and outcomes of each sector in a particular direction.

> Distinct broadcasting types, each uniquely motivated by internal values and dynamics, coexist in any given country, and the specific mix is open to considerable influence.

> Policy and regulation aim to influence the dynamics and motivations of each type of broadcaster within the mix, and can steer the overall media sector toward a public interest approach.

At the simplest level of analysis, the business model of each broadcasting type, its sources of sustainability and internal growth dynamic, is distinct. Each confronts pressures from various directions, and a course must be navigated between sometimes conflicting demands: for instance, public service broadcasters must balance the need to produce high-quality independent content reflecting the full diversity of views against the need to avoid influence from the governments which are its main source of income. Commercial broadcasting must navigate a course between establishing a significant market share through quality programs and the drive to maximize profits through lowest-cost content and advertising-maximizing audiences. And community broadcasters, the most economically precarious of the three, must strike a balance between their mandate to give voice to the community in a participatory and diverse manner and their constant struggle with the capacity to deliver. In the absence of a stable economic base, community broadcasters may have to steer a course between insularity and potentially compromising their independence and legitimacy.

But in reality these underlying forces are interwoven with more complex trends and interactions between the sectors, which are far more than mere nuances. Presented in isolation these dynamics court caricature, failing to reflect any given broadcasting system's flexibility and environmental specificity. Broadcast policy and regulation do not attempt to reduce broadcasting to its simplest constituent forms; but rather strive to create an appropriate mixture that best contributes to the public interest by influencing how, in their unique circumstances, these diverse sectors mesh in a particular national system. Policy makers and regulators have developed a range of instruments to achieve this, and some good practices are outlined in Part III.

An independent regulator can be a vital instrument in achieving the right mix. Regulators are subject to various forms of failure, but the type of regulation and capacity of the regulator are key factors in successfully implementing a public interest approach.

At this point a word on the different types of regulatory agencies is relevant, as these can substantially affect the shape and functioning of broadcasting.

This guide makes a case for an independent regulator. This concept, which is discussed in depth in Part III, can be briefly defined as a regulator that can pursue stated, accepted, legitimate goals in a manner that is free of undue political influence. This kind of regulation can be differentiated from direct government regulation, for instance through a Ministry of Information or Ministry of Communication. But this sharp distinction disguises other trends. Regulatory agencies can be subject to "capture," that is, excess influence from the industries that are subject to supervision. Some agencies are "converged," having oversight across many forms of communication (including telecommunication) as the actual distribution processes and infrastructures become intermeshed. Some regulatory agencies have what is termed external pluralism, and make a conscious effort to ensure many stakeholders are represented on their boards. Often the regulation (or self-regulation) of the public service broadcaster is distinct from that of the rest of broadcasting. Many of these differences are raised again later in this guide. The point here is that the nature of the regulator and its capacity to fulfill legitimate objectives can be critical factors in determining the specificity of any given configuration of broadcasting and its ability to fulfill the public interest.

The diversity of circumstances, approaches, and institutions gives rise to variations of each of the broadcasting types, and some hybrids.

For instance, the line between community broadcasting and public service broadcasting is thin in countries like the Netherlands, where local authorities hold both television and radio "community" licenses and provide funding, but local communities have a decisive influence on structures and content. In Sri Lanka, the few "community" radio stations are formally owned by the public broadcaster, SLBC, though the community maintains a high degree of local participation. In a number of countries local commercial radio and community radio are barely distinguishable, particularly where they arise from, or become part of, a wider social movement for change where radio can and has played a key role. They can evolve later into either commercial or community forms.

Furthermore, regulation of the community sector need not preclude market-based mechanisms and instruments, even ones that do not discriminate between the commercial and community sectors while recognizing the specificity of each. Some poor communities, for instance, neither can attract the advertising revenue needed to sustain a local commercial radio station nor do they have the level of capacity and organization needed to sustain the collective effort of building a community station. Policy measures to address "market failure" can be devised to enhance the feasibility of either or both sectors to provide a service to such underserved communities. An incentive package could offer a subsidy to a local broadcaster subject to license conditions to provide at least a modicum of news and development-related content. What emerges can be a local station run by an individual entrepreneur; or a community channel run by the more active local groups—or even a hybrid where a local commercial enterprise works closely with a board of community interests.

Public service television also has variants, including a second "tier" that represents a distinct model. It has been described as "alternative public broadcasting" and operates successfully in a number of countries as a complement to traditional public service.[16] Like public service television such stations are established initially by government and exist independently of government as a nonprofit entity or corporation. But they are distinguished usually by a specific mandate to provide a finely focused service. Channel 4 in the United Kingdom has a mandate to broadcast distinctive innovative and creative programs, and to enhance cultural diversity, but it operates in a commercial environment and commissions all its programs.[17] The French/German cultural channel Arte[18] delivers cultural output; and the Australian Special Broadcasting Service (SBS) provides exclusively multilingual and multicultural radio and television services in up to sixty languages.[19] In Mexico, the closest thing to a public service broadcaster is run by the National Polytechnic Institute.[20] A number of regional publicly funded broadcasters in Canada, Spain, and elsewhere fall into the same category.

> The interaction between funding bases of different broadcasting types can influence their shape.

The interaction between the funding bases of commercial broadcasting sectors and public service broadcasting also influences the shape of the broadcasting

---

[16]Marc Raboy, "The World Situation of Public Service Broadcasting: Overview and Analysis," Ch. 1, *Public Service Broadcasting: Cultural and Educational Dimensions* (Paris: UNESCO, 1997), 19–56.

[17]Channel 4 in the United Kingdom, available at: *http://www.channel4.com/about4/overview.html*.

[18]French/German cultural channel Arte, available at: *www.arte.tv*.

[19]Australian Special Broadcasting Service, available at: *http://www20.sbs.com.au/sbscorporate/index.php?id=*.

[20]National Polytechnic Institute of Mexico, available at: *http://www.oncetv.ipn.mx/*.

system. Efforts to distance the financing of public service broadcasters from government control can pit them against commercial broadcasters. In small or poor countries a license fee or other funding mechanism is often insufficient to ensure the viability of public service broadcasting, and a regulated volume and form of advertising is permitted. A heavy reliance on advertising, however, puts public service broadcasters into direct competition with commercial broadcasters, while potentially subjecting them to similar pressures from advertisers.

Thus there are many gradations and overlaps to be found outside the three-sector model, and these can be accentuated and shaped by policy and regulation so as to open a wider spectrum of possible combinations in different circumstances.

Regional Broadcasting Characteristics and Trends

What do broadcasting systems look like in reality, in different regions? What are their main dynamics and trends?

What follows is a review of broadcasting in the different regions. The aim is to assess the extent to which commonalities in broadcasting trends and dynamics can be distinguished, with a view to contextualizing the legal, policy, and regulatory good practice outlined in Parts II and III.

The conclusion focuses on an emerging paradigm in broadcasting shared by much of the world, though often more as aspiration than implementation.

The Media Environment Regionally

At the regional level, the overall environment for media varies considerably.

There is a paucity of comparative empirical and analytical data on broadcasting at the global level, and indeed most research in the area bemoans the lack of such material. There is no consistent global review of broadcasting, and only very few statistical indicators—covering the availability of television sets and radios at national level and little else. In terms of the enabling environment for media, however, there are a few sources.

Table 3.1 offers a comparative view of general press freedom in the different regions, developed by Freedom House using a methodology that covers the legal, political, and economic environment for all media. A picture emerges of virtually ubiquitous restrictions on media freedom in the Middle East and North Africa (MENA), and over 50 percent of the population of Asia Pacific and Central and Eastern Europe (CEE) living in countries with restricted media freedom.

TABLE 3.1 Press Freedom 2006: Countries and Percentage of Population "Not Free," by Region

Region	Total Countries	Number of Countries "Not Free"	% Population for Which Media Is "Not Free"
Americas	35	4	10
Sub-Saharan Africa	48	22	35
Asia Pacific	40	15	52
Central and Eastern Europe	27	10	56
Middle East and North Africa	19	16	96

Source: Freedom House, *Map of Press Freedom*, 2006. http://www.freedomhouse.org/.

FIGURE 3.1

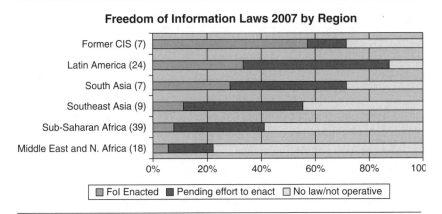

Freedom of Information Laws 2007 by Region

Source: Privacy International. *http://www.privacyinternational.org/issues/foia/foia-laws.jpg*
Number of countries counted in parentheses.

The MENA region also comes in at the bottom of Figure 3.1, on the enactment of freedom of information laws, as monitored by Privacy International.

More directly related to broadcasting, a team of researchers undertook a study in 2001 of the ownership of the top five

In terms of the legal, political, and economic environment for press freedom, the MENA region comes in as least free, followed at a distance by CEE and Asia Pacific.

TABLE 3.2 Television Ownership Distribution 1999

Region	Ownership of Top 5 Channels (regional average)		Division of Market Share of Top 5 Channels (regional average)	
	State	Private	State	Private
Africa	78%	19%	85%	15%
Americas	17%	78%	11%	85%
Asia Pacific	65%	34%	70%	30%
Middle East and North Africa	93%	7%	94%	6%
Central and Eastern Europe, Transition countries	80%	20%	73%	27%
Western Europe	48%	52%	55%	45%

Note: Where figures do not add up to 100%, an "other" category comprises the remainder.

television channels in 97 countries around the world.[1] Table 3.2 summarizes the regional comparison in 1999.

MENA countries were rated highest in 1999 in terms of state ownership and market share, followed by CEE and former Soviet countries, then Asia Pacific and Western Europe. The Americas exhibit a strong bias toward private ownership.

> In relation to freedom of information, the MENA region, Sub-Saharan Africa and Southeast Asia are closely clustered at the bottom.

While offering a useful snapshot of ownership, these figures do not differentiate between state control and public service television, in which major regional differences also exist. The figures are also somewhat dated.

Despite the absence of consistent global data on the broadcasting sector, a partial comparative regional overview can be pieced together from a variety of sources, including some recent multicountry comparative surveys in Europe, transition countries and Africa, several partial global databases and surveys, and a variety of reports. A number of regions or subregions are considered below, with a focus—data permitting—on the overall broadcasting environment, the broadcasting sectoral composition, the legal/regulatory environment and the reality of its implementation, and dynamics and trends. The emphasis is on developing countries and regions in which the

---

[1] Simeon Djankov, Caralee McLiesh, Tatiana Nenova, and Andrei Shleifer, "Who Owns the Media?" (Harvard Institute of Economic Research Paper No. 1919; World Bank Policy Research Working Paper No. 2620, April 19, 2001), extracted from table 2, available at SSRN: *http://ssrn.com/abstract=267386.*

broadcasting sector is undergoing change driven either by external factors or by a demonstrable government desire to reform.

Region by Region

Sub-Saharan Africa

Sub-Saharan Africa is probably the least researched of regions,[2] but seventeen countries there were the subject of recent comparative research by the African Media Development Initiative (AMDI).[3] Sub-Saharan Africa is characterized by a young and growing population, with low literacy rates in many countries. In nine of the countries surveyed, over 60 percent of the population is rural, often with poor transport and no electricity. Radio, the AMDI study found, is the dominant medium in Africa:

> Sub-Saharan Africa, with its large rural population, prefers radio, but television is growing.

> Radio dominates the mass media spectrum with state-controlled radio services still commanding the biggest audiences in most countries but regional (within country) commercial stations demonstrating the largest consistent increases in numbers, followed by community radio, where growth,

> A move is under way toward independent regulatory agencies, the adoption of freedom of information legislation, and the transformation of state-controlled into public service broadcasters.

although significant in certain countries, has been inconsistent. Television is less widely available, especially in rural areas, although it is seen as a growing force.[4]

---

[2]The AMDI Research Summary Report notes: ". . . despite the wealth of valuable insights available from other published research, systematic and reliable data on the sector is underdeveloped or non-existent. There is a lack of robust research, on a continental scale, demonstrating what is and is not working in the attempts by many players to strengthen African media. The lack of reliable information has been a factor constraining private and public (donor) investment" (13).

[3]The countries covered are: Angola, Botswana, Cameroon, Democratic Republic of Congo, Ethiopia, Ghana, Kenya, Mozambique, Nigeria, Senegal, Sierra Leone, Somalia, South Africa, Tanzania, Uganda, Zambia, and Zimbabwe. African Media Development Initiative, *Summary and Seventeen National Reports* (BBC World Service Trust, 2006), available at: *http://www.bbcworldservicetrust.org/amdi*.

[4]Ibid., 33.

Religious broadcasters, especially in radio, play a major role in several countries and account for the main growth in non-state broadcasting since 2000.

Africa has seen a gradual movement in the media regulatory paradigm over the past decade:

It is now generally based on a democratic model of separation of powers—the establishment of independent broadcasting regulatory bodies—while acknowledging the right of the broadcasting media in general to regulate themselves (media councils). This is accompanied by adopting freedom of information legislation and pursuing the goal of transforming state broadcasting into public-service broadcasting.[5]

> But effective implementation of these faces serious challenges in terms of . . . the independence of the regulator . . .

The shift is neither complete nor unproblematic and countries exhibit varying levels of commitment to the model's principles and to its implementation in practice. Eight of the seventeen countries have legislated for independent media regulators, but there is widespread skepticism regarding their independence.[6] A number of others have state-run regulatory bodies. Legislation aiming to secure the independence of publicly owned broadcasting was in place in six of the seventeen, with three more working toward it. However, few of the public service broadcasters created are fully independent of government, and most are subject to interference and patronage. Community broadcasting is given basic recognition in ten of the countries in the study, but often on a piecemeal basis and with little support offered.

In terms of the overall environment for media, five of the seventeen countries retain criminal defamation and libel laws, and even where repressive laws have been removed, state-sponsored mecha-

> . . . defamation laws . . .

nisms for sanctioning journalists were found to persist in at least eight countries. All but three (South Africa, Tanzania, and Uganda) have no freedom of information legislation. Laws are pending in a further six—in the case of Ghana and Nigeria for over six years.

Although the past decade has seen a welcome and significant increase in diversity of broadcasting content, serious shortcomings remain

---

[5]Ibid., 15.
[6]The report singles out South Africa and possibly Ghana as the most independent (56–57).

regarding its quality. The content of many government controlled broadcasters coincides too closely to the government or ruling party perspective, and there is a tendency among most media to reflect the view of the urban educated elite:

> . . . quality of programs and independence of broadcasters . . .

> Community and private media are widely acknowledged to cater to populations and regions under-served by other outlets, and— particularly through radio—to provide an important educational and information source for those areas marked by low literacy or low access to mainstream media.[7]

> . . . and impartiality of public broadcasters.

The principal challenge for state-owned media, the research concludes, is to serve all sectors of the population as impartial public service broadcasters, free from government interference. It calls for action to legislate for freedom of expression and access to information; develop a consistent policy on the independent allocation of licenses; reinforce the protection of journalists; and strengthen independent regulatory frameworks. The report also notes that those surveyed placed the community media sector, especially radio, amongst the highest priorities for new funding, precisely because of its development role.

> Nevertheless progress is in the right direction, and radio, especially local and community radio, is widely recognized as having major development potential.

The report concludes on a relatively optimistic note:

> In all of the countries surveyed, significant changes were reported in the media regulatory environment as a result of increasing levels of democratisation, more conducive political and economic environments, and increased national and international media development activity.[8]

CEE and Former CIS

Former Soviet Union, Eastern bloc, and some Central European countries[9] are

> With the collapse of the Soviet Union, the media structures of former members and CEE countries underwent sudden and massive change.

---

[7]Ibid., 88.

[8]Ibid., 59.

[9]Considered here are "transition countries" as defined by the European Economic Area, but no consideration is given to Afghanistan, Belarus, or Turkmenistan. See *http://www .eeassoc.org/transition_countries_list.asp*.

unique in having undergone a sudden, more or less simultaneous and radical break from existing media structures with the collapse of the Soviet Union. The process and outcomes are partly documented in two recent comparative studies: an Open Society Institute (OSI) study of television in twenty mainly transitional countries in Europe,[10] and a European Audiovisual Observatory (EAO) study of broadcasting in five Commonwealth of Independent States (CIS) countries.[11] Central and Eastern European countries and most CIS countries experienced an immediate and massive growth in commercial and private broadcasters. For a period, many pioneered investigative reporting and news, opening up wide areas of society and economy previously out of bounds to public scrutiny. In many countries, the dismantling of state control and the opening up to commercial interests led to a massive influx of Western capital into the television industry, that often relegated domestic players to the margins of the market and is still a major factor today.[12]

> The collapse of state-controlled media was followed by an influx of Western capital much of it in pursuit solely of commercial gain. In response many governments tried to reinvent broadcasters as public service rather than state controlled.

But in the largely unregulated context and lacking local experience of a diverse commercial media:

. . . freedom of the media soon came to mean first of all freedom to run the media as a private business. Private broadcasters pursuing above all commercial gains rapidly outperformed State broadcasters, which were mostly reluctant or unable to keep up.[13]

---

[10]Open Society Institute *Television across Europe: Regulation, Policy and Independence,* four volumes (Hungary, 2005), available at: *http://www.eumap.org.*

[11]Andrei Richter and Dmitry Golovanov, *Public Service Broadcasting Regulation in the Commonwealth of Independent States Special Report on the Legal Framework for Public Service Broadcasting in Azerbaijan, Georgia, Moldova, Russia and Ukraine* (European Audiovisual Observatory, Strasbourg, France, November 2006).

[12]Open Society Institute, *Television across Europe: Regulation, Policy and Independence* (2005), summary, 33. Hereinafter cited as OSI, 2005.

[13]Ibid.

These developments provoked a variety of concerns among governments of newly independent states. The exodus of audiences from state to commercial channels, the desire to strengthen post-Soviet national identities among the populace, and the collapse of the traditional system of financing and program production led to an effort to replace the bankrupt—in many senses—state-run television and radio systems with a more appealing system of public service broadcasting[14] (EAO, 2006, p. 1). Public service broadcasters, radio and television, were established in one CIS country after another from 1994 onward, and were accompanied by the closure of the state broadcasters in all but two countries (Azerbaijan and Kyrgyzstan).[15] All CEE countries covered in the OSI study now have public service broadcasters in place.[16] Some were strongly influenced in the choice by external factors, especially where there was a prospect of EU membership. The Council of Europe and the Organization for Economic Cooperation on Security in Europe (OSCE) both brought significant pressure on governments seeking to become members.

Thus the transition and post-transition countries considered here have for the most part now adopted a so-called "European framework" for broadcasting. This is a mixed system. It includes public service broadcasters of varying degrees of capacity and strength, operationally independent from the state but ultimately accountable to elected officials. Alongside them are commercial broadcasters subject to local laws and regulation. In a few countries there is also a more recent opening for community media consisting of "local media outlets run by NGOs, non-profit organisations or minority communities."[17]

All sectors confront challenges. Public service broadcasters, for instance, saw a steep decline in viewing figures that has only recently

---

[14]EAD, 2006, 1.

[15]Public service television was established in Estonia in 1994; Latvia in 1995; Moldova in 1995; Lithuania in 1996; Armenia in 2000; Georgia in 2004; Azerbaijan in 2005, and Kyrgyzstan in 2005. In Ukraine a public service broadcasting law was passed in 1997 but has not been enforced, and an attempt to pass a law in Russia failed. From time to time discussions on the issue take place in Belarus, Kazakhstan, Tajikistan, and Uzbekistan. Only in Turkmenistan is there no such discussion. See EAO, 2006, p. 1.

[16]See OSI, 2005, table 9 for details of Albania, Bosnia and Herzegovina, Bulgaria, Croatia, Czech Republic, Estonia, Hungary, Latvia, Lithuania, Macedonia, Poland, Romania, Serbia, Slovakia, and Slovenia.

[17]OSI, 2005, 78.

been arrested or reversed in a few countries.[18] In the area of news, they have nevertheless achieved some success:

> [A] fact confirmed far and wide is that public service television remains the main source of news for the largest part of the population in most of the countries covered by this report. Only in a few countries, such as the Czech Republic, Slovakia and Hungary, do private channels attract more viewers for newscasts.[19]

> The transition to a European mixed model is not easy. Key issues include: . . . a retention of state control and influence in various ways . . .

The transition to the new broadcasting environment was and remains problematic and the overall broadcasting system of many CEE and CIS countries exhibits serious problems. As compared to Western Europe, the OSI study notes:

> [t]he essential difference now lies in the greater vulnerability of public service broadcasting within transition (and post-transition) countries to political and economic pressures alike.[20]

The EAO report concludes regarding the process of the transformation of state broadcasters into public service broadcasters in CIS countries:

> It is a common practice . . . to change some "details" of the originally envisaged public service broadcasting laws in the course of the legislative process so that most of its provisions meant to secure the independence of public service broadcasting have no effect. Another "scholastic" way to counteract public service broadcasting is to lay stress on declarative provisions, without providing their actual enforcement. [21]

> . . . compounded by an insecure funding base . . .

Legal flaws are compounded in some countries by the absence of effective funding mechanisms. Some Eastern and

---

[18]Public service television is now picking up in countries such as Poland, the Czech Republic, Slovakia, Serbia, and Hungary. See OSI, 2005, p. 54, and table 13.
[19]OSI, 2005, 40.
[20]OSI, 2005, 38.
[21]EAO, 2006, 41.

Central European countries[22] have introduced a license fee that provides over 50 percent of total funding of public service broadcasters.[23] However, many other former CIS countries, including the Baltics, have no license fee system[24] and almost all are funded directly from state finances, resulting in a potentially much higher level of state control over the nominally independent channels.

There is little doubt that editorial independence is compromised in many public service broadcasters. Some offer "politically slanted, inaccurate, partisan reporting" and journalists in some countries experience "direct or indirect political interference and pressures in their work,"[25] which can be especially prevalent during election campaigns.[26]

> . . . leading to compromises in editorial independence and slanted journalism.

Furthermore, despite pioneering news, political, and investigative reporting in the early days, commercial television now is usually "not a reference for solid investigative journalism and quality news programmes." Pressures to attract large audiences and reduce costs have led to sensationalism in news and a focus on low-quality entertainment. Effective self-regulatory mechanisms are few in number, and journalists are often poorly paid and suffer from poor labor regulations and fear for their jobs. "In such a precarious environment, and against the background of widespread political interference in programming and economic pressures, self-censorship thrives."[27]

> Commercial television too has declined in the quality of news, and self-censorship is common.

Among the key recommendations of the OSI report are ones emphasizing the need to reinforce the independence and transparency of the regulator, to ensure the independence of public service media in practice and in law, and to develop means to make ownership in all media more transparent.

---

[22]Including Croatia, Czech Republic, the Republic of Macedonia, Romania, Slovakia, and Slovenia.
[23]OSI, 2005, 60, table 1.
[24]EAO, 2006, 42.
[25]OSI, 2005, 64–65.
[26]The World Press Freedom Index reports a number of cases of bias in many of these countries in both public and private media. Available at: *http://www.freedomhouse.org/template.cfm?page=251&year=2006.*
[27]OSI, 2005, 71.

Latin America

More than 90 percent of Latin Americans listen to radio every day, making it the most ubiquitous of media in the region.[28] Latin America also has the most unequal income distribution of any region, almost 45 percent of the population living below the poverty line.[29]

In broad terms, Latin American countries, with the exception of Cuba, adopted the U.S. model of largely unrestrained private commercial broadcasting, though there are differences. The larger countries also support significant content production industries and export around the region and further afield.

> Private sector interests are dominant in Latin America with relatively weak public service broadcasting.

Public service broadcasting in Latin America is limited. Almost every country, however, has state-run channels, most of which are poorly funded and subject to government manipulation or control.[30] A number of publicly owned channels offer cultural and educational programs; some channels are run by political parties (in opposition or government); a few by religious organizations; and there are a handful of nonprofit and foundation-based channels. No country, however, has formally independent, well-funded, public service broadcasting with a broad remit to include news and current affairs: among the closest are TVN in Chile and Once TV in Mexico.[31] The vast majority of broadcasting is commercial. Ownership of the sector is highly concentrated at the national level with significant cross-ownership across audiovisual and media sectors.

The radio sector differs from television in one crucial respect: although community television does exist in a minor way, community radio broadcasting is diverse, numerically significant, and widespread. Pioneers go back over fifty years, long before the term community radio was coined. They include stations set up by tin miners in

---

[28]Juan Pablo Cárdenas, "América Latina y las Fortalezas de la Radiodifusión," *Diario electrónico "Radio Universidad de Chile"* (March 22, 2005), available at: *http://www.radio.uchile.cl/notas.aspx?idNota=18169.*

[29]Dr. Jennifer McCoy, Carter Center, *Las Vulnerabilidades de la Democracia, Democracia y Cumbre de las Américas, Panel sobre la Carta Democrática Interamericana* (Buenos Aires, Argentina, March 11, 2005).

[30]Based on the BBC Country Profiles, available at: *http://news.bbc.co.uk/1/hi/country_profiles/default.stm.*

[31]See respectively *http://www.tvn.cl/* and *http://www.oncetv.ipn.mx/.*

Bolivia in the 1940s and 1950s that contributed hugely to community organization and political empowerment, and the hundreds of educational stations inspired by Radio Sutenza, which was founded in 1947 by a Catholic priest to bring practical education to rural and marginalized groups. Such is the influence of the sector that it has been argued that community radio and to some extent even community television, occupy the space of public service broadcasting. For irrespective of their actual legal status, as community or commercial media, they are driven by the same ethos and fulfill many of the same functions as public service broadcasters.[32] Although these channels emerged for the most part in a regulatory vacuum, or in direct opposition to the law, they are now being recognized and regulated in a growing number of countries, among them Colombia, Bolivia, Peru, Venezuela, Mexico, and Argentina. Many older and more established community stations continue to operate with commercial or cultural licenses. Legal recognition can, however, be a mixed blessing. Some countries, sensitive not to encroach on commercial media, impose restrictions on the community sector that threaten viability. Chile, for instance, limits transmission power to just one watt (enough to broadcast only a few hundred meters, in good conditions), and other countries prohibit advertising.

> Community radio has a long history, and is claimed even to occupy the space of public service, but has yet to achieve full legal recognition and a positive regulatory environment.

Most countries in Latin America have formally independent broadcast regulators (about half of them combined with the telecoms regulator), though among the larger exceptions are Brazil, Peru, Mexico, and Colombia. The process of issuing licenses in many countries, however, lacks transparency, is sometimes corrupt, and follows procedures that elsewhere are considered bad practice. The issuing of lengthy broadcast licenses, with options to

> While formally independent regulators are common, the process of issuing licenses, and other areas, are problematic.

renew, is commonplace. In Argentina in May 2005, for example, President Kirchner renewed television broadcast licenses that grant the

---

[32]See Rafael Roncagliolo, "Latin America: Community Radio and Television as Public Service Broadcasting," in Public Service Broadcasting (UNESCO, Paris, 1996), available at: *www.cidh.oas.org/relatoria/docListCat.asp?catID=24&llD=1.*

holders a total of 35 years, in one case to 2025. In Uruguay the five cable licenses were granted in 1994—four to existing commercial television licensees—without any competition or call for tenders. Also, Uruguayan broadcast licenses often have no specific time limits or in practice renewal is automatic. But legally they are "precarious and revocable," subject to government decision. Many other countries follow similar practices.

Politics is sometimes too central an issue in decisions regarding licensees. The Venezuelan government's decision in 2007 not to renew the license of a private television channel, Radio Caracas Television (RCTV)—a 20-year license initially obtained in 1987 by presidential decree—was widely criticized and may have been politically motivated. The station took an antigovernment stance, but it was not merely editorially critical: in 2002, it actively backed a failed coup against the elected president. The president was criticized both for political motivation in the failure to renew and for not following properly the system for assessing whether a channel should retain its license. Also relevant in this context is a government decision to fold the regulator back into the Ministry of Communication, resulting in the loss of its arm's-length status. The dispute illustrates the intense connections between politics, due process, and the award of valuable instruments for communication in society. Meanwhile, in neighboring Colombia, the government in 2004 closed down the public Instituto de Radio y Televisión (Inravisión), which produced programs and broadcast on three channels about educational, cultural, and social issues, including documentaries critical of the government.[33]

> Debate on human rights issues relating to media are influential, relating to poverty, freedom of expression, issuing of licenses and concessions, and concentration of ownership.

There is now considerable activity and impetus in Latin America to reform the broadcasting sector, and the media sector as a whole. With growing recognition of community media, a three-sector broadcast environment is becoming the norm, with the important caveat that the public sector

---

[33]Diana Cariboni, "Easy to See the Speck in the Other's Eye" (1996), available at: *http://other-news.info/index.php?p=1988#more-1988; Juan Forero*, "Pulling the Plug on Anti-Chavez TV" (Washington Post Foreign Service, Thursday, January 18, 2007) A16; and the AMARC statement and other IFEX alerts at: *http://www.ifex.org/en/ content/view/full/82665.*

is largely state controlled. The possibility of public service broadcasting is the subject of debate in just a few countries, among them Uruguay, where the public broadcaster does have some independence, but none of these countries is close to developing the appropriate legislation and mechanisms. A key issue in such debates is how to devise funding mechanisms that can generate sufficient funding in societies with large poor populations and high skewed income distribution. But the general move toward independent regulators is continuing with growing effort to reinforce their independence from political pressures and to reform the process of issuing licenses.

Political issues are integral to media developments in Latin America in one way or another. Telesur is a regional television channel established in 2005 by Venezuela, Argentina, Cuba, and Uruguay (later joined by Bolivia) to broadcast news and current affairs from a regional perspective, deliberately countering what it sees as biased coverage from northern-based satellite channels, such as CNN. It is accused by some of promoting government propaganda. In the channel's defense, it is worth noting that its management board comprises government appointed media professionals, its advisory board is made up of prominent international intellectuals, and its remit draws heavily on public service principles. It does not seem, however, to be structured as an autonomous entity protected from government intervention.

Also important in debates supporting the process of reform in Latin America is the focus on human rights issues and references to a right to communicate. The Special Rapporteur for Freedom of Expression of the Inter-American Commission on Human Rights, an autonomous organ of the Organization of American States (OAS), is a significant regional actor here and has considerable moral authority and political influence. Successive annual reports[34] have forcefully raised issues such as links between media, freedom of expression and poverty (2002), democratic criteria for the concession of radio and television broadcast frequencies, and freedom of information (2003) and concentration of media ownership (2004).

---

[34]For all OAS annual reports see: *http://www.cidh.oas.org/relatoria/docListCat.asp?catID=24&lID=1*; for Freedom of expression and poverty see: 2002 Ch IV at: *http://www.cidh.oas.org/relatoria/showarticle.asp?artID=309&lID=1*.

South and Southeast Asia

Broadcasting in South and Southeast Asia is hugely diverse, driven by a variety of dynamics, and only a schematic outline is possible here. If it is possible to generalize at all, it is about the trend towards commercialization.

> Asia is hugely varied but can be grouped in terms of their structure:

While the debate over the "responsible" and the "free" press continues to rage, a common feature in Asian countries is commercialisation of the media. In the wake of economic liberalisation, media is undergoing a transition beyond politics, to information and consumerism. Media has also become a platform for advertising clients and a supporter of economic reconstruction, while creating demand for new consumer goods.[35]

The major countries of South and Southeast Asia can be loosely grouped in terms of the structure of their broadcasting sectors.

In Bhutan, Myanmar (Burma), Laos, and Vietnam the state maintains direct control of national broadcasting, both radio and television, though the degree of control and censorship varies. Described as a "paradise for censors"[36] Burma relentlessly practices prior censorship across all media. Broadcasting in Laos is under heavy-handed direct government control. Virtually no criticism of the government is permitted in Bhutan, though the press sector is opening up slowly. Vietnam's elaborate national and regional broadcasting system of around 100 radio and television services all remain under different forms of state control, though a dissident press manages to survive.

> . . . from extreme control of broadcasting and intolerance of government criticism . . .

Foreign broadcasting in these countries is available in border areas, and through long-wave radio, satellite, or carefully monitored cable access.

---

[35]Werner vom Busch, ed., *The Asia Media Directory* (Konrad-Adenauer Foundation Singapore, 2004), 8–9, available at: *http://www.kas-asia.org/pub_bkg/Asia%20Media%20Directory.pdf.*
[36]Raporteurs sans Frontiers, *Burma Annual Report 2006*, available at: *http://www.rsf.org/article.php3?id_article=17346.*

China has opened its broadcasting sector significantly in recent years, though the Communist Party of China (CPC) and government continue to exercise stringent control and censorship. Broadcasting is dominated by state-run Chinese Central Television (CCTV), as the only national service, and offers numerous satellite and pay television channels. Over 2,000 provincial and municipal stations exist, run by local government, although most now rely on advertising and commercial income and focus heavily on commercial fare. They all also carry CCTV's main news program. Agreements are in place to allow major global corporations, such as AOL Time Warner and News Corp, to broadcast via cable, though programs are vetted by the regulator, and criticism of the CPC is not permitted. China National Radio is the only national channel but every province, autonomous region, and municipality has its own radio stations run by local government. Within the strict parameters set, there is fairly open discussion of social concerns and policy options.

Countries such as Bangladesh, Cambodia, and Pakistan operate a mixed state-controlled and private broadcasting, with little in the way of independent regulation. In Bangladesh, the state runs terrestrial television and radio over the national territory, but four commercial television

> . . . to a mixed public and private system regulated by the state, with implicit and explicit state control of both and as yet no opening to community . . .

channels are licensed on satellite and cable, and there are a number of FM radio stations. For private broadcasters, however, "keeping their licences depends on their demonstrating a certain compliance with the government."[37] Vocal opposition comes only from newspapers. In Cambodia, the combination of state-controlled and commercial radio and television is further complicated by the fact that much of the private media is actually under political party control. Corruption and political bias of both state and private broadcasting limit the contribution of the broadcast media, and a heavy criminal code hangs over the press. Pakistan has issued over twenty satellite television licenses,

---

[37]Raporteurs sans Frontiers, *Bangladesh Annual Report 2006*, available at: *http://www .rsf.org/article.php3?id_article=17344.*

though terrestrial television remains state controlled; and over 100 licenses have also been issued for private FM radio stations with many more promised. At the same time, and somewhat paradoxically, the broadcasting and censorship laws are being tightened and intimidation is rife, though the print media remains far freer. None of these countries currently permit community broadcasting, though the issue is hotly debated in several and is likely to appear sooner or later.

In India, Nepal, Sri Lanka, Thailand, and Indonesia community radio is an emerging feature of a broadcasting environment that includes commercial, state, but also, in some cases, aspects of public service broadcasting. The commercial sector in India's media has expanded exponentially in recent years, first television and then radio. Although private commercial radio is not permitted to broadcast news, cable and satellite television news is popular. The public broadcasting corporation, Prasar Bharati, established in 1997 as an independent body with a public service

> ... to a mixed public, private, and community system in a variety of configurations, and a movement toward independent regulation ...

mandate, oversees the very extensive national television service, *Doordarshan*, and All India Radio. But Prasar Bharati's links to government are numerous and its funding base compromises its independence. In 2006, a policy statement was approved to open up the licensing of community radio, and the sector is expected to see rapid growth. In Nepal community radio came into being in the mid-1990s, pioneering the concept in South Asia, and it has established a major role in the broadcasting landscape. It is credited with having played a part in the recent return to democracy. Commercial radio and television also exist alongside the state broadcasters. Indonesia opened up to commercial broadcasting after the fall of the Soeharto regime in 1998. In 2002, a new broadcasting law[38] provided for the establishment of the Indonesian Broadcasting Commission (KPI—Komisi Penyiaran Indonesia) and for the recognition of community radio. There are about a dozen national commercial television services and hundreds of local commercial and community radio and television services.

The ongoing civil war has created a fraught media environment in Sri Lanka. It has a mixed system of state and commercial broadcasting,

---

[38]Law number 32/2002.

with numerous commercial radio and television channels. The Sri Lanka Broadcasting Corporation (SLBC) has a public service mandate in radio, though it comes under a ministry and has little editorial autonomy. SLBC operates a number of local stations with some community radio characteristics, but SLBC control ensures they rarely carry coverage critical of the government. Thailand's 1997 constitution enshrined a broadcasting system with an independent regulator and three basic forms, reserving 20 percent of broadcast frequencies for not-for-profit community broadcasting, the rest to be divided equally between public service and commercial sectors. Implementation has yet to live up to this, but many hundreds of private and community radio stations sprang up. The independence of all broadcasting was whittled away under the leadership of Prime Minister Thaksin Shinawatra. The coup that removed him in 2006 introduced more extreme media controls and censorship, including the shutting down of hundreds of community radio stations.

To varying degrees, what distinguishes these countries is the opening to community radio, some development of public service broadcasters alongside ongoing and widespread debate on the concept, and movement toward independent regulation.

Among Southeast Asian countries, the Philippines stands out for its dominance by powerful commercial interests. Dozens of commercial television services are grouped mainly into five major networks, with virtually no direct state or public broadcasting. The government-owned National Broadcasting Network (NBN) has a public service charter but receives no public funding and is widely criticized for being partisan in favor of the government. But radio is still the most popular medium,

> . . . to a highly commercialized system, with public service and regulation in practice largely controlled by government, but with a vibrant community and local radio sector.

and NBN exists alongside innumerable commercial stations, as well as a vibrant though underfunded community and nonprofit radio sector, including many religious stations.

Middle Eastern and North African Countries

Media in the MENA region might seem to be an entirely exceptional case, for the most part under direct control of the state. There are

> Broadcasting in the MENA region, by contrast, straddles a narrower spectrum.

widespread abuses of freedom of expression in many countries, including Saudi Arabia, Syria, Yemen, and Libya, and the concept of freedom of information is alien to most.

At one end of this narrow spectrum is Saudi Arabia, a pioneer of pan-Arab satellite television but long one of the most tightly controlled media environments in the Middle East, with no private radio or television and a government minister chairing the national channels. Criticism of the government or royal family and the questioning of religious tenets are not generally tolerated. Broadcasting in a number of other countries, such as Iran and Libya, is barely more liberal, and, in some respects, is less so. Algeria's broadcasting is all state controlled, though there is a lively and critical press. Bahrain's radio and TV stations are state run. The country's first private radio station—Sawt al-Ghad—was launched in 2005, but the authorities closed it in 2006, alleging irregularities. A number of others, including Jordan and Syria permit commercial radio, though content is limited to music and license holders are often close to the state.

> . . . At one is a cluster of highly controlled and censored broadcasting systems, under state ownership or strict regulation at the national level, though with some openings in the press or satellite . . .

> . . . at the other is a group of countries opening to commercial, and even community, broadcasting; with the possibility of an independent regulator. However, all broadcasters refrain from serious political debate analysis.

Lebanon is one of the more liberalized states whose broadcasters reflect a diversity of social and political interests. Jordan has introduced licensing for commercial broadcasting and is the only country in the region so far to have licensed community broadcasting services. There are some gestures toward pluralization in Kuwait and Egypt, both of which combine state-run broadcasting with commercial services in both television and radio. Morocco can be said to be considering the installation of a liberalized model and has established a relatively independent broadcast regulator. A number of others, including Syria, permit commercial radio, though license holders are fairly close to the state. Almost all national commercial media in Middle Eastern and North African countries, through direct or self-censorship, refrain from serious political debate and analysis.

An IREX Media Sustainability Index covering eighteen MENA countries[39] found that the combination at a constitutional level of relatively progressive laws but poor implementation by the government and the courts was typical of the region, and that editors and journalists exercise restraint even after the regulatory environment and the political climate loosens. It also concludes that:

> Relatively progressive constitutional laws are undermined by weak implementation; though the absence of broadcasting critical of the government has not constrained the development of a media industry.

> These oil-rich countries and their neighbors have demonstrated the ability to develop a media industry without loosening press freedoms beyond points that threaten the governing monarchies and regimes of the region.[40]

What appears almost entirely absent is a challenging national public service broadcasting, or a confident commercial broadcasting critical of the government and stimulating debate. Recent developments, however, suggest that change is coming and these developments are led by television, not nationally but at the regional level. Satellite services have had a transformative influence across the region. What has been described as a new Arab public is leading to significant change in the political culture:

> Change may be on the horizon as public opinion in MENA countries begins to open out under the stimulus of such influences as regional satellite television.

> Rather than imposing a single, overwhelming consensus, the new satellite television channels, along with newspapers, Internet sites, and many other sites of public communication, challenged Arabs to argue, to disagree, and to question the status quo . . . . [the new Arab public] has conclusively shattered the state's monopoly over the of information and the oppressive state censorship that was smothering public discourse well into the 1990s. The new public rejects

---

[39]IREX (International Research & Exchanges Board), *The Development of Sustainable Independent Media in the Middle East and North Africa*, Media Sustainability Index 2005 (IREX, 2006), Executive Summary, x, available at: *http://www.irex.org/programs/MSI_MENA/index.asp.*
[40]Ibid.

the long, dismal traditions of enforced public consensus, insisting on the legitimacy of challenging official policies and proclamations.[41]

The most influential of the new satellite channels, al-Jazeera, models itself on public service broadcasting in terms of its principles, ethos, and modus operandi, though it relies on the continuing support of the Emir of Qatar. Pan-Arab media, especially television, is likely to continue to have a transformative role in the media landscape, including at national level, though at this stage the contours of the outcomes are unclear. The IREX study, referring to the satellite and Internet news dissemination, concludes that "this struggle over control of the information space . . . will be a major factor determining how the countries of the region develop both politically and economically."[42]

Conclusion: An Emerging Paradigm

Chapter 1 identified a set of characteristics that can, potentially, enable the media sector to contribute to good governance and development. These are: freedom of expression, ready and timely access to information both public and private, independence of the media, diverse media content reflecting a wide range of views especially of marginalized groups, broad media coverage and reach, and a sustainable media resource base.

The analysis of broadcasting systems in each region conveys a sense of the degree to which these characteristics are present and might be encouraged and reinforced. It confirms that broadcast media in developing countries and regions have by far the greatest reach, especially into rural and remote areas in which a large proportion of the poorer population often resides, and that these media comprise the primary source of information and news for most people.

The current status of many of the above features is far from ideal, although there are some encouraging trends.

The last decade has seen a pronounced decline in the legitimacy of direct government control of broadcasting, especially in Africa and in transition countries of Central and Eastern Europe but also, and to

---

[41]Marc Lynch, *Voices of the New Arab Public: Iraq, al-Jazeera, and Middle East Politics Today* (New York, Chichester: Columbia University Press, 2006), 2–3.
[42]Ibid., 9.

a lesser extent, in Latin America, parts of Asia, the Middle East, and North Africa. In its place, there is a growing aspiration to develop a mixed model that combines public service broadcasting with private commercial and community broadcasting, under the scrutiny of an independent regulator. This trend is most pronounced in Africa and transition countries, but there is evidence that, starting from a very different point, key characteristics of the system are moving to the foreground in Latin America where the community sector is growing in size and the idea of public service is being revisited. Parts of Asia are also moving in this direction, though commercial dynamics dominate at present. In the Middle East and North Africa the main sign of movement comes from pan-regional television, which is consciously casting itself as public service in its ethos; and government control over broadcasting at the national level is coming under pressure and is the subject of growing debate and tentative moves toward reform.

> The legitimacy of direct state control of broadcasting is in decline, and an aspiration towards a mixed model emerging. Although clearest in Africa and CEE countries, other regions are moving forward in certain dimensions.

Both legislation and implementation, however, leave a lot to be desired even in those regions that are most actively pursuing reform, and there is often doubt as to the level of underlying political commitment. Nevertheless many governments have accepted, in principle, the legitimacy of such a media trajectory, and this offers an important opening for policy change. Movement toward this emerging media paradigm is sometimes halting, and often selective, as it encounters resistance among interests that would prefer to retain firm control of decisive media components. It is not inevitable that broadcasting should progress in a direction that maximizes its contribution to good governance and development. A prognosis must factor in a number of issues and trends.

> Likely long-term outcomes must factor in a number of issues:

First, basic freedom of expression remains a serious concern in many developing countries across all regions, with governments exerting subtle and not-so-subtle pressures and barriers of various kinds. This seriously hampers the emergence of a positive media environment insofar as it

> First, serious concerns remain concerning basic freedom of expression in many countries.

compromises media independence and impedes reporting on corruption and maladministration, and the gathering of information.

Second, and related to the first issue, are obstacles that prevent the media, and the population, in most countries from gaining access to information in a timely manner—especially government information but also information from nongovernment sources that pertains to issues of public concern. Freedom of information legislation and its effective implementation is still the exception, not the rule, though the trend is positive here, and many countries are engaged in the process of developing and implementing such legislation.

> Second, freedom of information legislation, though becoming more widespread, is still the exception, not the rule.

Third, few countries have yet to establish an authoritative independent regulator. This cannot be stressed enough. Even where appropriate policy and legal instruments are in place, the reality on the ground is often very different. The capacity of nominally independent regulators to be effective can be undermined by corruption, negligence, or bureaucratic inertia. Regulators can suffer "capture" by partisan interests, especially government. The risk of regulatory failure is heightened by a lack of capacity and experience of regulatory issues in many countries in which regulators may confront well-funded national and international media interests. And only a handful of governments have demonstrated conclusive willingness to fully renounce their capacity to influence the broadcast media, and the ability to follow through on it.

> Third, independent regulators, with the authority and resources to build the broadcasting sector, are few and far between.

Fourth, the transformation of the landscape into the thriving clusters of public service, commercial and community broadcasting, with a viable economic base for each, is not straightforward.

Converting state-controlled broadcasting to public service broadcasting is no mere adaptation, and demands a fundamental shift in government culture and perception of broadcasting. Few have succeeded in fully severing the link to government to establish an arms-length relationship. Devising a sustainable source of funding without compromising independence or the viability of the commercial broadcast sector has been achieved only rarely. Although improvements over state-controlled media are evident,

> Fourth, creating an economically viable three-pillar broadcasting system faces many obstacles . . .

achieving the ideal of public service broadcasting has a considerable way to go.

Commercial broadcasting has added considerably to diversity in many countries from national to local levels, but it is not reaching its full potential in terms of promoting good governance and development. In some transition countries, a "reckless commercialisation of content"[43] needs to be constructively addressed.

> ... in transforming state-controlled broadcasters into sustainable and independent public services broadcasters ...

Although there is growing recognition that a community broadcasting sector can be especially valuable to enhancing participation in governance and in supporting development, further policy and regulatory change is needed, the capacities of communities and civil society to build the sector are not always present, and creating a sustainable funding base is a challenge.

> ... in enabling private-sector broadcasting to reach its full potential in terms of serving the public interest ...

In addition to these four trends, all of which directly influence broadcasting, the sector will inevitably also continue to be

> ... and in providing the environment for and building the capacity of the community broadcasting sector.

impacted by wider global events. The terrorist attacks on New York and Washington in September 2001 and related events have had significant repercussions internationally on media freedom and the use of defamation, treason, and hate speech laws, and have sometimes added impetus to repressive policies pursued with other agendas. The World Association of Newspapers (WAN) claims that there is "a legitimate and growing concern that in too many instances tightening of security and surveillance measures, whether old or newly introduced, are being used to stifle debate and the free flow of information about political decisions, or that they are being implemented with too little concern for the overriding necessity to protect individual liberties and, notably, freedom of the press."[44] The rise of

---

[43]OSI, 2005, 72.

[44]Cited are: new antiterrorism and official secrets laws, criminalization of speech judged to justify terrorism, criminal prosecution of journalists for disclosing classified information, surveillance of communications without judicial authorization, restrictions on access to government data, and stricter security classifications. "All these measures can severely erode the capacity of journalists to investigate and report accurately and critically, and thus the ability of the press to inform," according to WAN (2007), available at: *http://www .wan-press.org/3may/2007/downloads.php?type=doc&file_name=3MayDogma.*

China as a major world power and its unique state-led yet highly commercialized approach to media will also undoubtedly have a profound influence on debates concerning the appropriate media environment.

Nevertheless this apparently widespread convergence toward a broadcast system that includes a mix of independent public service, private commercial, and not-for-profit community broadcasters has significant potential to promote good governance and to generate other public interest outcomes, including development benefits of broadcast media. At the same time, there are also specific obstacles that could stall the emergence of these benefits and stunt the potential of the model in important ways.

> Achieving the right mix of, and balance between, the sectors within a public interest approach, will demand the design and implementation of both a positive overall media environment and the right legal, policy, and regulatory measures.

In any given country, such a system will necessarily vary in the weight and composition of the constituent broadcast sectors, each sector producing its own hybrid as influenced by history, culture, local circumstances, level and nature of economic and institutional development, and so forth. The extent and form of the application of market and competitive principles within this overall public interest framework will vary. The balance of size and influence can shift between the sectors, and between underlying approaches, as policy makers and regulators experiment and implement new ideas. There is no single, fixed set of rules on how to maximize the potential of the system to contribute to the public interest, and broadcasting policy and regulation will undoubtedly remain a dynamic area of change and development.

Yet many of the key challenges facing broadcasting reform can be addressed by devising the appropriate policy, legislative, and regulatory framework. This can operate at two levels.

1. Certain aspects of the enabling environment affect all media and extend beyond media per se, encompassing freedom of expression, limits to free speech, defamation laws, and access to information. These features of the policy environment can greatly enhance the prospects for media to

contribute to good governance and development, and go to the heart of open communication in the society and polity.

2. Other policy issues are specific to media and to broadcasting, in particular. These include creating an independent regulator capable of exerting its several functions effectively and creating the space within which the various media sectors and subsectors can thrive. They also include expectations regarding the governance and accountabilities of diverse broadcasting subsectors.

Parts II and III, respectively, address these challenges.

Part II

The Enabling Environment for Media

Overview

In the absence of a conducive wider environment, even the finest guidelines on broadcast policies, laws, and regulations are of little use. Part III addresses the broadcasting sector directly, while Part II outlines some key elements of the enabling environment media in more detail. Without solid guarantees of the right to freedom of expression, media cannot say what they need to say. Without timely access to information, they lack the raw material essential for their job. The overzealous application of—indeed the mere existence of—criminal defamation laws can greatly restrain reporting and end in self-censorship. And while everyone accepts that laws to limit certain media content are justified, preventing the abuse of such laws demands very careful design and implementation. Finally, journalists and the conditions in which they operate hold particular influence over the quality of the media landscape.

All of these issues are covered in Part II: guarantees of freedom of expression, enabling access to information, the use and misuse of defamation laws, content rules and limits to free speech, and the role and regulation of journalists. Most of the territory covered relates to wider concerns for freedom of expression and general openness in society, and some is relevant to media in general, Internet, and print as well as broadcasting. Thus the broadcasting specific regulation and policy are left as the dedicated focus of Part III.

The first three areas for discussion—freedom of expression, access to information, and defamation laws—are particularly important for the achievement of an atmosphere in which everyone, all sectors and people, can have a voice and openly contribute to public discussion. Each of them protects or advances the rights of individuals as well as of the media. In the discussion, these rights are addressed primarily in terms of their impact on the media and their role in society.

Chapter 4 addresses the importance of effective guarantees for freedom of expression, normally at the constitutional level. Progressive guarantees for freedom of expression are a key general underpinning of broadcasting in the public interest. Most countries do have some form of constitutional guarantee of freedom of expression, but they vary considerably in their scope, strength, and means of applicability, and Chapter 4 outlines the key features of a robust system to protect freedom of expression.

Chapter 5 highlights the importance of access to information legislation, granting a right to individuals as well as to the media to access information held by public bodies. Access to information is central to the ability of broadcasters to hold governments to account and to expose corruption. By enabling informed opinions and decisions, it also contributes to people's empowerment and participation. In practice, the law must set out the manner in which this right may be exercised, key features of which include a broad presumption of access, good process guarantees, a narrow regime of exceptions, and the right to appeal a refusal to an independent oversight body.

Appropriate content constraints, the subject of Chapter 6, are a central feature of public interest broadcasting. Unfortunately, many countries still have very restrictive rules in place regarding what may be published or broadcast. Defamation laws, in particular, are often the tool of choice for politicians, officials, and powerful private actors to discourage critical or simply unwelcome reporting.

Although defamation laws are a particular concern in many countries, a number of other restrictions on content—such as national security laws, prohibition against publishing false news and hate speech, and rules governing reporting during elections—can also be abused to prevent critical reporting. These are covered in Chapter 7.

Rules governing journalists, irrespective of the media sector for which they work, are also an important component of the wider environment for broadcasting. Government control over the profession impacts directly on the ability of broadcasters to report. Given their special role in informing all citizens, the right of journalists to protect the confidentiality of their sources of information is one of the few special rights recognized for the profession. These legal and regulatory issues are outlined in Chapter 8. Also covered here are certain systems that are widely used to deal with harmful content in the media. A right of correction and/or reply, in particular, provides quick and accessible redress for victims, while minimizing interference with media freedom.

In its presentation of material in Parts II and III, the guide draws heavily on international standards relating to the right to freedom of expression, as established by various authoritative international bodies. The guide also makes considerable use of country examples to demonstrate how these standards have been implemented in practice. This includes a description of various practical means by which regulatory approaches have been put into place, as well as legal and policy prescriptions and directions, and rulings by superior and constitutional courts regarding appropriate standards.

Guarantees of Freedom of Expression

Good Practice Checklist

- Freedom of expression is a fundamental human right, widely recognized as essential for good development practice and guaranteed in international law and practically all national constitutions. Although freedom of the press is already implicit in this right, it is useful to have it explicitly included among constitutional guarantees.
- Constitutions should ideally provide explicit guarantees for freedom of the media, in recognition of the crucial role of the media in giving practical effect to the free flow of information and ideas in society.
- Incorporation into national legal systems of international guarantees of freedom of expression, which have been subject to extensive and positive elaboration by various authoritative international bodies, can help provide a strong minimum basis of protection for this right.

Introduction

Freedom of expression is a fundamental human right and, as such, should receive formal recognition as a basic value in every society. Guarantees of freedom of expression can be found in almost all modern constitutions and receive strong support under international human rights law and generally among the public.

Although guarantees at the constitutional level are not in themselves sufficient—without political will and more detailed laws and regulations they cannot always be relied on to lead to implementation—they are a vital precondition. Strong guarantees of freedom of expression, when they are respected and implemented, can also have significant developmental consequences, by providing an underpinning for improvements in governance and for the adoption of legal and regulatory frameworks.

The review and improvement of the terms of constitutional guarantees of freedom of expression can be part of a wider process of constitutional reform, common at times of transition to democracy or other significant change to open the governance system to public accountability. From a developmental perspective, such periods of change can provide a critical window of opportunity to strengthen commitments to the right to freedom of expression.

The existence and the terms of constitutional guarantees carry both juridical and social significance. At one level, constitutional provisions are formal legal guarantees setting out the scope of the right and the standards, in respect of this right, to which other laws and official practice must conform. As such, these guarantees are an underpinning for all of the public interest regulatory approaches described in this guide.

Their character as formal legal guarantees also means that constitutional protections can be used to provide practical protection for freedom of expression. In many countries, these guarantees are directly enforceable through the courts, providing a concrete means of redress against laws and official practices that unduly limit freedom of expression. Even where they are not directly applicable, constitutional guarantees can be relied upon to promote an interpretation of other laws that is consistent with freedom of expression.

At another level, constitutional guarantees are peak standard-setting documents, providing a reference point for acceptable government behavior. They are important social documents that create public expectations about what constitutes appropriate official action. They can help give people the confidence to critique government actions or inaction publicly, influence others, and demand improvements in governance and service delivery, without fear of retribution. Even if implementation is legally flawed, failure to conform to the standards is seen as unacceptable. This can help build momentum for change, both by providing clear direction as to an appropriate solution or direction, and by giving authority to challenge occasions when the state or its agents are in breach of the provision.

Most constitutional guarantees of freedom of expression are very brief—normally just a few lines—and it is through judicial interpretation and, in some cases, more detailed legislation, that the precise contours of this rather complex right are more fully elaborated. Constitutional guarantees, if strong, can play a number of key

---

BOX 1. South Africa: Constitutional Guarantees

In apartheid South Africa, the 1983 constitution contained neither a Bill of Rights nor guarantees for freedom of expression. Broadcasting was operated through the South African Broadcasting Corporation (SABC) as a state monopoly and as a mouthpiece of government. During the transitional government of 1993, an interim constitution was adopted which, for the first time, provided an explicit guarantee of the right to freedom of expression. The 1993 constitution signaled the liberalization of broadcasting and stated explicitly that "all media financed by or under the control of the state shall be regulated in a manner which ensures impartiality and the expression of a diversity of opinion." In accordance with the interim constitution, the transitional government adopted the Independent Broadcasting Act of 1993, establishing an independent regulatory body to oversee broadcasting, including community and private commercial services. The present day constitutional guarantees of freedom of expression in South Africa are contained in the postapartheid constitution of 1996, which was the culmination of two years of intensive consultation said to be "the largest public participation programme ever carried out in South Africa."[1]

---

1. Constitution of the Republic of South Africa 1996.

---

standard-setting roles in relation to freedom of expression. Among others, they can include:

- Affirmation of the right to freedom of expression
- Affirmation of the freedom of the press/media
- Provision for the applicability of international law

This chapter examines the scope and nature of these guarantees, their relevance to good development practice, and the mechanisms for their implementation. It provides country examples that offer comparative illustrations of the guarantees and it includes references to the relevant international law and standards.

Guarantees of Freedom of Expression

Freedom of expression is a fundamental human right. It is guaranteed in international law and practically all national constitutions. It is widely recognized today as being an essential foundation for good development practice.

> **BOX 2. Thailand, Mali, Columbia: Constitutional Guarantees**
>
> Section 39 of the Constitution of Thailand, states, in part: "A person shall enjoy the liberty to express his or her opinion, make speeches, write, print, publicize, and make expression by other means." Article 4 of the Constitution of Mali, adopted after the 1991 revolution, states: "Every person has the right to freedom of thought, conscience, religion, opinion, expression and creation in respect to the law." Article 20(1) of the Constitution of Columbia states: "Everyone is guaranteed the right to express and disseminate their thoughts and opinions, freedom to inform and receive truthful and impartial information, and freedom to establish mass communication media."

The right to freedom of expression is explicitly guaranteed in various international declarations and treaties and in most national constitutions. In some countries where there is no explicit guarantee, courts have found an implicit right to freedom of expression. Australia, for example, does not have a bill of rights, although it does have a written constitution. The High Court has held that there is an implied constitutional freedom of political communication, based on the guarantee of elected government. This protection is, however, given its basis, limited to "political discussion," including "discussion of the conduct, policies or fitness for office of government, political parties, public bodies, public officers and those seeking public office."[1]

National guarantees of freedom of expression vary considerably. Constitutional guarantees that are too narrowly defined, in terms either of the types of expression or the modalities of communication covered, fail to provide a sufficient underpinning for realizing developmental, participatory, and accountability needs. Qualities that enhance the guarantee, taking into account judicial interpretation, include the following:

- it applies to everyone, not just citizens or residents;
- it applies to seeking and receiving, as well as imparting, information and ideas;
- it is understood broadly to protect all content, not only that which is deemed socially useful; false, offensive and even harmful speech should be covered; and
- it is understood broadly to protect all forms of communication.

---

[1]See *Lange v. Australian Broadcasting Corporation*, 71 ALJR 818 (1997).

The principle of universal application can contribute to strengthening equitable development, preventing the exclusion of marginalized groups, such as migrant workers and refugees, and avoiding discrimination in access to the means of communication.

Although freedom of expression is most commonly associated with protecting the "speaker," under international law the "listener" is also protected through the right to seek and receive information. As noted previously, the dual aspect to the right is fundamentally important as an underpinning of both access to information legislation and media regulation in the public interest.

The protection of all content (subject to certain limited restrictions described in more detail subsequently) deters the prohibition or restriction of legitimate forms of expression, whether because officials may find it inconvenient, because it is considered offensive by some even though it represents the opinions of others, or because it might harm the popularity of the party in power. The broad protection of content is needed to ensure that different points of view can be heard and criticisms can be aired, including criticisms of those in positions of public authority.

The protection of all forms of communications means the guarantee applies not only to traditional means of communications—such as the press and public speaking—but also to electronic media, such as radio, television, and the Internet.

Constitutions represent societies' fundamental values and are often difficult to amend. The exercise of the right to freedom of expression, on the other hand, is enormously dynamic, particularly in recent years, aided by very rapid changes in technologies and the way these are being used. As a result, textual guarantees should be sufficiently general and flexible to ensure their continued relevance over time.

Guarantees of Freedom of the Press/Media

It is desirable for constitutions to provide explicit guarantees for freedom of the media, in recognition of the crucial role of the media in giving practical effect to the free flow of information and ideas in society.

As with freedom of information, freedom of the press and media is implicit in the right to freedom of expression. At the same time, it has

BOX 3. Argentina: Constitutional Decision to Allow Noncommercial Media

In September 2003, the Argentine Supreme Court declared Article 45 of the Radio Broadcasting Law to contravene the country's constitutional provision for freedom of expression. Article 45 stipulated that only individuals or legally recognized commercial entities could apply for and receive authorization to operate an FM radio station. This excluded cooperatives, community-based groups, and charitable organizations. The judges stated:

> This is an unacceptable restriction of the right to freedom of expression and imposes unreasonable limitations on the choice of whether to incorporate or not. The system . . . should not preclude non-profit entities, who contribute to the social good, from accessing this medium of communication.[1]

The ruling led to amendment of the Radio Broadcasting Law to reflect the Supreme Court decision.

---

1. Discrimination in allocation of radio broadcasting licenses unconstitutional, says Supreme Court, reported on September 4, 2003, available at: *http://www.ifex.org.*

---

been found useful to include specific reference to it at the constitutional level.

Section 2(b) of the Canadian constitution,[2] for instance, states: "Everyone has the following fundamental freedoms: . . . b) freedom of thought, belief, opinion and expression, including freedom of the press and other media of communication." Article 32 of the constitution of Argentina[3] states: "The Federal Congress shall not enact laws restricting the freedom of printing or establishing federal jurisdiction over it."

In Sweden, which is a rather unique case, the entirety of its lengthy Freedom of the Press Act, running to some thirty-eight pages, is part of its constitution. This act sets out detailed rules relating to press freedom, including the right to print and disseminate publications, the right to publish anonymously, and the right to access information held by public authorities. It also includes a section on offenses against freedom of the press.

---

[2] Available at: *http://www.solon.org/constitutions/canada/english/ca_1982.html.*
[3] Available at: *http://www.oefre.unibe.ch/law/icl/ar00000_html.*

The Thai constitution,[4] too, includes detailed provisions specifically aimed at protection of freedom of the press/media. Article 39 includes the following provisions:

(3) The closure of a pressing house or a radio or television station in deprivation of the liberty under this section shall not be made.

(4) The censorship by a competent official of news or articles before their publication in a newspaper, printed matter or radio or television broadcasting shall not be made except during the time when the country is in a state of war or armed conflict; provided that it must be made by virtue of the law enacted under the provisions of paragraph two.

The constitution also includes detailed provisions regarding broadcast regulation, in Article 40, as follows:

(1) Transmission frequencies for radio or television broadcasting and radio telecommunication are national communication resources for public interest.

(2) There shall be an independent regulatory body having the duty to distribute the frequencies under paragraph one and supervise radio or television broadcasting and telecommunication businesses as provided by law.

(3) In carrying out the act under paragraph two, regard shall be had to utmost public benefit at national and local levels in education, culture, State security, and other public interests including fair and free competition.

Unfortunately, implementation of these provisions has been problematic; for example, no independent regulatory body has yet been appointed for broadcasting.

Direct Applicability of International Law

International law provides for strong guarantees of freedom of expression and these have been subject to extensive and positive elaboration by various authoritative international bodies. If the national legal system directly incorporates these guarantees, that can help provide a strong minimum basis of protection for this right.

---

[4]Available at: *http://www.servat.unibe.ch/icl/th00000_.html.*

> **BOX 4. France, United Kingdom: Direct Applicability of International Human Rights Agreements**
>
> Article 55 of the French Constitution provides: "Treaties or agreements duly ratified or approved shall, upon publication, prevail over Acts of Parliament, subject, in regard to each agreement or treaty, to its application by the other party." Article 75(22) of the Argentinean constitution provides that Congress shall have the power:
>
>> To approve or reject treaties entered with other nations and with international organizations, and concordats with the Holy See. Treaties and concordats have higher standing than laws.
>
> The same article goes on to provide that a long list of human rights treaties and declarations have the constitutional status, and complement the rights guaranteed in the constitution, although they shall not be understood as repealing any constitutionally guaranteed rights.
>
> In 1998, the United Kingdom adopted the Human Rights Act, which effectively incorporated the human rights guarantees of the European Convention for the Protection of Human Rights and Fundamental Freedoms into national law. This law gives courts the power to rule out secondary legislation and official practice but not to "strike down" primary legislation. Instead, courts are required to interpret legislation, as far as this is possible, in accordance with human rights guarantees and, where this is not possible, they can enter a declaration of incompatibility, which then empowers a minister to take such action as may be necessary to remove the incompatibility.

In many civil law systems, international law is directly applicable as part of the national legal system, and usually has superior status to ordinary legislation so that, in case of conflict, international law prevails. In common law systems, however, it is rare for the constitution to provide for the general incorporation of international law. International law may specifically be incorporated by statute, but such statutes cannot generally override other legislation.

Even where international law has not been incorporated, the decisions of international courts—such as the European Court of Human Rights and the Inter-American Court of Human Rights—are binding on states. States are, therefore, formally obliged to give effect to these judgments.

The benefits of direct applicability of international law are fairly obvious. It helps to ensure that the state respects its international legal obligations, and thereby lends force to those obligations. More importantly, however, it ensures the formal applicability of a progressive body of standards that has been established through independent mechanisms and by individuals with internationally recognized expertise in the field. It is important to note, however, that very few national courts apply these standards on a regular basis.

5 Enabling Access to Information

Good Practice Checklist

- Constitutional guarantees of the right to information, either specifically or as part of a general right to seek, receive, and impart information, are important both as legal guarantees and to signal the importance of access as a human right.
- The starting point for good practice in access to information laws is the principle of maximum disclosure, which establishes a presumption that all information, defined broadly, held by any public body, again defined broadly, is subject to disclosure.
- An important part of an access to information regime is an obligation for public bodies to publish certain key categories of information, even in the absence of a request, known as proactive or routine disclosure.
- Certain public and private interests may override the right to access information, and good practice access to information laws provide for comprehensive but narrowly and clearly drafted exceptions to the right of access.
- International standards establish that a refusal to disclose information is justified only when a public body can show that disclosure would cause harm to one of the legitimate interests listed and that this harm is greater than the public benefit of disclosing the information.
- To facilitate access to information in practice, an access to information law should set out clearly the manner in which requests will be processed, it should respect minimum due process guarantees, and it should ensure the fair, timely, and inexpensive processing of requests.
- Where a request for information has been refused, the requester should have the right to appeal this refusal to an independent body for adjudication.
- In most countries, one may ultimately appeal to the courts, but in practice, it is very important that an administrative system of appeals be provided which operates rapidly and at low cost.

(continued)

Good Practice Checklist (continued)

- Individuals who, in good faith, release information on wrongdoing, known as whistle-blowers, should be protected from legal, administrative, or employment-related sanctions for so doing.
- Promotional measures can help to overcome the culture of secrecy that exists in many countries and to ensure that the public is properly informed about the new access to information law.

Introduction

The idea that public bodies hold information not for themselves but on behalf of the public is now widely recognized as a fundamental underpinning of democracy and good governance. Numerous recent statements by international human rights bodies assert the importance of the right to know and it has also been recognized as a human right in many national constitutions around the world, particularly those adopted in the last ten to fifteen years. To give practical effect to this right, a growing number of countries—over seventy as of April 2006—have already adopted access to information legislation, with many other countries taking steps in that direction.

Access to information held by public bodies has also been widely promoted as an essential underpinning of equitable and sustainable development. Puddephatt lists five key reasons why access to information is important:

1. it is necessary for informed political debate;
2. secrecy leads to a culture of rumor and conspiracy;
3. secrecy leads to corruption;
4. it is a key tool in combating ignorance, for example in the area of health, which undermines development; and
5. it is crucial to holding governments accountable.[1]

Numerous commentators have noted the role of openness in combating corruption and particularly in providing civil society and the media with a key tool to investigate and expose corrupt practices. As Pope has noted: "Secrecy still strikes at the concerns of civil society

---

[1]A. Puddephatt, Preface in R. Calland and A. Tilley, *The Right to Know, the Right to Live: Access to Information and Socio-Economic Justice* (Cape Town: ODAC, 2002), xi–xii.

everywhere, and most significantly it perpetuates an environment in which corruption can flourish unhindered."[2] There are numerous examples of access to official information being effectively used to combat corruption, some of which have been outlined in Chapter 3.

The crucial importance of access to information as an underpinning of democratic participation is also widely acknowledged. Stiglitz, whose work on the economic implications of asymmetries of information won him a Nobel Prize, has stated: "Essentially, meaningful participation in democratic processes requires informed participants. Secrecy reduces the information available to the citizenry, hobbling people's ability to participate meaningfully."[3] This applies at all levels of participation, whether it be electing a government, sitting on a local school board, or providing feedback to a proposed development project.

Information is equally central to holding government accountable. Unless citizens are properly informed about what government is doing, how it is spending public funds, and its own assessment of its successes and failures, they cannot ensure that it is acting for the general public good, or in accordance with its public promises.[4] Once again, this is relevant at all levels of governance, from the national to the provincial to the local.

Constitutional guarantees of the right to information, either specifically or as part of a general right to seek, receive, and impart information, are important both as legal guarantees and to signal the importance of access as a human right. But detailed access to information legislation is also needed:

- to spell out the practical means by which this right may be exercised (i.e., how requests are to be processed, within what time lines, etc.);

- to elaborate clearly the scope of exceptions to the right of access; and

- to establish the right to appeal any refusals to disclose information to an independent body.

---

[2]J. Pope, "Access to Information: Whose Right and Whose Information?" in Transparency International, *Global Corruption Report 2003: Special Focus: Access to Information* (London: Profile Books, 2003), 21.
[3]J. Stiglitz, "Transparency in Government" in the World Bank, *The Right To Tell: The Role of the Mass Media in Economic Development* (Washington, DC: World Bank, 2002), 30.
[4]T. Mendel, *Freedom of Information: A Comparative Legal Survey* (New Delhi: UNESCO, 2003), iv.

In many countries, specific provisions on access to information in different contexts apply. For example, consumer protection laws and legislation on the environment often include rules providing for access to information or the disclosure of certain specific types of information, including on commercial entities such as corporations. These are important complements to more generic access to information legislation.

The four main features of a good access to information law, reflecting the need for such legislation as just noted, are:

1. a presumption that all information held by public bodies shall be subject to public disclosure;
2. a procedure clarifying the manner in which individuals may place requests for information and how officials should respond;
3. the elaboration of clear grounds for refusing a request for information (the regime of exceptions); and
4. the right to appeal any refusal to disclose information to an independent body.

Other important issues to consider in an access to information law include:

- an obligation to publish information proactively, even in the absence of a request;
- protection for whistle-blowers, individuals who release information on wrongdoing;
- systems for the proper maintenance of the records held by public bodies; and
- measures to promote effective implementation of the legislation.

This last issue is central to the success of an access to information regime. Indeed, it has often been noted that getting an access law adopted, even a very good law, is only the first, and often the easiest, step in terms of putting into place an effective access to information regime.

Numerous international statements provide guidance as to good practices in this area. These include official documents, such as the Recommendation 2002(2) of the Committee of Ministers of the Council of Europe on Access to Official Documents[5] and the African

---

[5]Adopted February 21, 2002.

BOX 5. Sweden: The First to Grant Access

Sweden was the first country in the world to adopt a law granting citizens the right to access information held by public bodies, having adopted its Freedom of the Press Act in 1776.[1] The act, part of the Swedish constitution, guarantees the right of access through Chapter 2 "On the Public Nature of Official Documents." Despite the act's title, the right is available to everyone, not just the press. Article 1 of Chapter 2 of the act states that "every Swedish subject shall have free access to official documents." In practice, however, anyone can claim this right, and Sweden has developed a reputation, for example, for being a good country to access European Union documents. The right to access, and to correct, personal data is provided for by the Personal Data Act, 1998.

---

1. Available at: *http://www.oefre.unibe.ch/law/icl/sw03000_.html.*

Commission on Human and Peoples' Rights' *Declaration of Principles on Freedom of Expression in Africa,*[6] as well as NGO statements, such as Article 19's *The Public's Right to Know: Principles on Freedom of Information Legislation.*[7]

Constitutional Guarantees of Access to Information

Although some argue it is implicit in the guarantee of freedom of expression, explicit constitutional protection regarding the right to access information makes this absolutely clear.

In some countries, courts have held that a right to access information is implicit in more general guarantees of freedom of expression.[8] In other cases, however, courts have declined to find a right of access in more general guarantees.[9] As a result, explicit recognition of this right is important. Although rare in older constitutions, many recent ones

---

[6]Adopted at the 32nd Session, October, 17–23, 2002.

[7](London: ARTICLE 19, 1999), available at: *http://www.article19.org/docimages/ 512.htm.*

[8]For example, as early as 1969, the Supreme Court of Japan established in two high-profile cases the principle that *shiru kenri* (the "right to know") is protected by the guarantee of freedom of expression in Article 21 of the constitution. See Lawrence Repeta, *Local Government Disclosure Systems in Japan* (National Bureau of Asian Research, paper no.16, October 1999), 3.

[9]See, for example, *Houchins v. KQED, Inc.,* 438 US 1 (1978) (United States Supreme Court).

explicitly provide for it. For example, Article 61(1) of the 1997 Polish constitution provides:

> A citizen shall have the right to obtain information on the activities of organs of public authority as well as persons discharging public functions. Such right shall also include receipt of information on the activities of self-governing economic or professional organs and other persons or organizational units relating to the field in which they perform the duties of public authorities and manage communal assets or property of the State Treasury.

Some constitutions also provide for the adoption of legislation implementing the right to information, in some cases even setting time limits on the adoption of such legislation. For example, the South African constitution contains not only the right of access to information but a requirement that national legislation be enacted to give effect to this right. Section 23 of Schedule 6 of the South African constitution provides that implementing legislation on the right of access to information be adopted within three years of the constitution coming into effect, which was indeed done.

Section 7 of Article III of the Philippine constitution provides:

> The right of the people to information on matters of public concern shall be recognized. Access to official records, and to documents and papers pertaining to official acts, transactions, or decisions, as well as to government research data used as basis for policy development, shall be afforded the citizen, subject to such limitations as may be provided by law.

Principle of Maximum Disclosure

> *The starting point for good practice access to information laws is the principle of maximum disclosure, which establishes a presumption that all information, defined broadly, held by any public body, again defined broadly, is subject to disclosure.*

The central idea behind access to information legislation is to provide the general public with access to information held by government institutions. This is reflected in the principle of maximum disclosure, which implies that the law covers all information and all public bodies.

Good practice access to information laws define the scope of information covered very broadly to include all records held by the public body, regardless of the form in which the information is stored—printed document, tape, electronic recording, and so on—its source—whether it was produced by the public body or some other body—and the date of production.

Legislation should cover all branches and levels of government, including local government, elected bodies, bodies that operate under a statutory mandate, nationalized industries and public corporations, nondepartmental public bodies or quangos (quasi nongovernmental organizations), and even private bodies that carry out public functions (such as maintaining roads or operating rail lines).

However, in some cases private bodies can also become subject to access laws. In South Africa, for instance, the African law provides for a right to access to information held by both public and private bodies. A public body is defined as a department of state or administration in the national, provincial, or municipal spheres, and any other institution exercising a power in terms of the constitution or a provincial constitution, or exercising a public power or performing a public function in terms of any legislation. Private bodies are defined as bodies that engage in commercial activities; they are required to provide access to information where this is required for the exercise or protection of any right.

A slightly different approach is taken in the United Kingdom, where the main means for designating public bodies is through a list of bodies covered—set out in Schedule 1 of the act, which runs to some eighteen pages—rather than a generic definition. The list includes all government departments, the various legislative bodies,[10] the armed forces, and numerous other bodies listed individually by name. Publicly owned corporations are also classified as public bodies. The act does not, however, cover the secret services (intelligence operations) or, with a few small exceptions, the court system. The act also grants the secretary of state the power to designate further public bodies.

The 1997 Official Information Act of Thailand defines information to include any material that communicates anything, regardless of the form that material takes. Official information, in turn, is defined simply as information in the possession of a public body,

---

[10]The act does not cover Scotland, which has its own law, the Freedom of Information (Scotland) Act of 2002.

whether relating to the operation of the state or to a private individual. The latter is very important given that exposure of corruption will often be through information relating to a private individual.

Proactive or Routine Disclosure

An important part of an access to information regime is an obligation for public bodies to publish certain key categories of information, even in the absence of a request, known as proactive or routine disclosure.

Supplementing direct requests for information, the proactive dissemination of key information by public bodies is a central component of most modern access to information regimes. Routine disclosure serves a number of goals relating to democratic participation and sustainable development. For example, information relating to participatory mechanisms, such as school councils or public discussions around a development project or strategy, needs to be widely disseminated if it is to be effective and accessible to all segments of the population. More generally, the success of moves toward e-government hinges on proactive information disclosure. For these goals to be served, the information must be disseminated in a manner that ensures it is accessible to the intended beneficiaries and is in a form in which they can understand and can make use of it. The growth of new information technologies has also made it easier to publish more and more information electronically.

In principle, any information that may be of public interest, and which is clearly not subject to an exception, should be provided electronically and, in practice, many public bodies are in fact moving in this direction. Good practice laws vary in the specific information they require public bodies to publish, but certain categories of information are normally included. These are derived directly from the broader goals of development, participation, and accountability, for the realization of which access to information is so important. The following categories are subject to routine disclosure in most access laws:

- operational information about how the public body functions, including costs, objectives, audited accounts, standards, achievements, and so on, particularly where the body provides direct services to the public;

BOX 6.   Innovative Approaches to Routine Disclosure

Article 14(2) of the Bulgarian Access to Public Information Act, 2000, contains a public interest rule governing proactive disclosure. It requires public bodies to disseminate information that may prevent a threat to life, health, security, or property, or that could be of public interest, even if it is otherwise confidential, where the public interest in receiving it outweighs the risk of harm to the confidential interest. This public interest override in relation to the duty to publish is an interesting innovation not found in most other laws.

The Thai Official Information Act of 1997 specifies two means of routine disclosure; some information must be published in the *Government Gazette*, while other information must be made available for inspection at the organization's premises.

The UK Freedom of Information Act includes a unique system for levering up over time the amount of information subject to routine disclosure. Rather than providing for a list of information that each public body must publish, every public body is required to develop and implement a publication scheme. This must set out the classes of information that the public body will publish, the manner in which it will publish them, and whether or not it intends to charge for any particular publication. Importantly, the scheme must be approved by the Information Commissioner, who may put a time limit on his or her approval, or withdraw the approval at any time. This system promotes the progressive improvement of publication schemes, so that they may encompass more and more information over time.

A very practical measure in Mexico's 2002 Federal Transparency and Access to Public Government Information Law requires all public bodies to establish accessible computer terminals on their premises, and to provide assistance to the public in using them.

- information on any requests, complaints, or other direct actions that members of the public may take in relation to the public body;
- guidance on processes by which members of the public may provide input into major policy or legislative proposals;
- the types of information that the body holds and the form in which this information is held; and
- the content of any decision or policy affecting the public, along with reasons for the decision and background material of importance in framing the decision.

Narrow Regime of Exceptions

It is recognized that certain public and private interests override the right to access information, and all access to information laws provide for exceptions to the right of access. The exceptions should be comprehensive, and drafted narrowly and clearly. International standards establish that a refusal to disclose information is justified only where a public body can show that disclosure would cause harm to one of the legitimate interests listed and that this harm is greater than the public benefit of disclosing the information.

The regime of exceptions is a key part of any access to information law. On the one hand, the law must protect a number of legitimate, both public and private, secrecy interests. On the other hand, if the regime of exceptions is too broad, it will significantly undermine the right to information.

It is recognized that some degree of confidentiality around internal decision making and advice is legitimate; civil servants might be inhibited from providing free and frank advice if this were automatically subject to open public scrutiny. At the same time, many laws cast this exception in unduly broad terms. For example, the Swedish Freedom of the Press Act, which is also an access to information law, provides, at Article 7 of Chapter 2, that a document has been drawn up by a public authority only if the matter to which it relates has been "finally settled by the authority," "finally checked and approved," or "finalized in some other manner." Critics argue that this represents an unnecessarily complicated and broad way of protecting the free and frank provision of advice. In many cases, the access to information law overrides secrecy laws in case of conflict. This is true, for example, in India, South Africa, and Pakistan, but not in Mexico or the United Kingdom.

Yet no matter how carefully drafted, exceptions cannot accommodate every situation where information should, on public interest grounds, be disclosed. As a result, many laws provide that, even if disclosure of information would cause harm to a legitimate interest, the information should still be disclosed if the benefits of disclosure outweigh the harm—a provision known as the public interest override. For example, certain information may be private in nature but at the same time expose high-level corruption within government. These interests should be weighed against each other when determining whether or not the public interest override applies.

BOX 7.   The Council of Europe Standards on Exceptions

Recommendation 2002(2) of the Committee of Ministers of the Council of Europe on Access to Official Documents sets out very clearly the standards to be applied to exceptions in Principle IV:

1. Member states may limit the right of access to official documents. Limitations should be set down precisely in law, be necessary in a democratic society and be proportionate to the aim of protecting:

    i.   national security, defence, and international relations;
    ii. public safety;
    iii. the prevention, investigation, and prosecution of criminal activities;
    iv. privacy and other legitimate private interests;
    v.   commercial and other economic interests, be they private or public;
    vi. the equality of parties concerning court proceedings;
    vii. nature;
    viii. inspection, control and supervision by public authorities;
    ix. the economic, monetary and exchange rate policies of the state;
    x.   the confidentiality of deliberations within or between public authorities during the internal preparation of a matter.

2. Access to a document may be refused if the disclosure of the information contained in the official document would or would be likely to harm any of the interests mentioned in paragraph 1, unless there is an overriding public interest in disclosure.
3. Member states should consider setting time limits beyond which the limitations mentioned in paragraph 1 would no longer apply.

Three principles governing exceptions are evident from this recommendation. In particular, exceptions should only apply where:

- the information relates to a legitimate interest listed in the law;
- disclosure threatens to cause harm to that interest; and
- the harm to the legitimate interest is greater than the public interest in having the information.

Furthermore, the recommendation stipulates that overall time limits should be established, beyond which exceptions, or certain exceptions, no longer apply. This is particularly important for certain types of exceptions, particularly those protecting public interests, and which the authorities have a systematic tendency to interpret broadly, such as national security.[1]

---

1. See Toby Mendel, "National Security vs. Openness: An Overview and Status Report on the Johannesburg Principles" in *National Security and Open Government: Striking the Right Balance* (New York: Campbell Public Affairs Institute, Maxwell School of Syracuse Univesity, 2003), p. 1.

All of the exceptions in the South African law, for example, are subject to a public interest override. This applies whenever the disclosure of the record would reveal evidence of a substantial contravention of, or failure to comply with, the law or an imminent and serious risk to public safety or the environment, and where the public interest in disclosure "clearly outweighs" the harm. The Thai law requires public officials to consider the public interest when assessing exceptions. The UK law includes a good, and broad, public interest override, providing that nondisclosure is justified only where, "in all the

---

BOX 8.   India: Exceptions in the Right to Information Act

The Indian Right to Information Act of 2005 provides for the following exceptions to the right of access:

   i. information, disclosure of which would prejudicially affect the sovereignty and integrity of India, the security, strategic, scientific, or economic interests of the state or relations with foreign state, or would incite to an offence;
   ii. information which has been expressly forbidden to be published by any court of law or tribunal or the disclosure of which may constitute contempt of court;
   iii. information, the disclosure of which would cause a breach of privilege of Parliament or a state legislature;
   iv. cabinet papers including records of deliberations of the Council of Ministers, Secretaries and other officers;
   v. information received in confidence from a foreign government; and
   vi. information, including commercial confidences, trade secrets or intellectual property, the disclosure of which would harm the competitive position of a third party, unless the competent authority is satisfied that the larger public interest warrants the disclosure of such information.

Most of these exceptions include a harm test, and all are subject to a general public interest override. There is an overall 20-year time limit on most exceptions.

Importantly, the Right to Information Act specifically overrides secrecy laws to the extent of any inconsistency, explicitly referring in this context to the infamous Official Secrets Act of 1923, passed during the period of British rule, and stating:

> The provisions of this Act shall have effect notwithstanding anything inconsistent therewith contained in the Official Secrets Act, 1923, and any other law for the time being in force or in any instrument having effect by virtue of any law other than this Act.

circumstances of the case, the public interest in maintaining the exemption outweighs the public interest in disclosing the information."

Good Process Guarantees

To facilitate practical access to information, an access to information law should set out clearly the manner in which requests will be processed. This should respect minimum due process guarantees and ensure the fair, timely, and inexpensive processing of requests.

Good process guarantees help ensure the proper application of the law, whereas poor procedural mechanisms can result in delay and confusion, undermining the right of access.

In good practice access to information laws, requests can be made in a number of different formats, including orally and by email. The Bulgarian Access to Public Information Act, for example, provides that requests may be made in either oral or written form. Requests must be registered by the public body in question, ensuring a paper trail for even oral requests.

To ensure that all citizens can make information disclosure requests, measures to promote equitable access outside of the capital region, such as providing for ministries with a presence throughout the country to serve as general points for receipt of information

---

BOX 9. Sweden: Facilitating Access by Listing Holdings

The Swedish access to information system includes a particularly useful feature, set out in Chapter 15 of the Secrecy Act, 1981, requiring all public authorities to produce a register of all documents held.[1] In general these registers are open for public inspection and an effort is now under way to ensure that they are available electronically. This system enormously facilitates access, by letting requesters know in advance what information the public body holds.

---

1. There are four exceptions to this rule:

   1. documents that are obviously of little importance, such as press cuttings;
   2. documents that are not secret and that are kept in a manner which makes it easy to ascertain whether they have been received or drawn up by a public authority;
   3. documents found in large numbers that have been exempted; and
   4. electronic records kept in a central registry.

requests, should be considered. Public bodies should also be required to provide assistance to those who are having difficultly formulating their requests. Special assistance may be needed for illiterate or disabled requesters. This is stipulated, for example, in the South African law. An official receipt should be provided as evidence of a request having been made, among other things, to serve as the basis for an appeal if the request is not responded to in time or at all.

Public bodies should be required to respond to requests as soon as possible, and a maximum time limit for responding to requests should be established. The Bulgarian act, for example, provides that requesters must be notified in writing of a decision regarding their request as quickly as possible but in any case within fourteen days. Where the request is for a large number of documents and more time is needed to respond, an extension of up to ten days may be made, provided that the requester be notified of this.

Where requests have been refused, in full or in part, the requester should be provided with the reasons why his or her request was refused, including the specific exception relied upon, as well as information about the right to appeal the refusal. This is necessary for requesters to frame an effective appeal against any refusal to provide access.

BOX 10. United States: Varied Fee Scales

The 1966 U.S. Freedom of Information Act sets out detailed rules on the fees that may be charged for requests for information, which must conform to central guidelines providing a uniform schedule of fees for all public bodies. The law provides for three different fee systems. Requests for commercial use may be billed "reasonable standard charges for document search, duplication, and review." Requests by educational or scientific institutions may be billed only "reasonable standard charges for document duplication," and all other requests may be charged for search and duplication. For the latter two categories of requester, no fees may be charged for the first 2 hours of search or for the first 100 pages of documents, or where the cost of collecting the fee would exceed the value of the fee. Furthermore, where disclosure is in the public interest because it is "likely to contribute significantly to public understanding of the operations or activities of the government," information must be provided without charge or at a lower charge than would otherwise be the case. This is, in effect, a waiver for the media, as well as for NGOs who can show a public interest use.

BOX 11.   Japan: Progressive Process Provision

The Japanese Law Concerning Access to Information Held by Administrative Organs, 1999, includes a number of progressive provisions on process. A request should describe the record sought in sufficient detail to enable it to be found, but where this is not the case, the administrative organ notifies the requester and gives him or her a suitable amount of time to remedy the problem, while also "endeavoring" to provide assistance.

A decision to disclose must normally be made within 30 days and the requester must be notified of this decision in writing. This period may be extended for another 30 days, "when there are justifiable grounds such as difficulties arising from the conduct of business," provided that the requester must be notified of any such extension in writing, along with the reasons. Requesters may ask to inspect the record and to be provided with copies or other forms of access, and this should be respected unless it would pose a risk of harm to the record.

Fees may be charged for both processing the request and for providing the information, provided that these do not exceed the actual cost. The fee structure must take into account the desirability of keeping fees to as "affordable an amount as possible," and the head of the administrative organ may reduce or waive the fee in cases of economic hardship or for other special reasons.

Fees may be charged for lodging a request and/or for being given access to the information but, if these are excessive, they will undermine the right of access. A common provision in national laws is that fees should not, in any circumstances, exceed the actual costs of providing access. If fee schedules are set centrally, this will avoid a patchwork of fee systems across the public service, with some ministries and public bodies providing access at lower rates and some at higher ones.

Right to Independent Review of Refusals to Grant Access

Where a request for information has been refused, the requester should have the right to appeal this refusal to an independent body for adjudication. An administrative system of appeals that operates rapidly and at low cost should be provided for.

Requesters should have the right to appeal to an independent body against any refusal by a public body to grant access. If public bodies themselves make the final decision as to whether or not the information requested is exempt from disclosure, the right of access, or at least the power to determine the scope of the exceptions, is effectively at the discretion of officials. In most countries, the courts act as the final arbiters of such disputes, and this is important as a means of providing fully reasoned and authoritative answers to the many complex questions an access to information regime can be expected to generate. At the same time, court challenges are expensive and time consuming; few requesters are prepared to devote so much time and money simply to get the desired information. Administrative appeals, on the other hand, can be rapid and low cost, making them far more accessible, and hence effective.

To realize these benefits, many access to information laws provide for appeals to an independent administrative body. As in the case of the courts, it is clearly important that such an administrative body be independent of government. Otherwise, it cannot be expected to provide effective oversight of the system and, in particular, to overrule refusals by officials to disclose information.

BOX 12.   Pakistan and Mexico: Rules on Refusal

Pakistan's Freedom of Information Ordinance, 2002, provides for two levels of appeals, one internal and one to an administrative body. Requesters have 30 days after being refused information to appeal this refusal to the head of the public body concerned and, upon failing to get the information from him or her "within the prescribed time," from there to the Mohtasib (ombudsman) or, in cases involving the Revenue Division, to the federal tax ombudsman. These officials may either direct the public body to release the information or reject the complaint. Although the law does not specify this, requesters presumably also have a right to appeal from there to the courts.

Under the Mexican Act, appeals from any refusal to provide information go first to the Federal Institute of Access to Information, established under the act, and from there to the courts. The institute is an independent body. The five commissioners are nominated by the executive branch, but nominations may be vetoed by a majority vote of either the Senate or the Permanent Commission. Individuals may not be appointed as commissioners unless they are citizens, have not been convicted of a crime of fraud, are at least 35 years old, do not have strong political connections, and have "performed outstandingly in the professional activities." Commissioners hold office for 6 years, but may be removed for serious or repeated violations of the constitution or the act, where their actions or failure to act undermine the work of the institute, or if they have been convicted of a crime subject to imprisonment.

Protection for Whistle-blowers

Individuals who, in good faith, release information on wrongdoing, known as whistle-blowers, should be protected from legal, administrative, or employment-related sanctions for so doing.

Whistle-blowers act as an important information safety valve, making sure that key information on wrongdoing reaches the public. They are a key supplement to the other information disclosures systems insofar as they bring to light information that would otherwise remain hidden, and they can play a particularly important role in relation to the exposure of corruption, promote greater public accountability, expose corporate crimes, and bring environmental harms to light.

To encourage this practice, it is important to protect whistle-blowers from sanction, as long as they acted in good faith. This protection may be triggered, for example, by the exposure of the commission of a criminal offense, a failure to comply with a legal obligation, a miscarriage of justice, corruption or dishonesty, or serious maladministration regarding a public body. It should also extend to those who release information disclosing a serious threat to health, safety, or the environment, whether linked to individual wrongdoing or not. Such protection should apply even where disclosure would otherwise be in breach of a legal or employment requirement.

Few countries include general protection for whistle-blowers within their access to information laws, but rather in separate laws specifically devoted to this.

In South Africa, the Protected Disclosures Act of 2000 provides protection to those who, in good faith, disclose information on wrongdoing. The access law also protects individuals who, in good faith, disclose information pursuant to a request. Similarly, in the United Kingdom, the Public Interest Disclosure Act of 1998, rather than the Freedom of Information Act, provides protection for whistle-blowers. The access law, however, protects those who provide information in response to a request from any liability in defamation.

An interesting proposal in this area was tabled in the Philippines, although it has not been passed into law. In 2004, Senator Mar Roxas filed a bill in the Senate that would have not only protected whistle-blowers but would actually have provided rewards to anyone who uncovered and divulged corrupt practices or acts of graft in government. The amount of the award would have depended on a combination of the nature of the offense exposed, the sum of money recovered, and the salary of the official in question.

Promotional Measures

A number of promotional measures are needed to overcome the culture of secrecy that exists in many countries and to ensure that the public is properly informed about the new access to information law.

Deeply entrenched cultures of secrecy, founded on the idea that public bodies, or even individual officials, rather than the public as a whole, own the information they hold or have created, can seriously undermine even the most progressive access legislation. Promotional measures, both among the public bodies and the public, can help to address this.

The appropriate measures will depend on the context, but they may include:

- requiring public bodies, or one central body, to publish and widely disseminate a public guide to using the access to information law;
- placing positive obligations on information officers to take the lead in ensuring that the public body in question meets its obligations under the law;
- making provision for adequate training of public officials; and
- requiring public bodies to report annually on their activities to implement the access to information law, including by providing an overview of requests made and how they were resolved.

Many access to information laws provide for criminal sanctions for those who wilfully obstruct access, for instance in India, Mexico, the United Kingdom, and South Africa.

Guides and public provision of other types of information to facilitate public access are an important promotional measure. Requiring public bodies to report on their access to information activities can be central to enabling civic engagement with those bodies around information disclosure issues, as well as to facilitating the monitoring of openness trends, bottlenecks, and so on.

It may be noted that changing cultures, including those internal to government, is never an easy or short-term task and that changing cultures of secrecy has proven to be one of the most significant implementation challenges for access to information advocates.

BOX 13.   United States: Producing a Guide and Reporting Requirements

In the United States, the head of each public body is required to prepare and make publicly available a guide for requesting records, including an index of all major information systems, a description of the main information locator systems, and a handbook for obtaining various types of public information from the body.

Public bodies are required to submit annual reports to the attorney general on their activities under the act, and these annual reports must be made publicly available, including via electronic means. The reports must, in particular, cover:

- the number of refusals to disclose information, along with the reasons given;
- the number of appeals, their outcome, and the grounds for each appeal that does not result in disclosure of information;
- a list of all statutes relied upon to withhold information, whether the court has upheld the refusal to disclose, and the scope of information withheld;
- the number of requests pending and the average number of days they have been pending;
- the number of requests both received and processed, along with the average number of days to process requests of different types;
- the total amount of fees charged; and
- the number of full-time staff working on access to information.

BOX 14. South Africa: Protections for Officials Who Disclose Information

The South African Promotion of Access to Information Act, 2001, protects anyone against liability for anything done in good faith pursuant to the act. This is designed to protect public officials who make progressive decisions to disclose information. Furthermore, it is a criminal offense to destroy, damage, alter, conceal, or falsify a record with intent to deny a right of access, punishable by up to two years imprisonment.

Every public body must compile, in at least three official languages, a manual with information about its information disclosure processes. The precise contents of the manual are set out in section 14 of the act, including information about the structure of the body, how to make information requests, services available to the public, any consultative or participatory processes, and a description of all remedies. Public bodies are also required to submit an annual report with detailed information about the number of information requests, whether or not they were granted, the provisions of the act relied upon to deny access, appeals, and so on, to the Human Rights Commission.

The Human Rights Commission is tasked with a number of promotional duties under the Act, including:

- publishing a guide on how to use the act;
- providing an annual report to the National Assembly on the functioning of the act, including any recommendations and detailed information, in relation to each public body, about requests received, granted, refused, appealed, and so on;
- undertaking educational and training programs;
- promoting the timely dissemination of accurate information;
- making recommendations to improve the functioning of the act, including to public bodies;
- monitoring implementation; and
- assisting individuals to exercise their rights under the act.

6

Use and Misuse of Defamation Law

Good Practice Checklist

- Public bodies—including all bodies that form part of the legislative, executive, or judicial branches of government or that otherwise perform public functions—should not be able to bring defamation actions.
- There is a growing trend to repeal criminal defamation laws and to replace them, where necessary, with civil defamation laws.
- In many countries, proof of the truth of any statements alleged to be defamatory completely absolves the defendant of liability.
- In some counties, the person bringing the defamation action bears the burden of proving that the statement is false, at least in relation to statements on matters of public interest.
- Defamation laws should not provide any special protection for public officials, whatever their rank or status, and in some countries it is extremely difficult for public officials to win defamation cases based on statements about their public functions.
- Statements of opinion—understood broadly to include all statements that do not contain a factually provable allegation, as well as statements that cannot reasonably be interpreted as stating actual fact (e.g., because they are satirical)—normally benefit from a greater degree of protection under defamation law than statements of fact.
- In many countries, a defense against a charge of defamation relating to a statement on a matter of public interest can be entered by showing that it was reasonable in all the circumstances for the defendant to have disseminated the statement, even if that statement has been shown to be false.
- The overriding goal of providing a remedy for defamatory statements is to redress the harm done to the reputation of the plaintiff, not to punish those responsible for the dissemination of the statement.
- Remedies or sanctions for defamation should be proportionate to the harm done.

Introduction

The need to protect reputations means that some limits are always imposed on the right to freedom of expression. The term defamation is used here to refer to all such laws, recognizing that they go by a number of different names in different countries, including libel, slander, insult, *desacato,* and so on.

Freedom of expression plays a central role in exposing corruption, in holding governments to account, and in underpinning democratic participation. To do so, individuals, and particularly journalists, must be able to publish what they know without fear of prosecution.

A scientific study in the United Kingdom, based on research of actual defamation cases brought to court, *Libel and the Media: The Chilling Effect,* concluded that the defamation law in that country "significantly restricts what the public is able to read and hear."[1] Furthermore, it noted the "deeper, and subtler way in which libel inhibits media publication," which functions in a "preventive manner: preventing the creation of certain material,"[2] often referred to as the "chilling effect."

This problem is certainly not restricted to the United Kingdom. In many countries, defamation is the restriction on content that exerts the most serious chilling effect on freedom of expression, undermining the ability of the media and others to report in the public interest. In countries in transition to democracy, the erstwhile direct forms of control by the authorities over the media—such as licensing publications, prior censorship, and ministerial control over broadcast licensing—have often been done away with. In this context, authorities often look to defamation law to prevent criticism of their actions. Croatia presents a typical example of this. In that country, there was an explosion of cases in the mid- to late-1990s, with a huge number against just one critical independent newspaper, *Feral Tribune.*[3]

In a similar vein, unduly harsh defamation laws also undermine civic participation and development, since these also often involve

---

[1]E. Barendt, L. Lustgarten, K. Norrie, and H. Stephenson (Oxford: Oxford University Press, 1997), 193.

[2]*Ibid.,* p. 194.

[3]See International Press Institute, 1999 World Press Freedom Review, Croatia. Excerpts available at: *http://archiv.medienhilfe.ch/Reports/ipi1999/IPI-CRO.htm.*

BOX 15. Indonesia: Misuse of Criminal Defamation

The case of Bambang Harymurti, editor of *Tempo*, a leading Indonesian news magazine, is illustrative. Bambang was charged with criminal defamation for an article published in *Tempo* alleging corruption on the part of a local businessman in relation to a market fire. Despite the obvious public interest nature of the article, and the lack of bad faith, Bambang was originally convicted and sentenced to a year's imprisonment. Although he was finally acquitted by the Indonesian Supreme Court, the case exerted a serious chilling effect on the media. It also provides a good illustration of how the powerful, whether they be businessmen or political figures, can abuse defamation laws to prevent criticism.

---

unwanted criticism. Criticism by locals of a development project, for example, may have political implications and hence attract defamation suits, undermining participatory processes and the two-way flow of information.

The central challenge of defamation law is to provide an appropriate balance between the right to freedom of expression and everyone's interest in maintaining their reputation. But certain kinds of statements, in particular, statements about matters of public concern, including those relating to public figures, should benefit from greater protection. The importance, in a democracy, of open discussion about such matters justifies a different balancing approach in these cases.

Who May Sue

Public bodies—including all bodies that form part of the legislative, executive, or judicial branches of government or that otherwise perform public functions—should not be able to bring defamation actions.

In a democracy, open criticism of government and public authorities is of vital importance. These bodies play a central role in development and must be held to account, even if doing so sometimes involves robust, and even unjustified, criticism. As the Supreme Court of Nepal noted, in a case involving criticism of the government:

> So long as citizens are not involved in violent activities, do not jeopardize the peace and order situation, or create anarchism or intend to do so and if the objective of such

---

BOX 16. United Kingdom: Rationale for Restricting the Right of Elected Bodies to Sue

In the UK case of *Derbyshire County Council v. Times Newspapers Ltd.*, the House of Lords ruled that the common law does not allow a local authority to maintain an action for damages for libel. As an elected body, it "should be open to uninhibited public criticism. The threat of a civil action for defamation must inevitably have an inhibiting effect on freedom of speech."[1]

The House of Lords put forward a threefold rationale for restricting the ability of elected bodies to sue. First, criticism of government is vital to the success of a democracy, and defamation suits inhibit free debate about vital matters of public concern. Second, defamation laws are designed to protect reputations. Elected bodies should not be entitled to sue in defamation because any reputation they might have would belong to the public as a whole, which on balance benefits from uninhibited criticism. Furthermore, elected bodies regularly change membership, so "it is difficult to say the local authority as such has any reputation of its own." Finally, the government has ample ability to defend itself from harsh criticism by other means, for example by responding directly to any allegations. Allowing public bodies to sue is an inappropriate use of taxpayers' money, one which may well be open to abuse by governments intolerant of criticism.

1. [1993] 1 All ER 1011, p. 1017.

---

criticism is to effect changes in the work and policy of the government to improve the condition of the general public he or she has the freedom to speak out against the government.[4]

Courts in a number of countries have specifically ruled against the possibility of defamation suits by public bodies. The Indian Supreme Court, for example, in *Rajagopal v. State of Tamil Nadu*, held that "the Government, local authority and other organs and institutions exercising governmental power" cannot bring a defamation suit.[5] This has been extended by some courts to elected bodies and state-owned corporations. State-owned corporations, for example, have failed to win standing in South Africa and Zimbabwe.[6]

---

[4]*Dr. K. I. Singh v. His Majesty's Government of Nepal (HMG/N)* (1965) Nepal Kanun Patra (NKP) (*Nepal Law Journal*) (NKP, 2022 B.S.: Decision No. 279, pg. 58). A similar position has been taken in the United States. See *City of Chicago v. Tribune Co.*, 307 Ill 595 (1923).
[5]6 Supreme Court Cases 632 (1994), 650.
[6]See *Die Spoorbond and Anor. v. South African Railways*, AD 999 (1946) and *Posts and Telecommunications Co. v. Modus Publications (Private) Ltd.*, No. SC 199/97 (Supreme Court of Zimbabwe, November 25, 1997).

The international trend is to extend the scope of this prohibition to an ever-wider range of public bodies, and even to include political parties.[7]

Criminal Defamation

There is a growing trend to repeal criminal defamation laws and to replace them, where necessary, with civil defamation laws.

The threat of potentially much harsher sanctions, especially imprisonment, in those countries that treat defamation as a criminal offense exerts a profound chilling effect on freedom of expression and reinforces many of the problems outlined previously.

Furthermore, the experience of the growing number of countries where defamation is exclusively a civil matter (see the following box), either by law or as a matter of practice, demonstrates the adequacy of noncriminal sanctions in redressing harm to reputation. The experience

---

BOX 17. Countries That Have Abolished or Limited Criminal Defamation

A number of countries have completely abolished criminal defamation laws recently. These include Bosnia-Herzegovina (2002), Central African Republic (2004), Georgia (2004), Ghana (2001), Sri Lanka (2002), Togo (2004), and the Ukraine (2001). Albania is also about to decriminalize defamation.

Some countries—such as France and Bulgaria—have done away with the possibility of imprisonment for defamation. Countries such as Argentina, Chile, Costa Rica, Honduras, Paraguay, and Peru have done away with their notorious *desacato* laws, which provided special criminal law protection for public officials. The Cambodian government has recently pledged to do the same. In a growing number of other jurisdictions, civil defamation laws are the preferred means of redress, even though criminal defamation laws are still on the books. This is the case, for example, in many European countries. In other countries, criminal defamation laws have fallen into virtual desuetude. There has been no successful attempt to bring a criminal prosecution for defamation in the United Kingdom for many years. In the United States, criminal defamation laws have been repealed or ruled unconstitutional in most states, and there has been no successful prosecution for many years.

---

[7]See the United Kingdom case, *Goldsmith and Anor. v. Bhoyrul and Others*, 4 All ER 268 (1997).

of these countries, which have not witnessed any increase in defamation cases or in the seriousness of defamation complaints, refutes the argument that criminal sanctions are necessary to punish defamatory statements.

> *These national developments have been accompanied by a growing body of authoritative international commentary to the effect that criminal defamation laws cannot be justified as a restriction on freedom of expression.*

The three special international mandates for promoting freedom of expression—the UN Special Rapporteur, the OSCE Representative on Freedom of the Media, and the OAS Special Rapporteur on Freedom of Expression—called on states to repeal their criminal defamation laws in their joint declarations of November 1999, November 2000, and December 2002. The 2002 statement read:

> Criminal defamation is not a justifiable restriction on freedom of expression; all criminal defamation laws should be abolished and replaced, where necessary, with appropriate civil defamation laws.[8]

The Inter-American Commission on Human Rights, in its report on the compatibility of *desacato* laws with the American Convention on Human Rights, suggested that all matters relating to the protection of reputation should be dealt with as a matter of civil law:

> The Commission considers that the State's obligation to protect the rights of others is served by providing statutory protection against intentional infringement on honor and reputation through civil actions and by implementing laws that guarantee the right of reply.[9]

In two recent cases involving criminal defamation laws, the Inter-American Court of Human Rights has found a violation of the right to freedom of expression. These decisions make it clear that its use will be very hard to justify, particularly in the context of statements relating to matters of public interest.[10]

---

[8]Joint Declaration of December 10, 2002.

[9]1994 Annual Report of the Inter-American Commission on Human Rights, Chapter V, Conclusion.

[10]See *Herrera-Ulloa vs. Costa Rica*, July 2, Series C, No. 107 (2004) and *Ricardo Canese vs. Paraguay*, Series C, No. 111 (August 31, 2004) (both Inter-American Court of Human Rights).

Proof of Truth

In many countries, proof of the truth of any statements alleged to be defamatory completely absolves the defendant of liability. In some counties, the person bringing the defamation action bears the burden of proving that the statement is false, at least in relation to statements on matters of public interest.

No one should be subject to liability in defamation law for disseminating a true statement. This is reflected, for example, in Principle XII of the *Declaration of Principles on Freedom of Expression in Africa*, which states, in part:

1. States should ensure that their laws relating to defamation conform to the following standards:

   - *no one shall be found liable for true statements* . . .[11]

The right to publish truths also derives from basic principles of freedom of expression, as well as the obvious principle that one cannot defend a reputation one does not deserve. In other words, if someone writes the truth about another person, which harms the latter's reputation, in fact that person had been enjoying a reputation he or she did not deserve in the first place. Protecting true statements under defamation law does not necessarily rule out the possibility of other sorts of legal action for true statements, such as protection of privacy.

At the very minimum, defendants should always be given a full opportunity to prove that their statements were true. In *Castells v. Spain*,[12] for example, the European Court of Human Rights ruled that the failure of the Spanish courts to allow Castells to prove the truth of his statements in a defamation case was a violation of his right to freedom of expression, which could not be justified in a democratic society.

Requiring statements not only to be true but also to be in the public interest, as in the case with some defamation laws, places an unacceptable burden on journalists and others wishing to publish. It also runs counter to the basic thrust of the right to freedom of expression, which requires restrictions to be in the public interest, not

---

[11] Adopted by the African Commission on Human and Peoples' Rights at its 32nd Session, October 17–23, 2002.

[12] *Castells v. Spain*, 236 Eur. Ct. H.R. (ser.A) (1992), available at *http://www.world lii.org/eu/cases/ECHR/1992/48.html*.

BOX 18.   United States: The Onus on the Plaintiff to Prove the Case

In the leading U.S. case, *New York Times Co. v. Sullivan*,[1] the U.S. Supreme Court held that, in relation to statements about public officials, the onus was on the plaintiff to prove that the statements were false. Furthermore, the plaintiff also had to prove that the statements had been published in malice, or with reckless disregard for the truth to succeed in the action. Subsequent cases have extended the scope of this rule, for example to candidates for public office[2] and public figures who do not hold official or government positions.[3]

---

1. 376 US 254, 279 (1964).
2. *Monitor Patriot Co. v. Roy* (1971) 401 US 265.
3. *Curtis Publishing Co. v. Butts* (1967) 388 US 130.

---

the exercise of the right. This was pointed out by the House of Lords in the UK case *Gleaves v. Deakin*. At issue in this case was a criminal defamation rule that required not only proof of the truth of the statements, but also proof that publication was for the public benefit. As Lord Diplock stated: "This is to turn article 10 of the [European Convention on Human Rights, guaranteeing freedom of expression] on its head . . . article 10 requires that freedom of expression shall be untrammelled [unless interference] is necessary for the protection of the public interest."[13]

No Special Protection for Public Officials

> *Defamation laws should not provide any special protection for public officials, whatever their rank or status. In some countries, it is extremely difficult for public officials to win defamation cases based on statements about their public functions.*

It is now well established in international law that public officials should be required to tolerate more, rather than less, criticism than ordinary citizens. In its very first defamation case, the European Court of Human Rights stated:

> The limits of acceptable criticism are . . . wider as regards a politician as such than as regards a private individual. Unlike the latter, the former inevitably and knowingly lays himself

[13]*Gleaves v. Deakin* [1980] A.C. 477 (House of Lords).

open to close scrutiny of his every word and deed by both journalists and the public at large, and must consequently display a greater degree of tolerance.[14]

This has become a fundamental tenet of the court's case law.

Similarly, the Inter-American Commission of Human Rights has stated:

> The use of *desacato* laws to protect the honor of public functionaries acting in their official capacities unjustifiably grants a right to protection to public officials that is not available to other members of society. This distinction inverts the fundamental principle in a democratic system that holds the Government subject to controls, such as public scrutiny, in order to preclude or control abuse of its coercive powers.[15]

There are three key reasons for this. First, and most important, the role that such officials play in a democracy means that there is a heightened need for open public debate regarding their actions and views. They must be accountable to the public, and this includes responding openly to criticism rather than attempting to suppress it. Such accountability is perhaps most obviously manifested when they tolerate criticism of their own decisions, irrespective of how intemperate such criticism may be. This tolerance is not only central to democracy but also to facilitating participation in development work since criticism of official action is inherent in open engagement around development issues.

Second, officials have, by virtue of their positions, voluntarily accepted that they should be subjected to greater public scrutiny. Third, officials normally have adequate means at their disposal to refute any false or misleading allegations, making defamation cases unnecessary, although this does not apply to all officials (e.g., judicial officers may be precluded by professional obligations from responding to criticism of their public functions).

The precise standard that should apply to defamation of public officials is less clear. However, in striking a balance between

---

[14]*Lingens v. Austria*, Application No. 9815/82, 8 EHRR 407 (July 8, 1986).
[15]*Report on the Compatibility of "Desacato" Laws With the American Convention on Human Rights*, 1994 Annual Report of the Inter-American Commission on Human Rights, Chapter V [emphasis added].

protecting the reputation of public officials and encouraging a robust and open debate on public issues, legislators, and courts have often taken into account the importance of vigorous reporting on public issues, as well as the need to protect officials from malicious and unwarranted attacks on their reputation.

In a Croatian case, a member of parliament sued the *Feral Tribune* newspaper for having defamed him by publishing a cartoon of him suggesting a litigious disease was inflicting the country, a reference to the numerous cases that he had already brought against them. The Zagreb Municipal Court dismissed the case, holding: "The plaintiff is a public and political figure and his conduct and activity is open to public eyes and subject to critic, humour and satire."[16] Similarly, in a case involving the publication of a letter from a politician in South Korea to the leader of North Korea, Kim Jung-il, the Korean Constitutional Court held that different standards apply when criticism of public officials is involved. In particular, their right to their reputation had to be balanced against the public interest in the news story.[17]

Opinions

> *Statements of opinion—understood broadly to include all statements that do not contain a factually provable allegation, as well as statements that cannot reasonably be interpreted as stating actual facts, for example because they are satirical—normally benefit from a greater degree of protection under defamation law than statements of fact.*

Wide latitude is often given to those expressing statements of opinion, and, in some jurisdictions these do not attract any liability under defamation law. This is particularly important when expressing views about public officials. As previously noted, democracy depends on the toleration of robust criticism of officials, most obviously during elections but also at other times, and of all attempts to hold officials accountable.

---

[16]*Tomislav Mercep v. "Feral Tribune,"* XL-PN-1444-95 (1995).
[17]11-1 KCCR (Korean Constitutional Court Report) 768, 97 Hun-Ma 265, Decisions of the Korean Constitutional Court (English) 83 (2001), 7 Collection of Court Cases on the Press 345 (2000), Constitutional Court of Korea (1999).

BOX 19.   European Court of Human Rights: Tolerating Statements of Opinion

The European Court of Human Rights has signaled a high degree of tolerance in relation to statements of opinion, although it has not gone quite so far as to protect them absolutely. In the case of *Dichand and others v. Austria*, for example, at issue was a national decision holding the applicant liable in defamation for an article alleging that a national politician who also practiced as a lawyer had proposed legislation in parliament in order to serve the needs of his private clients. The European Court held that the statements were protected by the guarantee of freedom of expression even though there were no underlying facts to sustain them and very strong language had been used.[1] The Court also reiterated its long-standing view that no one should be required to prove the truth of an opinion: "The requirement to prove the truth of a value judgment is impossible to fulfil and infringes freedom of opinion itself, which is a fundamental part of the right to [freedom of expression]."[2]

---

1. February 26, 2002, Application No. 29271/95.
2. *Dichand and others v. Austria, ibid.*, para. 42. See also *Nikula v. Finland*, March 21, 2002, Application No. 31611/96 (European Court of Human Rights).

In the United States, it is now well established that opinions in relation to matters of public concern are not actionable, that is to say, they receive full constitutional protection. Two types of statements receive this type of protection: those that "do not contain a provably false factual connotation" and those that "cannot reasonably [be] interpreted as stating actual facts."[18]

Under international law, everyone has an absolute right to hold opinions, and this provides a strong basis for protection of the expression of those opinions. Opinions are, almost by definition, highly subjective; it is not possible to prove them to be true, and even the question of whether or not they are "reasonable" or founded on provable facts is highly elusive. This argues in favor of either absolute protection or at least a very high level of protection.

---

[18]*Milkovich v. Lorain Journal*, 497 US 1 (U.S. Supreme Court, 1990), 20.

BOX 20. Germany: Some Greater Protection for Opinions

The German Federal Constitutional Court, in a case involving allegations that someone had been involved in Nazi activities in Poland during the Second World War, found that:

> The flyer distributed by the complainant contained facts and personal opinions which were determined to be and capable of creating opinions.[1]

Opinions received greater protection under the constitutional guarantee of freedom of expression in the context of a defamation case than statements of fact. The lower courts had failed to take this into account and thus breached the right to freedom of expression.

---

1. Bundesverfassungsgericht (German Federal Constitutional Court), BVerfGE 43, 130, 1 BvR 460/72 of December 7, 1976, p. 137.

Defense of Reasonable Publication

In many countries, it is a defense to a claim of defamation regarding a statement on a matter of public interest to show that it was reasonable in all the circumstances for the defendant to have disseminated the statement, even if that statement has been shown to be false.

An increasing number of jurisdictions are recognizing a "reasonableness" defense—or an analogous defense based on the ideas of "due diligence," "good faith," or an absence of malice—due to the harsh nature of traditional strict liability rules whereby defendants were liable whenever they disseminated false statements, or statements that they could not prove to be true in a court of law. The traditional rule is particularly unfair for the media and other social commentators, which are under a duty to satisfy the public's right to know and often cannot wait until they are absolutely sure that every fact alleged is true before they publish or broadcast a story. Even the best journalists make honest mistakes, and to leave them open to punishment for every false allegation would be to undermine the public interest in receiving timely information. This is often particularly true in cases involving allegations of wrongdoing, given that such contexts are, almost by definition, characterized by secrecy, making such allegations hard to prove to court standards. Furthermore, journalists may

---

BOX 21.   The Need for a Good Faith Defense

A case from Thailand illustrates the importance of this defense. In that case, an NGO activist, Supinya Klangnarong, made statements that were quoted in a local newspaper to the effect that, as prime minister, Thaksin had adopted policies that helped Shin Corp grow and that this growth, in turn, helped Thaksin's Thai Rak Thai party. Shin Corp was founded by Thaksin and, when he was elected prime minister, he divested his shares to family members. Shin Corp sued Supinya for both criminal and civil defamation.

Thai law provides for a defense for a good faith and fair comment upon any person or thing that should be subject to public criticism. The Court held that the matter was one of general public interest due to the nature of Shin Corp as a "national resource" (as well as a major corporation) and the prime minister's close links to it. Supinya had acted reasonably and in good faith in making the statements, which were not motivated by malice. As a result, she was held to be innocent in the criminal case, and the civil case against her was dropped. Absent the good faith defense, there would have been a much greater likelihood of Supinya being convicted.

---

rely on confidential sources of information, which professional ethics prevent them from using to defend themselves in court.

A more appropriate balance between the right to freedom of expression and reputations is to protect those who have acted reasonably, in good faith, or without malice, while allowing plaintiffs to sue those who have not. In determining whether dissemination was reasonable in the circumstances of a particular case, courts have considered the importance of freedom of expression with respect to matters of public concern and the right of the public to receive timely information relating to such matters. For the media, acting in accordance with accepted professional standards should normally satisfy a reasonableness test.

Different jurisdictions have taken different approaches on this issue, both as to the standard to be applied and the breadth of the protection.

Perhaps the strongest standard in terms of defending freedom of expression was established by the U.S. Supreme Court in the *New York Times Co. v. Sullivan* case. In that case, the impugned statements contained factual errors. However, as "erroneous statement is inevitable in free debate," the Court ruled that a public official could only recover damages if he or she could prove "the statement was made with 'actual malice'—that is, with knowledge that it was false or with reckless disregard for whether it was false or not."[19]

The "malice standard" was adopted in a decision of the Supreme Court of Argentinean Justice on November 12, 1996,[20] in acquitting the defendant of charges of defamation. The court stated:

> This Court adopted the standard jurisprudential created by the Supreme Court of the United States in the case New York Times vs. Sullivan (376 U.S. 255; 1964) that has been given in calling the doctrine of the real malice and whose objective is to offer a reasonable balance among the function of the press and the individual rights that had been affected by prejudicial comments to public officials, public figures and even matters that had intervened in questions of public interest, object of the information or of the chronicle.

Courts in Australia, South Africa, and the UK have instead opted for what might be termed a reasonable publication rule. In *Lange v. Australian Broadcasting Corporation*, the Australian High Court held that political communications were covered by the defense of qualified privilege. This could be defeated, however, where the defendant failed to meet a standard "of reasonableness . . . which goes beyond mere honesty." In Australia, the onus is on the defendant to prove reasonableness.[21]

Civil law jurisdictions often opt for a defense based on good faith, as in the Thai case noted previously. A similar rule applies in French defamation law, where it is a defense to show that one acted in good faith, at least where the goal is to inform the public. In a 1997 case, the *Cour de Cassation*, the highest appellate court, upheld this principle and reaffirmed that the notion of reporting in the public interest is a broad one.[22]

---

[19]*New York Times Co. v. Sullivan*, 376 US 254, 279 (1964), 279–280.

[20]Available at: *http://www.legalmania.com/rincon_estudiantes/el_rincon/morales_sola.htm*.

[21](1997) 71 ALJR 818, 832-3.

[22]*X v. Y and others*, 15 January 1997, Cour de Cassation—Deuxiéme chamber civile, no. 94-19.767.

Redress

The overriding goal of providing a remedy for defamatory statements is to redress the harm done to the reputation of the plaintiff, not to punish those responsible for the dissemination of the statement. As a result, remedies or sanctions for defamation should be proportionate to the harm done.

International law requires remedies or sanctions, like the restrictions from which they flow, to be proportionate. Excessive sanctions, on their own, may represent a breach of the right to freedom of expression due to the disproportionate chilling effect they exert and the fact that they can significantly limit the free flow of information and ideas. This impact is felt not only by the party to whom the sanctions apply but also the broader community, as individuals will steer well clear of the potential zone of liability to ensure that they do not expose themselves to a risk of attracting these harsh sanctions.

Nonpecuniary remedies—such as a right of correction—are often effective in terms of redressing harm to reputation and yet are less

---

BOX 22.   International Standards on Sanctions

In the case of *Tolstoy Miloslavsky v. the United Kingdom*, the European Court of Human Rights stated that "the award of damages and the injunction clearly constitute an interference with the exercise [of the] right to freedom of expression." Even though it was accepted that the statements in question were highly defamatory, sanctions must bear a "reasonable relationship of proportionality to the injury to reputation suffered" and this should be specified in national defamation laws.[1]

The African Commission on Human and Peoples' Rights recently adopted a Declaration of Principles on Freedom of Expression in Africa. Principle XII of the Declaration, entitled "Protecting Reputations," states, in part:

1. States should ensure that their laws relating to defamation conform to the following standards:

   . . .

   • sanctions shall never be so severe as to inhibit the right to freedom of expression, including by others.[2]

---

1. July 13, 1995, Application No. 18139/91, para. 49.
2. Adopted by the African Commission on Human and Peoples' Rights at its 32nd Session, October 17–23, 2002.

intrusive from the perspective of freedom of expression than financial awards; courts should, as a result, prioritize their use. Furthermore, courts should, when assessing legal remedies, also take into account any voluntary or self-regulatory remedies that may have been provided in redressing any harm to reputation. In a *Declaration on Freedom of Political Debate in the Media*, the Committee of Ministers of the Council of Europe stressed the need for sanctions both to be proportionate and to take into account any other remedies provided:

> Damages and fines for defamation or insult must bear a reasonable relationship of proportionality to the violation of the rights or reputation of others, taking into consideration any possible effective and adequate voluntary remedies.[23]

Many countries provide for a right of reply and/or correction for attacks on reputation. At the same time, unduly broad rights of reply or an obligation to apologize may themselves represent a breach of the right to freedom of expression. (See Box 23 for an example.)

BOX 23.   Korea: Notice of Apology a Breach of the Right to Freedom of Opinion

Article 764 of the Korean Civil Code authorizes courts, upon the application of the plaintiff, to order the defendant "to take suitable measures" to restore the defamed party's reputation, "either in lieu of or together with damages." Courts have recognized a requirement to publish an apology as one such suitable measure. In a 1991 case, the constitutional court ruled that this was a breach of the right to freedom of opinion, stating:

> A notice of apology compels a person to make a humiliating public expression in the mass media like newspapers, magazines, etc. This is a violation of his freedom of conscience. Although the contents of the apology are specifically dictated by the State authorities in the course of the judicial proceedings, the public apparently views them as a voluntary expression of opinion.[1]

---

1. 3 KCCR [Korean Constitutional Court Report] 139, 89 Hun-Ma 160. The First Ten Years of the Korean Constitutional Court (English) 138 (2001), Press Arbitration Quarterly 162 (summer 1991), 1991, p. 164.

---

[23]Adopted February 12, 2004.

7 Content Rules and Limits to Free Speech

Good Practice Checklist

- Restrictions may be imposed on freedom of expression to protect national security/public order, but these should be carefully and narrowly drawn so that they only prohibit expression that poses a serious risk of imminent and substantial harm to a legitimate national security/public order interest.
- International law requires states to prohibit advocacy of hatred that constitutes incitement to discrimination, hostility, or violence (International Convention for Civil and Political Rights [CCPR], Article 20(2)) but this does not include true statements or statements that, while offensive, do not constitute incitement.
- Restrictions on obscene materials should apply only to material that either depicts a criminal act or that poses a serious and direct risk of harm, for example to children.
- Restrictions on freedom of expression to protect the impartiality and fairness of the system of justice should be carefully drawn so as not to protect judges against legitimate criticism or prevent open public discussion about the administration of justice.
- Blanket bans on the publication of false material, simply because it is inaccurate, are illegitimate.
- Political expression is at the heart of the guarantee of freedom of expression and should receive particular protection.
- It is especially important to protect political expression during elections, and effective measures should be taken to ensure that the electorate is informed about both how to vote and the various issues at stake in the election.

Introduction

In order to protect various public or private interests, countries around the world impose a wide range of restrictions on the content of what may be published or broadcast. In this chapter, a number of

BOX 24.   International Standards: The Three-Part Test

Article 19(3) of the International Covenant on Civil and Political Rights (ICCPR) allows for restrictions on freedom of expression in the following terms:

> The exercise of the rights provided for in paragraph 2 of this article carries with it special duties and responsibilities. It may therefore be subject to certain restrictions, but these shall only be such as are provided by law and are necessary:
> (a) For respect of the rights or reputations of others;
> (b) For the protection of national security or of public order (ordre public), or of public health or morals.

A similar formulation is found in the European and American regional human rights treaties. These have been interpreted as requiring restrictions to meet the strict three-part test elaborated subsequently. International jurisprudence makes it clear that this test presents a high standard that any interference in freedom of expression must overcome.

First, the interference must be provided for by law. This requirement will be fulfilled only where the law is accessible and formulated with sufficient precision for the citizens to be able to regulate their conduct accordingly. Second, the interference must pursue a legitimate aim. The list of aims in Article 19(3) of the ICCPR is exclusive in the sense that no other aims are considered legitimate as grounds for restricting freedom of expression. Third, the restriction must be necessary to secure one of those aims. The word *necessary* means that there must be a "pressing social need" for the restriction. The reasons given by the state to justify the restriction must be "relevant and sufficient" and the restriction must be proportionate to the aim pursued.

the more common content restrictions are outlined. Under international law, all of these are recognized as legitimate grounds for restricting freedom of expression. At the same time, all may, if not clearly and narrowly drawn, be abused to limit the free flow of information and ideas in the public interest.

Constitutionally Authorized Limitations on the Right to Freedom of Expression

Restrictions to freedom of expression must be subject to certain limits if the guarantee of freedom of expression is to be effective. Under international law, restrictions must meet a stringent three-part test

that requires them to be explicitly provided by law, to pursue a
legitimate aim, and to be no more restrictive than necessary to
protect that aim.

The question of the scope of restrictions on freedom of expression is central to the question of how effectively this key right is guaranteed: If unduly broad restrictions are permitted, the right will be undermined. At a minimum, the constitution should provide a clear framework for restrictions that ensures an appropriate balance between freedom of expression and other public and private interests. A clear framework for exceptions will facilitate media regulation in the public interest by helping to draw the line between what constitutes legitimate public interest regulation and what is excessive interference with media freedom.

Ideally, the constitution should set clear limits on when and how ordinary legislative restrictions on freedom of expression will be legitimate. For example, Article 39(2) of the constitution of Thailand provides for restrictions on freedom of expression as follows:

> The restriction on liberty under paragraph one shall not be imposed except by virtue of the provisions of the law specifically enacted for the purpose of maintaining the security of the state, safeguarding the rights, liberties, dignity, reputation, family or privacy rights of other persons, maintaining public order or good morals or preventing the deterioration of the mind or health of the public.

South Africa too covers the issue: The constitution states in chapter 2, section 36:

(1) The rights in the Bill of Rights may be limited only in terms of law of general application to the extent that the limitation is reasonable and justifiable in an open and democratic society based on human dignity, equality and freedom, taking into account all relevant factors including—

    (a) the nature of the right;
    (b) the importance of the purpose of the limitation;
    (c) the nature and extent of the limitation;
    (d) the relation between the limitation and its purpose; and
    (e) less restrictive means to achieve the purpose.

(2) Except as provided in subsection (1) or in any other provision of the Constitution, no law may limit any right entrenched in the Bill of Rights.

In practice, the constitutional court has interpreted this so as to permit only very limited restrictions on the right to freedom of expression

General Principles of Content Restrictions

Some general principles regarding content restrictions may be derived from international and good practice national jurisprudence. First, prior restraints or prior censorship, whereby material is reviewed by a controlling body before it is disseminated, while not absolutely forbidden under international law, are regarded with a great deal of suspicion, due to their highly intrusive nature and the obvious opportunity for abuse that they represent. The Inter-American Convention on Human Rights, for example, prohibits all prior censorship except where this is aimed at protecting children.[1] In practice, systems of prior restraint are applied increasingly rarely in democracies, and never to the media.

Second, as noted previously in relation to defamation, it is widely recognized that political speech, due to its importance as an underpinning of democracy, deserves special protection. International courts have made it clear that they are not prepared to allow states much latitude in terms of the interpretation and application of restrictions on political speech. The European Court of Human Rights, for example, allows states a "margin of appreciation" in the interpretation of rights. This margin, however, is very narrow in relation to political speech.[2]

Third, restrictions that are overly broad in the sense that they capture not only the offending expression but also legitimate speech will fail to pass muster under the necessity part of the test for restrictions. States have an obligation, when pursuing legitimate aims, to give due regard to the right to freedom of expression by tailoring restrictions as narrowly as possible.

Fourth, it is a fundamental principle of criminal law, based on the presumption of innocence, that mere commission of a criminal act is not enough for conviction; instead, the act must be accompanied by a mental element of will so that there is mental, as well as physical,

---

[1] Article 13(4).

[2] See, for example, *Refah Partisi and others v. Turkey*, Application Nos. 41340/98, 41342/98, 41343/98, and 41344/98 (February 13, 2003), para. 81.

guilt. Any crimes of expression should respect this fundamental criminal rule.

Fifth, as noted previously in relation to defamation, excessive sanctions, even where some sanction is warranted, represent an independent breach of the right to freedom of expression, given the chilling effect they exert. In particular, individuals will steer well clear of the actual zone of prohibited speech to avoid unduly harsh sanctions, so that the effect is analogous to an overbroad restriction.

National Security/Public Order

Restrictions may be imposed on freedom of expression to protect national security/public order, but these should be carefully and narrowly drawn so that they only prohibit expression that poses a serious risk of imminent and substantial harm to a legitimate national security/public order interest.

As with all restrictions on freedom of expression, restrictions in the name of national security/public order are permitted under international law only if they can be shown to be necessary to protect a legitimate interest. Although security and public order are social interests of the highest order, without which all rights are at risk, they are at the same time almost impossible to define precisely and are hence inherently susceptible to abuse.

Public oversight is crucial to ensuring sensible policy-making and decision making, specifically in relation to national security.

International jurisprudence has established a number of principles relating to national security/public order. First, courts have consistently ruled out unduly broad restrictions on freedom of expression in the name of national security or public order. It is not legitimate, for example, to ban opposition party activities on grounds of public order simply because a state of emergency is in force, even if that state of emergency is itself legitimate. Vague appeals to some purported social interest will not suffice to justify national security restrictions on freedom of expression. In *Mukong v. Cameroon*, for example, the author, who was critical of the president and the government, was arrested twice under the provisions of an ordinance that criminalized statements "intoxicat[ing] national or international public opinion." The UN Human Rights Committee found a breach of the

---

BOX 25.   Abuse of National Security/Public Order Rules

The abuse of national security and public order laws by the powerful to silence minorities, those espousing unpopular political causes, or just critical voices is a very serious problem around the world. In Malaysia, for example, arrests under the Sedition Act of 1948 are commonly used for political purposes. The popular online newspaper, *Malaysiakini*, famous for its independent reporting, was raided by the Malaysian police on January 20, 2003, and nineteen computers, including four servers, were seized for allegedly being in breach of the Sedition Act. Its crime was to publish a letter that satirized nationalist policies in favor of ethnic Malays, through a comparison with the United States, on the basis that this could cause racial disharmony.

Similarly, Article 7(1) of the South Korean National Security Act of 1980 provided, in part, that any person who, with the knowledge that he might endanger the existence or security of the state, praised, encouraged, propagandized, or sided with the activities of an anti-state organization committed an offense punishable by imprisonment of up to seven years. In finding these provisions unconstitutional, the constitutional court noted:

> [I]f criticism of the government and its leader happens to parallel what North Korea claims, it may fall within the crime of praising and encouraging North Korea. Also, if an individual is aware that criticism of the South Korean government's policy can be used by North Korea for its propaganda, he or she can be punished for benefiting the enemy.

---

right to freedom of expression, noting that even in "difficult political circumstances," a law like this could not be justified and was a threat to "multi-party democracy, democratic tenets and human rights."[3]

Second, the onus rests on the state imposing the restriction to justify it as legitimate. This is true of all restrictions on freedom of expression but is perhaps particularly relevant in relation to national security/public order restrictions, given their almost inherently broad nature. Courts have required states to show that a restriction is necessary to avoid a particular threat to a specific legitimate national security/public order interest, rather than simply to allege that a legitimate interest is at risk.[4]

---

[3]Communication No. 44/1979, views adopted March 27, 1981, para. 9.7.
[4]See *Laptsevich v. Belarus*, Communication No. 780/1997 (UN Human Rights Committee) (March 20, 2000), para. 8.

Third, information that is already in the public domain may not be restricted on alleged grounds of national security/public order. The reason for this is fairly obvious: if the information is already available, further distribution of it may cause embarrassment but cannot endanger national security/public order. This is particularly relevant in the Internet era, where information published anywhere is easily accessible to people everywhere. In the *Spycatcher* case before the European Court of Human Rights, at issue were injunctions against reprinted passages from the unauthorized memoirs of a former member of the British security service, which had already been published in the United States. The court held that to continue to restrict publication, once the materials were effectively available to UK audiences, was illegitimate.[5]

Finally, and most importantly, courts have upheld restrictions on freedom of expression to protect national security/public order interests only where there is a close nexus between the particular expression and the risk of harm to those interests. The idea is to mitigate the inherently vague and general nature of the concepts of national security and public order. Requiring a close nexus between the expression and the risk is a means of concretizing the matter and avoiding vague appeals to some unspecified national security interest.

Hate Speech

International law requires states to prohibit advocacy of hatred that constitutes incitement to discrimination, hostility or violence (ICCPR, Article 20[2]). However, true statements or statements which, while offensive, do not constitute incitement are not covered.

The right of a person to express him- or herself may conflict with the rights to equality and nondiscrimination. As a result, international law recognizes that expression that constitutes incitement to discrimination, hostility, or violence through advocacy of national, racial, or religious hatred should be prohibited. At the same time, the role of freedom of expression in safeguarding the exercise of other rights, including the right to equality and nondiscrimination, has been recognized.

---

[5]The *Observer and Guardian v. UK* and the *Sunday Times v. UK* (No. 2), Application No. 13585/88 (November 26, 1991).

As with all restrictions on content, overly broad or vague hate speech laws may be abused. They have, in particular, been used to target, rather than defend, minorities; to deny them voice; and to undermine their ability to participate in the political process. A clear example of this is the case of *Incal v. Turkey*, where the applicant was convicted in Turkey of hate speech for protesting, in strong terms, against official measures he believed were aimed at oppressing the

---

BOX 26. National Standards on Incitement

A French case involved a claim that some pornographic cartoons depicting Jesus Christ, the pope, and priests in various compromising situations constituted hate speech and/or incitement to violence against Catholics. The *Cour de Cassation* rejected the appeal in part on the ground that the cartoons, although insulting, contained no incitement to hatred or violence against any ethnic or religious group.[1]

In the leading Canadian case, *R. v. Keegstra*,[2] the supreme court upheld a criminal provision that "prohibited the wilful promotion of hatred, other than in private conversation, towards any section of the public distinguished by colour, race, religion or ethnic origin." The court stressed a number of factors in upholding this rule. First, the term *wilful* posed a substantial barrier to conviction, requiring proof that the "accused subjectively desires the promotion of hatred or foresees such a consequence as certain or substantially certain to result. . . ." Further: "The hatemonger must intend or foresee as substantially certain a direct and active stimulation of hatred against an identifiable group."

Second, the term *hatred* was an extreme term:

> Hatred is predicated on destruction, and hatred against identifiable groups and therefore thrives on insensitivity, bigotry and destruction of both the target group and of the values of our society. Hatred in this sense is a most extreme emotion that belies reason; an emotion that, if exercised against members of an identifiable group, implies that those individuals are to be despised, scorned, denied respect and made subject to ill-treatment on the basis of group affiliation.

Finally, the impugned provision included a number of defenses, including that the statements were true, that they were a good faith attempt to express an opinion on a religious subject, that the statements were relevant to a matter of public interest and the accused reasonably believed them to be true, and that, in good faith, the accused intended to point out, for purposes of removal, matters tending to produce feelings of hatred.

---

1. Arrêt no. 242 du 8 mars 2001, Cour de Cassation—Deuxième chambre civil.
2. [1990] 3 S.C.R. 697.

Kurds. The European Court of Human Rights recognized that the impugned statements appealed to Kurds, urging them to band together to defend their rights. But it held that there was nothing in the text that incited to "violence, hostility or hatred between citizens."[6]

Courts have also refused to tell journalists how to do their job, respecting their right to decide how best to communicate information and ideas to the public, including when they are reporting on racism and intolerance. This may include reporting the racist statements of others, for example, to illustrate that such views exist within society. This was at issue in the *Jersild* case, where a journalist was convicted in Denmark for a television program that included statements by racist extremists. The European Court of Human Rights held that the applicant had acted with a view to exposing the problem of racism and to generating public debate and, as such, should not be held liable.[7]

Obscenity

Restrictions on obscene materials should apply only to material that either depicts a criminal act or that poses a serious and direct risk of harm, for example, to children.

Although infrequently the subject of political abuse, laws restricting the portrayal of sexual material do have relevance to cultural issues and equality concerns. Sexual minorities, for example, have been targeted by obscenity laws, undermining their ability to participate as equals in society.

Historically, courts in many countries have defined obscenity by reference to community standards, but the clear trend in this area is toward more permissive rules, which take into account globalization and the revolution in access to information, including sexually explicit material, occasioned by the Internet. At the same time, international courts tend to award a margin of appreciation to individual states to address obscenity concerns rather than attempting to lay down clear, universally binding norms in this area. In *Müller and*

---

[6]Application No. 22678/93 (June 9, 1998), para. 50.
[7]Application No. 15890/89 (September 1994).

BOX 27.   National Courts' Definitions of Obscenity

The Canadian Supreme Court, in *R. v. Butler*, noted that in assessing whether something was obscene, it "is the standards of the community as a whole which must be considered and not the standards of a small segment of that community." Only material that unduly exploits sexual material may be deemed to be obscene. Furthermore: "Even material which by itself offends community standards will not be considered 'undue,' if it is required for the serious treatment of a theme."[1]

An analogous approach, taken by the South Korean Constitutional Court, is to distinguish between obscene material and less extreme forms of sexually explicit material. The court has distinguished between obscene material and material that is simply indecent:

> Obscenity is a sexually blatant and undisguised expression that distorts human dignity or humanity. It only appeals to prurient interests and, if taken as a whole, does not possess any literary, artistic, scientific, or political value. Obscenity not only undermines the healthy societal morality on sex, but its harmful impact is also difficult to eliminate through the open competition of ideas. Accordingly, obscene expression, if strictly interpreted as suggested here, is not within the area of constitutionally protected speech or press.[2]

---

1. *R. v. Butler*, [1992] 1 SCR 452, pp. 477, 485.
2. 10-1 KCCR 327, 95 Hun-Ka 16, The First Ten Years of the Korean Constitutional Court.

---

others v. Switzerland, a case involving sanctions under an obscenity law, the European Court stated:

> State authorities are in principle in a better position than the international judge to give an opinion on the exact content of [moral requirements].[8]

Courts have, while accepting that the definition of obscenity should be judged by community standards, also placed some limits on the implications of this.

Many countries impose restrictions on the display and sale of pornography, with a view to protecting children. Self-regulatory approaches and systems for informing readers/viewers in advance of the potentially offensive nature of the material are also commonly employed. For example, many countries require films and videos to provide a rating to indicate to audiences what sort of material, including sexual material, they contain. Such a system may either be

---

[8]May 24, 1988, Application no. 10737/84, para. 35.

> **BOX 28. India: Obscene Material**
>
> The Indian Supreme Court adverted to community standards in *Samaresh Bose v. Amal Mitra*, which assessed the legitimacy of a law prohibiting the distribution of "obscene" material defined as that which is "lascivious or appeals to the prurient interest or its effect . . . is, if taken as a whole, such as to tend to deprave and corrupt persons who are likely, having regard to all relevant circumstances, to read, see or hear the matter contained or embodied in it."[1] The court held: "[T]he concept of obscenity is moulded to a very great extent by the social outlook of the people who are generally expected to read the book. It is beyond dispute that the concept of obscenity usually differs from country to country. . . ."[2] However, the court also placed some parameters of the notion of community standards: "Our standards must be so framed that we are not reduced to a level where the protection of the least capable and the most depraved amongst us determines what the morally healthy cannot view or read."
>
> In the *Bose* case, the Indian Supreme Court held that the book before it was not obscene, in part because, "[i]f we place ourselves in the position of readers, who are likely to read this book . . . we do not think that any reader on reading this book *would become* depraved, debased and encouraged to lasciviousness" (emphasis added). In the absence of a strong likelihood that exposure to the allegedly obscene material would actually result in the harms that the law was designed to prevent, the court could not conclude that the material before it was obscene.
>
> ---
>
> 1. *Samaresh Bose & Another v. Amal Mitra & Another* [1986] AIR 967.
> 2. *K.A. Abbas v. Union of India*, [1971] AIR (SC) 481.

self-regulatory or overseen by an independent administrative body. The idea is that this allows viewers to decide for themselves whether or not they wish to view the material. The rules governing broadcasters may also address sexual content, for example, by limiting programming containing such content to times when the youth do not generally watch TV.

Protection of the Administration of Justice

> *Restrictions on freedom of expression to protect the impartiality and fairness of the system of justice should be carefully drawn so as not to protect judges against legitimate criticism or prevent open public discussion about the administration of justice.*

International law recognizes two legitimate goals pursuant to which restrictions on freedom of expression may be justified by reference to the administration of justice, namely protecting the impartiality and the authority of the judicial system. The first relates to the need for fairness within the judicial system and would be undermined by such things as intimidation of witnesses, biasing of judges and jurors, protection of litigants and other participants, and the like. The second relates to acceptance by society of the courts as the final arbiters of disputes. If this is not accepted, individuals may seek to resolve disputes in other, potentially illegal, ways.

These are undoubtedly important goals, worthy of some protection. At the same time, historically, judges have been unduly solicitous of them and too ready to condemn legitimate criticism of judges and courts, leading the UK Privy Council to declare:

> Justice is not a cloistered virtue: she must be allowed to suffer the scrutiny and the respectful even though outspoken comments of ordinary men.[9]

BOX 29.   Abuse of the Rules

In August 1999, Kenyan editor Tony Gachoka was jailed for six months for claiming in his publication, the *Post on Sunday*, that the chief justice and other senior judges had accepted a huge bribe in exchange for interfering in the course of justice to favor a local tycoon. Gachoka was, furthermore, tried directly and at the first instance by the court of appeal, the highest court in Kenya, which had the effect of denying him any opportunity to appeal against his conviction, contrary to international human rights guarantees. It also had the effect of ensuring that his case was heard by the very judges Gachoka had accused of corruption.

A study by the International Bar Association (IBA), for example, found that while the Malaysian courts operated impartially in commercial cases, they were subject to significant interference in more political cases, including cases involving freedom of expression.[1] Legal limitations on criticizing the judiciary in Malaysia are notorious, a point noted clearly in the IBA report.[2]

---

1. See *Justice in Jeopardy: Malaysia in 2000* (London: Human Rights Institute, International Bar Association, 2000), available at: *http://archive.ibanet.org/general/FindDocuments.asp.*
2. See, for example, *Murray Hiebert v. Chandra Sri Ram*, [1999] 4 MLJ 321, in which Hiebert, a reporter for the *Far Eastern Economic Review*, was jailed for six weeks for suggesting that a case brought by the wife of an appeals court judge moved through the system unusually quickly.

---

[9] *Ambard v. Attorney-General for Trinidad and Tobago*, AC 322 (1936), 335.

Furthermore, public oversight of the judiciary, a public institution, is particularly important to democracy. It can serve to root out corruption and incompetence. Equally importantly, it can serve to protect the independence and impartiality of the judiciary, a fundamental underpinning of both the rule of law and protection of all human rights, including freedom of expression.

BOX 30.   South Africa: Prohibitions on Criticizing Judges

In *S v. Mamabolo*,[1] the Constitutional Court of South Africa considered both the standards and the procedure applicable to prohibitions on criticizing judges. Given the constitutional importance of both the independence of the judiciary and freedom of expression, the court declined to hold that the offense was unconstitutional per se. However, the traditional standard, based on a tendency to bring the judiciary into contempt, was no longer appropriate. The court noted that it was of the greatest importance that the public be able to "discuss, endorse, criticise, applaud or castigate the conduct of their courts. And, ultimately, such free and frank debate about judicial proceedings serves more than one vital public purpose. Self-evidently such informed and vocal public scrutiny promotes impartiality, accessibility and effectiveness, three of the important aspirational attributes prescribed for the judiciary by the Constitution."[2]

The "tendency to harm" test should be replaced by one based on the effect of the statement judged objectively:

> The threshold for a conviction on a charge of scandalising the court is now even higher than before the super-imposition of constitutional values on common law principles; and prosecutions are likely to be instituted only in clear cases of impeachment of judicial integrity. . . . . Ultimately the test is whether the offending conduct, viewed contextually, really was likely to damage the administration of justice.[3]

With regard to procedure, the court considered that where the case in question had already been decided, "there is no pressing need for firm or swift measures to preserve the integrity of the judicial process." The court held that "it is inherently inappropriate for a court of law, the constitutionally designated primary protector of personal rights and freedoms," to employ a summary procedure save where ordinary prosecution at the instance of the prosecuting authority is impossible or highly undesirable.[4]

---

1. 2001 (3) SA 409 (CC); 2001 (5) BCLR 449 (CC).
2. *Ibid.*, paras. 29–30.
3. *Ibid.*, para. 45.
4. *Ibid.*, para. 57.

Restrictions designed to serve the first goal just noted, the impartiality of the judiciary, fall into two main categories. First, general limits may be imposed on reporting on proceedings that are *sub judice*, or ongoing before the courts. Courts have held that this should only be done where the material in question poses a serious risk of actual prejudice to an ongoing case. In assessing that risk, judges are presumed not to be susceptible to being swayed by media reporting, given their professional training.[10]

The second goal noted previously, maintaining the authority of the judiciary, is increasingly contentious. Some countries still impose restrictions on criticism of judges and courts, on the basis that these are considered necessary to maintain the authority of the judiciary. In many countries, however, the possibility of conviction on this basis has either been formally repealed or defined so narrowly that it has fallen into disuse. In these countries, such restrictions are not considered necessary; the judiciary as an institution have proven themselves to be above unjustified criticism and do not need legal restrictions of this sort to maintain their status.

False News

Blanket bans on the publication of false material, simply because it is inaccurate, are illegitimate.

It is well established that guarantees of freedom of expression protect incorrect, as well as correct, statements. In many circumstances, the truth is a contested matter, and prohibitions on publishing false news may be abused in an attempt to suppress unwanted allegations, whether or not they are true. For example, in January 1999, the *Standard* newspaper in Zimbabwe published an article about a coup attempt within the Zimbabwe National Army, citing "highly-placed sources within the military" as sources. The author and editor were detained by the military and later charged with disseminating false news.[11]

---

[10]See *Vine Products Ltd. v. MacKenzie & Co. Ltd.*, 3 All ER 58 (1965), 62.

[11]The Supreme Court of Zimbabwe later struck down the false news provision under which they were charged. See *Chavunduka & Choto v. Minister of Home Affairs & Attorney General*, Judgment No. S.C. 36/2000, Civil Application No. 156/99 (May 22, 2000).

BOX 31. Protection for Inaccurate Statements

Principle 7 of the Inter-American Declaration of Principles on Freedom of Expression explicitly recognizes that false statements are prima facie covered by the guarantee of freedom of expression:

> Prior conditioning of expressions, such as truthfulness, timeliness, or impartiality, is incompatible with the right to freedom of expression recognized in international instruments.[1]

The Peruvian Constitutional Tribunal has held that the right to freedom of expression covers inaccurate statements. A bank brought a case alleging that a radio station, by disseminating false statements, had caused financial panic in the population. The court refused to intervene, saying that this would breach the radio's rights. The plaintiff retained his right to seek a rectification of the information or to bring a civil case, for example in defamation.[2]

In a 2004 decision, the Ugandan Supreme Court struck down the criminal offense of publishing false news. In doing so, it noted:

> [T]he right to freedom of expression extends to holding, receiving and imparting all forms of opinions, ideas and information. It is not confined to categories, such as correct opinions, sound ideas or truthful information . . . [A] person's expression or statement is not precluded from the constitutional protection simply because it is thought by another or others to be false, erroneous, controversial or unpleasant . . . Indeed, the protection is most relevant and required where a person's views are opposed or objected to by society or any part thereof, as "false" or "wrong."[3]

---

1. Adopted by the Inter-American Commission on Human Rights at its 108th Regular Session, October 19, 2000.
2. *San Martin's Rural Bank of Savings and Credit v. Radio Imagen*, Exp. No. 905-2001-AA/TC San Martín.
3. *Onyango-Obbo and Mwenda v. AG*, Constitutional Appeal No. 2, 2002, February 11, 2004 (not yet published).

Inaccurate statements, by themselves, are unlikely to cause any tangible harm to society. Harms that may result from false statements, such as defamation or a risk of public disorder, may be addressed through restrictions specifically tailored to address these harms. There is, therefore, no need for a general prohibition on incorrect statements. On the other hand, banning false statements per se exerts a significant chilling effect on freedom of expression.

BOX 32.   Chilling Effect

In 1992, the Canadian Supreme Court, in *R. v. Zundel*,[1] struck down a false news provision. In its decision, it expounded at some length on the chilling effect of false news provisions as contrary to the constitutional guarantee of freedom of expression:

> The danger is magnified because the prohibition affects not only those caught and prosecuted, but those who may refrain from saying what they would like to because of the fear that they will be caught. Thus worthy minority groups or individuals may be inhibited from saying what they desire to say for fear that they might be prosecuted. Should an activist be prevented from saying "the rainforest of British Columbia is being destroyed" because she fears criminal prosecution for spreading "false news" in the event that scientists conclude and a jury accepts that the statement is false . . .?

The Judicial Committee of the Privy Council[2] has similarly noted the chilling effect of a rule that penalizes any statement that is inaccurate:

> [I]t was submitted that it was unobjectionable to penalise false statements made without taking due care to verify their accuracy. . . . [I]t would on any view be a grave impediment to the freedom of the press if those who print, or *a fortiori* those who distribute, matter reflecting critically on the conduct of public authorities could only do so with impunity if they could first verify the accuracy of all statements of fact on which the criticism was based.[3]

---

1. [1992] 2 SCR 731.
2. This is the final court of appeal for a number of common law countries and is comprised of judges from the House of Lords.
3. *Hector v. Attorney-General of Antigua and Barbuda*, [1990] 2 AC 312 (PC), p. 318.

Political Expression/Elections

> *Political expression is at the heart of the guarantee of freedom of expression and should receive particular protection. This is especially true during elections, and effective measures should be taken to ensure that the electorate is informed about both how to vote and the various issues at stake in the election.*

Open debate about political matters, understood broadly as matters of public concern, is essential in a democracy and the guarantee of freedom of expression provides particular protection to political expression. Such speech lies at the heart of the media's role as the watchdog of government and as a facilitator of public participation and democratic development. In many countries, statements made in legislative bodies benefit from absolute immunity from sanction. High levels of protection may also be afforded to statements made in the context of an election campaign.

It may be necessary to put in place particular rules relating to freedom of expression during elections. It is of the greatest importance that the electorate understands the right to vote, as well as the modalities by which this right may be exercised. The public media should be under a strict obligation to be balanced and impartial during elections; it is clearly inappropriate for a publicly funded body to

---

BOX 33.   Obligations of Balance

The Italian Constitutional Court recently upheld regulations requiring all broadcasters to give equal time to all political parties during the election period.[1] Equal access during election periods was a prominent general interest. This obligation was analogous to requirements to carry news and children's programming and could not be considered a form of expropriation; rather, it was a legitimate part of the licensing concession. Particularly in the prevailing situation in Italy, which the court held was characterized by significant concentration of media ownership, free competition of views could not ensure equal access of all perspectives and the public's right to a diversity of information.

In a 1999 case,[2] the High Court of Malawi found that preferential coverage provided to the president during the election period by the national public service broadcaster violated the right of every person to equality and the right of every electoral competitor to equal access to public media. The court noted that free and equal access to public media is one of the prerequisites for the holding of free and fair elections. As the court noted:

> If campaign messages are broadcast live at a presidential function, then equal treatment means that campaign rallies of other political parties or at least campaign rallies of other presidential candidates be broadcast live. That would give other political parties or other presidential candidates an opportunity to reply to some of the matters raised. This is what equitable treatment of political parties and elections candidates would entail.

---

1. Decision of the constitutional court no. 155 of April 24–May 7, 2002.
2. *Kafumba and others v. The Electoral Commission and Malawi Broadcasting Corporation*, Miscellaneous Cause Number 35 of 1999.

do otherwise. In many countries, all broadcasters are required to be impartial and to provide equal access to all parties.

It is also important that competing parties and candidates have an adequate opportunity to put their views to the public, including, as appropriate, direct access slots on public media. Any such slots should be allocated on an equitable basis to all parties. Where political advertising is allowed, all media should be required to provide it to all parties on a nondiscriminatory basis to preserve a level playing field during the elections.

8 Regulation of Journalists

Good Practice Checklist

- No conditions should be placed on who may practice journalism, and individual journalists should not be subject to either licensing or registration requirements.
- Journalists should be free to establish professional associations of their own choosing.
- Journalists have a right to protect their confidential sources of information, without which the flow of information to them, and hence to the public, would be undermined.

A right of correction/reply can provide an effective and appropriate response to media errors and other wrongs. However, they represent a limitation on freedom of expression and so should be clearly defined in a manner that limits the potential for abuse. A right of correction/reply relates to a publisher, not to a journalist.

Introduction

Few if any established democracies impose licensing or registration requirements on individual journalists, or mandatory systems for promoting professional standards or entertaining complaints from the public, and transitional democracies are quickly moving in this direction as well. Promoting professionalism is achieved, instead, by protecting the freedom of journalists to establish professional associations of their own choice, which employ a range of self-regulatory means for promoting high standards, including training, ethical auditing, and setting ethical standards. As regards the latter, it is generally recognized that it is both more appropriate and more effective for complaints to be directed at media outlets than at individual journalists since it is, after all, the publication or broadcast of the material by a media outlet that is responsible for any harm caused.

Statutory registration systems for individual journalists almost always compromise independence, unduly limit access to the profession, and undermine rather than promote professionalism. Often, these systems are justified on the basis that journalism is a profession and, like other professions, needs to be regulated. Unlike other professions, such as law and medicine, however, the practice that defines journalism, namely engaging in expressive activity, is protected as a fundamental human right. Everyone has a fundamental right to express themselves, including through the media, that is, to do what journalists do.

All professions make a contribution to development, and regulatory systems can often enhance their impact by promoting minimum professional standards. Journalism differs from other professions, nevertheless, insofar as journalists' ability to contribute to development depends, in key ways, not just on their professionalism but also on their independence. But, as has been made clear previously, there are important incentives for governments to abuse any regulatory systems governing journalists precisely to undermine that independence, and those incentives play a far less important role in other professions. As a result, content regulation, far from promoting professionalism, is more likely to threaten it.

As a general rule, journalists do not enjoy special rights, over and above the rights that freedom of expression guarantees to everyone. One area where laws and courts have recognized such special rights is in the protection of confidential sources of information. This special recognition is based on the role journalists play in acting as "middlemen" between sources and the general public, conveying information of public interest disclosed by the former while protecting their identity, which is a precondition for the information being provided in the first place.

This chapter begins by considering democracies' approach to licensing and registration of journalists, as well as the issue of accreditation. It then looks at self-regulatory systems and the role of independent professional and self-regulatory bodies in promoting higher standards of journalism. Certain specific regulatory approaches for individual journalists—namely, the right to protect confidential sources of information—are highlighted. Finally, it considers a right of reply and a right of correction as they apply to publishers.

Absence of Licensing and/or Registration Requirements

No conditions should be placed on who may practice journalism, and individual journalists should not be subject to either licensing or registration requirements.

It is extremely doubtful whether a licensing system could ever be an effective means of promoting professional journalism. The possible conditions that may be placed on who may practice journalism— requiring an individual to be of a certain age, to have a certain type of training or to be a citizen, common licensing requirements in those countries which maintain such systems—simply do not provide any assurance against poor journalism. Furthermore, it is not journalists but media outlets that ultimately print or broadcast information and so, as noted previously, complaints are more properly directed at those outlets than at individual journalists.

Accreditation of journalists, whereby they are given privileged access to certain places and events with limited public capacity, raises rather different issues than licensing or registration, although in some cases, governments have tried to dress up licensing regimes by presenting them as accreditation schemes.[1] Accreditation, in its legitimate guise, is designed to provide special access for journalists to restricted capacity places and events on the basis that they will, in turn, provide wider access for the public at large, through publication or broadcast in the media. At the same time, accreditation schemes, like any regulatory system, can be abused. Once again, the three special mandates on freedom of expression provide guidance on this stating, in their 2003 Joint Declaration:

- Accreditation schemes for journalists are appropriate only where necessary to provide them with privileged access to certain places and/or events; such schemes should be overseen by an independent body and accreditation decisions should be taken pursuant to a fair and transparent process, based on clear and nondiscriminatory criteria published in advance.

- Accreditation should never be subject to withdrawal based only on the content of an individual journalist's work.

---

[1]See, for example, the Zimbabwean Access to Information and Protection of Privacy Act of 2002.

BOX 34. The Legitimacy of Licensing

International standards in this area are quite clear. A joint declaration by the three special mandates for protecting freedom of expression—the UN Special Rapporteur on Freedom of Opinion and Expression, the OSCE Representative on Freedom of the Media, and the OAS Special Rapporteur on Freedom of Expression—makes it clear that registration of journalists is not legitimate, noting also the particular problem of registration systems that allow for discretion to refuse (i.e., licensing systems).

In an advisory opinion, the Inter-American Court of Human Rights held that imposing a license requirement on journalists, along with conditions for membership, was a breach of the right to freedom of expression, stating:

> The argument that licensing is a way to guarantee society objective and truthful information by means of codes of professional responsibility and ethics is based on considerations of general welfare. But, in truth, as has been shown, general welfare requires the greatest possible amount of information, and it is the full exercise of the right of expression that benefits this general welfare.[1]

In practice, very few if any democratic countries impose licensing or even registration requirements on journalists. In a decision of August 1997, the high court of Zambia struck down an attempt to establish a statutory body to regulate and license journalists.[2] The court stressed that statutory licensing of journalists, as proposed in the legislation, would breach the rights to freedom of expression and association:

> I do not in my view consider the decision to constitute the Media Council of Zambia to be in furtherance of . . . freedom of expression, and press freedom in particular. . . . The decision to create the Media Council of Zambia is no doubt going to have an impact . . . on freedom of expression in that failure of one to affiliate himself to the Media Council of Zambia, or in the event of breach of any moral code determined by the Council would entail losing his status as a journalist, and with the denial of the opportunity to express and communicate his ideas through the media. In the light of the above it cannot be seriously argued that the creation of the Media Association or any other regulatory body by the Government would be in furtherance of the ideal embodied in the Constitution, vis-à-vis freedom of expression and association.

The decision is particularly noteworthy for its extremely wide application. In effect, the court ruled that any statutory attempt to license journalists would breach the right to freedom of expression, regardless of the form that attempt took.

---

1. *Compulsory Membership in an Association Prescribed by Law for the Practice of Journalism,* Advisory Opinion OC-5/85 of November 13, 1985, Series A. No. 5, para. 77.
2. *Kasoma v. Attorney General,* August 22, 1997, 95/HP/29/59.

BOX 35.   The United Kingdom Accreditation System

In the United Kingdom, the UK Press Card Authority[1] operates a scheme for issuing press/media cards to professional media workers. The scheme was facilitated by the London Metropolitan Police in 1992, with the co-operation of all major industry bodies, with the aims of ending the proliferation of press cards and of promoting agreement on a universally recognized press card.

The authority is made up of sixteen "gatekeepers," all of which are national trade unions and professional associations representing journalists and other media personnel covering the print and broadcast media. The gatekeepers issue cards to their members and are responsible for ensuring that the conditions are adhered to. The card is formally recognized by all police forces in the United Kingdom and de facto by other public bodies.

1. See *http://www.presscard.uk.com/*.

Self-Regulation

Self-regulatory systems are the most effective means of promoting professional standards, and, where such systems are in place, there is no need for statutory systems to be imposed. Where statutory systems for promoting professional standards are imposed, they should apply to print media outlets rather than individual journalists and be overseen by independent bodies. Journalists should be free to establish professional associations of their own choosing.

Systems for promoting professional standards in the media are an important way not only of protecting against harmful or inaccurate media reporting but also for enhancing the overall quality of media output. As such, they can contribute to building trust in the media and to facilitating its ability to promote participatory and equitable development. At the same time, when such systems allow officials to play an oversight role, they can seriously undermine media independence and hence its ability to act as watch-dog of government.

Journalists' right to establish professional bodies derives from both the right to freedom of association and the right to freedom of expression. Such bodies can play an important role in defending freedom of the media generally in society, as well as protecting their individual members.

On the other hand, a requirement for journalists to belong to a certain professional or other body has been held by international courts to breach the right to freedom of expression. Unlike other professions, everyone has the right to practice journalism and, as with licensing systems, this should not be subject to formal requirements, including a requirement to belong to a specific professional body.[2] Imposing professional standards on journalists by law is oppressive, serves no legitimate aim, and is unlikely to be workable in practice. As noted previously, statutory complaints systems aimed at media outlets provide adequate redress, so there is no need to extend their coverage to individual journalists.

In Indonesia, for example, journalists are free to organize themselves into professional associations or unions. Article 7 of the 1999 Indonesian Press Law, for example, states:

(1) Journalists are free to choose a journalist's association.

(2) Journalists possess and adhere to a Journalistic Code of Ethics.[3]

Many journalists' associations set professional standards for their members. In some cases, these rules are just voluntary guidelines, whereas in other cases, they are conditions of membership. The Hong Kong Journalists' Association, for example, has a Code of Ethics with some 11 sections setting standards for journalists' activities. An example is section 4:

A journalist shall rectify promptly any harmful inaccuracies, ensure that correction and apologies receive due prominence and afford the right of reply to persons criticized when the issue is of sufficient importance.

For a serious breach of these standards, a journalist can ultimately be expelled from the association, but this does not deprive the individual of the right to work as a journalist. Similar professional associations and/or unions exist in many countries.

Protection of Sources

Journalists have a right to protect their confidential sources of information, without which the flow of information to them, and hence to the public, would be undermined.

---

[2] See *Compulsory Membership in an Association Prescribed by Law for the Practice of Journalism*, note.
[3] An unofficial translation of National Law of the Republic of Indonesia, no. 40/1999 on the Press, available at: *http://web.amnesty.org/library/index/engasa210442003.*

The ability of the media to inform the public depends on a free flow of information to the media. Journalists often depend on others for the supply of information on issues of public interest, including individuals who come forward with secret or sensitive information, known as confidential sources. In many instances, anonymity is a precondition of the information being conveyed from the source to the journalist, for example, because of fear of repercussions that might adversely affect the source's physical safety or job security. If journalists cannot keep the identity of their sources confidential, these sources will dry up, and the journalists' ability to report in the public interest will be seriously impaired.

Source protection is most closely associated with the media's role as watch-dog of government and other powerful social actors. The disclosure of information by sources to journalists acts as an important informational safety valve, helping to ensure that information of public interest, particularly on wrongdoing, reaches the public. It is in precisely these situations that sources are most likely to demand protection of the confidentiality of their identity before they are willing to disclose information in the first place.

Many journalists are bound by professional codes of ethics from revealing confidential sources. But, pursuant to international guarantees of freedom of expression, they should also benefit from legal protection in this area. Indeed, all those involved in a significant way in maintaining the flow of information to the public should benefit from this right.

In some countries, source protection is constitutionally guaranteed. This is the case, for example, in Argentina, where Article 43(3) provides for the "secrecy of journalistic information sources." In other cases, the right has received statutory protection,[4] while in still other cases, national courts have based a right to protect confidential sources of information on constitutional guarantees of freedom of expression. For example, in Nigeria, the High Court of Lagos State

---

[4]In the United Kingdom, for example, section 10 of the Contempt of Court Act of 1981 provides some protection against mandatory source disclosure, as follows:

> No court may require a person to disclose, nor is the person guilty of contempt of court for refusing to disclose the source information contained in the publication for which he is responsible, unless it is established to the satisfaction of the court that disclosure is necessary in the interests of justice or national security or for the prevention of disorder or crime.

BOX 36. International Standards on the Protection of Source Confidentiality

The European Court of Human Rights clearly established the right of journalists to protect the confidentiality of their sources of information:

> Protection of journalistic sources is one of the basic conditions for press freedom as is reflected in the laws and professional codes of conduct in a number of Contracting States and is affirmed in several international instruments on journalistic freedoms. Without such protection, sources may be deterred from assisting the press in informing the public on matters of public interest. As a result, the vital public-watchdog role of the press may be undermined and the ability of the press to provide accurate and reliable information may be adversely affected. Having regard to the importance of the protection of journalistic sources for press freedom in a democratic society and the potential chilling effect an order of source disclosure has on the exercise of that freedom, such a measure cannot be compatible with Article 10 unless it is justified by an overriding requirement in the public interest.[1]

In part due to that case, the Committee of Ministers adopted Recommendation R(2000)7 on the right of journalists not to disclose their sources of information.[2] The recommendation elaborates in some detail on the nature of this right.

Similarly, Principle 15 of the *Declaration of Principles on Freedom of Expression in Africa* states:

> Media practitioners shall not be required to reveal confidential sources of information or to disclose other material held for journalistic purposes except in accordance with the following principles:
>
> - the identity of the source is necessary for the investigation or prosecution of a serious crime, or the defence of a person accused of a criminal offence;
> - the information or similar information leading to the same result cannot be obtained elsewhere;
> - the public interest in disclosure outweighs the harm to freedom of expression; and
> - disclosure has been ordered by a court, after a full hearing.[3]

The International Criminal Tribunal for Yugoslavia also recognized a special right for war correspondents not to have to testify against their informants, based on the same principles outlined in the European Court case.[4]

---

1. *Goodwin v. United Kingdom,* March 27, 1996, Application No. 17488/90, para. 39.
2. Adopted March 8, 2000.
3. Adopted by the African Commission on Human and Peoples' Rights at its 32nd Session, October 17–23, 2002.
4. *Prosecutor v. Radoslav Brdjanin & Momir Talic ("Randal Case"),* International Criminal Tribunal for the Former Yugoslavia, (Appeals Chamber), JL/P.I.S/715-e (December 11, 2002).

BOX 37.   Germany: Journalists' Right to Confidentiality of Sources

Regulation of the press in Germany is a matter in the first instance for the Länder (states). The press laws of most Länder include a provision granting journalists a right to refuse to divulge the identity of their confidential sources. Article 24(1) of North Rhine Westphalia's Press Law is typical.[1] It provides:

> Editors, journalists, publishers, printers and others involved in the production or publication of periodical literature in a professional capacity can refuse to give evidence as to the person of the author, sender or confidant of an item published in the editorial section of the paper or communication intended wholly or partly for such publication or about its contents.

This provides an absolute privilege, admitting of no exceptions. Subparagraphs (2), (3), and (4) render evidence that discloses a confidential source inadmissible in court if obtained via confiscation of materials or a search of premises unless,

> [the party to whom the evidence belongs] is urgently suspected of being the perpetrator of or participant in a criminal offence.

Federal law also provides strong support for the protection of confidential sources, especially in civil cases. Section 383 of the Civil Procedure Code provides that when facts are confided to persons because of their profession, including journalism, these persons are entitled to refuse to give testimony on these facts unless their source consents to disclosure. Section 53 of the Criminal Procedure Code authorizes journalists to refuse to testify concerning the content or source of information given in confidence.

---

1. North Rhine Westphalia Press Law, 24 May 1966, in Pamphlet on the Press Law of Germany, issued by the Ministry of Information (1989), p. 14. See also, Article 19, *Press Law and Practice* (London: Article 19, 1993), pp. 92–93.

---

ruled that the Senate of the National Assembly had exceeded its authority in summoning a journalist to disclose the confidential sources of an article he had written. In concluding that the summons had interfered with the journalist's right to freedom of expression as guaranteed by the constitution, the Court stated:

> It is a matter of common knowledge that those who express their opinions or impart ideas and information through the medium of a newspaper or any other medium for the dissemination of information enjoy by customary law and convention a degree of confidentiality. How else is a disseminator of

information to operate if those who supply him with such information are not assured of protection from identification and/or disclosure?[5]

Similarly, the Supreme Court of Bermuda upheld the right of journalists to protect confidential sources of information in a case involving a journalist as a witness.[6]

Both international law and national practice thus recognize the importance of protection of source confidentiality as an aspect of freedom of expression. It may legitimately be overridden but only in limited circumstances. In particular, mandatory source disclosure should be permitted only by court order and to serve an overriding interest, such as the right of an accused person to defend him- or herself. Where similar information may be obtained by other means, mandatory source disclosure cannot be justified as necessary. Furthermore, an order for source disclosure can only be justified where the public interest in obtaining the information clearly outweighs the harm to freedom of expression.

Right of Correction/Reply

A right of correction/reply can provide an effective and appropriate response to media errors and other wrongs. However, it represents a limitation on freedom of expression and so should be clearly defined in a manner that limits the potential for abuse.

Both a right of correction and a right of reply are designed to promote redress for media inaccuracies and other wrongs without the need to resort to lengthy and costly court cases. As such, they can promote more professional standards in the media while intruding relatively little on media freedom. Greater professionalism, as noted previously, is likely to promote greater trust in the media and hence facilitate its ability to contribute to development goals and democratic participation.

It should be noted, however, that such a right of reply refers to the media organization as the publisher, and not to the individual journalist involved.

---

[5]*Tony Momoh v. Senate of the National Assembly*, [1981] 1 NCLR 105.
[6]*The Bermuda Fire & Marine Insurance Company Limited (in liquidation) v. F&M Limited and Others*, Civil Jurisdiction 1995 No. 7 (Supreme Court of Bermuda).

Although they are often referred to in combination, the right of correction and the right of reply are very different remedies. A right of correction implies a right to complain of inaccuracies in the media and to have such complaints, where upheld, lead to the correction of the inaccuracies. In most cases, a quick right of correction represents an effective and appropriate means to redress any factual errors in the media. It poses little threat to independence—since it applies only in very clear and limited circumstances and the content of the correction is controlled by the media outlet—and yet it provides a quick and low-cost means to resolve inaccuracies.

A right of reply, on the other hand, effectively grants a right of access to the media to make one's own statement. As a result, it is more contentious and open to possible abuse.[7] While a right of reply may be less onerous for the media than lengthy and expensive court proceedings, advocates of media freedom generally suggest that it should be voluntary rather than prescribed by law. In some countries, the right of reply may be claimed in a wide range of circumstances that do not involve any harm to the claimant. This is open to abuse and may result in the media being reluctant to engage in criticism, for fear of this leading to claims of a right of reply, and hence unable effectively to perform its watchdog role.

International standards and national law and practice (Box 38) suggest the following conditions for any right of reply:

1. A reply should be required to be provided only in response to statements that are false or misleading and that breach an important interest of the claimant; a reply should not be permitted to be used to comment on opinions that the reader or viewer simply does not like.

2. A reply should receive similar prominence to the original article or broadcast.

---

[7]The United States Supreme Court, for example, struck down a mandatory right of reply for the print media on the grounds that it is an unconstitutional interference with the First Amendment right to free speech. See *Miami Herald Publishing Co. v. Tornillo*, 418 U.S. 241 (1974). The U.S. Supreme Court has, however, upheld a right of reply for the broadcast media. See *Red Lion Broadcasting Co. v. Federal Communications Commission*, 395 US 367 (1969). No legal right of reply for print media outlets exists in countries such as Canada and the United Kingdom.

BOX 38.   International and Comparative Standards on the Right of Reply

A right of reply is a favored form of redress in many parts of the world. Article 14(1) of the *American Convention on Human Rights*, for example, actually requires state parties to introduce either a right of reply or a right of correction.[1] A resolution of the Committee of Ministers of the Council of Europe similarly supports the institution of a right of reply, setting out detailed rules for its exercise, including that it may be overridden by a countervailing public interest.[2]

The Argentinean Supreme Court has held that a number of requirements must be met before the right may become operative:

1) there must be a "substantial serious offense";
2) the offense must arise from a statement unsupported by reasonable argument;
3) in the case of "ideological interests," the person who replies assumes a "collective representation"; only one person, the first to reply, will have the right to reply in the name of all those who may have been offended by the same statement;
4) the rectification or reply must be published in the same medium of communication, in the same place and with the same prominence as the offending statement; and
5) the space given to the reply must be adequate to its goal.[3]

In a later case, the same court held that the right could not be used to respond to the expression of ideas, only facts.[4]

1. See also *Enforceability of the Right to Reply or Correction*, Advisory Opinion OC-7/85, Series A, No. 7 (August 29, 1986).
2. See Resolution (74) 26 on the right of reply—position of the individual in relation to the press, adopted July 2, 1974.
3. *Ekmekdjian v. Sofovich*, Fallos 315:1492 (July 7, 1992).
4. *Petric v. Pagina 12*, Fallos 315:1492, CSJN, Supreme Court of Justice of the Nation, (April 16, 1998).

3. A reply should be proportionate in length to the original article or broadcast.

4. A reply should be restricted to addressing the incorrect or misleading facts in the original text and not be taken as an opportunity to introduce new issues or comment on correct facts.

5. The media should not be required to carry a reply that is abusive or illegal.

Part III

Promoting Plural and Independent Broadcasting

Overview

Broadcasting, as we noted in Part I, can play a significant role in the delivery of public service goals, not only by informing, educating, and entertaining, but also by providing a platform for the views of all people, facilitating participation in governance, holding leaders and officials to account, and contributing to sustainable, equitable, and participatory development.

Governments cannot achieve these objectives alone. But they can introduce specific policies tailored to create a framework for broadcasting that, taken as a whole, will have the capacity to produce a diverse range of high-quality services. These services should be accessible to all, serve the goals of equitable and sustainable development, and promote access to information, accountability, and participation.

There is no doubt that broadcasting can be a powerful force for good governance, but it may also serve as an instrument of social control, a vehicle for the pursuit of political or sectarian interests, or even a means of fomenting conflict and war. The interwoven tensions generated by competing desires to enhance accountability, retain broadcasting as an instrument of state policy, exploit the media for sectional interests, satisfy the demands of civil society and social movements for media reform, and realize the economic opportunities offered by broadcasting underlie the different trends in broadcast policy and practice throughout the world.

Part I argued that a media landscape that promotes accountability, participation, and development requires a diversity of content but also a diversity of ownership and forms of ownership, including commercial, noncommercial, public, and community ownership at both the national and local levels. Specific policy interventions, largely through the regulatory system, are needed to promote a multifaceted broadcasting sector that recognizes the different interests at stake and the respective merits and values of different types of broadcasting, each with its own distinct social, economic, and political logic.

Development of a multilayered broadcasting sector is feasible, evidenced by its historical emergence in most regions of the world, with significantly different emphases depending on the context. Its emergence also reflects widely held aspirations among governments and people that this is an approach worth striving for, even if many are failing to implement it effectively.

In the following chapters, we set out the essential elements of good practice that constitute a broad policy, legal, and regulatory framework for broadcasting in the public interest, as discussed in Part I. We draw from internationally recognized legal guarantees on freedom of expression and access to information, along with concrete examples from different countries of how these have been put into effect.

Chapter 9 discusses good practices in the structure, mandate, staffing, and procedures of broadcast regulatory agencies and identifies core principles, including independence, authority and competence. It also acknowledges that the risk of regulatory failure, including capture by vested interests, is ever present and needs to be offset by a vigilant, robust, and authoritative institutional structure.

Chapter 10 looks specifically at the regulation of broadcast content. When and where is it justified for policy and regulation to attempt to influence broadcast content, either directly, through regulation of the general nature of content, or indirectly, through interventions relating to the technical means to broadcast? This question, and some answers to it, are explored in some depth.

Chapters 11 through 13 focus respectively on the three main broadcasting sectors: public service, community, and commercial broadcasting. In each case, we explore the relevant institutional, licensing, and regulatory structures, the checks and balances needed to ensure the promotion of public interest goals, and the possible and appropriate funding structures.

9 Regulation and the Government Role

Good Practice Checklist

- The regulation of broadcasting should be the responsibility of an independent regulatory body established on a statutory basis with powers and duties set out explicitly in law.
- The independence of the broadcast regulatory body should be adequately and explicitly protected from interference, particularly of a political or economic nature.
- Any independent body that exercises regulatory powers in broadcasting should have a principal duty to further the public interest and should have particular regard for the right to freedom of opinion and expression and the desirability of fostering a plurality and diversity of services.
- The appointment process for members of an independent broadcast regulator should be fair, open, transparent, and set out in law. It should be designed to ensure relevant expertise or experience and a diversity of interests and opinions representative of society as a whole.
- The appointments process should not be dominated by any particular political party or commercial interest and the members appointed should be required to serve in an individual capacity and to exercise their functions in the public interest at all times.
- In exercising its powers, the independent broadcast regulator should be required by law to operate openly and transparently and to facilitate public participation in their affairs, including through public consultation on their policies and procedures.
- All decisions of the independent broadcast regulator should be accompanied by written reasons.
- The independent broadcast regulator should be subject to judicial oversight and should be formally accountable to the public through a multiparty body such as the parliament or a parliamentary committee in which all major parties are represented.
- The independent broadcast regulator should be required by law to publish an annual report.
- The independent broadcast regulator should be ensured a reliable and recurrent income provided for in law and sufficient to carry out its activities effectively and without interference.

Introduction

In the hands of governments, or under the influence of powerful economic interests, the regulation of broadcasting can in effect become a gatekeeping exercise and an obstacle to enhanced media pluralism and diversity. The selective distribution of broadcast concessions with the intention of rewarding certain groups over others can stifle democratic debate and the plurality of opinion. Similarly, regulatory sanctions can discourage the exercise of freedom of expression and limit the independence of the media. The trend in most regions is thus toward a system whereby broadcasting regulation is placed in the hands of an independent regulator constituted in such a way as to reflect a diversity of interests, with clearly defined powers and duties and transparent and accountable operating procedures.

An independent broadcast regulator provides a means to promote and develop a balanced broadcasting sector in which a plurality of broadcasters, commercial, public service, nonprofit, or community in their various incarnations, can exist alongside one another. It may have a duty, among other things, to encourage multiple forms of ownership; to promote local and public service content; to meet the needs of particular groups, including cultural and linguistic minorities; to consider equality of opportunity; and to ensure that broadcasting respects generally accepted community standards, for example, those established for the protection of children.

BOX 39.   France: From Monopoly to Diversity

In France, until 1982, the state retained a monopoly control over broadcasting. In 1986 the Law on Freedom of Communication (No. 86-1087) was adopted providing for the creation of a new regulatory body, the Conseil Superieur de l'Audiovisuel (CSA). The CSA came into existence on February 13, 1989, tasked with the dual role of guaranteeing and promoting broadcasting freedom in France. Article 3.1 states that the CSA is an independent authority that "guarantees the exercise of the freedom of audiovisual communication with regard to radio and television by any means of electronic communication under conditions defined by the present law."[1] Alongside the publicly owned broadcasters, the CSA established the current regulatory framework for the licensing of commercial and community broadcasting.

---

1. Law on Freedom of Communication No 86-1087 of 1986 (modified). Available at: www.csa.fr.

The functions of broadcast regulation may be the responsibility of a stand-alone body, they may be located within the responsibilities of different bodies, or they may constitute just one part of the functions of a communications regulator with wider responsibilities.

Vesting the various functions of broadcast regulation—spectrum planning, broadcast licensing, content standards, and complaints handling—in more than one regulatory body can lead to duplication of effort and cost and may also be confusing for the public. On the other hand, it may be desirable, when adapting good practice to particular country circumstances, to have some division of regulatory responsibilities between different bodies. This may be considered preferable to an excessively powerful regulatory body that is not sufficiently independent of the government or of other particular interests.

In most countries broadcast regulation has historically been distinct from the regulation of telecommunications and the radio spectrum. In recent years the trend has been to replace distinct regulatory regimes for broadcasting, telecommunications, and radio frequencies with a single communications regulator as, for example, ICASA in South Africa and Ofcom in the United Kingdom. The single regulator idea, however, is by no means new. The U.S. Federal Communications Commission was set up on these lines in 1934.

While a single regulator responsible for both telecommunications and broadcasting can be expected to produce greater policy coherence in communications regulation, the vesting of a wide range of regulatory powers in a single regulator makes it all the more important for the regulator to be capable of clearly distinguishing the specificities of each of its areas of responsibility and meeting the highest standards of good practice in each.

Threats to Independence

As stressed earlier, the independence of a regulator can be threatened from several directions.

The risk of "capture" of the regulator by partisan interests is high and ongoing.[1] "Capture" occurs when the positions and actions of a

---

[1] There is a very considerable literature by "capture theorists," much, though not all of it, emanating from the United States. Only a very limited literature, however, is available on the specificities of regulatory capture of the broadcast sector in developing countries.

government regulatory agency are overly influenced by the vested interests of the industry it regulates to the detriment of the public interest it is intended to serve. A higher risk of capture can be built into flawed founding legal and institutional structures of a regulator or can emerge gradually over an extended period of time, and wealthy countries with long experience of independent regulation are not exempt.[2]

Regulators take decisions that have far-reaching economic implications for private media entities, granting or withdrawing licenses, imposing and policing more or less onerous conditions that, although aimed at protecting the public interest, can greatly influence the growth potential, income, and profitability of media enterprises. This influence inevitably entails a risk of corruption among regulatory staff and decision-making processes[3] and thus also underlines the importance of safeguards such as transparency and "whistle-blower" mechanisms. Powerful lobbying of the regulator by media interests can also result in regulatory decisions and outcomes that favor private media interests, especially where the regulator has limited research, analytical, and public relations capacity. When directed at governments, such media industry lobbying can also diminish the independence of the regulatory body vis-à-vis the regulated, whether at the time of its establishment or through amending legislation.

Furthermore, media interests are particularly well placed to influence public opinion and, hence, the actions of publicly elected officials and members of government. And a "revolving door" between the regulator and the regulated, where key staff shuttle between one and the other with scant protection against conflicts of interests, can be a problem for regulators everywhere. Sustained and varied contact, formal and informal, between regulators and commercial broadcasters, as well as the considerable economic power of media, may be among the causes of what has been described as a "soft" approach toward regulating commercial

---

[2]For a view of the issue in U.S. broadcasting see: Anthony E. Varona, "Changing Channels and Bridging Divides: The Failure and Redemption of American Broadcast Television Regulation," *Minnesota Journal of Law, Science & Technology*, Vol. 6, No. 1, 2004–2005, available at SSRN: http://ssrn.com/abstract=921132.

[3]The Polish regulator became enmeshed in a corruption scandal in 2003, in which cross-ownership was the issue. Open Society Institute EU Monitoring and Advocacy Program, *Television Across Europe: Regulation, Policy and Independence* (OSI: New York/Budapest, 2005), 52, available at: *http://www.eumap.org*.

broadcasters in Western Europe. This approach is characterized by laxity in the enforcement of license conditions and a reluctance to use the powers available, among other things.[4]

Legislating to avoid such capture is neither simple nor direct, and aspects of the enabling environment in Part II are relevant here, in particular, robust access to information legislation. Adequate funding, training, and capacity-building can be important alongside the legal measures outlined in the following section.

Excessive government influence over the regulator, however, is very often a larger problem. The policy and statutory measures presented here, including formal guarantees of independence and transparency, appropriate appointment procedures, and adequate enforcement mechanisms, can go a long way toward addressing this, as can the implementation of an effective enabling environment outlined in Part II. Yet many regulators succumb, willingly or not, to government pressures, many of which are informal and concealed from public view. Less tangible challenges facing regulatory independence may be related to attitudes and cultures. In some environments, acquiescence to and practical implementation of an authority established by legislation and subject to law, but independent of government influence, can take some time to evolve among members of government and regulators alike.

In the following, it should be borne in mind that good practice in one area, such as exemplary legislating for independence, may be undermined by weaknesses in others, such as inadequate funding or a culture of inertia or corruption.

An Independent Regulatory Body

The regulation of broadcasting should be the responsibility of an independent regulatory body established on a statutory basis with powers and duties set out explicitly in law. The independence and institutional autonomy of the regulatory body should be adequately and explicitly protected from interference, particularly interference of a political or economic nature.

---

[4]Open Society Institute EU Monitoring and Advocacy Program, *Television Across Europe: Regulation, Policy and Independence* (OSI: New York/Budapest, 2005), 53, 1031.

The independence of the regulatory body is central to its effectiveness. Though insufficient in itself, it should be guaranteed in the legislation under which it is established. This legislation should set out clearly the powers and duties that have been assigned to the regulatory body and that it is entitled to exercise independently of government or any other entity or person. Any change to these powers and duties should be permissible only through amendment by the parliament of the relevant legislation.

The legislation should also guarantee the independence of the regulator by identifying clear and explicit rules for appointment of its members and the terms under which they serve, and by requiring formal accountability to the public and funding arrangements that ensure its operational and administrative autonomy from government or politicians. The regulator must also maintain impartiality with respect to those whom it regulates, and in particular avoid undue influence by the major broadcast licensees and private media owners.

In some countries the independence of the broadcast regulator is constitutionally prescribed. For example, the South African constitution states, in Section 192: "National legislation must establish an independent authority to regulate broadcasting in the public interest, and to ensure fairness and a diversity of views broadly representing South African society." Section 192 expressly obliges Parliament to establish an independent authority to regulate broadcasting. To this end, Parliament has enacted the Independent Communications Authority of South Africa 2000 Act (ICASA Act). ICASA took over the function of two previous regulators, the South African Telecommunications Regulatory Authority (SATRA) and the Independent Broadcasting Authority (IBA). The preamble to the ICASA Act acknowledges "that the establishment of an independent body to regulate broadcasting and telecommunications is required." The act describes ICASA in the following clear terms:[5]

(3) The Authority is independent and subject only to the Constitution and the law, and must be impartial and must perform its functions without fear, favour or prejudice.

(4) The Authority must function without any political or commercial interference.

---

[5]The Independent Communications Authority of South Africa Act No. 13 of 2000, available at: *www.icasa.org.za.*

> **BOX 40. Benin: Constitutional Support for an Independent Regulatory Body**
>
> The creation of a regulatory body, the *Haute Authorité de l'Audiovisuel et de la Communication* (HAAC), on August 21, 1992 (Law No. 92-021), was a recommendation of the *Conference Nationale Souveraine* (February 19 to 28, 1990), imposed by civil society organizations on the then-military regime to review the governance of the country. The conference laid the foundations of a system based on the rule of law and the respect of fundamental human rights. The conference appointed an interim prime minister charged with the preparation of a referendum on a new constitution. The new constitution adopted by referendum in December 1990 sought to protect the media from government interference and make it a watchdog of government. It recommended that the regulatory body be rooted in the constitution in order to give it legitimacy comparable to that of the Executive. It established that "the *Haute Autorité de l'Audiovisuel et de la Communication* is an institution independent of all political powers, organization or lobby of any sort."

Powers and Duties

> *Any independent body that exercises regulatory powers in broadcasting should have a principal duty to further the public interest in relation to broadcasting and should have particular concern for the right to freedom of opinion and expression and the desirability of fostering a plurality and diversity of services.*

The legislation under which the regulatory body is established should describe its principal duties in clear terms together with the specific functions that it is required to carry out. It should be framed in such a way that the regulator is able to operate in a manner that is fair, open, transparent, and consistent with its principal duties.

Although broadcasting's ability to contribute to development is increased within a regulatory framework that gives precedence to the goal of furthering the public interest, other additional and more specific duties of the regulator should also be set out. These may include, for example:

- the availability throughout the territory of a wide range of broadcasting services of a high quality and appealing to a variety of tastes and interest;
- the maintenance of a plurality of providers of different broadcasting services;

- protection of the public from offensive and harmful program material;
- protection from unfair treatment or unwarranted intrusions of privacy.

The powers in relation to broadcasting that are assigned to an independent regulatory body should also be set out clearly and should, inter alia, include the powers:

- to grant and to suspend or revoke broadcast licenses;
- to assign those frequencies that are designated for broadcast use;
- to set standards and rules within clearly defined areas of responsibility; and
- to hear and to adjudicate on complaints relating to broadcast content.

The Broadcasting Commission of Ireland (BCI)—previously the Irish Radio and Television Commission but renamed under the Broadcasting Act of 2001—is responsible for the licensing, regulation, and oversight of all private and independent broadcasting, including community broadcasting. In addition to licensing, it develops codes

---

BOX 41.   Mali: Dual Regulatory Bodies

Two regulatory bodies, the *Conseil Superieur de la Communication* (CSC), which was set up in December 1992, and the *Comité National de l'Egal Accès aux Médias d'Etat* (CNEAME), set up in January 1993, are in charge of the implementation of Article 7 of the 1992 constitution, which states that freedom of expression is guaranteed under the law. The CNEAME is concerned only with the access of political parties to state media and its activities are developed mainly during electoral campaigns. All other regulatory oversight of the broadcast media and print media rest with the CSC. The powers and duties of the CSC are set out in the CSC Act of 1992 (No. 92-038). The CSC decides on the allocation and withdrawal of frequencies to radio and television broadcasting stations and ensures that stations abide by their service commitments. It has powers to suspend or withdraw broadcast authorizations in the event of noncompliance. The CSC undertakes research into the media and communications sector and also has powers to prevent undue dominance or control of the market for print and broadcast communications.

and rules with respect to programming and advertising standards; it monitors services to ensure compliance; it provides support for training and development initiatives; and it undertakes or commissions research to assist the development of broadcast policy.

In the Republic of Korea, all of the regulatory functions relating to the broadcast media have been consolidated within the Korean Broadcasting Commission (KBC) established as an independent body under the terms of the Broadcasting Law of 2000. The KBC took over the administrative functions, previously reserved by government, for licensing and authorization of terrestrial, cable, and satellite broadcasters and relay cable operators. It is also responsible, among other matters, for regulation of broadcast content, nomination of board members of the main public broadcasting institutions, broadcast policy-making, and management of the Broadcasting Development Fund.

Appointment of Members

The appointments process for members of a regulatory body with responsibility for broadcasting should be fair, open, transparent, and set out in law. It should be designed to ensure that members have relevant expertise or experience and carry a diversity of interests and opinions representative of society as a whole. The appointments process should not be dominated by any particular political party or commercial interest, and the members appointed should be required to serve in an individual capacity and to exercise their functions in the public interest at all times.

Members of the regulatory body should be appointed for a fixed term and should be protected from dismissal during this term unless they cease to meet explicit conditions of eligibility for office or fail to discharge their responsibilities as set out in law. There should be clear rules of eligibility for membership of the regulatory body to avoid incompatibility with the responsibilities of office. No one should be appointed who:

- is an employee in the civil service or other branch of government;
- is an officeholder or employee of a political party;
- is an elected or appointed member of the government;
- is an elected or appointed member of the legislature;
- is an employee, or has financial interests, in broadcasting or communications; or

- has been convicted, after due process in accordance with internationally accepted legal principles, of a violent crime or a crime of dishonesty, unless five years has passed since the sentence was discharged.

In carrying out their duties and responsibilities, members of the regulatory body should be required to act according to the principles of public office and not to accept any instructions, terms, conditions, gifts, or payment from any party other than those that are explicitly provided for in law for the effective discharge of their responsibilities.

The size and composition of the board vary significantly from country to country. In the Netherlands, the independent Media Authority (*Commissariaat voor de Media*) has only three commissioners, although their independence is guaranteed by the Media Act of 1987. The commissioners are appointed by Royal Decree on the Recommendation of the Minister for Education, Culture, and Science. In contrast, in France, the CSA has a board of nine members. Three members are appointed by the president, three by the National Assembly, and the remainder appointed by the chairman of the Senate. They are confirmed by presidential decree, and the chairman of the CSA is appointed by the president. A third of the members of the CSA are renewed every two years. The term of office for all members is six years, which can neither be revoked nor renewed.

In Benin, the president of the *Haute Authorité de l'Audiovisuel et de la Communication* (HAAC) is appointed, after consultation with the president of the Parliament, by decree in the Council of Ministers. The other members of the HAAC board consist of three appointees of the head of state and three appointees of the Cabinet of the Parliament.

BOX 42.   Canada: Procedures for Appointment of Members

The Canadian Radio-television and Telecommunications Commission (CRTC) is responsible for overseeing broadcasting licensing in Canada. It consists of not more than thirteen full-time members and not more than six part-time members, appointed by the prime minister. In practice, although not in law, this is a broad public process involving public consultations. Members are appointed for five years and may be reappointed. There are strict conflict-of-interest rules for members, which exclude anyone who has interests in telecommunications or broadcasting from membership. The law does not set out prohibitions on politically active individuals from becoming members, but this is respected in practice.

Each set of appointments is to include a communicator, a lawyer, and a personality from civil society. In addition, it includes two professional journalists and one telecommunications technician appointed in a general assembly of their peers. The mandate of the nine members of the HAAC board is five years and may neither be revoked nor renewed.

Transparency and Consultation

In exercising regulatory powers over broadcasting, regulatory bodies should be required by law to operate openly and transparently and to facilitate public participation in their affairs, including through public consultation on their policies and procedures. All decisions of regulatory bodies should be accompanied by written reasons.

Regulatory bodies should operate according to the principles of good governance and the highest standards of public administration and in accordance with the principles of natural justice. The regulatory body should conduct its affairs on the basis of an explicit commitment to access to information and should not withhold information from the public unless this is justified by reference to a clear, explicit, and overriding reason for doing so. Exceptions to the general principle of disclosure might include information of a commercially sensitive nature provided in confidence by a license applicant.

Transparency can be achieved through various means, including: publishing details of the interests and affiliations of members of the regulatory body; publishing proceedings of meetings; open licensing processes (including licensing decisions and reasons for those decisions); engaging in public consultation on the annual plan and priorities of the regulatory body; and conducting public consultation on licensing and regulatory policies, codes, and procedures. Decision making on all major policy matters should include, as a minimum, a three-stage public consultation process that includes the following:

- notice of a new decision that is to be made
- collection of public input on the possible decision
- final decision issued publicly

The Canadian Radio-television and Telecommunications Commission, for example, issues public notice of all new decisions to be taken. This is followed by a consultation period in which comments can be filed by interested parties and in which there may also be public hearings and consultative workshops. After consultation the decision is made and publicized.

In countries where access to information legislation is in force, the independent regulatory body should be subject to the same rules that apply to government departments and public bodies. It is also good practice for provisions on transparency and consultation to be made explicit in the legislation providing for the independent regulatory body.

The Independent Communications Authority of South Africa (ICASA), for example, is defined as a "public body" within the terms of the Promotion of Access to Information Act of 2000. ICASA publishes a manual setting out its compliance with access to information legislation as this applies to public bodies.[6] With respect to broadcast

---

BOX 43.   United Kingdom: Consultation Policies

In a published guide to their consultation processes, Ofcom states: "Consultation is an essential part of regulatory accountability—the means by which those people and organizations affected by our decisions can judge what we do and why we do it."[1] The Communications Act of 2003 sets out, in Section 3, a general requirement on Ofcom to have regard to:[2]

  (a) the principles under which regulatory activities should be transparent, accountable, proportionate, consistent and targeted only at cases in which action is needed; and
  (b) any other principles appearing to Ofcom to represent the best regulatory practice.

In addition, the act includes seventy-seven specific requirements on matters where consultation is required before a decision is taken. Ofcom consultation policy draws on current good practice in public administration set out in guidelines published by the Cabinet Office, a body of central government.[3]

---

1. From *Commencement to 1st quarter 2004: Foundation and Framework*, Ofcom, 2004.
2. Communications Act of 2003, available at: *www.communicationsact.gov.uk.*
3. For example, *Cabinet Office Code of Practice on Written Consultation*, available at: *www.cabinet-office.gov.uk/guidanceconsult/index.asp.*

---

[6]*Promotion of Access to Information: Manual in terms of Section 14 in respect of the Independent Communications Authority of South Africa*, ICASA.

regulation ICASA is obliged under the Broadcasting Act of 1993 to engage in public consultation with respect to any inquiry it conducts; with respect to frequency planning; and with respect to license applications, license renewals, and amendments to licenses.

Public Accountability

Any public body that exercises regulatory powers in broadcasting should be subject to judicial oversight and should be formally accountable to the public through a multiparty body, such as the parliament or a parliamentary committee, in which all major parties are represented. The regulatory body should be required by law to publish an annual report.

Decisions taken by a regulatory body responsible for broadcasting should be subject to judicial oversight and any individual or organization affected by such a decision should have the right to seek judicial review of that decision through the appropriate court.

Formal accountability should focus on review of the past activities and performance of the regulatory body and should not have the purpose of seeking to influence individual decisions. The annual report of the regulatory body should include a detailed account of their licensing and regulatory activities together with audited financial accounts. It should be published in a manner that ensures it to be easily accessible to the public.

BOX 44.   South Africa: The Regulator's Annual Report

The Independent Communications Authority of South Africa (ICASA) Act 2000 requires, under Section 16, that ICASA prepare an annual report, within three months of the financial year, to include "information regarding licences granted, renewed, amended, transferred, suspended or revoked and such other information as the Minister may in writing require."[1] The minister is required to table the report in Parliament within fixed time limits. ICASA is also required to produce annual financial statements and the auditor-general's report on those statements. All decisions of ICASA are subject to judicial review.

---

1. The Independent Communications Authority of South Africa Act No. 13 of 2000, available at: *www.icasa.org.za*.

Funding Arrangements

Regulatory bodies responsible for broadcasting should be ensured a reliable and recurrent income provided for in law and sufficient to carry out their activities effectively and without interference.

The legal framework for funding regulators should be transparent and include protections against arbitrary interference. Funding to, or the withdrawal of funding from, a regulatory body should never be used as a means to influence decision making. A variety of mechanisms can be used to fund regulatory bodies, including direct funding by government from taxation or funding through charges applied to licensees.

In Benin, for example, the budget of the *Haute Authorite de l'Audiovisuel et de la Communication* (HAAC) is provided for by the National Assembly upon request of the president of HAAC and administered through the Ministry of Finance.

Although direct funding is a common model it can be used to undermine the independence of the regulator. It is therefore desirable to have an independent funding mechanism provided this can guarantee adequate resources for the regulatory function.

The revenues of the UK communications regulator, Ofcom, for example, are derived from payments received in respect of license

---

BOX 45.   Lithuania: Financing the Regulator

The Radio and Television Commission of Lithuania (LRTK), established under the Mass Media Law of 1996, is financed from the funds of the commercial broadcasters. All broadcasters earning income from commercial broadcasting activities—with the exception of the public broadcaster, LRT—must pay the commission on a monthly basis: 0.8 percent of their incomes received from advertising, subscription fees, and other commercial activities related to broadcasting and/or retransmission. If broadcasters fail to pay for three months after a deadline specified in writing by the commission, such amounts are to be recovered in court. The LRTK is responsible for establishing its own budget within the funds thus made available.[1]

---

1. Open Society Institute EU Monitoring and Advocacy Program, *Television Across Europe: Regulation, Policy and Independence* (OSI: New York/Budapest, 2005), 1031.

fees from and penalties applied to license holders. The Office of Communications Act 2002 states, in Schedule 1, Paragraph 8(1):[7] "It shall be the duty of Ofcom . . . so to conduct their affairs as to secure that their revenues become at the earliest possible date, and continue at all times after that to be, at least sufficient to enable them to meet their obligations and to carry out their functions."

---

[7]Office of Communications Act 2002, available at: *http://www.hmso.gov.uk/acts/acts2002/20020011.htm.*

10 Regulating Broadcast Content and Distribution

Good Practice Checklist

- General positive content obligations, requiring them to carry certain material or types of material, may be placed on commercial and community broadcasters for the purpose of promoting broadcast diversity and the range of material available to the public, though more onerous obligations may be placed on public service broadcasters.
- Positive content obligations should not have the effect of stifling creativity or threatening viability.
- Special content rules may apply during elections.
- Broadcasting laws should not impose content restrictions of a civil or criminal nature on broadcasters, over and above those that apply to all forms of expression.
- Codes of conduct rules should be developed in close consultation with broadcasters and should be applied either on a self-regulatory basis or by an independent regulatory body.
- A range of sanctions should be available for breach of rules on broadcast content so that any sanctions that are applied may be proportionate to the harm done.
- Spectrum planning for broadcast services should ensure a fair and equitable distribution between public service, commercial, and community broadcasters.
- "Must-carry" rules are a useful regulatory mechanism to guarantee access to cable and satellite networks for public interest uses, including public service and community broadcasters. Broadcast law should ensure that broadcast regulators have powers to make "must-carry" rulings and a duty to do so where such rulings are in the public interest.
- Public access channels are channels on cable or satellite networks that have been set aside for noncommercial public use such as educational, community, or public service programming. Broadcast law should ensure the regulator is able to insist on the inclusion of public access channels as a condition of licensing a cable or satellite operator.

Introduction

The characteristics of the general enabling legal and institutional environment outlined in Part II constitute essential prerequisites to broadcasting that can promote good governance and development. The specific regulatory role appropriate to broadcasting, including its overall goals and structures, is outlined above. But an immediate question confronting any form of broadcast regulation is whether and where it is justified to attempt to influence broadcast content, either directly through rules on the broad nature of content or indirectly through interventions relating to the technical means to broadcast, specifically radio spectrum and cable. Beyond question is the fact that such justification must conform fully to the general legal environment relating to freedom of expression. But allowing for this, what is the case for specific measures to influence content?

In a regulatory environment that provides for independent media, free of government control, it is, in the first instance, the responsibility of broadcasters themselves to decide, on a day-to-day basis, what content they should or should not carry. There should be no prior censorship.

Are there circumstances that justify measures to directly influence content? More specifically, can the state regulate to promote in broadcasting those characteristics that can enhance governance and participation, for instance by increasing the likelihood of a wide diversity of content across broadcasting? Is regulation of commercial broadcasting a feasible way of augmenting public participation?

Regulation of the means of broadcast transmission, radio spectrum and cable, poses another set of questions. If restrictions on the means to broadcast should be kept to a minimum, and maximum opportunities offered to those wishing to broadcast, what circumstances justify regulatory interventions in the conditions of access to them? Can and should the regulation of these scarce resources be used to broadly influence content in this direction?

There are clear dangers in the overregulation of content. Apart from the obvious risk of state censorship by another name, content rules should not be so onerous as to restrict creativity or impose excessive costs on a broadcaster. Nor should they be more stringent than those applying to other media, though they can take account of and be adapted to the particular nature of broadcasting. Many countries have developed systems to directly and indirectly influence broadcast content, with the goal of enhancing the quality and diversity of content, while fully respecting freedom of expression.

Some aspects of broadcasting standards are by their nature contextually dependent. The level of obscenity, sex, or violence considered acceptable on television not only depends on the particular circumstances of each broadcast but is subject to changing social values over time and different cultural interpretations and contexts. The goal of broadcasting standards systems is to clarify and articulate the generally pertaining social standards and acceptable behavior, in order to set program standards for broadcasters. Though sanctions may be a necessary part of such a system, more serious sanctions should be applied only relatively rarely, for instance to address the problem of a persistently offending broadcaster. Good practice examples of these systems are characterized by a code of conduct, developed by or in close consultation with broadcasters and other interested stakeholders; an independent body with oversight, monitoring, and sanction powers and the opportunity for public complaints; and a graduated system of sanctions for breach of the rules.

Positive content rules, for instance where a license to broadcast is accompanied by obligations to show certain general types of content, have the purpose of promoting diversity by extending the range of material available and improving its quality. Public service broadcasters in particular are subject to these rules, but they may be brought to bear on all forms of broadcasting.

In the case of allocating radio spectrum to broadcasting, the fundamental justification for regulation in the first place is usually that radio spectrum is a scarce resource that requires overall management. To that extent it comprises part of the technical enabling environment. But at a nontechnical level, rules regarding the allocation of spectrum to particular types of broadcasters can be motivated by a desire to enhance the diversity of content, and especially to improve the balance of different forms of ownership and participation. A similar case can be made for certain measures that regulate the cable broadcast system.

Positive Content Rules

General positive content obligations, requiring them to carry certain material or types of material, may be placed on commercial and community broadcasters but only where the purpose and effect of the rules is to promote broadcast diversity by enhancing the range of material available to the public. More onerous obligations may be placed on public service broadcasters, given their primary obligation to promote the public interest through a diversity of voices and perspectives in broadcasting. Positive content obligations should not have the effect of stifling creativity or threatening viability. Special content rules may apply during elections.

Positive content regulation can be particularly useful in encouraging the productions of programs with educational value; ensuring high quality news and current affairs coverage; promoting local and national culture, including minority cultures; providing programming for children; encouraging investment in local content production; and covering other matters of development concern such as health, welfare, and economic development.

Positive content regulation should not specify in detail what is to be broadcast. Such an approach would put the independence of the broadcaster at risk and place the regulator in a position of making editorial decisions. Positive content rules should instead be set out in the form of general obligations concerning the type of programming to be carried.

Different types of broadcasters may be subject to different positive content obligations. They should be proportionate to the broadcaster's coverage, the scarcity of the transmission resources available, and their ability to meet the obligations without danger to their viability. For example, a local broadcaster could not be expected to invest in costly program production, such as drama, but might be required to carry a certain proportion of locally produced content or local news.

For commercial or community broadcasters content obligations will normally be set out in the license terms and conditions. Public service broadcasters can be expected to have a higher obligation with respect to public interest content than commercial and community broadcasters, and their content requirements will generally be set out as the law establishes them.

Public service broadcasters have a particular obligation to promote broadcast diversity, and it is legitimate, even necessary, to provide for this in their mandates. This may involve requiring them generally to carry programming considered to be of national importance, such as children's programming, educational programming,

programming of interest to different sectors of society, comprehensive news programming, and so on. At the same time, as with private broadcasters, specific obligations to carry messages by officials are susceptible to abuse and should be avoided.

Special considerations may apply during elections, where it is of the greatest importance that the electorate be exposed to the views of the competing candidates and parties, so as to be able to make an informed voting choice. It is common for broadcasters, particularly public broadcasters, but often private broadcasters as well, to be required to carry election material, often in the form of direct access slots by parties and candidates.

In Italy, a case decided in 2002 challenged the requirement for broadcasters to provide equal access to all political parties, arguing that it infringed the freedom of expression of broadcasters and constituted discrimination against them in relation to newspapers, which did not have this obligation. The constitutional court rejected these arguments, noting the key importance of broadcasting in forming the public's political views. The court also noted the special situation in Italy, which is characterized by concentration of ownership of private broadcasting in the hands of politically active individuals, existing alongside public broadcasting. It also noted the limited nature of the restrictions, which applied only during elections and only to certain types of broadcasts.[1]

Some countries include specific provision to promote indigenous program production or to ensure broadcasting in the national language. For example, in Indonesia the broadcasting law includes detailed language rules. In general, broadcasting must be in standard Indonesian, although there are exceptions for other local and foreign languages. Foreign language programs must be either subtitled or dubbed into Indonesian, although the latter is restricted to 30 percent of all foreign programs.

In the *Yatama* case the Inter-American Court of Human Rights set an important precedent in ruling that a decision of the court concerning the political rights of indigenous communities on the Atlantic coast of Nicaragua must be disseminated through community radio and in the local indigenous languages of Miskito, Sumo, and Rama.[2]

---

[1]Decision of the Italian Constitutional Court, no. 155 (Apr. 24–May 7, 2002).
[2]*Yatama v. Nicaragua*, Inter-American Court of Human Rights (June 23, 2003), available at: *http://www.corteidh.or.cr/docs/casos/articulos/seriec_127_esp.pdf.*

Rules on national and linguistic content should not be such that they restrict the rights of minorities. Latvian law, for example, provided that no more that 25 percent of broadcast time on any particular broadcaster could be in a foreign language, thereby effectively denying the large Russian minority a broadcaster of their own. In a 2003 decision, the constitutional court struck down the law as an unreasonable restriction on freedom of expression. In doing so, the court noted the law did not in fact increase the use of the Latvian language but, to the contrary, many Russian speakers simply listened to the widely available Russian channels, meaning that they lost any exposure to Latvian.[3]

Positive content obligations must not have the effect of undermining broadcast development or threaten the viability of the service, for example, by being unrealistic or excessively onerous. They must also be sufficiently general in nature as to remain politically neutral, and they must unambiguously define the type of material covered.

BOX 46. United Kingdom: Public Service Objectives among Different Broadcasters

In the United Kingdom, the rules for public service broadcasters (BBC, Channel 4, and the Welsh language channel, S4C) are much more detailed and onerous than for commercial broadcasting, but the main national commercial terrestrial broadcaster (ITV) is also required by law and licensing agreement to meet a number of public service objectives, including the carriage of news and information, children's and educational programming, and international affairs. Lesser requirements apply to the commercial Channel 5. Local commercial broadcasters are obliged to carry an agreed proportion of local programming while community broadcasters are obliged to demonstrate "social gain" through their programming output and other activities. The broadcast regulator, Ofcom, has the power to set rules relating to party political broadcasts (during elections but also less frequently on an ongoing basis) for all broadcasters. All broadcasters are required to maintain "due impartiality" on matters of public policy or political or industrial controversy.

---

[3]Restriction on broadcasting in foreign languages, decisions of the Latvian Constitutional Court, no. 2003-02-0106 (2003) and no. 2003-02-0106 (2003).

Content Restrictions and Codes of Conduct

Broadcasting laws should not impose content restrictions of a civil or criminal nature on broadcasters, over and above, or duplicating, those that apply to all forms of expression. Codes of conduct for broadcast content should be developed in close consultation with broadcasters and should be applied either on a self-regulatory basis or by an independent regulatory body.

To meet the "provided by law" part of the three-part test for restrictions on freedom of expression, any content restrictions should be based on a clear, detailed, and preestablished code of conduct. Such codes should be developed in close consultation with broadcasters in order to be firmly based in broadcasting reality and should also provide for input from the public, including viewers' and listeners' associations. Codes of conduct can be effective in setting clear professional standards and in preventing more intrusive forms of regulation. Different codes may be developed for radio and television, given the important differences between them. In adopting codes of conduct, a range of considerations should be taken into account, including the likelihood and seriousness of harm and the importance of maintaining independent editorial control over program content.

Codes of conduct for broadcast content may relate to a number of different content objectives, such as ensuring protection of children and youth; impartiality in news and current affairs; responsible religious programming; obscenity, hate speech, or other offensive material; invasion of privacy; and fairness in political advertising. Specific rules may apply to the content of commercial advertising and sponsorship in order to avoid undue exploitation of listeners, not to be misleading, to avoid promoting harmful products such as tobacco, and to avoid unfair discrimination between advertisers.

Codes of conduct may be applied through self-regulatory mechanisms such as a body established by the broadcasters themselves, through an independent regulatory body, or through some combination of both mechanisms (co-regulation). In some countries broadcast content codes have been developed by the broadcasters associations or journalists organizations and adopted directly by the regulatory body.

In Mali, for example, the *Conseil Superieur de la Communication* (CSC) does not have its own broadcast content code but enforces the Code of Conduct of the Observatory for Press Ethics, which is a self-regulatory body jointly sponsored by the Malian journalists union *(Union Nationale des Journalists du Mali)* and the Malian broadcasters association *(Union des Radios et Televisions Libres du Mali)*.

As with all forms of media regulation, any system relating to the regulation of broadcast content should be overseen by a body that is protected against political or commercial interference in its work. It should not operate on the basis of prior censorship but should rather act on complaints through a transparent complaints procedure that provides prompt, independent, and fair arbitration or adjudication of the complaint.

In Indonesia, broadcast content regulation is the responsibility of the Indonesian Broadcasting Commission (KPI), an independent body established under the Broadcasting Act of 2002.[4] KPI is tasked with developing a broadcasting code dealing with a wide range of topics, including respect for religion and privacy, appropriate taste and decency, limits on sexual and violent material, protection for youth and women, program classification based on age groups, broadcasting in foreign languages, timing and neutrality of news programs, live broadcasts, and advertising. The code is kept under constant review to ensure compatibility with legal developments and changing social norms.

Australia has put in place an interesting system of co-regulation,[5] with two parallel mechanisms, one involving codes of practice, overseen by so-called peak bodies representing different broadcasting sectors (six sectors are specified in the law, including commercial and community broadcasters), and one involving standards, overseen by the Australian Broadcasting Authority (ABA), a statutory body. Codes are registered by the ABA if they meet certain standards, notably requirements of public consultation and of providing adequate safeguards to the community. Where the codes are not deemed to be providing appropriate safeguards, such as, for example, when there is a widespread breach of certain types of rules, the ABA must adopt a standard to remedy this problem.

---

[4]KPI has both a national body and regional bodies. We focus here on the national one.
[5]Set out in Part 9 of the Broadcasting Services Act of 1942.

BOX 47.   Mozambique: Community Radio Self-Regulation Code

In Mozambique the growing community radio sector managed to respond in a mature manner to political tensions over the responsibilities of the media in political reporting in the run up to the 2003 municipal elections and the 2004 presidential and national elections. The absence of legal regulation on the role and responsibilities of community radio during elections became a subject of heated debate in parliament as politicians saw that community radio had come to constitute a powerful voice for the people, covering all the major cities and more than one third of the rural areas. In response, the Coordination Group (the forerunner of the community radio sector body FORCOM) initiated a series of national consultations with all community radio actors, which resulted in agreement on "the ten rules"—a code for self-regulation of the use of community radio during election periods. These rules were launched nationally, with involvement of the Director of the Government Press Office (GABINFO), and provincially by the radios themselves. Most radio stations followed the rules laid down, except the state-owned radio stations, which responded to decrees from their national leadership to include additional coverage of the ruling Frelimo party.[1]

---

1. "Participation by Community Radios in Civic Education and Electoral Coverage—The experience of the Community Radios in Mozambique's 2003 Local Elections. Specific Cases of: Dondo, Chimoio, and Cuamba," UNESCO/UNDP (2003) referenced in Jallov, "Voice, Media, and Empowerment," commissioned paper (2006) .

The amount of advertising that broadcasters can carry may be subject to overall limits, or specific restrictions, for example, in relation to alcoholic beverages or tobacco. Care should be taken, however, not to impose such stringent limits on advertising as to undermine the viability of the broadcasting sector as a whole.

In setting rules relating to advertising, consideration may be given to the different financial structures of different types of broadcasters. It is, for example, not appropriate for public service broadcasters to take advantage of their public funding to offer advertising at below-market rates and so it may be appropriate to subject them to fair competition rules in relation to any advertising they carry.

Sanctions

A range of sanctions should be available for breach of rules on broadcast content so that any sanctions that are applied may be proportionate to the harm done.

Regulators should have a range of sanctions available to them that can be applied proportionately and flexibly enough to take account of specific circumstances. Warnings, fines of varying magnitudes, and license suspensions, for example, provide the regulator with penalties proportionate to the infraction and also the scope to increase the sanction when lesser penalties have not induced compliance. A "gap" in the intensity of sanctions available can undermine the regulator's ability to respond effectively. If the regulator is obliged to choose a sanction that is too feeble, this can increase the risk of further infractions and of damaging public confidence. If the regulator's alternative is too severe, it can have a chilling effect on broadcasters' freedom of expression, may undermine the flow of information to the public, and/or may be found upon review to be unconstitutional.

Sanctions should be imposed only after an investigation in which the regulator has concluded that a broadcaster has repeatedly, deliberately, or seriously breached the terms of its license. In most cases, sanctions for breach of a rule relating to content should be applied in a graduated fashion. Normally, the sanction for an initial breach will be a warning stating the nature of the breach and the need to not repeat it. Other low to midrange sanctions might include requiring an on-air correction or statement of the regulator's findings, or other undertakings, such as refraining from again broadcasting the program.

In assessing the type of sanction to impose, regulatory bodies should bear in mind that the purpose of regulation is not primarily to "police" broadcasters but rather to protect the public interest by ensuring that the sector operates smoothly and by promoting the range and quality of broadcasting services that are available to the public.

In Indonesia any member of the public may complain of a breach of the broadcasting code, and KPI is required to assess the legitimacy of such complaints. The affected broadcaster must be notified in writing and given an adequate opportunity to be heard in the matter. In a case in which the code has been breached, KPI may require a broadcaster to publish a correction and a statement prepared by KPI.[6] Broadcasters are also required to provide a correction, within 24 hours where possible, when an inaccuracy in their programming has been brought to their attention.

---

[6]The law also provides for license revocation for breach of the code, if ordered by the courts.

In Benin, the *Haute Authorité de l'Audiovisuel et de la Communication* (HAAC) has a range of sanctions available under Article 47 of its law of establishment (No. 92-021, August 1992). In the case that publicized warnings have not been acted upon, the HAAC can pronounce against the offending broadcaster one of the following sanctions, depending on the gravity of the offense:

(a) the suspension of broadcast authorization or of part of a program for a maximum of one month

(b) the reduction of the duration of the authorization for a maximum of one year

(c) the withdrawal of the authorization

Given the relatively more intrusive nature of sanctions such as fines, or suspension or revocation of a license, conditions should be placed on their application for breach of a rule relating to content. To be justifiable as necessary, fines should be imposed only after other measures have failed to redress the problem.

Suspension or revocation of a license represents the most serious sanctions possible, with extremely grave consequences for the broadcaster. As a result, these sanctions should be imposed only where the broadcaster has repeatedly been found to have committed serious abuses and other sanctions have proved inadequate to redress the problem.

Such a case arose in Canada in 2004, when the Canadian Radio-television and Telecommunications Commission refused to renew the license of a radio station in Quebec City that was persistently broadcasting abusive content denigrating specific social groups. The regulatory decision has been upheld by the federal court of appeal.[7]

In all cases the broadcaster in question should have a right to make written representation on the complaint and may also be invited to make oral representation in cases where a fine or more serious sanction is being considered. As with all regulatory decisions the broadcaster should have a right of judicial review in the courts, which may consider questions such as compliance with the standards of natural justice or human rights norms.

---

[7]See *http://www.crtc.gc.ca/eng/NEWS/RELEASES/2004/r040713.htm.*

> **BOX 48.   Australia: Sanctions for Breaching Codes**
>
> In Australia there is no sanction for breach of a code of conduct. However, persistent breach may lead to a condition being imposed on a licensee. Pursuant to section 139 of the Broadcasting Services Act of 1942, it is an offense to breach a program standard. Breach will lead to different levels of fines for different types of broadcasters. The ABA may direct a licensee to stop committing a breach (Section 141). Where a licensee fails to respond to a notice to stop a breach, the ABA can suspend the license for up to three months or may cancel it altogether (Section 143).

Spectrum Planning for Broadcast Services

Spectrum planning for broadcast services should ensure a fair and equitable distribution between public service, commercial, and community broadcasters.

International frequency planning designates a number of spectrum blocks for sound broadcasting and television. However the allocation of these blocks between public service, commercial, and community broadcasters is the responsibility of national administrations and may be assigned by them to the broadcast regulatory body. One of the goals of radio spectrum management in broadcasting should be to ensure an appropriate balance between commercial, community, and public service broadcasters. The goal is to enhance diversity by ensuring that each of the different forms of ownership and control has reasonable access to the spectrum, according to what they can usefully contribute to broadcasting.

In practice this usually means ensuring that sufficient spectrum is available free or at affordable cost for public service and community broadcasting. There should be open public consultation on the use of frequencies and their allocation between different uses, including public service, commercial, and community broadcasters.

International practice shows that the allocation of a minimum of 10–15 percent of the FM band to community broadcasting (2–3 MHz out of the 20 MHz contained in the FM band that runs from 88 to 108 MHz) should be adequate, while 20 percent is optimal. Countries as diverse as Thailand, France, and the United States allocate around 20 percent of the FM band to nonprofit local and community broadcasting.

BOX 49.   Thailand: Frequencies as Resources for the Public Interest

Article 40 of the 1997 Thai Constitution states:

> Transmission frequencies for radio or television broadcasting and radio telecommunication are national communication resources for public interest.

The Allocation of Telecommunication and Broadcasting Frequencies Act, passed in March 2000, lays down specific rules by which the public interest in broadcasting may be safeguarded. It assigns 40 percent of the available broadcast frequencies to the state sector, 40 percent to the commercial sector, and reserves 20 percent for not-for-profit community broadcasting. This model won over alternative suggestions made in the drafting process of having one community radio station per province or of allocating 2 percent of airtime to community broadcasting.

The radio sector in France offers five different categories of licensees: community radios, eligible for public funding; local commercial radios; local or regional radios affiliated into a national network; national radios; and a special category for three radio stations that existed prior to 1982 and that transmit abroad. The priority attached to community radio can be observed by the percentage this sector makes up of all radio stations, which is over 50 percent, or 545 of 1,070 licensees as of January 1, 2005, utilizing nearly 25 percent, or 874 of 3,538, frequencies.

Efficient use of the spectrum requires a comprehensive national plan for national and regional services, whereas local services may be accommodated more flexibly according to demand, population distribution, and spectrum availability. With the advent of new modes of digital distribution some early assumptions in spectrum planning have come under scrutiny. In particular it is increasingly recognized that there can be efficient spectrum use without requiring each individual service to be part of a national planning and licensing framework. Building on the experience of WiFi and other license-exempt, shared-spectrum technologies on an "open spectrum" model may become appropriate for low-power local broadcasting services where a part of the radio spectrum is set aside specifically for these services within agreed technical parameters.

In the medium to long term, digital broadcasting of television and radio will bring other challenges. The move to digital not only allows many more channels to be broadcast over the same spectrum—which can, where the paucity of channels is a constraint, facilitate greater content diversity—but it also allows for additional functionality such as electronic program guides. Such additions to functionality create new concerns for regulators, such as how to ensure that due prominence is given to all types of broadcasters and programs rather than preferential treatment to certain services.

From the regulatory perspective satellite and cable broadcasting have had a relatively seamless transition to digital, enabling them to offer additional channels and greater functionality. Terrestrial broadcasting is also under strong pressure to digitalize, in part because the spectrum it currently occupies is suited for other high-demand usage such as mobile telephony and wireless broadband. Yet the move to digital has been complicated by the fact that international spectrum planning has decided that it is not feasible to identify a large new area of spectrum for digital television services to commence while continuing to retain the spectrum required for analog television. Instead, digital services will commence within existing bands and eventually replace the analog services after a "switch-off" date.[8]

Further complicating matters is the fact that several competing digital standards already exist in both radio and television and are being promoted by different groups of developed countries, each trying to recruit developing countries to their standard. In the long term, public interest issues for regulators will include the question of which standards to select, including how they affect the need for and price of new televisions or radio sets, how to ensure universal coverage, and how best to migrate from analog to digital.

All these future issues will affect content in the broadest sense of allocating, or otherwise distributing, sufficient channels to the different broadcasting sectors and ensuring content is accessible and affordable. Yet in most developing and transitional countries questions arising from digitization are for the future: at the moment the priority remains ensuring that the current structures can be appropriately reformed, revised, and refined.

---

[8]ITU (1993) International Telecommunications Union Radio Recommendations—Digital Terrestrial Television Broadcasting in the VHF/UHF Bands (BT.798.1), approved July 1994.

Must-Carry Rules

"Must-carry" rules are a useful regulatory mechanism to guarantee access to cable and satellite networks for public interest uses, including public service and community broadcasters. Broadcast law should ensure that broadcast regulators have powers to make "must-carry" rulings and a duty to do so where such rulings are in the public interest.

Private cable network and satellite operators are often disinclined, usually for commercial reasons, to provide access to public service and community broadcasting. "Must-carry" rules can be applied where a cable network or a satellite operator has, or is likely to have, a dominant market position in providing access to viewers. They should be used in cases where, without guaranteed carriage, public service and community broadcasters face the likelihood of being excluded from access to cable or satellite distribution. Alongside the inclusion of must-carry rules for certain program services, cable network and satellite operators should be prohibited from unfairly discriminating on grounds of content between different program services, for example on grounds of religion.

In Spain, for example, cable operators are required under Article 11 of the Cable Telecommunications Act 1995[9] and Article 26 of the Royal Decree 2066/1996 to carry the following channels:

- the television programs transmitted by the two channels of the public service broadcasting company, *Radio Télévision España* (RTVE)
- the television programs transmitted by the three channels of private broadcasting companies
- the television programs transmitted by the channels of public service broadcasting companies of the autonomous regions
- television programs transmitted by local television channels, if they so request

---

[9]Cable Telecommunications Act (Act 42/1995 of December 22, 1995).

BOX 50. Germany: Must-Carry Obligations on Cable Networks

The Inter-State Agreement on Broadcasting Services (RStV)[1] concluded between the sixteen German *Länder* set out the principles of must-carry arrangements on cable networks. Different rules apply on analog and digital cable distribution networks.[2]

For analog cable networks, the application of must-carry rules and the order of priority are determined by the regional broadcasting regulations, although the rules are similar from one region to another. In North Rhine-Westphalia, for example, there is a requirement to carry public broadcasters throughout the region and to carry local broadcasting services within the dissemination area of the local broadcaster. If the cable capacity is not sufficient to carry all other channels receivable the Media Agency of North Rhine-Westphalia determines the priority according to criteria that include plurality of programs, of special interests, and of opinion, the extent to which events in the political, economic, social, and cultural domain are presented, and contribution to the cultural and linguistic diversity of the entire program offer.

For digital cable networks there is a common set of rules established within the framework of the Inter-State Agreement on Broadcasting Services. There is a general rule that broadcasts available in analog form should be allocated digital channel capacity. In addition, the operator of a digitized cable network must ensure:

- transmission capacity is reserved for the dissemination of broadcasters established under public law, including their program packages or "bouquets"; and
- transmission capacity is available for regional and local television stations and for "open channels" licensed in the particular *Länder*.

---

1. Rundfunkänderungsstaatsvertrag, consolidated text Jan. 1, 2001, available at: *http://www.artikel5.de/gesetze/rstv.html*.
2. The information on Germany and Spain in this section is based on *Inventory of EU Must Carry Regulations: A Report to the European Commission, Information Society Directorate*, 2001, available at: *http://europa.eu.int/ISPO/infosoc/telecompolicy/en/OVUM-mustcarry.pdf*.

Public Access Channels

Public access channels are channels on cable or satellite networks that have been set aside for noncommercial public use such as educational, community, or public service programming. Broadcast law should ensure the regulator is able to insist on the inclusion of public access channels as a condition of licensing a cable or satellite operator.

BOX 51. United States: Public Access Channels and Cable Operators

Although no federal law requires public access channels to be carried on local cable networks, such channels may be required by agreements between cable operators and local franchising organizations (normally local authorities). In return for their use of local public rights of way (streets, highways, parks, etc.), cable operators agree to provide channel capacity, services, facilities, and equipment for public access, educational, and governmental (PEG) channels. The compensation rights given to the local franchising authority can assist in providing access to the media for the local population. Public access channels have built and maintained an extensive presence in the United States as a result of the enabling legal framework of the Communications Act of 1934 and an extensive body of case law.

The legal framework is set out in Section 611 of the Communications Act of 1934 (as amended by 1984, 1992, and 1996 acts) entitled "Cable channels for public, educational or governmental use." Section 611 states that "a franchising authority may establish requirements in a franchise with respect to the designation or use of channel capacity for public, educational or governmental use." Franchising authorities may require the cable network operators to provide services, facilities, or equipment for the use of PEG channels. In accordance with the local franchise agreement the cable operator or the franchising authority may adopt rules governing the use of PEG channels; however, the Federal Communications Commission (FCC) specifies that these must not be content based. They may include rules for allocating time between competing applicants "on a reasonable basis other than the content of the program." They may also require minimum production standards and that users undergo training.

PEG channels are editorially independent of the cable network operator with very limited exceptions. Federal law provides, in Section 611(e) that: "A cable operator shall not exercise any editorial control over any public, educational, or governmental use of channel capacity provided pursuant to this section, except a cable operator may refuse to transmit any public access program or portion of a public access program which contains obscenity, indecency or nudity." However, the Supreme Court has determined that these powers are unconstitutional.[1] The Federal Communications Commission subsequently issued guidance in which the exception is further limited: "A cable operator may refuse to transmit any public access program or portion of a public access program that the operator reasonably believes contains obscenity."[2]

There have also been a number of court decisions that are supportive of limiting local government interference in public access channels;[3] however, the legislative and regulatory framework for public access channels remains weak in this respect.

---

1. FCC guidance on PEG channels, available at: *http://www.fcc.gov/mb/facts/pegfacts.html.*
2. Code of Federal Regulations (1997) 47 C.F.R. Section 76.702 Public Access.
3. Norwood, James, *Public Policy Update: Court Decisions and Legal Rulings*, Spiegal and McDiarmad (2002), *http://www.spiege/mcd.com/publications/default.asp.*

Cable and satellite operators receive valuable public resource concessions that can be usefully linked to an obligation to provide public access channels. Cable operators require a right to lay extensive
communications cabling under public rights of way while satellite
operators require international radio spectrum allocation for transmission of their signal and access to orbital satellite paths or fixed
geostationary satellite positions. Orbital paths constitute an additional finite resource that merits public compensation.

Obligating a cable or satellite operator to provide a proportion of
available capacity for public access channels is an effective means of
achieving public interest objectives in broadcasting, whether or not
there is a must-carry requirement to include particular channels.

The first public access television channels in Germany (*Offener
Kanale*) started in 1984 and there are now more than 80 such channels.
They are provided for within the powers of regional broadcasting
regulation rather than at federal state level. *Offener Kanale* are operated on a not-for-profit open access basis in which the program pro-
ducer is legally and editorially responsible for the program that is
aired. They are considered to be a contribution to freedom of expression and media pluralism.

Offene Kanal Berlin,[10] for example, provides fully staffed technical
facilities. The staff are employed directly by the regional regulatory
body, *Medienanstalt Berlin-Brandenburg* (MABB).[11] Advertising is not
allowed, and program producers are obliged to ensure that their programs conform with legal minimum standards. Airtime is offered to
program producers on a first-come first-served basis. In those *Länder*
where the regulatory body provides one or more open channels, a
part of the license fee paid by viewers and listeners is reserved for
meeting costs of provision.

---

[10]Offene Kanal Berlin website: *http://www.okb.de.*
[11]Medienanstalt Berlin-Brandeburg website: *http://www.mabb.de/.*

11 Public Service Broadcasting

Good Practice Checklist

- Public service broadcasters should be prescribed in law as bodies that are editorially independent of government, serve the public interest, and are protected against political and commercial interference.
- The duty of a national public service broadcaster should be to serve the public interest in broadcasting throughout the territory and for the whole of the population of the country in which it is established.
- The public service broadcaster should provide a wide range of innovative and high quality programs designed to educate, inform, and entertain the general public while taking account of ethnic, cultural, religious, and regional diversity.
- The public service broadcaster should be governed by an independent governing board with powers and duties set out in law. These should include monitoring and ensuring compliance with public service duties and responsibilities, ensuring highest standards of probity and value for money, and providing formal accountability to the general public.
- The appointments process for the governing board should be fair, open, transparent, and set out in law. It should be designed to ensure the members have relevant expertise or experience and carry a diversity of interests and opinions representative of society as a whole.
- The appointments process should not be dominated by any particular political party or commercial interest, and the members appointed should be required to serve in an individual capacity and to exercise their functions in the public interest at all times.
- Day-to-day management of the public service broadcaster should be the responsibility of a chief executive officer appointed by the governing board for a fixed term, whose tenure may be renewed. The chief executive officer, along with his or her editorial staff, should have responsibility for setting editorial policy and making editorial decisions.
- The public service broadcaster should be predominantly funded from public funding through a funding mechanism designed to protect its independence. It may raise additional revenues from direct subsidies, commercial activities, and donations.

Introduction

> *The relative merits of public service broadcasting institutions are widely and vigorously debated. But it is generally accepted that public service broadcasting has a particular role to play in meeting public interest objectives and contributing to media pluralism, and that where broadcasting services are in public ownership they should be editorially independent of the state and the government of the day, managed in the public interest, and accountable to the public they serve. These principles form the basis for the recommendations of good practice in public service broadcasting set out in this section.*

The BBC is perhaps the most famous of public service broadcasters. When granted editorial independence in 1926, the BBC's guiding principles were nonprofit status, universality of service, unified control, and the maintenance of high program standards.[1] The editorial independence of the BBC is safeguarded by its Royal Charter and specifically guaranteed by a written agreement with the government. Its economic base is secured through payment by viewers of a license fee. This has allowed it to produce a great variety of high-quality programming designed to serve the public interest. Although appointments to the board of directors remain under government control, the BBC operates largely free of day-to-day government interference. Yet in times of war and other serious conflict, the BBC has come under pressure to side with the government. In 2005 the director general of the BBC resigned, under pressure from the government, following an official inquiry into the death of weapons expert, Dr. David Kelly, a key source for BBC reports on government policy making in the period leading up to the war on Iraq.

Thus, maintaining editorial independence in practice remains a challenge even in those countries where it is accepted in principle and in law. As we have seen in Part I, in many countries editorial independence is too often only apparent, with no real independence from government and other interests.

---

[1]Peter M. Lewis and J. Booth, *The Invisible Medium: Public, Commercial and Community Radio* (London: Macmillan, 1989).

Funding is a key factor that influences independence and the ability of public broadcasters to play a positive social role. Many public broadcasters face serious funding constraints. Audience fees, levied on television or radio receiver ownership, represent a stable, independent, and often relatively rich source of funding. Where this option is not feasible, as in many developing countries, devising other effective funding mechanisms is a central challenge for the sector.

The growth of private commercial broadcasting can also pose a deep challenge to the future of public service broadcasting. In countries with traditions of public service broadcasting, opening up to commercial competition has led to declining audiences which, in turn, has led to pressure to reduce public subsidies; to "dumbing down" of programming, including the provision of more populist and less costly productions; and, in some cases, to partial or full privatization. Private broadcast owners have also attacked state aid to public service broadcasters, for example in the form of compulsory license fees levied on domestic receivers, as "unfair competition."

In the face of these challenges, public service broadcasters and some governments have mounted a vigorous defense of public service values, notably achieving significant legal support in the Amsterdam Protocol to the Treaty on European Union, in the "audio-visual exemption" to the General Agreement on Trade in Services, and in the UNESCO Convention on Diversity of Cultural and Artistic Expressions. In some countries, such as Canada and the United Kingdom, citizens' campaigns have emerged to defend public service broadcasters. These developments are indicative of the continuing relevance of the public service broadcasting model in an environment of media pluralism.

Public service broadcasting has become a favored component in an evolving multisector broadcasting system in most transition countries and a growing number of developing countries. Even so, it contends with major challenges: to achieve genuine independence and gain a secure financial base, all the while struggling to compete with commercial broadcasting.

There is no standard definition of public service broadcasting, and models vary from country to country; however, there are some widely accepted characteristics. The 2000 report of the World Radio and Television Council, *Public Broadcasting: Why? How?* describes the principles of independent public service broadcasting as being universality, diversity, independence, and distinctiveness, and explains them as follows:

- It is accessible to every citizen, not merely in technological terms, but also in terms of the intelligibility of the programming.

- It demonstrates diversity in the genres of programs offered, the audiences targeted, and the subjects discussed.

- It is independent of commercial pressures and political influence. This includes editorial independence, protections for freedom of expression, adequate, predictable, and independent mechanisms of financing, and the independence of governing bodies and the selection process for their boards and chief executives.

- It not only produces types of programs and subject matter other services ignore and targets audiences others neglect but, without excluding any genre, it aims to innovate, create new genres, and set the pace in the audiovisual world.[2]

Other characteristics ascribed to public service broadcasting include a concern for national identity and culture, the impartiality as well as the independence of programs, and its role in quality "standard setting."[3]

Among the most important issues in determining the quality, diversity, independence, and distinctiveness of public service broadcasting are: the legal framework in which the broadcaster operates, including the powers and duties set down in law; the governance arrangements, including the process for appointment of the governing board and the senior management staff; and the funding arrangements. In the sections that follow, this chapter examines these and related issues and the approaches to implementation that are best designed to assure an effective and high-quality public service broadcasting.

---

[2]World Radio and Television Council, *Public Broadcasting: Why? How?* (2000), quoted in Monroe E. Price and Marc Raboy, eds., *Public Service Broadcasting in Transition* (The Hague: Kluwer Law International, 2003), 2–4.

[3]UNDP, *Supporting Public Service Broadcasting: Learning from Bosnia and Herzegovina's experience* (Bureau for Development Policy, 2004), available at: *http://www.undp.org/governance/docs/A2I_Pub_PublicServiceBroadcasting.pdf*.

Status and Independence

Public service broadcasters should be prescribed in law as bodies that are editorially independent of government, serve the public interest, and are protected against political and commercial interference.

The status of public service broadcasters is normally defined by legislation setting out its duties, responsibilities, lines of accountability, and guarantees of editorial independence from government and protection from political or commercial interference. These are defining characteristics of public service broadcasting. The governing legislation provides the first means of assurance that the broadcaster will operate in the public interest with public service objectives and accountability to the public.

The framework for public service broadcasting balances the principles of independence and accountability. Accountability of the public service broadcaster should be to the public, through Parliament. If there is an independent regulator with responsibility over all of broadcasting, then accountability may be through the regulator.

In France, for example, the *Conseil Superieur de l'Audiovisuel* (CSA) evaluates how the public networks have fulfilled their obligations under their terms of reference. In Canada, the Canadian Radio-television and Telecommunications Commission (CRTC) issues licenses to the Canadian Broadcasting Corporation (CBC) and comments on how the CBC should carry out its responsibilities. The CBC has also created the post of Ombudsperson—a person to whom citizens direct their concerns and submit criticisms of CBC, for review and potential action and public dissemination of how the concerns were addressed.

In Georgia the creation of a public broadcasting company was a recommendation of the Council of Europe whose experts assisted Georgian legislators in drawing up the Law on Broadcasting.[4] Under the terms of the law, passed in December 2004, the state-owned State TV and Radio Broadcasting of Georgia was transformed into "Georgian Public Broadcasting," an independent public corporation that operates two television channels and two radio stations. Georgian Public

---

[4]Internews, "Broadcast Field in Georgia," commissioned report (2006).

Broadcasting is governed by a board of trustees consisting of nine members who are appointed by Parliament for a period of six years and who in turn appoint the director general. The broadcaster is funded from the state budget.

Duties and Responsibilities

The duty of a national public service broadcaster should be to serve the public interest in broadcasting throughout the territory and for the whole of the population of the country in which it is established. In particular, the public service broadcaster should provide a wide range of innovative and high quality programs designed to educate, inform, and entertain the general public, taking account of ethnic, cultural, religious, and regional diversity.

The mandate of the public service broadcaster should be set out in law and may include a range of duties and responsibilities designed to serve the public interest, such as:

- provide comprehensive, balanced, and impartial news and current affairs programs, including national and international affairs of general public interest;
- provide programming of wide appeal as well as specialized programming;
- contribute to national identity while also reflecting cultural and regional diversity;
- give a voice to minority groups, including minority languages;
- provide a reasonable proportion of educational programs;
- provide a reasonable proportion of programs for children; and
- promote program-making by in-country producers, including regional production.

Context strongly influences what particular programming is most appropriate to each public service broadcaster's mission. However, some general approaches to programming are commonly taken to be the duty of most public service broadcasters: to maintain balance and impartiality; to include general interest programming as well as news and current affairs; to promote the arts and culture; to have significant "in-house" production capacity to allow it to provide programs of diversity, uniqueness, and quality; and to reflect the ideas, opinions, and values of the society and nation that it serves.

The Chilean public television, TVN (*Televisión Nacional de Chile*), is widely considered to be a leading example of public service broadcasting in Latin America. Although it commenced in 1969 as a state broadcaster TVN was transformed in 1992, following the country's return to democracy, into an autonomous public channel obliged to be pluralistic and representative and to operate on a self-financed basis. It aims:

- to promote national culture, identity, and values in all their diversity;
- to be plural and objective in the representation of the cultural, social, economic, religious, and political realities of the country;
- to be independent of the diverse powers that act in society;
- to connect to Chileans throughout its territory and Chileans who live abroad; and
- to represent all Chileans in their social, cultural, and religious diversity.

Finland is a good example of how legislation governing public service broadcasting can address the needs and interests of persons belonging to minorities.[5] Section 7 of the Act on *Yleisradio Oy* (Finnish Broadcasting Company), as amended in 2005,[6] describes the duties of the public service broadcaster in the following terms:

> The company shall be responsible for the provision of comprehensive television and radio programming with the related additional and extra services for all citizens under equal conditions. These and other content services related to public

---

[5] Case study provided by Tarlach McGonagle, commissioned paper (2006).
[6] Act on the Amendment of the Act on Yleisradio Oy, Act No. 635/2005 of August 19, 2005, available at: *http://www.finlex.fi/en/laki/kaannokset/1993/en19931380.pdf.*

service may be provided in all telecommunications networks. The public service programming shall in particular:

1. support democracy and everyone's opportunity to partici-pate by providing a wide variety of information, opinions, and debates as well as opportunities to interact;
2. produce, create, and develop Finnish culture, art, and in-spiring entertainment;
3. take educational and equality aspects into consideration in the programs, provide an opportunity to learn and study, give focus on programming for children, and offer devo-tional programs;
4. treat in its broadcasting Finnish-speaking and Swedish-speaking citizens on equal grounds and produce services in the Sami, Romany, and sign languages, as well as, where applicable, in the languages of other language groups in the country;
5. support tolerance and multiculturalism and provide pro-gramming for minority and special groups;
6. promote cultural interaction and provide programming di-rected abroad; and
7. broadcast official announcements, for which further provi-sions shall be issued by decree, and make provision for tele-vision and radio broadcasting in exceptional circumstances.

In concrete terms, these amendments aim to promote democratic val-ues and practices, as well as participatory and interactive opportuni-ties, and thus support tolerance, multiculturalism, and programming for minorities and special groups. Taken together, they are very im-portant for fostering intergroup understanding and societal cohesion. Cultural and educational goals are also likely to benefit minorities, and the various language provisions will certainly do so.

In Mali, the focus was developing quality programs, promoting pluralism, and culture, and extending coverage.[7] After the 1991 revo-lution, a contract of service was established between the government and the *Office de radiodiffusion et de télévision du Mali* (ORTM) defining the public service obligations of the ORTM. A 1996 Decree (no. 96-284 taken on October 23) commits ORTM to devoting at least 80 percent

---

[7]Alimany Bathily, unpublished report commissioned for the World Bank (2005).

of its radio programming and 60 percent of its television programming to public service content. It also commits ORTM to progressively extending radio coverage of 65 percent of the country in 2003 to 100 percent in 2015 and to extend television coverage from 35 percent to 75 percent in the same period. The governing board of the ORTM specifies its mandate as follows:

1. Develop radio and television programs in line with the objectives of the economic, social, and cultural development objectives of the country.

2. Promote the use of national languages; promote science, technology, and the protection of the environment.

3. Develop entertaining programs based on quality shows.

4. Promote pluralist, civic, and useful information.

5. Produce magazines and live reporting, debates, and investigations.

Specific social and development objectives of ORTM include: to combat poverty; to increase the literacy rate; to contribute to health awareness and the development of health services; to strengthen formal education, including adult education; and the de-marginalization of geographically isolated communities. The ORTM network is comprised of one national television service, two FM stations broadcasting from the capital city Bamako, ten regional FM stations based in the regional capitals, and about thirty "rural stations."

Governance

The public service broadcaster should be governed by an independent governing board with powers and duties set out in law and which include monitoring and ensuring compliance with public service duties and responsibilities, ensuring highest standards of probity and value for money, and providing formal accountability to the general public.

Governance arrangements must balance two principles: independence and accountability. This can be achieved through various arrangements. The usual one involves an independent governing board, whose members are appointed in a fair and transparent manner, with the involvement of civil society. In turn, the chief executive is responsible only to the board, rather than the government, and the board is responsible for approving the budget and all general policies, and appointing the most senior executive officers. In this way, the board and its chairperson serve as a buffer between management and government.

The powers of the governing board in exercising its duties should include:

- the power to appoint and remove all senior staff;
- the power to set the overall strategy and to propose the budget;
- the power to determine internal policies; and
- the power to undertake internal audit.

In exercising its powers, the governing board should not interfere with day-to-day management or with the editorial independence of the chief executive and his or her staff. The governing board should be responsible for preparing an annual report and should be formally accountable to the public through a multiparty body such as the parliament or a parliamentary committee in which all major parties are represented.

The Australian Broadcasting Corporation (ABC), for example, is governed by a board of directors established under the ABC Act. Its duties include:

a. to ensure that the functions of the corporation are performed efficiently and with the maximum benefit to the people of Australia;
b. to maintain the independence and integrity of the corporation; and
c. to ensure that the gathering and presentation by the corporation of news and information is accurate and impartial according to the recognized standards of objective journalism.

The board is also obliged to ensure that the ABC complies with relevant legislation. The federal government of Australia has ultimate legislative control over the ABC and has control over the annual public grants on which the ABC depends. The ABC is not subject to direction by the government except in relation to the broadcasting of matters of national interest or as provided for in other legislation. But particulars of each such broadcast must be contained in the ABC annual report. It must also include codes of practice, details of any gift, device, or bequest accepted during the year, any advice received from the advisory council, a summary of the activities of the community affairs officers, and any actions taken in response to complaints.

A different arrangement exists in South Africa. The South African Broadcasting Corporation (SABC) is governed by a board of directors, established under the Broadcasting Act of 1999, which is the accountable authority for SABC and controls their affairs. It appoints an executive committee consisting of the chief executive and eleven other members to administer the affairs of the corporation. The executive committee is accountable to the board.

The Independent Communications Authority of South Africa (ICASA) is a broadcast regulatory body, which itself has constitutionally guaranteed independence, and significant regulatory powers with regard to the SABC. The Broadcasting Act of 1999 gives ICASA overall responsibility for ensuring that it complies with the terms of its charter. The act requires all broadcasting SABC services to be licensees of ICASA. In addition, all broadcasters, including SABC, must comply with the ICASA Code of Conduct, set out in the Independent Broadcasting Authority Act of 1993.

Formal accountability of the SABC is to Parliament through the minister. The SABC board furnishes the minister with an annual report on its work, together with a balance sheet and a complete statement of revenue and expenditure for that financial year. Financial accounts must be audited and accompanied by the auditor's report. The minister tables the report in Parliament, within seven days after receiving it.

Membership of the Governing Board

The appointment process for the governing board should be fair, open, transparent, and set out in law. It should be designed to ensure the members have relevant expertise or experience and carry a diversity of interests and opinions representative of society as a whole. It should not be dominated by any particular political party or commercial interest, and the members appointed should serve in an individual capacity and exercise their functions in the public interest at all times.

The appointment process of the government board cannot guarantee that a governing board will be free from partisan influence and undue pressures and suitably diverse in nature. But it can help to avoid some of the pitfalls.

Governing board members should be appointed for a fixed term and protected from dismissal during this term unless they cease to meet explicit conditions of eligibility for office or fail to discharge their responsibilities as set out in law. Rules of eligibility for membership of the board of governors should be clear and explicit, to avoid incompatibility with the responsibilities of office. The diversity of the board should take account of the desirability of reflecting different regional and cultural backgrounds and achieving a fair balance of women and men. Certain groups should be precluded from membership:

- employees in the civil service or other branch of government;
- officeholders or employees of a political party;
- elected or appointed members of the government;
- elected or appointed members of the legislature;
- employees of, or those with financial interests in, broadcasting or communications; and
- those convicted, after due process in accordance with internationally accepted legal principles, of a violent crime or a crime of dishonesty unless a period (e.g., five years) has passed since the sentence was discharged.

The presence of appropriate expertise on the governing board is useful, with knowledge of broadcasting, public service, management, and other relevant matters.

A few examples illustrate some variations:

- The Australian Broadcasting Corporation (ABC) is governed by a board of directors who are appointed and hold office under the terms of the Australian Broadcasting Act of 1983. The board consists of a managing director who is appointed by the board for a 5-year term and between six and eight other directors who are appointed by the governor general. In appointing the directors, account is taken of their experience relating to the provision of broadcasting services, experience in communications or management, expertise in financial or technical matters, and cultural or other interests relevant to the oversight of a public service broadcasting organization.

- NHK (Japan Broadcasting Corporation), Japan's sole public broadcaster, is governed by a board of governors consisting of twelve people who are appointed by the Prime Minister and approved by both Houses of the Diet on behalf of the Japanese public. They are selected to bring a broad range of experience and expertise. The board of governors is the decision-making body for every important matter of management policy and operation, including the annual budget, operational plan, and basic programming policy.

- Lithuanian Radio and Television (LRT) is governed by the Lithuanian Radio and Television Council (LRTT), consisting of twelve members representing diverse backgrounds. The law on LRT, adopted in 1996, requires that four of the members be appointed by the president of the Republic, four by Parliament, including two members from candidates recommended by opposition parties, and the remaining four by civil society organizations, namely the Lithuanian Science Council, the Lithuanian Board of Education, the Lithuanian Association of Art Creators, and the Lithuanian Congregation of Bishops. All must be "prominent individuals in the social, scientific and cultural spheres." LRTT members cannot be members of Parliament, the government, or of the LRTK, the broadcast regulatory body. They are appointed for a period of six years and may serve a maximum of two terms. Initial appointments to the LRTT in 1996 were staggered so that not all members are replaced at the same time and the appointments do not coincide with the electoral cycle. The council has strongly resisted attempts by politicians to interfere in its activities.

Director General

Day-to-day management of the public service broadcaster is the responsibility of a chief executive officer appointed by the governing board for a fixed term, whose tenure may be renewed. He or she, along with editorial staff, has responsibility for setting editorial policy and making editorial decisions.

The chief executive is responsible for management within the framework of the overall duties and responsibilities of the public service broadcaster, the strategy approved by the board of governors, the budget, and the internal policies currently in force. In the performance of his or her duties, the chief executive may seek or accept instructions only from the governing board, except as provided by law, and has final responsibility in relation to all editorial decisions.

Variations often depend on the local circumstances. For example:

- A director general of the BBC is appointed by the BBC Board of Governors, and in turn appoints nine other executive directors, who make up the BBC Executive Board responsible for operational management and editorial decisions.

- In the German regional public service broadcasting system, grouped together in the ARD (Association of Public Service Broadcasters in Germany), a director general is appointed by its regional broadcasting council to each public service broadcaster. The normal term of office of the director general is four years and the contract may be renewed.

- The president and chief executive officer of the Korean Broadcasting Service is appointed by the president of Korea but on the recommendation of the board of governors. The executive vice president is appointed by the president/CEO with the consent of the board of governors, while the managing directors are appointed by the president/CEO. The term of the president/CEO and of other members of the executive body is 3 years. The officeholders are eligible for reappointment.

- The affairs of the Australian Broadcasting Corporation (ABC) are managed by the managing director, who must act in accordance with any policies determined, and any directions given to him or her by the ABC Board. The managing director is appointed by the board for a period of five years and is eligible for reappointment for a further five years. The ABC Act includes a requirement that the remuneration of the managing director be determined by the Remuneration Tribunal and that he or she not take part in a meeting of the board at which the appointment or terms and conditions of employment of the managing director are discussed.

Funding

*The public service broadcaster should be predominantly funded
from public funding through a funding mechanism designed to protect its independence. It may raise additional revenues from direct
subsidies, commercial activities, and donations.*

The mechanisms by which public service broadcasting is funded are of
critical importance both to its independence and to the quality of its
output, but they are often among the most difficult ones to get right.
The financing system must be insulated from political pressures, permit some form of accountability, and be sufficiently predictable to allow for the multiyear investments that the public service broadcaster
needs to make to deliver on its mandate.

A variety of financial models are used to provide the principal
public funding mechanism. These include a household levy (a license
fee), direct government funding, a levy on commercial broadcasting,
and advertising. The amount of public funding for the sector varies
significantly even between countries with strong public broadcasters.
One study looked at financing of the sector in eighteen developed
countries and found that on average public broadcasters received
US$80 equivalent per year per resident, but the figure ranged from a
high of $154 in Switzerland to a low of $5 in the United States. Among
others included in the study were Germany ($134), UK ($124),
Finland ($111), Ireland ($67), Australia ($44), Spain ($36), and Canada
($33).[8] However, developing countries in particular, confronted with
a tax base overstretched across many priorities, a low household income for most of the population (though often a wealthy middle
class), and limited media advertising markets, will probably have to
look beyond the obvious to determine potential sources of income.

Any model chosen strives to both guarantee independence and
ensure an adequate financial base for the fulfillment of its duties and
responsibilities. There are pros and cons to the current options. Direct
government funding entails a risk of government interference.

---

[8]Analysis of Government Support for Public Broadcasting and Other Culture in Canada,
prepared for the Canadian Broadcasting Corporation by the Nordicity Group (2006),
available at: *http://www.cbc.radio-canada.ca/submissions/crtc/2006/BNPH_2006-5_CBC_RC_
Public_Broadcaster_Comparison.pdf.*

Overdependence on advertising subjects the public broadcaster to some of the same pressures as commercial broadcasters, which can undermine its scope to develop diverse informational programming and in-depth news coverage.

The household levy is usually based on a license fee for ownership of a television or radio receiver. Other means of collecting receipts from households include a levy linked to electricity supply. The fee may operate as a flat rate per household or may be progressive and linked to the ability to pay. The advantage of this form of parafiscal arrangement is that the revenues can be collected and distributed to the broadcaster by an independent collection and distribution body in a manner that further assures the operational independence of the broadcaster. On the other hand it can be costly and difficult to collect a household levy and it may be politically unpopular to introduce one for the first time.

NHK (Japan Broadcasting Corporation), Japan's sole public broadcaster, is financed by the receiving fee paid by each household that owns a television set. Germany's regional public broadcasters, grouped together in the ARD (Association of Public Service Broadcasters in Germany), are similarly funded almost entirely by the license fee. In Ireland, the main public broadcaster, RTÉ, receives license fee revenues, but this is supplemented by advertising sales, sponsorship, charges for the facilities and transmission network, program sales, merchandising, and related revenue. The Chilean public service broadcaster, TVN, is funded almost entirely through advertising.

Estonia developed a model for financing public service television by means of fees collected from private broadcasters. Launched in 1998 it was widely praised for allowing the public service broadcaster to shift its focus away from commercial and toward cultural programs while also diverting advertising funding toward private stations. (The failure of a private television station to pay its annual contribution on time led to its withdrawal in 1999—suggesting a weakness in regulation.)[8]

Depending on the proportion of revenue raised through a guaranteed public funding mechanism, the public service broadcaster may be subject to certain restrictions on its power to raise funds from other sources, in particular from commercial sources. Such restrictions may be designed to protect the character of the service as a public service or to ensure fair competition with commercial broadcasting services.

---

[8]OSI 2005, 59.

For example, the British Broadcasting Corporation (BBC) is funded almost entirely through the collection of television receiver set license fees. The BBC is precluded from selling advertising or sponsorship in its broadcasts, but it has an expanding portfolio of commercial business activities mainly based on the commercial exploitation of BBC programs, other assets, and skill base. The BBC World Service is separately funded.

In France, too, advertising revenues are strictly controlled with an overall limit set by Parliament. French public service broadcasting, consisting of six national programming companies and a publicly funded satellite channel, gets about 70 percent of its income from the annual license fee on television owners. The remainder is derived mainly from sale of advertising and program sponsorship. The license fee is set annually by Parliament as is the distribution of the fee between the national programming companies and other institutions with functions related to broadcasting. The proportion of the annual expenditure met by the license fee varies between program companies from around 50 percent for *France2*, to nearly 100 percent for *Radio France Internationale* and the European satellite channel, *La Sept-ARTE*. The most popular channels derive a larger proportion of their revenue from advertising.

But the television license fee is not a guaranteed solution. In Ghana, for example, the license fee has remained at a static level for many years due to the reluctance of politicians to vote for an increase. The effects of inflation have served to reduce the value of the license fee collected to a very low level that barely exceeds the costs of collection and is insufficient to fund Ghana Broadcasting Corporation (GBC), the public broadcaster. This has led to a growing dependence on commercial revenue sources and reduction in investment in quality program making. Some countries, to prevent this, have instituted automatic fee adjustments based on the cost-of-living index.

12 Community Nonprofit Broadcasting

Good Practice Checklist

- Community broadcasting should be recognized in law as a distinct type of broadcasting to be supported and encouraged through specific and explicit licensing arrangements that guarantee fair and equitable access to radio spectrum for civil-society and community-based organizations.
- Community broadcasting can be defined as independent broadcasting that is provided by and for the members of a community in a particular geographical location or that belongs to a particular community of interest. Its primary purpose is to deliver social benefit and not to operate for private commercial profit. It should be owned by and accountable to the community that it seeks to serve and it should provide for participation by the community at all levels.
- Licensing processes for community broadcasting should be fair, open, transparent, and set out in law and should be under the responsibility of an independent licensing body. Criteria for application and selection should be established openly and in consultation with civil society.
- License terms and conditions for community broadcasting should be consistent with the objectives of broadcast regulation and be designed to ensure that the community broadcasting service characteristics are protected and maintained for the duration of the license period.
- Community broadcasting services should have access to a diversity of funding sources according to local circumstances. There should be no restrictions on funding sources other than those deemed necessary to maintain the character of the service and to avoid unfair competition.
- Community broadcasting may be supported by public funding, including direct public subsidies. Where there is a regular and guaranteed system of public funding this should be fair, open, and transparent in its administration and under the responsibility of an independent public body.

Introduction

Community broadcasting refers to broadcast media that are independent and civil-society–based and that operate for social objectives rather than for private financial profit. They are run by community-based organizations, local nongovernmental organizations, workers organizations, educational institutions, religious or cultural organizations, or associations comprised of one or more of these forms of civil society organization.

Community broadcasting was initially developed, often without state authorization, by social movements and community-based organizations seeking to express their own issues, concerns, cultures, and languages, and to create an alternative both to public broadcasters, who were often under government control, and to private commercial media. There is no single definition of community broadcasting, and there are almost as many models as there are stations. Each community broadcasting initiative is a hybrid, a unique communication process shaped by its environment and the distinct culture, history, and reality of the community it serves. Indeed the term *community broadcasting* is applied to a wide range of noncommercial initiatives, including rural, cooperative, participatory, free, citizens', alternative, popular, and educational broadcasting. Community radio stations are located in isolated rural villages but also in the heart of the largest cities, and the communities they represent and serve may be geographically defined as the residents of a given town, or they may be defined by shared cultural, linguistic, or other interests. Depending on the nature of the community, the broadcast signal may reach only a kilometer, cover a whole country, or be carried on the Internet to community members on the other side of the world.

Community broadcasting, and particularly radio, can provide communities with access to information and voice, facilitating community-level debate, information sharing, and input into decision-making. Community broadcasting is also a process that engages the community in capacity building and empowering activities. If public broadcasting is a window through which viewers and listeners can understand their country and the world, then community broadcasting is a mirror that reflects a community's own knowledge and experience back at it and invites the community to know itself, to engage in dialogue, to find solutions to its problems, and to develop agendas for action.

As we have seen in Part I, community broadcasting is gaining recognition as an essential component of a pluralist media landscape, particularly for its role in giving access to voice and information, and promoting participation among communities and groups facing social and economic exclusion. In 2003, for example, the Ninth United Nations Roundtable on Communications for Development referred to community media in the following terms:

> Governments should implement a legal and supportive framework favoring the right to free expression and the emergence of free and pluralistic information systems, including the recognition of the specific and crucial role of community media in providing access to communication for isolated and marginalized groups.[1]

A growing number of countries do make explicit provision for community broadcasting in their broadcast law and/or in published decisions of the regulatory body responsible for broadcasting. Typically this framework describes the characteristics of community broadcasting and sets out the arrangements for licensing and funding. Legal and regulatory provision for community radio is more widespread than for community television. In some countries the framework for community broadcasting includes both radio and television, whereas in others there are separate arrangements for each.

A number of studies have compared and evaluated the policy, legal, and regulatory frameworks that are most conducive to enabling community broadcasting to flourish.[2] From this diverse and widespread experience some characteristics of good practice in law and regulation can be identified. In the sections that follow, the elements of good practices in regulation of community broadcasting are discussed in more detail.

---

[1] Ninth United Nations Roundtable on Communications for Development (Rome, September 2004).

[2] E. Price-Davies and J. Tacchi, *Community Radio in a Global Context: A Comparative Analysis in Six Countries* (Sheffield: Community Media Association, 2001) Sanchez, G. C., Legislation on Community Radio Broadcasting: A Comparative Study of the Legislation of 13 Countries (Paris: UNESCO 2001) AMARC-LAC, Best practices on community broadcasting regulatory frameworks—a comparative study regulatory and legal frameworks and national policies in 14 countries, unpublished draft report (Montevideo, Uruguay: AMARC-LAC 2006).

Recognition and Differentiation

Community broadcasting should be recognized in law as a distinct type of broadcasting to be supported and encouraged through specific and explicit licensing arrangements that guarantee fair and equitable access to radio spectrum and to economic resources.

Clear and explicit legal and policy recognition of community broadcasting as a distinct sector is desirable since policies relevant to community broadcasting differ from those relevant to other sectors, such as those relating to its economic base, its forms of accountability and participation, and its relationship to the community. The fair distribution of radio spectrum, a valuable and scarce resource, requires special mechanisms to reach beyond commercial and public service allocations and to guarantee access for civil society and community-based organizations.

BOX 52.   Mali: Building a Diverse Radio Landscape

As in most West African countries, broadcasting in Mali has traditionally been a state monopoly with the ORTM (Office de Radiodiffusion au Television de Mali) broadcasting from the capital to the entire country.

Following the introduction of multiparty democracy in 1991, Mali formally allowed private radio and television stations and adopted one of the most democratic broadcast laws in Africa. Within a few years dozens of private radio stations, both commercial and community, were established, most of them local stations.

Fifteen years ago the state monopoly broadcaster (ORTM—*Office de radiodiffusion et de télévision du Mali*) broadcast programming primarily produced in Bamako, and primarily in French, via repeater transmitters across the country. Now Mali has one of the strongest and most diverse radio systems in Africa, with as many as 300 radio stations broadcasting local programming throughout the country in more than a dozen local languages.

One reason for the growth of the sector is the lack of bureaucratic and financial hurdles to obtaining a license. There are no license fees to establish a radio station in Mali and the only requirements are that you be Malian and that you fill out a simple form. The form is sent to the *Conseil Superieur de la Communication* (CSC), which checks frequency availability and technical integrity of the proposal by informing the *Comité de Regulation de Telecommunication*. If the proposal is technically sound and the requested frequency is available, the radio station is allowed to use it. Each year, a frequency allowance of about US$20 is paid by each radio station.

Community radio *(servicio comunitario de radiodifusión sonora)* has received such recognition in Colombia since 1995 by successive presidential decrees. The most recent[3] provides a clear definition and permits the licensing of community radio on AM and FM. In Venezuela community broadcasting is recognized in the *Ley Orgánica de Telecomunicaciones 2000* and the Regulation No. 1521 of 2002 *(servicio de radiodifusión sonora y televisión abierta comunitarias de servicio público sin fines de lucro).*

Mali was the first country in Africa to enable the licensing of community broadcasting through a general provision for private broadcasting services.[4] The Malian regulatory body, the *Conseil Superieur de la Communication*, provides for a specific licensing category of community radio defined as "not for profit and owned by local communities." Within a few years of opening the airwaves there, hundreds of independent and community radio stations had been established throughout the country, largely aided by the decision to eliminate financial and bureaucratic hurdles.[5]

In South Africa, the Independent Broadcasting Authority Act of 1993 set out an explicit licensing framework for community broadcasting, now superseded by similar provisions in the Electronic Communications Act of 2006. The South African Broadcasting Act of 1999 includes additional provisions for licensing community broadcasting services in South Africa. The *Declaration of Principles on Freedom of Expression in Africa*, adopted by the African Commission on Human and People's Rights in 2002, calls on African states to ensure: "an equitable allocation of frequencies between private broadcast uses, both commercial and community" and that "Community broadcasting shall be encouraged given its potential to broaden access by poor and rural communities to the airwaves."[6]

It should be noted that achieving an equitable allocation of frequencies will usually require laws and regulations that differentiate

---

[3]Presidential Decree No. 1981 of 2003, available at: *http://www.mincomunicaciones.gov.co/.*

[4]Presidency of the Republic of Mali (2002) Décret no. 02-22 7 /P-RM du 10 mai 2002 *portant statut des services privés de radiodiffusion sonore par voie hertzienne terrestre et modulation de fréquence.*

[5]A sample application is available online at: *http://urtel.radio.org.ml/IMG/doc/Cahier_de_charges.doc.*

[6]African Commission on Human and People's Rights (2002) Declaration of Principles on Freedom of Expression in Africa, adopted at the 32nd Session (Banjul,October 17–23, 2002).

between community and commercial broadcasting and that specifically encourage community broadcasting and take their social objectives and noncommercial nature into account. For example, Mali, Venezuela, and Colombia reduced or waived license fees for noncommercial radio and implemented simplified license application procedures. It is equally important to use appropriate criteria for evaluating community broadcast applications.

Recognition and differentiation of community broadcasting in law and regulation are desirable features but not in themselves sufficient conditions of good practice. Indeed, in some cases, the legal framework has been operated as a means to limit the viability or influence of community broadcasters by, for example, imposing excessive constraints on transmission power or unreasonable limitations on sources of finance. The Special Rapporteur for Freedom of Expression of the Inter-American Commission on Human Rights addressed this problem in its 2002 annual report: "Given the potential importance of these community channels for freedom of expression, the establishment of discriminatory legal frameworks that hinder the allocation of frequencies to community radio stations is unacceptable."[7] It is essential therefore that the legal and regulatory framework also offers fair and equitable access to frequencies and also to economic and other resources.

BOX 53. United States: Noncommercial Radio Licenses

In the United States, community broadcasting has its roots in a historic decision of the Federal Communications Commission in 1945 to reserve 20 percent of the FM radio spectrum (from 88.0 to 92.0 MHz) for nonprofit services.[1] The first nonprofit radio services in the United States were limited to educational institutions, but the launch in 1949 of KPFA in Berkeley, California, marked the beginning of a wider opening for community radio. Today, over 2,500 licenses have been issued to noncommercial FM radio services and around 400 licenses to noncommercial public and educational television services.

---

1. Federal Communications Commission (1945) Allocation of Frequencies to the Various Classes of Nongovernmental Services in the Radio Spectrum from 10 Kilocycles to 30,000,000 Kilocycles, Docket No. 6651 (June 27, 1945).

---

[7]Annual Report of the Special Rapporteur for Freedom of Expression, p. 128, 2002, available at: *http://www.cidh.org/Relatoria/showarticle.asp?artID=138&lID=1.*

Definition and Characteristics

Community broadcasting can be defined as independent broadcasting that is provided by and for the members of a community in a particular geographical location or belonging to a particular community of interest. Its primary purpose is to deliver social benefit and not to operate for private commercial profit. It should be owned by and accountable to the community that it seeks to serve and it should provide for participation by the community in the making of programs and in management. There should be no a priori or unreasonable limitations on the extent of coverage, transmission power, or the nature of the community to be served.

Community broadcasters are independent media operated for social purposes by not-for-profit organizations. They should not face any content restrictions beyond those that legitimately apply to all broadcast media. They have a responsibility to respond to the issues, expectations, and proposals of their community, in all their diversity, and are committed to enabling and promoting participation at all levels.

The right to establish community broadcasting services should be available for community-based organizations and other civil society groups in rural and urban areas and for geographical and interest-based communities. They should not face a priori or arbitrary limitations on transmission power or coverage area, nor should they be reserved exclusively for particular social groups or communities, rural or urban.

Characteristics that should be included in any legal or regulatory definition of community broadcasting—and derived from countries where specific licensing arrangements for community broadcasting are in place—include requirements that they:

- remain independent of the government and of commercial organizations;
- serve specific communities, either geographical or communities of interest;
- have ownership and management representative of that community;
- operate for purposes of social benefit rather than private financial profit; and
- enable participation by the community in program-making and management.

These characteristics form the basis for a legal or regulatory definition. The regulatory framework, including the terms and conditions of licensing, should require that these characteristics are respected, while allowing flexibility for the broadcaster to adapt its service to best meet the needs and conditions of the community it is intended to serve.

The independence of the service means that it should not be directly or indirectly controlled by any body of central or local government or face undue influence by such bodies through ownership or funding. It should also be independent of commercial interests, and no commercial broadcaster or other commercial entity should be able to own or otherwise exercise effective control over the service.

The community orientation of the service means that it provides programming intended to serve one or more communities and that it promotes and supports participation by members of the community in its operation and management. This should include measures to ensure that the provider of the service is accountable to the community it serves.

The characteristic of operating for purposes of social benefit means that any profit from operations is used wholly and exclusively for securing the future provision of the service or for the delivery of social gain to the members of the public or community that it is intended to serve. Social benefit means the achievement of objectives that contribute to the social and economic well-being of the community served. These may include:

- the provision of access to broadcast facilities by the community;
- the encouragement of dialogue, opinion, and expression;
- the improvement of access to information and knowledge;
- the provision of education or training for members of the community;
- the promotion of inclusion of and access by disadvantaged groups;
- the promotion of cultural and linguistic diversity;
- the promotion of equality between men and women;
- the promotion of the rights of children and young people;
- the promotion of civic participation and volunteerism;
- the promotion of employment and work experience; and
- the promotion of sustainable social and economic development.

In practice there are significant variations in the definitions of community broadcasting, but most definitions include some or all of these characteristics. The Canadian Radio-television and Telecommunications Commission (CRTC) regulates broadcasting in Canada and defines community radio in Public Notice CRTC 2000-13 as follows:

> A community radio station is owned and controlled by a not-for-profit organization, the structure of which provides for membership, management, operation and programming primarily by members of the community at large. Programming should reflect the diversity of the market that the station is licensed to serve.[8]

The African Charter on Broadcasting, adopted in 2002 by media practitioners and freedom of expression advocates from all over Africa, has become a widely referenced statement of good practice. It includes the following definition:

> Community broadcasting is broadcasting which is for, by and about the community, whose ownership and management is representative of the community, which pursues a social development agenda, and which is non-profit.[9]

Policy guidelines adopted by the Indian government in 2006 state the following:

> An organisation desirous of operating a Community Radio Station (CRS) must be able to satisfy and adhere to the following principles:
>
> a.   It should be explicitly constituted as a "non-profit" organisation and should have a proven record of at least three years of service to the local community.
> b.   The CRS to be operated by it should be designed to serve a specific well-defined local community.
> c.   It should have an ownership and management structure that is reflective of the community that the CRS seeks to serve.

---

[8]Public Notice CRTC 2000-13.
[9]The African Charter on Broadcasting was adopted in Windhoek, Namibia, in May 2001.

    d.   Programmes for broadcast should be relevant to the educational, developmental, social and cultural needs of the community.

    e.   It must be a Legal Entity, i.e., it should be registered (under the registration of Societies Act or any other such act relevant to the purpose).[10]

The requirement to be an NGO with three years of community service is intended to gauge an applicant's level of community involvement and support. But it is a burden to innovative projects and excludes applications from associations formed specifically to operate a community radio, regardless of the experience the members of the new association might have. A better way of achieving this is found in Colombia and Venezuela, which require that the applicant demonstrate that it has the support of established organizations in the community rather than the history of the legal entity making the application. However, in other respects this statement of principles is consistent with a good practice definition.

In South Africa, the Broadcasting Act number 4 of 1999 states that community broadcasting license holders for radio and television: must democratically elect a board from members of the community; must reflect their cultural, religious, language, and demographic needs; must provide a unique and diverse service, including a focus on grassroots community issues such as developmental, health care, and environmental affairs; and must promote a common sense of purpose. All surplus funds must also be reinvested for the benefit of the community.[11]

Licensing Process

Licensing processes for community broadcasting should be fair, open, transparent, and set out in law and should be the responsibility of an independent licensing body. Criteria for application and selection should be established openly and in consultation with civil society.

Licensing is necessary to ensure fair and equitable access to a limited resource, the radio spectrum. Licensing of community broadcasting should normally be separate from licensing of commercial broadcasting

---

[10]Government of India, Ministry of Information and Broadcasting (2006) Policy guidelines for setting up Community Radio stations in India (updated December 4, 2006).
[11]Broadcasting Act number 4 of 1999, Section 32.

services, and sufficient broadcast spectrum ring-fenced for community services. Allocation of spectrum and licenses to community broadcasting should be a straightforward and transparent process, responsive to demand from community-based organizations that meet the characteristics set out in the definition. There should be no unnecessary obstacles to communities seeking a license, and the process should be independent of political interference. Licensing should consider issues of community participation, ownership, and operation and its social purpose.

The process of applying for a license should be set out clearly in law. This may take the form of a call for applications for a particular locality, or applicants may be able to define for themselves the localities they propose to cover. The information to be provided by applicants should be specified by the licensing body and may include:

- legal status and membership of the applicant;
- proposed coverage and intended audience;
- content of the program service to be provided;
- involvement of and accountability to the community;
- proposals to ensure the delivery of social gain; and
- financial plans and sources of finance.

The application requirements, selection criteria, and mode of assessment should be established prior to the invitation to apply for licensing and should be developed in a manner that includes open and public consultation involving civil society groups.

Decisions on license applications should be taken within a reasonable timeframe and allow for public comments to be submitted, and a refusal should be accompanied by written reasons and made subject to judicial review. The characteristics of the frequency assignment should be specified and adequate to the proposed coverage.

Aside from long-term community broadcasting licenses it can be useful to offer short-term or experimental licenses that provide an opportunity to new community broadcasters to gain experience and demonstrate their ability to operate a full-time service.

In Benin, the *Haute Autorité de l'Audiovisuel et de la Communication* (HAAC) is an independent regulatory body responsible for the licensing of private radio and television services. The HAAC distinguishes between commercial radio and noncommercial radio, and it publishes a *Cahiers des Charges* setting out the procedure and criteria for licensing of noncommercial radio services. In addition to the not-for-profit status, the HAAC identifies community radio by its range; its focus on a specific community; its use of specific languages; and its focus on local information and mobilization, cultural development, and further education. The licensing process for community radio starts with the HAAC publishing the list of available frequencies based on its frequency map and issuing a published call for applications from all sectors, public, private, and commercial. Applications are processed and frequencies allocated based on the proposed program content and the viability of the service.

In Ireland, community radio licenses are awarded under a two-stage procedure. First the Broadcasting Commission of Ireland (BCI) invites expressions of interest. Subsequently it invites applications by public notice for a contract to provide a service in a specific area for which a frequency has been assigned by the Commission for Communications Regulation, a statutory body responsible for regulation of telecommunications, radio-communications, and broadcast transmission.

The licensing process for community radio is the same as that for private commercial broadcasters though different selection criteria and licensing terms apply. For instance, in considering expressions of interest, the BCI examines the level of participation by the community in the station and the program service envisaged. If it decides to proceed with a public invitation for applications, the area to be covered and the community nature of the service will be specified and a "Guide to Submissions" published. Criteria include: the character of the applicant; its expertise and financial resource; the quality of program proposals, including provisions for Irish language and culture; and the desirability of having a diversity of services and ownership.

License Terms and Conditions

License terms and conditions for community broadcasting should be consistent with the objectives of broadcast regulation and designed to ensure that the community broadcasting service characteristics are protected and maintained for the duration of the license period.

Licenses may contain certain terms and conditions, either of a general nature, for example set out in the law or in regulations, or specific to an individual broadcaster. They can include:

- specification of the technical characteristics of the service;
- specification of the duration of the license;
- a requirement to comply with general broadcast law and regulations;
- a requirement to provide the service proposed in the license application; and
- a provision for sanctions in the case of noncompliance.

Normally, the transfer of the license to another person or group would not be permitted without the permission of the regulator, which should be given only where it can be shown that the new owner would continue to operate it as a community broadcasting service.

In Australia, for example, community broadcasting services are subject to general license conditions, which apply to all broadcasting services and to more specific license conditions that are relevant to community broadcasting. These conditions are set out in the Broadcasting Services Act of 1992 and include the following specific requirements:

a. the licensee will remain a suitable licensee;
b. the licensee will continue to represent the community interest that it represented at the time when the license was allocated or was last renewed;
c. the licensee will encourage members of the community that it serves to participate in:
   i. the operations of the licensee in providing the service; and
   ii. the selection and provision of programs under the license;
d. the licensee will provide the service for community purposes; and
e. the licensee will not operate the service for profit or as part of a profit-making enterprise.[12]

Specifications for the technical characteristics of the service should not impose unreasonable constraints on transmission power, aerial height, or other distribution parameters that would restrict the

---

[12]Broadcasting Services Act of 1992.

viability of the service in achieving its purpose. They should be based on technical assumptions equivalent to those for other broadcasters.

In South Africa, the community broadcasting license specifies the licensee, the station name, the frequency and related technical parameters, the location and coverage area, the commencement date, and the expiry date. In addition the license requires compliance with a number of general license conditions for community sound broadcasting. The general license conditions include requirements:

- to have due regard to the character, control, management, objectives, intentions, undertakings, and representations made by the licensee in its application;
- to establish and maintain formal structures that provide for community participation in the control, management, operational, and programming aspects of the service;
- not to change the name or the ownership and control of the licensee or the control of the broadcasting service without written consent of the regulatory authority;
- to ensure the licensee is and remains under the control of a nonprofit and nonpolitical entity;
- to apply profits and any other income to the promotion of its broadcasting activities or in the service of the community; and
- to establish a procedure for handling complaints and to broadcast information on how to make a complaint.

Procedures for obtaining broadcast licenses can be lengthy and expensive, involving expensive technical studies and specialized legal expertise. Rural and lower-power licenses in particular can be allocated with simplified administrative procedures and effective yet less-expensive technical licenses, such as type-approved equipment. Countries as diverse as Canada and Peru have recognized this and simplified application procedures for rural and low-power broadcast initiatives. Even in urban areas where spectrum management is more complex, technical and legal requirements are often unnecessarily demanding and expensive and serve as an effective barrier to would-be community broadcasters.

Funding and Sustainability

> *Community broadcasting services should have fair and equitable access to a diversity of funding sources according to local circumstances. There should be no restrictions on funding sources other than what is necessary to maintain the character of the service and to avoid unfair competition.*

Ideally, community broadcasting should draw on a number of sources of funding and support, to reinforce its independence from vested interests and its capacity to serve exclusively the community. The regulatory framework should encourage this.

License fees should be waived or nominal so as not to exclude communities with few resources. There should be no unreasonable restrictions on sources of revenue such as advertising. Community broadcasters should be encouraged to develop economic support from within their own community, including sponsorships and announcements, but assistance may also be provided through independently administered public funding.

Support programs should also recognize that social, institutional, and technical sustainability are as important to the functioning and survival of community broadcasters as economic arrangements and capacity building is often required over a period of time.

Financial models for community broadcasting vary from one country to another and according to local circumstances.

In South Africa, for example, there are no funding restrictions imposed by the regulatory framework, and advertising and sponsorship are carried. Some international donors make a substantial commitment to the sector. Community radio stations are also able to apply for support from the Media Diversity and Development Agency (see the next section).

In the Netherlands, community radio stations are encouraged to seek funding from a wide range of sources, including advertising, sponsorship, membership fees, and donations. Advertising is limited to a maximum of fifteen percent of airtime on any given day and is also limited to a maximum of twelve minutes in any one hour. Some stations depend almost completely on advertising but most rely also on other sources of funding. More than one hundred municipalities provide public financial support.

An important measure of financial sustainability for a community broadcaster is the ability to secure contributions from its own community by, for example, generating fees from announcements by local organizations and businesses, developing sponsorships from community groups for special programs they request, or charging other organizations for airtime. External donors usually end financial support within a few years and should not be considered a principal source of long-term assistance.

In Canada, generalist community radio stations face no limits on revenue from advertising and sponsorship. Campus community radios and some native radio stations are limited to a maximum of four minutes of advertising in any one hour. Public funding for community radio in Canada is not extensive. Advertising is an important source for many of the larger urban stations, though some stations choose not to carry any. Most of the community radio stations draw significantly on direct support from listeners through on-air fund-raising drives and membership schemes.

Where there is a significant element of public funding, some limitations on funding from commercial sources, including the sale of advertising time, may be justified when it competes with commercial broadcasters. Such restrictions may also aim to guarantee the character of the service. Any such restrictions should be no more than is necessary to ensure fair competition, to avoid unfair subsidy, and/or to maintain the character of the service. Furthermore, they should be limited to sources of finance that form a significant proportion of commercial broadcasters' revenue and should not undermine the viability of operating the community broadcasting service.

Funding arrangements is one of several sets of issues that affects the viability and sustainability of community broadcasters. The social base, authenticity, and responsiveness of the broadcaster to its audience are crucial factors that are strengthened by interactive programming and by accountable and participatory management structures. Most community broadcasters depend heavily on volunteers to assist in program making, fund-raising, and other activities and rely on the active involvement of local groups and organizations to provide expertise and input on matters of local and community concern.

Public Funding

> *Community broadcasting may be supported by public funding, including direct public subsidies. Where there is a regular and guaranteed system of public funding this should be administered through an independent public body established for this purpose.*

If it is to succeed, community broadcasting, like any other sector, must have sufficient income, and in some circumstances public funding is necessary and justified. A special fund set up for this purpose is the preferred method for channeling public funding. This may be financed through direct taxation or through other mechanisms, such as a levy on cable concessions, a percentage of commercial broadcast revenue, or a proportion of a general license fee for public service broadcasting.

In the Netherlands, for example, the national government transfers funds to municipalities to support community broadcasting. Prior to 2000, municipalities had the option to levy an additional surcharge of 0.90 euro (US$1.20) on the license fee paid by all households with a radio or television receiver. About 100 municipalities opted to participate, generating 1.4 million euros per year for the community broadcasting sector. In 2000 the license fee was replaced by a system in which public broadcasting is paid out of the general budget. After strong pressure from OLON, the national community broadcast association, the government agreed to support the sector with approximately 7.7 million euros (US$10.5 million or US$1.50 per household) per year paid directly to the municipalities. Nevertheless the arrangement is not without flaws. According to OLON's director, Pieter de Wit,

> The problem is that municipalities are not obliged to use this money for local community media. In fact, only 30 percent of the 300 local media get the entire fee, 56 percent get less than the total, and 14 percent get nothing. Also some municipalities put restrictions on spending and act contrary to the Dutch legislation on public broadcasting, which forbids government influence in programming.[13]

New legislation expected to be passed in 2008 will overcome this problem by transferring the subsidy directly to the country's 300 local community broadcasters.

---

[13]Email from Pieter de Wit, April 26, 2007.

Public funding for community broadcasting should be operated independently of government and of the broadcast regulator through an independent public body. In Australia, for example, the Community Broadcasting Foundation Ltd. (CBF) was established in 1984 as an independent, nonprofit funding body.[14] Its primary aim is to act as a funding agency for the development of community broadcasting (radio and television) in Australia, and it receives an annual grant from the Department of Communications, Information Technology and the Arts. The CBF assesses applications for funding and distributes grants for development, programming, and infrastructure support for: aboriginal community broadcasting, ethnic community broadcasting, Radio for the Print Handicapped (RPH), general community broadcasting, the Australian Ethnic Radio Training Project (AERTP), and sector coordination and policy development. Government funding allocated to the CBF for the year 2006/2007 was A$7.88 (Australian) (US$6.5 million). Of this amount, 50 percent went to core support grants made directly to stations, 20 percent went to defray transmission costs, and the rest was in the form of targeted grants to support ethnic broadcasting and initiatives of the Community Broadcasting Organization. According to the Community Broadcasting Foundation, federal government funding of community radio in 2003–2004 amounted to 6 percent of total revenue with other levels of government contributing an additional 6 percent. This 12 percent "government support remains a vital catalyst to sector development. It supports the production of specialised program content . . . to meet community needs in the most cost-effective manner."[15]

The major source of finance for Community Radio in France is the *Fond de soutien à l'expression radiophonique* (Support Fund for Radio Expression), created in 1982. It draws from a levy on advertising placed on mainstream broadcast media. The fund provides support for start-up costs, equipment upgrades, and core functioning, with the major part going toward core functioning costs. In 2004 the fund provided total grants of 21 million euros (US$27 million).

---

[14]Community Broadcasting Foundation website: *www.cbf.com.au.*
[15]Sector Funding Trends, Community Broadcasting Foundation Ltd., available at: *http://www.cbf.com.au/Content/templates/sector.asp?articleid=66&zoneid=13.*

BOX 54. France: Support Fund for Local Noncommercial Radio

The *Fond de soutien à l'expression radiophonique* (Radio Expression Support Fund—FSER) is one of the most interesting aspects of French broadcast policy. The fund, which is made up of a special tax levied on radio and television advertising expenditures and paid by advertisers, is used to support the activities of local noncommercial radio. First established in 1982, the fund provides qualified stations with between US$5,000 and $150,000 annually. The actual amount received depends on a number of criteria, including the previous year's budget, the amount of funds secured from other sources (stations that can demonstrate local financial support receive more from the FSER), programming quality, and the purpose of the funds (new radio stations can get more to help defray the cost of their installations). In return for accessing the funds, the stations must agree to limit advertising revenue to not more than 20 percent of their total annual turnover. They must also broadcast at least four hours daily of local programming between 06:00 and 22:00.

In 2004 the fund distributed approximately 21 million euros:

- fourteen new radio stations received an average of 15,228 euros to help pay for their installations, for a total of 213,200 euros;
- five hundred and eighty-four (584) stations received an average of 40,496 euros to subsidize their operational costs, for a total of 23.65 million euros; and
- seventy-six stations received an average of 5,722 euros to subsidize equipment purchases, for a total of 434,870 euros.

South Africa adopted a unique approach by creating the Media Development and Diversity Agency (MDDA) in 2002 by an act of Parliament, to enable "historically disadvantaged communities and persons not adequately served by the media" to gain media access. Its beneficiaries include both community media and small commercial media. The MDDA has the following objectives:

- Encourage ownership and control of, and access to, media by historically disadvantaged communities, historically diminished indigenous language and cultural groups;
- Encourage the channeling of resources to community and small commercial media;
- Encourage human resource development and capacity building in the media industry, especially amongst historically disadvantaged groups; and
- Encourage research regarding media development and diversity.

MDDA is a partnership between the South African government and major print and broadcasting companies. Its funding comes from government, the media industry, and donors. The 2005 Electronic Communications Act has opened a new source of funding for MDDA, by stipulating that broadcasters' contributions to MDDA would be deducted from the obligatory contributions of telecommunications and broadcasting companies to the Universal Service and Access Agency.[16] At the time of this publication, MDDA is confirming a contribution of 1 percent of broadcasters' license fees, to be allocated to MDDA. This is being negotiated with broadcasting companies prior to promulgation of a formal regulation. In South Africa, there is great potential for the regulator, the Independent Communication Authority of South Africa (ICASA), MDDA, and the National Community Radio Forum (NCRF) to harmonize their responsibilities and reinforce each other, in developing the community broadcasting sector. For example, as NCRF, the National Community Radio Association, develops its systems for strengthening community radio stations through provincial hubs, it may become possible for MDDA to wholesale its support through NCRF, and for NCRF to handle the retail strengthening of individual stations. One of MDDA's potentially great strengths is its mandate to lace together relationships with partner agencies and organizations, to mobilize and align support for diversified media services.

Venezuela, Bolivia, and Colombia make funds available to support training and equipment purposes and/or provide indirect funding, particularly in the form of fee and tax waivers, and reductions are common in many countries.[17] Bolivia's community radio stations pay 10 percent of the amount charged to commercial stations for spectrum use and in Mali stations are charged only $20 per year.

---

[16]Since 1993, South Africa's Universal Service Agency (USA) funded the expansion of South Africa's telecommunications infrastructure through a mandatory levy of 0.2 percent on licensees' annual turnover. The Electronic Communications Act of 2005, section 89, provides that "the contributions to the Universal Service and Access Fund (the new name for the USA) must not exceed 1 percent of the licensee's annual turnover or such other percentage of the licensee's annual turnover as may be determined by the Minister after consultation with the affected parties, by notice in the *Gazette*." It also states, "Broadcasting service licensees contributing to the Media Development and Diversity Agency (MDDA) must have their annual MDDA contribution set off against their prescribed annual contribution to the Universal Service and Access Fund." *MDDA Strategic Focus and Plan 2007–2010, March 2007.*

[17]Best Practices in Regulation of Community Broadcasting, Programa de Legislacionesy Derecho a la Comunicación de AMARC-LAC (2007).

As in other areas, the application process and decisions for public funding should be fair, open, and transparent and based on clear public interest criteria. A substantial part of the fund could provide regular and guaranteed core financial support according to an agreed and transparent formula, for instance based on the amount of funds raised from other sources or the size of potential audience or some other objective measure. Funding may also be available for start-up and development costs and to support the provision of joint services to the sector through country-level associations of community broadcasters.

Community broadcasters should also be able to apply for direct public grants and contracts from other sources. Public funding arrangements should not be allowed to compromise the independence of the community broadcaster.

13 Commercial Private Sector Broadcasting

Good Practice Checklist

- Regulation of private commercial broadcasting should be designed to meet the public interest in a range and diversity of services and to ensure fair competition between private broadcasters. Commercial broadcasters normally require a license to operate a radio or television service.
- Licensing processes for commercial broadcasting should be fair and transparent, and should be overseen by an independent body. License conditions should serve the overall goals of broadcast regulation and should not be arbitrary or oppressive.
- Rules preventing undue concentration of ownership in the broadcast sector, or between that sector and the print media sector, are legitimate as long as their actual purpose and practical effect is to promote diversity in the provision of broadcast services.
- Restrictions may be imposed on the extent of foreign ownership and control over broadcasters, as long as these restrictions take into account the need for the broadcasting sector as a whole to develop and for broadcasting services to be economically viable. A total ban on foreign investment in the broadcasting sector is not legitimate.
- Private commercial broadcasters may be subject to public service requirements in exchange for access to a limited public resource, namely the airwaves. Such requirements should be designed to further public interest objectives and should not be disproportionate in scope such that they threaten the viability of the service.
- Public advertising budgets spent on commercial broadcasting should be allocated on a strictly nondiscriminatory and commercial basis.
- Public grants and subsidies may be offered to commercial broadcasters in order to promote a range and diversity of services and to encourage programming of public interest. They should be allocated according to set criteria and according to a fair and transparent process overseen by an independent body.

Introduction

In the United States, from the earliest days of radio broadcasting in the 1920s, competition and commercialism have been the rule. The U.S. model of largely private commercial broadcasting became the norm across much of Latin America. In more recent years, commercial broadcasting has become a key component of broadcasting throughout the world, and the dominant one in much of it.

Private commercial broadcasting has grown rapidly in those parts of the world where public broadcasting was once a monopoly, such as Europe, Africa, and parts of Asia and the Pacific. As outlined in Part I, it exerts a major impact on the media landscape, sometimes occupying a dominant role within the broadcasting sector as a whole. Within Europe, public broadcasting monopolies began to give way in the 1950s and 1960s, but it was not until the 1970s that commercial broadcasting really began to take root. The decision of the Italian Constitutional Court in 1976 to end the state broadcasting monopoly[1] opened the Italian airwaves to private broadcasting, from which emerged Silvio Berlusconi's Fininvest empire. Austria was the last western European state to liberalize its radio airwaves, following a landmark case brought by private and community broadcasters in 1993 in which the European Court of Human Rights found the state broadcasting monopoly to be in breach of the right to freedom of expression, as guaranteed by Article 10 of the European Convention of Human Rights.[2] In Eastern Europe, private broadcasting emerged rapidly after the end of the cold war. Belarus is now the last remaining European country to maintain a state broadcasting monopoly.

In the 1980s, there were only a handful of private broadcasters on the African continent, whereas today there are thousands of private commercial radios, and almost every African country allows some degree of private sector broadcasting. In Asia and the Pacific, private broadcasting is less widespread. Several East and Southeast Asian countries have promoted private sector broadcasting, including Japan, the Philippines, and Indonesia. China, however, maintains a state broadcasting monopoly, and India only recently began to open its airwaves to private terrestrial radio stations and has been cautious in licensing new services.

---

[1] Decision 202/76 of the Italian Constitutional Court, July 28, 1976.
[2] *Informationsverein Lentia and others v. Austria*, May 25, 1993, Application Nos. 13914/88, 15041/89, 15717/89, 15779/89, 17207/90 (European Court of Human Rights).

Private commercial broadcasting has also gained strength from new forms of broadcast distribution, particularly cable and satellite and, more recently, the Internet. Satellite broadcasters have circumvented state control by using internationally assigned frequencies and uplinks in countries friendly to satellite operators. Star TV, for example, was established in 1991 and now broadcasts more than fifty channels to over fifty Asian countries, including India and China.

The growth of private commercial broadcasting has attracted significant entrepreneurial energy, as well as significant funding, to the sector. It has generally, as a result, increased media pluralism and choice and provided greater opportunities for different voices to be heard. Commercial broadcasting, and the competition it involves, has contributed to the growth of entertainment and talk programs available to the general public.

Although commercial broadcasters can play a role in promoting the public interest, by their very nature, this role must be somewhat limited. Having, legally, a primary obligation to their shareholders, they face pressures to maximize profit that can affect program content, as well as demands by advertisers, whose commercial interests may be at odds with public interest programming. In the absence of public interest regulation, more costly programs, such as those involving international reporting, investigative journalism, education, and high quality drama, as well as programs serving smaller populations, tend to lose out to cheaper programming with mass appeal. News reporting and analysis may also become influenced by the same profit-making imperatives as entertainment, with accurate and factual reporting being replaced by favorable editorial coverage of commercial sponsors and their products.

Furthermore, whenever the regulatory framework does not provide adequate safeguards, there has been a tendency toward increased concentration of ownership that, over time, can lead to a reduction in diversity, access, and quality in broadcasting and allow dominance by a small number of commercial broadcast owners. Poor regulatory frameworks can also result in private commercial broadcasting licenses being allocated under systems of political patronage, a practice evident in many countries.

According to a background study for the World Development Report 2002, 85 percent of private commercial radio and televisions broadcasters are owned by families rather than a wide range of shareholders.[3] A combination of media concentration and a narrow shareholder base can lead to disproportionate political influence by certain media owners. This kind of ownership arrangement runs contrary to the public interest in media pluralism and diversity.

In Guatemala, for example, four out of the six terrestrial television channels are owned by one businessman, a Mexican citizen living in Miami, without whose support few politicians could hope to be president. In El Salvador, the results of the 2004 presidential elections were widely attributed to the influence of the commercial media.[4] The new president is himself the owner of a chain of commercial radio stations.

Because of the important role the media can play in forming and influencing public opinion, it is widely accepted that rules to prevent concentration of the media, over and above general competition rules, can form a legitimate part of public interest regulation. In many countries, regulatory mechanisms for commercial broadcasting also mandate, in exchange for access to the publicly owned airwaves, minimum time requirements for news broadcasts, public service announcements, guaranteed access to political candidates under equal-time rules, and commitments to a proportion of public interest programming.

A few overriding principles apply to commercial broadcasting and are evident in the trends described in Part I, including the use of the licensing system to promote broadcast diversity and to prevent undue concentration of ownership in the broadcast sector. These principles are normally set out in law, but implementation is left to individual decision making by the regulator. As a result, and in a fashion analogous to content regulation, commercial broadcast regulation should be closely tailored to meeting local needs and interests.

Regulation

Regulation of private commercial broadcasting should be designed to meet the public interest in a range and diversity of services and to ensure fair competition between private broadcasters. Commercial broadcasters normally require a license to operate a radio or television service.

---

[3]Djankov, McLiesh, and others, 2001, *World Development Report 2002*, background paper.
[4]Proceso No. 1091, March 24, 2004. Translated from Spanish.

As with all regulation of the media, licensing should be overseen by a body that is independent of political or commercial control. There should be no blanket prohibitions on who may hold or participate in ownership of a broadcasting license based on either form or nature, except in relation to political parties, where a ban may be legitimate. The licensing body should have the power to make licensing decisions on a case-by-case basis while ensuring that there is no unfair discrimination against one applicant or another.

On this last point, the Inter-American Commission on Human Rights in its Principles on Freedom of Expression states explicitly, among other matters, that "the concession of radio and television broadcast frequencies should take into account democratic criteria that provide equal opportunity of access for all individuals."[5]

In the licensing of commercial broadcasting services the main objectives should be:

- to ensure a range and diversity of services at local and national level;
- to ensure, as far as possible, the provision of services that meet the needs and interests of listeners and viewers and that are of a high quality; and
- to ensure fair and effective competition in the provision of services.

Although the regulatory body should not discriminate unfairly for or against any applicant, a concession to operate a radio or television service may specify that the service should either be of a local or of a national character. Specific provision may also be included to encourage services to be established that serve minority groups lacking in financial or technological resources. In Poland, for example, a broadcaster qualifying as a "social broadcaster" (according to criteria set out in the Broadcasting Act) is exempt from "fees payable for awarding or altering the licence" on the strength of the social role it fulfills.[6]

---

[5]Inter-American Commission of Human Rights (2000) Declaration of Principles on Freedom of Expression, quoted in Loreti (2006) "Broadcast Law and Regulation in Latin America," commissioned paper.
[6]McGonagle (2006) "Minorities and the Media," commissioned paper.

The distribution of licenses for television channels and radio frequencies solely through auction to the highest bidder is unlikely to produce a range and diversity of services that meet the needs of all sections of society. In considering such arrangements in Guatemala (and also in Paraguay), the Special Rapporteur on Freedom of Expression of the Organization of American States has stated:

> Bidding procedures that do not go beyond economic considerations, or that do not give a chance to all social sectors, are incompatible with participatory democracy and the right of freedom of expression and information enshrined in the American Convention on Human Rights.[7]

Licensing Process

Licensing processes for commercial broadcasting should be fair, open, and transparent and should be overseen by an independent regulatory body. License conditions should serve the overall goals of broadcast regulation and should not be arbitrary or oppressive.

The process for obtaining a broadcasting license should be set out clearly and precisely in law; it should be fair, open, and transparent, include clear time limits within which decisions must be made, and allow for effective public input and an opportunity for the applicant to be heard. It may involve either a call for tenders or ad hoc receipt by the licensing body of applications, depending on the situation, but where there is competition for limited frequencies, a tender process should be utilized.

License applications should be assessed according to clear criteria set out in advance in legal form (laws or regulations). The criteria should, as far as possible, be objective in nature, and should include promoting a wide range of viewpoints fairly reflecting the diversity of the population and preventing undue concentration of ownership, as well as an assessment of the financial and technical capacity of the applicant. Any refusal to issue a license should be accompanied by written reasons and should be subject to judicial review.

---

[7]Office of the Special Rapporteur on Freedom of Expression (2001) Guatemala Country Report, quoted in Loreti (2006).

A reasonable administrative fee for processing license applications may be charged. Furthermore, licensees may be charged a license fee, but this should not be excessive and should reflect the development of the sector, the competition for licenses, and general considerations of commercial viability. Fees for different types of licenses should be set out in advance, according to a schedule.

When licensees also need a broadcasting frequency, they should not have to go through a separate decision-making process to obtain this frequency; successful applicants should be guaranteed a frequency appropriate to their broadcasting license.

In South Africa, for example, license applications are initiated by a call for applications from the regulator, the Independent Communication Authority of South Africa (ICASA) by notice in the *Gazette*, setting out the relevant parameters for that license and the application fee. Applicants may also apply from time to time, even in the absence of a call, and these applications will also be published in the *Gazette*. Anyone may make representations in respect of license applications. In assessing license applications, ICASA takes into account the demand for the proposed service within the relevant area, the need for the service, the technical capacity of the applicant, the financial means of the applicant, and the ownership and control structure of the applicant. A successful applicant is guaranteed a frequency appropriate to his or her license. There is a strong presumption of license renewal, and ICASA may refuse to renew the license only if the licensee has materially failed to comply with the license conditions or the provisions of the broadcasting law and ICASA is satisfied that the licensee would not comply if his or her license were renewed.

In issuing a license, the Canadian Radio-television and Telecommunications Commission (CRTC) takes a number of criteria into account, including ownership, financial and technical capacity, and programming requirements. A key aspect of the latter is to ensure that new licenses contribute to diversity, and in so doing, the CRTC may require applicants to provide a market survey, showing that there is a demand for the new service and how it would increase diversity in the market. In all of its decision making, the CRTC is required to promote a long list of broadcasting principles, including that the system be effectively owned and controlled by Canadians; operate primarily in English and French; serve the needs of all Canadians; encourage the development of Canadian expression; and serve to safeguard, enrich, and strengthen the cultural, political, social, and economic fabric of Canada. Once the CRTC receives an application it may issue a call for competing applications. The application is considered at a public hearing and is published in the *Gazette* at least 60 days prior to the hearing. Anyone may provide written comments on the application and the CRTC may invite those who have done so to attend the hearing. The CRTC then reaches a decision to either approve or deny the application or to approve it in part.

Rules on Concentration of Ownership

Rules preventing undue concentration of ownership in the broadcast sector, or between that sector and the print media sector, are legitimate as long as their actual purpose and practical effect is to promote diversity in the provision of broadcast services.

Excessive concentration of ownership in broadcasting can have many of the same effects as a monopoly. It can lead to excessive and partisan political influence and constrain diversity of content. General rules on concentration of ownership, designed to enhance competition and so provide a lower cost and better services, are for reasons outlined in Part I insufficient for the broadcasting sector. They provide only minimum levels of diversity, far less than what is needed to maximize the capacity of the broadcasting sector to deliver social added value. Excessive concentration of ownership is to be avoided not simply because of its effects on competition, but because of its effects on the key role of broadcasting in society, and the latter requires specific and dedicated measures.

As a result, some countries limit such ownership, for example to a fixed number of channels or to a set overall percentage of market share. Such rules are legitimate as long as they are not unduly restrictive, taking particular account of such issues as viability and economies of scale, which can affect the quality of program content.

Other forms of cross-ownership where rules to restrict concentration are legitimate include measures to restrict vertical concentration, for example, ownership of broadcasters by advertising agencies; and cross-media concentration, for example, ownership of broadcasters by newspaper owners publishing in the same or overlapping markets.

For example, the Indonesian Broadcasting Act of 2002 includes a general prohibition on undue concentration of broadcast ownership. Cross-ownership both between different broadcasting sectors (radio, television, subscription services) and between the print and broadcast sectors is strictly prohibited. The law also prohibits more than one service being offered by a licensee in any particular area. These rules are applied both through the licensing process and through ongoing monitoring of the broadcast sector. Ownership is one of the criteria to be taken into account by the regulatory body when assessing applications for broadcasting licenses.

In South Africa, the law on concentration of ownership is more complex. First, no one may directly or indirectly exercise control over more than one private television license, or over more than two private FM or AM sound broadcasting licenses. Furthermore, no one may control substantially overlapping either FM or AM services (although overlapping ownership of one FM and one AM license would appear to be permitted). Cross-ownership rules prohibit anyone from controlling a newspaper and both a radio and a television license. And anyone in a position to control a newspaper with a circulation of 20 percent of the total newspaper's readership in a given area may not own a broadcasting license that substantially overlaps with the newspaper circulation: an overlap of 50 percent or more is deemed to be substantial and a 20 percent shareholding is deemed to constitute control. These rules may be waived in any particular case, as long as this does not run counter to the objects and principles of broadcast regulation, as set out in the law.

Rules on Foreign Ownership

Restrictions may be imposed on the extent of foreign ownership and control over broadcasters, as long as these restrictions take into account the need for the broadcasting sector as a whole to develop and for broadcasting services to be economically viable. A total ban on foreign investment in the broadcasting sector is not legitimate.

Restrictions on foreign ownership can be legitimately designed to promote local and national cultural production, ensuring the means for local and national opinions and cultural content to be expressed and heard. In many countries, dominant local control over such an important national resource is also considered necessary. Although such claims may be overstated, control may indeed be needed for the implementation of policies that are designed to foster a public interest approach to media.

But foreign ownership restrictions should not be used as a means to undermine the viability of services that provide alternative points of view: there are cases of restrictions on foreign funding designed to prevent donor support to independent media outlets. Furthermore, foreign investment can bring much-needed expertise and capital into the local market. Restrictions on this investment should not be so restrictive that they reduce the range and diversity of services available.

In Colombia, for example, foreign investment is allowed exclusively up to 40 percent of the stock of the broadcast concession holder. It is subject to reciprocal arrangements being in place with respect to the country of domicile of the foreign investor.[8]

The United States is generally considered to be among the most restrictive countries with respect to foreign ownership. Under the Communications Act of 1934 foreign ownership of a broadcasting license is denied to:

1) foreign government or representative;

2) alien or foreign registered companies;

3) companies in which foreign interests control more than 20 percent of voting capital; and

4) any company directly or indirectly controlled by another company in which more than 25 percent of the voting capital is owned by foreigners.

Public Service Requirements

Private commercial broadcasters may be subject to public service requirements in exchange for access to a limited public resource, namely the airwaves. Such requirements should be designed to further public interest objectives and should not be disproportionate in scope such that they threaten the viability of the service.

The limited capacity of the radio spectrum places overall limits on the number of broadcasters that may be licensed. This, along with the

---

[8]D. Loreti (2006), "Broadcast Law and Regulation in Latin America," commissioned paper.

fact that the radio spectrum is a public resource to which licensees have privileged access, justifies the imposition of limited public service requirements for commercial broadcasters. Such requirements are normally linked to promoting diversity of content in the airwaves, as well as maintaining quality. Often, such requirements are imposed as license conditions on a case-by-case basis for individual broadcasters. Although this provides flexibility to tailor these obligations to the specific market niche of each broadcaster, it also brings with it a risk of political interference.

The specific nature of such obligations will vary depending on the context. In some cases, license conditions may include specific public service content requirements to carry, for example, news and information or education and cultural programming. In the United Kingdom, for example, the main terrestrial television stations normally have their main news schedules fixed in their licenses and need to apply to the regulator if they wish to change the duration or timing of the news. This is used to ensure, for example, that banner evening news programs are available at different times for viewers.

An important public interest obligation in some countries is the requirement to carry a minimum percentage of locally produced programming. In many cases, it is far cheaper to purchase foreign programs, especially older ones, including films, than to produce programs in-house or purchase them from independent local producers. Local content requirements can counter a situation where all that is available to audiences is cheap, dated foreign programming. The African Charter on Broadcasting, adopted in 2002 by media practitioners and freedom of expression advocates from throughout Africa, for example, states: "Broadcasters should be required to promote and develop local content, which should be defined to include African content, including through the introduction of minimum quotas."

In Canada, general license conditions provide that Canadian content and news and public affairs programming must make up a minimum of 60 percent of private and public broadcasters' schedules, except overnight. Broadcasters must reflect cultural diversity and gender equality in content and character portrayals and reflect both English and French communities in their programming. To qualify as Canadian, entertainment music, for example, must meet the MAPL test, which requires the lyrics to be written by a Canadian, the music to be entirely composed and performed by a Canadian, and the production to be recorded in Canada.

In other cases, licensees may be required to provide certain guaranteed levels of geographical coverage to ensure rural and marginalized communities are properly served.

Public Grants, Subsidies, and Advertising

Public grants and subsidies may be offered to commercial broadcasters in order to promote a range and diversity of services and to encourage programming of public interest. They should be allocated according to set criteria and according to a fair and transparent process overseen by an independent body. Public advertising budgets spent on commercial broadcasting should be allocated on a strictly nondiscriminatory and best-value basis.

Public grants can provide an important role in funding the production of programs of public interest or by providing incentives for such programs by contributing a partial subsidy toward the total costs of production. Production funding may include, for example, support for programs of particular educational or cultural value that would otherwise be unlikely to be made. Public grants and subsidies can also help promote diversity by stimulating media output in underdeveloped sectors, such as small minority media, or by maintaining diverse media ownership in declining markets.

Grant schemes should be run in a fair and transparent manner to ensure equal access to the benefits they provide. This should include clear criteria set out in advance, which are designed to further the goals to be achieved. To prevent political interference with the scheme, it should, as with all regulatory powers, be overseen by an independent body, which may be the broadcast regulator or a body established specifically for the purpose of administering a scheme of financial support.

The Broadcasting Commission of Ireland (BCI), an independent regulatory body, administers financial support to independent broadcasters and producers in Ireland, including commercial broadcasters. Funding is provided on a competitive basis and is for public interest program making under the terms of the Broadcasting (Funding) Act of 2003,[9] to be broadcast by public service, commercial, or

---

[9]Broadcasting (Funding) Act of 2003, available at: *http://www.bci.ie/documents/2003fundingact.pdf.*

community license holders. The act provides that 5 percent of the receiver set license fee paid by television viewers should be allocated to the Sound and Vision Broadcasting Funding Scheme.[10] In 2006, this amounted to around US$10 million.

South Africa's Media Development and Diversity Agency (MDDA) provides technical and financial support to both community and small commercial media, to enable them to improve media services to historically underserved areas and people. As noted in the previous chapter, broadcasters' annual contributions to MDDA are deducted from their required contributions to South Africa's Universal Service and Access Agency, which supports expansion of telecommunications and broadcasting infrastructure.

Public advertising, often a very substantial part of total advertising spending, can also be subject to misuse as a discriminatory form of support, granted or withheld on the basis of editorial orientations toward the government. This is not a legitimate practice. Public advertising should be allocated in a nondiscriminatory manner to prevent political interference in the media sector. In South Africa, for example, the Government Communication Information System (GCIS) produces a large array of public service messages, in collaboration with sector ministries, which it sells to both commercial and nonprofit broadcasters. These are produced in different languages for listening audiences in different areas.

The criteria used to allocate public advertising should be related to the audience to be reached and follow principles of efficacy and best value, taking into account market considerations such as audience share or distribution and the target audience. Ideally, the allocation of such advertising should be done by a body that operates at arm's length from government.

---

[10]Broadcasting Commission of Ireland, Sound and Vision—Broadcasting Funding Scheme (2006), available at: *http://www.bci.ie/broadcast_funding_scheme/guide_submissions.html.*

Epilogue: Information Needs and Development Options

This final chapter returns to the need, raised at several points earlier, for further research and data to inform future development of effective broadcasting policies in developing countries. It also puts forward recommendations on the development assistance that is needed to support the growth of a robust, diversified broadcasting sector that answers public interest concerns. It concludes by pointing to convergence between fostering accountability, engaging citizens, and building effective processes of collective leadership and by highlighting some key policy reforms.

The Research Agenda

One overriding observation that emerged from the experience of researching and compiling this guide concerns the difficulty of obtaining data and useful research on many aspects of broadcasting, especially comparative research at global and regional levels. Anecdotes are found in abundance, and some in-depth research is available, although it tends to focus on narrowly delineated issues or territories. Most existing research looks at developed countries, with limited relevance to the very different circumstances in developing countries and poor communities.

This problem relates to data, an indispensable raw material for analysis. But it also relates to qualitative research on the dynamics and impact of policy and regulation, on the performance of the different broadcast sectors and the challenges they face, and on the place that broadcast media occupy in people's lives and their influence on people's social, cultural, and economic existence.

240

This dearth of material is surprising given the fact that the huge social impact and vitally important role of broadcast media are almost unanimously accepted. Perhaps the enormous, sprawling, and ever-changing nature of the sector and the diffuse and multifaceted nature of the impact lend themselves readily only to relatively abstract theorizing or a narrow empirical approach. A further challenge to generating comparative research is the need to develop and apply adequate and standardized categorization of institutional definitions and sectors and subsectors.

Research into the following areas would make a valuable contribution to concrete debates on media policy and regulation and to reinforcing the material contained in this guide:

- Generating a dynamic overview of the fundamental structural evolution of broadcasting requires basic numerical data and time series[1] such as statistics on the number of broadcasters in each sector and subsector at the various levels, local to international, and types of program broadcast. Also needed is data on independent broadcast regulators, differentiating those that also regulate other sectors.

- A more detailed level of description, however, is needed to go behind the statistics to discern the contours and drivers of sector dynamics. Descriptions and analyses of evolving government policy in broadcasting are a starting point. The legal and institutional structureof broadcast regulators, their sources of funding, and staff levels would be valuable, as would the formal institutional relationship between public service media and government, and their accountability, funding structures— especially innovative ones—and regulatory requirements imposed on them. Similar information is needed on com- mercial and community sectors, their hybrids and their variants. Again, identifying basic trends and milestones in these contexts would also be useful.

---

[1] UNESCO's Institute of Statistics is currently undertaking a global survey of broadcasting. Results will be available by the end of 2007. Although the questionnaire does not differentiate between public service and direct state control it will contain useful information on state/public, commercial, and community sectors in terms of: numbers of channels from local to international levels journalists employed, broadcast hours in different program categories, foreign programs, audience, and reach, etc. See *http://www.uis.unesco.org/ev.php?ID=6554_201&ID2=DO_TOPIC*.

Analytical studies would help illuminate the influences and motivations of actors at these levels and trace the opportunities and pitfalls faced by countries in achieving reforms and executing regulatory measures.

Public service broadcasting is confronting a crisis of identity and effectiveness in various parts of the world. More thinking is needed on how states should respond to the kinds of market failures that were at the heart of creating public service broadcasting entities in the past, and, also crucially, on the nature of the public interest in broadcasting. In a related vein, convergence and new technologies make it especially important to consider how regulators can be defined and redefined to perform their functions (with respect to commercial as well as public service broadcasters).[2]

How the dynamics of each sector influence the content it produces, in terms of subject matter, approach, and quality, is an area in which assertions are frequently made, most based on general analysis of sectoral motivations and dynamics, anecdotes, and a few studies usually of developed countries. Few are backed up by empirical content analysis. Methodologies for content analysis are well developed and are applied at the global level in some specific areas such as gender representation in media[3] and in some geographic domains, notably the United States.

In this guide we have assumed a correlation between media, especially independent media of the kind we describe, and improved governance. We have accepted the substantial writings that contend that giving people voice will lead to a stronger, healthier public sphere and will inform government so that its functioning can be enhanced. But we understand that even here, on matters that are fundamental to our understanding, more research will be helpful.

However, probably most neglected, and methodologically most challenging, is research that can tease out the everyday impact of broadcasting on society and on people: the benefits, the harm, and unintended consequences on people's economic, social, and cultural

---

[2]See for instance Carter Eltzroth (2006) "Broadcasting in Developing Countries: Elements of a Conceptual Framework for Reform," *Information Technologies and International Development*, Volume 3, Number 1, Fall 2006, 19–37. MIT.

[3]See Global Media Monitoring Project, World Association for Christian Communication. *http://www.wacc.org.uk/wacc/programmes/gender_and_media_justice/global_media_monitoring_project_2005.*

existence. Almost nothing is available to give us a direct insight into which media poor people actually consume; the value they attach to different broadcast content, including local and international news, entertainment, and educational and development material; the motivations behind their choices; and the impact on their lives. Even more difficult to discern is the cumulative impact of these individual experiences on broader communities and society.

In community radio, research is needed to document and monitor how participation in a community channel can empower poor communities and build their capacity to engage public officials and media, to articulate their concerns, and to mobilize information and expertise. Similarly, data on how local entrepreneurs can establish radio in underserved communities, and their contribution to empowerment, is almost nonexistent.

Direct interaction with broadcast consumers, and especially with poor and marginalized communities, is essential here. Approaches range from user and householder surveys through to ethnographic studies, but all are generally resource intensive and some are lengthy. Recent international studies on telephony and information and communication technology (ICT) use, a few of which also include broadcast media, might show the way here.[4]

Finally, research is required to understand how trends in media and communication as a whole will impinge on and possibly eventually transform the broadcasting sector. Key influences across many of the trends is the emerging "information society," the growing role of the Internet, and convergence of technologies. Issues requiring further investigation with a specific focus on developing countries include:

- The impact on the terrestrial broadcast sector, and on its regulation, of the growing use of the Internet to receive content, and the continuing growth of satellite broadcasting;

- The coming revolution in radio spectrum management and regulation, through the potential of "spread-spectrum" and other technologies to effectively eliminate scarcity as a factor;

---

[4]For recent surveys of telephony in Africa and Asia see: Research ICT Africa (2005) *Towards an African e-Index: Household and individual ICT access and usage in 10 African countries*, Research ICT Africa. Available at: *http://www.researchictafrica.net/images/ upload/Toward2.pdf*. A. Mooneshingh et al. (2006) *Telecom Use on a Shoestring: Expenditure and perceptions of costs amongst the financially constrained*, April 2006, available at: *http://www.regulateonline.org/content/view/713/31/*.

- The emergence of digital television and radio and pressures to move in this direction, including issues of the competing standards and different cost structures of digital; and

- The partial trend toward integration of telecommunications and broadcast regulation, and indeed multisector regulation.

These issues are not on the immediate agenda of broadcasting policy makers in developing countries. But the pace and technical complexity of development in the media and communication sectors is such that decision making is rarely exposed to adequate public scrutiny: when change happens it can be swift and, for most people, bewildering. More needs to be done by governments, communications regulators, and international bodies responsible to ensure that the impact of technical choices and regulatory approaches on the public interest is adequately assessed and subject to public consultation before policy decisions are taken. A first step would be to undertake basic research on emerging issues in a timely manner, so that it can feed into such a process of understanding and consultation.

Options for Development Assistance

What Donors Can Do

Assistance to developing countries is much needed, to improve their enabling environments for broadcasting and other media. This is integral to improving capacities for good governance, social accountability, and participatory development.

Reform media policy requires political will and citizen demand: compelling such reforms through "conditionality" is likely to be counterproductive for donors and development agencies.[5] The most fruitful opportunities for productive dialogue and assistance to improve the enabling environment for media functioning—and specifically for a robust, pluralistic broadcasting sector that serves public interest goals—tend to arise when countries are democratizing, opening their markets, decentralizing, or making other efforts to improve the transparency, accountability, and effectiveness of governance.

Media policy reforms can be facilitated by stakeholders sharing information and ideas, and by bringing pressure to bear on governments.

---

[5]Conditionality refers to the practice of placing requirements or "conditions" on the recipient government's access to further assistance.

Such coalitions can be important interlocutors and partners with development agencies and donors, and can provide a forum to define and agree on priorities and actions.

Forums, Analyses, Policy, and Technical Advice

Development efforts can provide information, encouragement and opportunities for stakeholders in developing countries to converge on policy reforms needed to make their broadcasting sector more vigorous, pluralistic, and independent. Consultations and fact-finding can lead to research and to policy and analysis and other diagnostic work. A broadcasting sector study in a specific country can analyze the policy, legal and regulatory, institutional and political economic context affecting the sector, compare current practices with global good practices, and offer recommendations. Such studies can be followed up by structured meetings and forums, to share analyses, assess and share good practices, and highlight issues. Projects—the processes of developing and implementing them—uncover issues and needs not previously addressed. The protagonists have an interest in solving the problems that emerge, and this engagement can lead to substantial policy dialogue and program change. Meanwhile, development assistance can strengthen the capacities of diverse institutions and organizations, from national media commissions and regulatory agencies to grassroots networks, through training and advice, study visits and "twinning" between organizations. Not only nongovernmental organizations, but increasingly, national and international associations and networks—community radio associations and networks are a case in point—are also providing assistance not only to their own constituencies and members, but to similar associations in other countries.

In this mix, symposia, workshops, and forums can provide a good "moment" for key stakeholders inside and outside government to get issues on the table that lack a single government constituency. They can enable potential allies to get a broader perspective and even develop a consensus for action. The Development Dialogue Series organized by the World Bank office in Accra, Ghana, on "Giving Access to the Airwaves" showcased a growing interest in broadcasting policy and regulatory reform, enabled stakeholders with widely divergent views to air their concerns, and provided opportunities to triangulate information and clarify facts. In some cases, a workshop provides the clarity and interest needed

---

BOX 55. Nigeria: A Forum Precipitates Action

In July 2006, the World Bank and the World Association of Community Radio Broadcasters (AMARC) co-convened a high-level symposium in Abuja, to discuss global good practice on broadcast policy that would enable development of a community radio sector. It followed a regional roundtable of AMARC and benefited from discussion of progress in other countries. This symposium was the first time that high-level Nigerian government officials—from both the Executive and the National Assembly—and civil society stakeholders, along with the President of the World Association of Community Radio Broadcasters, community radio expert-practitioners from the region, and the Bank, met together to discuss the role of community radio and the need for a better policy and regulatory framework that provided access to the airwaves. This workshop built upon previous World Bank discussions with the steering committee of Nigeria's coalition for community radio. It also benefitted from the Bank's collaboration with staff of the Fadama Project, which supports community-driven development in several regions of the country. At the end of the symposium, the president of AMARC, a representative of the World Bank country office, participants from the coalition, and Fadama's national coordination staff met with the Minister of Information, and briefed him on their findings.

Also in July 2006, the Fadama national coordination unit agreed to fund several community radio (CR) stations, and to contribute to policy development for CR. Six community radio stations are expected to be funded by the Fadama III Project, as pilots for potential further support.

In August 2006, Government established a Community Radio Policy Committee, including members of the CR coalition, with a mandate to draft a Community Radio Policy within two months.

In December 2006, the Community Radio Policy Drafting Committee submitted its report to the federal government of Nigeria. In receiving it, the Minister of Information stated that it was unacceptable for a few people to be able to participate in information management while the majority are forced to accept their voices and views. He said that government is convinced that opening up the airwaves to provide space for community radio would help address this situation and enrich governance as never before in the country.

---

to stimulate immediate action—as when Nigeria's Minister of Information called for a community radio policy to be drafted, established a policy committee composed of both government and nongovernmental representatives, and set a tight timetable for submission of the policy to government. The policy committee presented a draft consistent with global good practice in about three months. (See Box 55.)

For low income countries, the deliberations on the government's Poverty Reduction Strategy Program (PRSP) also provide an important forum to mobilize support for policies and action programs that contribute to civic participation and good governance.[6] The PRSP provides a framework for consultation and agreement with all the key donors and aid agencies working with the government, which tends to foster better collaboration and coherence in development support to a country.

Increasingly, PRSPs—as well as development frameworks produced in middle income countries—identify governance as a major focus area, and link this to civic participation. For example the Second Ghana Poverty Reduction Strategy (2006) has "Good Governance and Civic Responsibility" as one of its three main pillars.[7] The following matrix shows how several focus areas within that pillar align with the goal of promoting pluralistic broadcasting in the public interest, including community radio specifically.

------

[6]Since 1999, governments in low-income countries have prepared Poverty Reduction Strategy Papers (PRSPs) that describe the macroeconomic, structural, and social policies and programs that a country will pursue over several years to promote broad-based growth and reduce poverty, as well as external financing needs and the associated sources of financing. They are developed through a participatory process involving domestic stakeholders and external development partners, including the IMF and the World Bank, and are updated every three years. The ultimate outcome of a PRSP is not the paper, but rather, public and community actions to reduce poverty. PRSPs are produced according to a number of principles:

- They are country-driven, involving broad-based participation by civil society and the private sector as they are produced.
- They are directed toward achieving results and focused on outcomes that would benefit the poor.
- They recognize that tackling poverty requires a comprehensive approach because poverty is more than just a lack of income but that poor people also suffer from a lack of opportunity, security, and voice in decisions that affect their lives.
- They are partnership-oriented in that they encourage the coordinated involvement of bilateral, multilateral, and nongovernment organizations in the country's poverty reduction program.
- They are based on a long-term perspective for poverty reduction.
- PRSPs foster greater openness in policy making.

Governments have sought increasingly to include traditionally marginalized groups, the private sector, and civil society in developing them and because of this, poverty-reduction strategies developed through this process tend to have broader community and stakeholder support and are "owned" by the government. *http://web.worldbank.org/WBSITE/EXTERNAL/ TOPICS/EXTPOVERTY/EXTPRS/.*

[7]Available at: *http://siteresources.worldbank.org/INTPRS1/Resources/Ghana_PRSP(Nov-2005) .pdf.*

TABLE 1 Matrix: Ghana Poverty Reduction Strategy (GPRS) II and Its Relationship to Voice and Media Technical Assistance (TA)

GPRS II Focus Areas within Good Governance and Civic Responsibility	Relevant References in GPRS II	How Technical Assistance to Improve Broadcasting Policy and Regulation and Support for Community Radio Development Pluralism Relates to GPRS II
Strengthening the practice of democracy	"Foster Civic Advocacy to nurture the culture of democracy"; "Support institutions and schemes aimed at empowering civic participation"; "free access to public information"	TA will inform public opinion and build communities' skills in articulating issues important to them, developing a factual understanding and debating issues, and holding local government accountable.
Protecting rights under rule of law	"Promote the provision of legal aid for the poor"	Piloting would support partnership between GCRN and LRC,* to expand capacity-building in poor people's legal empowerment through radio programming.
Enhancing development communication	• "Promote Development Communication in state and civil society environments" • "Ensure commitment to enhance access to public information and enabling environment for media"; • Strategies: "Facilitate access and enabling environment [for media]"; "Involve the marginalized in governance through access to information" "Encourage private [nongovernmental] community radio stations" • Indicators include: "Number of additional community radio stations licensed & operational"	TA results, if successful, will reduce regulatory barriers to community radio development, allocate a portion of the radio-frequency spectrum to community broadcasting, and strengthen capacities of a regulator that will have the mandate and capacities to facilitate community radio development in order to meet the National Media Policy's objectives.

*Ghana Community Radio Network and Ghana's Legal Resources Center.

Voice and Rights Funds

Some farsighted donors make funds available to grassroots organizations to undertake actions that contribute to poor peoples' understanding of their rights and to building their capacity to exert those rights effectively. For example, an initiative of the UK's Department for International Development (DfID), Rights and Voice Initiative (RAVI), has been supporting the joint activities of the Ghana Legal Resources Centre and Ghana Community Radio Network to develop and broadcast social and legal empowerment programs, with active audience participation. As governance concerns are being translated into capacity building for civil society and the media, such efforts hold considerable future promise.

The Specific Role of the World Bank

The World Bank has a range of instruments it can potentially deploy to enhance an enabling broadcasting environment, and its strategic thinking is increasingly moving in this direction.

The World Bank's Governance and Anticorruption (GAC) Strategy

In early 2007, the World Bank's Board of Executive Directors approved a strategy for "Strengthening Bank Group Engagement on Governance and Anti-corruption" (March 21, 2007), a product of extensive consultations with governments and forums of civil society organizations, media, and the private sector in all regions. The report recognizes the Bank's lessons of experience that:

> Strengthening accountability requires capacity in government and institutions outside central government, such as parliament, civil society, media, and local communities, as well as an enabling environment in which these stakeholders can operate responsibly and effectively.[8]

The World Bank's primary clients for development assistance are still governments, but the governance strategy suggests that the Bank now has a mandate to help improve the enabling environment for media—the policies, laws, and regulations that enable media to contribute to broad social participation, oversight, and demand for good governance. In its "Strategy for Engaging Countries" the GAC report

---

[8]Executive Summary, iv, World Bank, "Strengthening Bank Group Engagement on Governance and Anti-corruption" (March 21, 2007).

notes that, depending on the country context, the range of governance interventions may include:

> Supporting more broadly participation and oversight by civil society, media and communities—and (a repeated theme in the GAC consultations) helping improve the enabling environment and capacity of these actors to play constructively their development role.[9]

The Bank's decision on a strategy for strengthening governance represents an important change in the authorizing environment for the Bank's country assistance programs. It will strengthen the Bank's multistakeholder engagement in client countries, and can shape multidonor assistance programs. Because the Bank convenes most of the consultative groups that marshal development assistance for the world's low-income countries, this breakthrough can have a considerable catalytic effect.

The GAC strategy report states:

> While government transparency can help to facilitate participation and oversight, *more proactive engagement* of society is also vital. Countries can achieve this by:
>
> - Creating concrete opportunities for participation and oversight, for example, through participatory development of policies and public spending priorities (the poverty reduction strategy process has provided a major impetus in this area in IDA-eligible countries), social accountability in the delivery of services, community-driven development, civil society and media oversight over public procurement, monitoring of income and asset declarations, and other arrangements that empower legitimate social groups;
> - Supporting the development of an enabling environment and of capacity so that civil society organizations can effectively take advantage of these opportunities; and
> - Enabling the development of independent and competitive media that can investigate, monitor, and provide feedback on government performance, including corruption.[10]

The strategy presents five entry points for its "Country Efforts: Entry Points for Anticorruption and Governance Reform." The second is to

---

[9]Op. cit., 18.
[10]Op. cit., 22.

"increase opportunities for participation and oversight by civil society, the media and communities."[11] Also, while continuing to "work with the government as its principal counterpart," the World Bank will use a variety of instruments more systematically "—policy dialogue, analytic work, capacity-building, policy-based lending, and community driven development—to scale up existing and good practice to increase opportunities for oversight."[12]

In December 2007, under President Robert Zoellick's leadership, the World Bank announced that it was launching a more proactive phase of work to implement the GAC strategy and mainstream it throughout World Bank operations. Implementation will focus on five areas; below we highlight the role that this guide can play in supporting them.

- *At the country level, Country Assistance Strategies (CASs) will begin to include GAC strategies. This will start in 26 countries, and will emphasize peer learning on effective approaches.* This step increases the scope to emphasize, actively assist and monitor governments' policies, institutional development, and capacities to improve their transparency and accountability to the public; of these, the *enabling environment for public scrutiny and voice* will need to play a role. The GAC country strategies are likely to include measures that can be put into place quickly in government systems, and also programs of analysis, dialogue and institutional development to promote transparency and the enabling environment for public scrutiny, including for independent media development. A significant part of this enabling environment concerns the policy, legal and regulatory environment for independent and pluralistic broadcasting that serves the public interest and enables society to engage. This guide should be a useful tool in the country assessments and assistance efforts ahead.

- *The Bank's sector assistance will mainstream governance and accountability measures.* This effort will expand opportunities for representative and accountable civil society organizations

---

[11]Op. cit., Annex B: "Country Efforts: Entry Points for Governance and Anticorruption Reform, 48.
[12]Ibid, 54.

to play specific management or implementation roles within projects, such as managing grants for local education or ensuring implementation of public works. Scaling up these measures will become increasingly feasible when they also strengthen platforms—such as community radio—for citizen information sharing, debate, decision making, and feedback to government, as discussed in this guide.

- *Anticorruption measures will be designed into Bank-financed projects to strengthen transparency and disclosure to the public.* This is likely to include agreements with governments to publicize revenues and planned expenditures; public works commitments; responsibilities for program implementation; and other information relating to Bank-financed projects. An inclusive broadcasting sector can play a core role in allowing broad segments of the population to access this sort of information and to voice their concerns. Hence, though the Bank may focus its efforts on project transparency, strengthening institutions and capacities to get this information to the people will need to play a role.

- *The Bank will strengthen its work on the demand side of governance—providing assistance to strengthen the role of civil society in demanding good governance and holding government to account.* Given the Bank's comparative advantage in helping governments to improve their policies and delivery of services, a key way for the Bank to support civil society's ability to exert demand will be to help governments improve the enabling environment for independent, robust, and pluralistic media. Complementing this could be World Bank financial and technical assistance to improve the independence, transparency and capabilities of broadcasting regulatory authorities, and project assistance to develop the community broadcasting sector as a vehicle for public voice and pressure.

- *The Bank will staff up to implement this strategy, in country offices and in an array of sectors.* This will include field-based GAC advisors and creation of regional hubs to support implementation of the above lines of work.

The Roles of the World Bank

The World Bank plays particular roles that can focus attention and galvanize action. It promotes new, common development platforms, such as the PRSP and Comprehensive Development Framework for donor assistance to a country. It convenes members of the development community and other diverse stakeholders to focus on particular issues and galvanize support to address them. It provides advice to governments. It mobilizes funds for the poorest countries through the International Development Association (IDA). Further, it provides substantial, integrated programs of support to national governments, to implement policy improvements, strengthen institutions, and develop capacities, and provide investment financing for specific development objectives.

Virtually all of the Bank's advisory and financial assistance is focused at the country level, normally with the government as the main client. The Bank's primary engagement focuses on

- the government's policy, legal, and regulatory framework, either focusing on specific sectors (telecommunications, roads, ports, railways; agriculture, natural resource management, and environmental sustainability) or improving broad government processes such as financial management and procurement, customs reforms, public access to information, and transparency;

- institutional changes, such as improvement in delivery systems, financing, and cost-recovery systems for key public services; adjustments in ministry and subnational government responsibilities; and reform of regulatory authorities; as well as

- investments targeted to improving the economic opportunities and well-being of poor and marginalized populations in society.

Country Assistance Strategy

The rolling three-year Country Assistance Strategy (CAS) is the primary determinant of the themes and key issues the Bank will address, and instruments it will deploy. It also is designed to promote collaboration and coordination among development partners in a country.

A growing number of CASs make governance one of their main pillars, including for instance the CASs for Indonesia, Albania, and Bangladesh. The Albania 2006 CAS cites "civil society voice and participation" as one of the four ingredients of good governance. The 2006 Cambodia CAS seeks to "promote a stronger demand for good governance by increasing citizens' voice and participation in the policy making process." The Country Assistance Program outlined in the CAS includes lending assistance, analytic support, and policy advice. In fiscal year 2006, almost half of new lending projects included governance and rule of law components, with 19.2 percent of total new lending, or $4.5 billion, dedicated to supporting this area.

Capacity Development and Nonlending Assistance

Providing longer-term programs of technical assistance and training, the World Bank Institute (WBI) supports operations by strengthening country capacity in areas of high priority that cannot be adequately addressed through normal projects. WBI's assistance is often not channeled through governments and can, in those cases, be carried out more flexibly than is possible through the Bank's country lending and related advisory support. WBI works with multiple stakeholders in countries, regionally and globally, to share good practice, stimulate networks and communities of practice, and support south-south assistance. "WBI particularly works to strengthen societal instruments of accountability by supporting media development, parliamentarians, legal and judicial reform, civic participation, private sector capacity for collective action against corruption, and youth leadership."[13] About half of WBI's work is focused on particular countries and supports the CAS through nonlending technical assistance, policy advice, training programs, and institutional development support for diverse stakeholders.

Sector Analysis and Policy Development

Before providing its first lending project to a particular sector, the Bank may carry out a sector assessment. When the policy framework for the sector is weak, perverse, or fragmented, the Bank may ask for

---

[13]Available at: *http://web.worldbank.org/WBSITE/EXTERNAL/NEWS/0,,contentMDK:20040922 ~menuPK:34480~pagePK:34370~theSitePK:4607,00.html.*

BOX 56. Ghana's National Telecommunications Policy and Development of a Broadcasting Law

In the lead-up to planning a substantial telecommunications project for Ghana, the government developed a Telecommunications Policy, and the World Bank advised on this effort through its Telecommunications Policy Review missions. One outgrowth of these discussions was that the National Telecommunications Policy adopted by the cabinet and published in January 2005 states the Government's intent to develop an appropriate legal and regulatory framework for broadcasting, and including in particular, for a three-tier system of public service, community and commercial radio and television stations. The Policy also expresses the Government's intention to undertake a comprehensive review of current broadcasting policy and legislation in Ghana, with the objective of further expanding access to broadcast radio and television media for all citizens, providing for the greatest diversity of voice and languages and for the preservation and ongoing creation of indigenous content. It describes community broadcasting as a priority which that should become a new area for development.

As discussions proceeded to the barriers to entry facing community radio applicants, the Government requested the Bank to assist in a study of Ghana's broadcasting sector, analyzing how Ghana's enabling environment for broadcasting could be better aligned with emerging international good practice. The broadcasting study drew upon the draft guide to good practice available at the time. The Government circulated the broadcasting study for comment, along with the draft guide, in late 2005. Stakeholder discussions proceeded in 2006 with these resources in hand, convened by the broad-based Advocacy Steering Committee for a New Broadcast Law, and in early 2007, a team of Ghanaian experts drafted a framework for a Broadcasting Law for formal government review.

---

a government policy statement. In the discussions on this policy, opportunities can appear to confer with senior government officials, including ministers, on issues that should be addressed.

Telecommunications policy is a case in point and of particular relevance to broadcasting development. Telecommunications policy dialogue can provide an important context in which to discuss and analyze broadcasting policies, regulatory responsibilities, and procedures, and can lead the government both to make formal policy statements and to propose changes in the legal and regulatory framework.

While telecommunications policy is often dominated by issues of technology and technical alternatives, expanding its perspective to encompass the broad public interests of developing an informed, engaged society can enable it to address broadcasting policy issues. The 2005 National Telecommunications Policy of Ghana (Box 56) demonstrates this point.

Governance, transparency, and civic participation projects are becoming an increasingly prominent part of the World Bank's work. (Examples appear in Box 57.) They offer appropriate opportunities for analysis, dialogue, and support to improve the policy, legal, regulatory, and institutional framework affecting media functioning and

---

Box 57.   Scaling up Citizen Feedback: Peru

In Peru, the Programmatic Social Reform Loan financed by the World Bank included training of community radio stations to promote citizen participation and social auditing, the facilitation of strategic planning meetings with rural and indigenous communities, and the preparation of a community radio program on social accountability and social auditing. The loan focused on improving the enabling environment for citizen participation in the social sectors through enhanced access to information and participatory budgeting. Many of the estimated 1,000 community radio stations in Peru have been promoting citizens' rights and participation by providing a channel for information and voice to poor people in their native languages. They became natural partners in the government's efforts to improve citizen feedback on social sector programs.

Demand for Good Governance: Cambodia. Cambodia's proposed Demand for Good Governance Project is devoted exclusively to developing demand-side approaches to governance issues, strengthening and linking the work of both governmental and nongovernmental actors. The project is in its early stages and would develop the extent and ability of citizens, civil society organizations, and other nonstate actors to hold the state accountable and to make it responsive to their needs. The project involves a process of four key elements: promotion, mediation, response, and monitoring of demand, with transparency, participation, and accountability mechanisms being key to the project. As part of the project's support to institutional development as well as to specific programs, it focuses on capacity building of the national radio broadcaster as an institution and on programming that promotes, mediates, and monitors good governance.

diversified broadcasting sector development. When Freedom of Information legislation is being considered, media freedoms and supportive policies should be addressed at the same time. The "Right to Tell" (as noted in the World Bank book of the same name) is inextricably related to making transparency measures work.

Community driven development (CDD) projects are evolving into very large programs that build capacities for local public service delivery and mechanisms for local government accountability. The development of community broadcasting would constitute a big-impact intervention that would build systems and capacities for local, usually poor, communities to raise issues of concern to them, have regular conversations with local government leaders, and have an open mike to identify instances of corruption or governmental high-handedness.

Because community radio stations develop their own programs, they provide a forum for the listening community to raise issues of importance to them and facilitate their own dialogue on these topics. They give communities an opportunity to strengthen their organizational capabilities and to build alliances for action through their programs. They enable poor communities to inform themselves about issues arising in public services, to mobilize and share information, engage each other, and to develop their skills in pressing government officials to be accountable. All of these aspects contribute to changing officials' calculus and incentives and encouraging them to behave as responsive public servants. In developing their skills in balanced reporting and analysis of issues, community radio stations can also play a vital role in conflict prevention and postconflict reconciliation.

Box 58 highlights CDD project support for community radio in Timor-Leste and the role of community radio in making local government accountable in Ghana. As noted in Box 55, a large CDD project in Nigeria—Fadama III—is also poised to finance community radio stations in several states.

Development Communications Assistance

Development communications is a growing area of donor assistance, and has evolved from equipping government with communications strategies to a much broader, strategic orientation to the

Box 58. Community Driven Development and Post-Conflict Reconstruction: Timor-Leste

Since 2000, the now completed World Bank supported Community Empowerment and Local Governance Projects (CEP) began assisting Timorese communities to reconstruct their physical, economic, and social infrastructures destroyed by the violence of 1999. This project gave communities small grants for infrastructure and economic activities, supported cultural heritage and social reconciliation activities, and also provided direct assistance to community radio. Under the last component, CEP was able to support and scale up grassroots media development, particularly community broadcasting, by funding the training of district reporters to support the national public broadcaster and helping establish eight community radios in selected districts afterward. As of April 2007, seven out of eight community radio stations were broadcasting (the eighth is facing technical problems that are being addressed). As part of this effort, CEP's community radio component also helped established a Community Radio Centre (CRC) in Dili, which continues to serve as a support hub for the network of community radios. The CRC is a member of the larger community radio association of Timor-Leste (ARKTL). The CRC's mandate is to support these stations with training, technical assistance (maintenance and operations), and to promote opportunities for partnership and networking with different groups—including donors—to build their capacity and support development of public interest media and civic voice. Community radio in Timor-Leste continues to be a dynamic, though struggling, sector given the lack of a conducive enabling environment and funding opportunities to grow and develop. But it plays a strategic role in the current process of nation building, social reconciliation and development, and local governance.

Making Local Government More Accountable: Ghana. In Ghana, a community radio station has begun to broadcast debate on a district assembly floor. Others have weekly call-in and write-in programs that put tough questions to the district chief executives (DCE) and raise concerns needing immediate government attention. This often provokes the DCE or assemblymen to call in and talk the issue through while the program is still on the air. The community radio stations broadcast follow-up meetings with officials, and the reporting of inaction can get fairly intense until the public service that was promised is delivered, or the public funds that were stolen are returned. These transformations affecting public servants' incentives are expected to spread quickly once community radio stations can be licensed appropriately.

communications sector as a whole.[14] This area of work has the potential to support not only communications sector assessments, as currently, but also communications sector projects. These efforts are promising when they are supported by government commitment to freedom of information and expression and the cultivation of an engaged and informed society. Given its focus on enhancement of communication with the public sector, development communication has great potential to create a platform for the reform of ministries of information or communication and to help the dissemination of information from government to citizens and vice versa.

Convergences: Fostering Accountability, Engaged Societies, and Collective Leadership

Fostering robust, diverse, and participatory media is an integral part of furthering good governance and accountability. Pluralistic broadcasting can play a particularly powerful role because of its ability to include and shape social perspectives and capabilities, and its unmatched reach, especially to rural populations. It can foster information exchange and airing and sharing of diverse perspectives, showcase

---

[14]The director for Development Communications in a speech in March 2007 summarized an "empowered communication environment" that would:

1. Reform Ministries of Information—including delivering information as a service, and turning state broadcasters into public broadcasters, as a "development communicator";
2. Decentralize communications—taking communication beyond the capitals both physically and in terms of language;
3. Improve the functioning of private media—how to build financial sustainability, and support the material infrastructure;
4. Find out how people receive information and the factors that influence trust;
5. Amend the legal environment for communication—regulatory and licensing; but also taxation and import regimes, freedom of information, and criminal liable laws;
6. Build a more sustainable market for media and associated sector;
7. Build the capacity of civil society in relation to communication;
8. Improve the training academic pipeline for media workers; and
9. Explore the potential of new media to leapfrog ahead. Available at: *http://web.worldbank.org/wbsite/external/topics/extdevcommeng*.

analyses, and stimulate public discussion and comment on government action or inaction. This ongoing feedback, analysis, and discussion through the media, and more inclusively through broadcasting, is an important complement to governments' efforts to support development and to improve their own transparency, accountability, and effectiveness. Genuine accountability is a *continuous* process of interaction between government and the people. Limited solely to election times, such opportunities for feedback and policy corrections would verge on formalistic tokenism.

While development agencies have promoted policies to extend access to information—through, for instance, freedom of information legislation—they have rarely devoted equal attention to media independence, pluralism, accessibility, and capacity building at the beginning of the democratization process. However, enhancing horizontal communication in society, and the means to share diverse perspectives, is arguably just as necessary.

The scale of the challenge facing developing countries, in particular in setting up the robust and sustainable institutional structures that constitute the backbone of an enabling media environment, should not be underestimated. The creation of a genuinely independent broadcast regulator with the capacity and authority to develop the sector in the public interest; the transformation of usually state-controlled broadcasters into public service broadcasters; the facilitation of the emergence of both private sector and nonprofit community broadcasting with maximum potential to contribute to the public interest together represent a major undertaking. These are likely to be tackled at times incrementally, at times only through taking bold steps forward.

Even partial progress can lead to significant improvements in participation and voice. Moreover, governance improvements are likely to be better implemented and sustained where they are submitted to analysis and public scrutiny from diverse points of view. It thus makes sense to address the enabling environment for robust, diverse, and independent media—including broadcasting—as an early step in governance reform.

Incentives for diverse news reporting and issue analysis, and capacity development to improve the quality of media content, including broadcast programming, are also needed. Mentoring and training of reporters and editors, orientation and awareness-raising regarding codes of conduct and self-regulation within the industry all play a role. Exposing journalists to international practices in the field can help. All these opportunities can sharpen skills in fact-finding and research, fact-checking with multiple sources, and interview techniques. A critical feature of the media's ability to sustain their key role in society is an ingrained understanding among media workers of the importance of maintaining trust, independence, and integrity.

For broadcasters, this is a particularly important responsibility. Whether intentionally or not, broadcasters influence their audiences' tendencies and outlook, and so have a very real effect on society at large. What people hear every day over the airwaves has a pervasive impact on people's sense of what is normal and acceptable. This includes their inclination and ability to think critically, to listen actively or passively, to express their views openly and clearly or to stay withdrawn, to discuss differences in points of view analytically and respectfully or to become hostile and *ad hominum*.

The content and style of broadcasting can have a strong impact on the listening public's skills and interest in civic engagement, its ability to manage and prevent conflict, and its confidence to participate in and help shape the directions of their communities and society. In 1998, a local nongovernmental organization in southern Albania put it this way, when explaining why they planned to start a community radio station:

> There's a lot of help going to parliament and other structures of government in Albania. But here, people generally don't disagree strongly and still stay calm so they can keep talking. They take it personally and get angry with each other, and then get violent. We need talk shows and roundtables on the air, to *model* how to debate issues and deliberate, even with very different views. We need this to develop a culture of democracy.[15]

This explanation underlines the role of broadcasting, and particularly of community radio, as a stimulant to local deliberation and debate.

---

[15]Auron Tare, speaking on behalf of plans for Radio Butrinti, established in Saranda, Albania in 2000.

Regional and national media, by their nature, generally fail to establish that connection with local level realities, especially in countries with large poor populations often pushed to the margins of mainstream public debate. Here is where community radio can have a huge impact, helping the less well connected majority to have their concerns discussed.

Key Policy Reforms

Of all the measures discussed in this guide, several stand out as ones that demand priority attention and where significant progress can potentially be made. Overall, protection of freedom of expression is fundamental. Without it citizens can neither engage each other effectively nor hold their governments to account. And without it, independent media development will be confounded. In that context, three areas of reform are extremely important for broadcasting sector development:

1. Developing an effective and accountable regulator, independent of both government and commercial pressure;
2. Enabling critique of public officials the media, without fear of prosecution or retaliation;
3. Promoting diversity and civic voice including through community nonprofit broadcasting.

1. Create an effective and accountable broadcasting regulator independent of both government and commercial pressures.

Often a first major step in reforming the broadcasting sector is the creation of a broadcasting regulator that is independent both of government and of commercial interests. The task is not easy but merits early and concerted effort. The threat of regulatory capture—either by government or commercial interests—is ever present, especially in the early days when the regulator is building its credibility and capacity. One strategy for addressing this is to institute specific mechanisms for public review of its decisions and procedures, including means by which the public can participate, and to generally ensure a high level of transparency and accountability within the organization. The effect is to build public confidence, which in turn can enhance authority and autonomy.

2. Decriminalize defamation and remove protections for public officials.

It is important to ensure that the wider legal environment enables and, if possible, facilitates public critique and investigative reporting. This has a number of components, such as respect for the right to freedom of expression, and freedom of information laws, discussed in Part II of this guide. However, of all the perverse policies interfering with the robust functioning of the media for the public good, the excessive protection of officials from criticism, and the use of criminal sanctions for defamation, can have a particularly chilling effect on free discourse and thwart media's contribution. Given the political will, remedying this distortion would face few technical difficulties, and can make a significant difference to the practice of broadcasting journalism.

3. Promote diversity and civic voice: Open space for community nonprofit broadcasting and promote sustainable funding mechanisms for nonprofits.

The overall goal proposed here is the creation of an environment in which a range of different broadcast subsectors can emerge, from public service, to private sector, to community nonprofit, and quite a few variations in between. The precise configurations possible will depend on local circumstances and needs. But community nonprofit broadcasting, especially community radio, has a particular relevance in the context of a public interest approach given its capacity to address and create dialogue on matters of local interest; to cultivate habits and skills of citizen participation, including interacting with those in power; and to empower marginalized communities, including in their local languages. The impact of community radio, where it is given the opportunity to thrive, can be both direct and highly visible.

An important first step is to recognize these different broadcasting subsectors in law, and for the licensing and taxation regime to differentiate requirements for community nonprofit broadcasters from those applied to commercial operators, with a view to eliminating barriers to entry and enhancing diverse vehicles for public debate, particularly for the poor. Licensing for community nonprofit broadcasters should not impose fees, and should be streamlined in procedure. It should eliminate or greatly reduce technical requirements, compared to commercial broadcasters, and instead emphasize community participation in the ownership, management, and operation of the broadcasting station and support to the development and communication needs of the community served. Licensing for community nonprofit broadcasters should not place restrictions on their news and current events coverage, or uniform restrictions on their power and coverage; these should be determined instead on the basis of the needs of the community to be served and the topographical context.

The community nonprofit sector is usually built initially on the energy and commitment of the community itself. It can attract considerable donor support in some circumstances, but protracted reliance on this can have a negative impact. It is important to allow nonprofit broadcasters to mobilize resources from diverse sources, such as sponsorships, membership fees, announcements, and local advertising. A central challenge is how to provide an ongoing core income and to create the conditions that will allow it to attract a diversity of other sources of funding. A good approach will also open a degree of distance between local commercial media and the community nonprofit model by ensuring they do not directly compete, while maintaining complete autonomy from political interest by using a mechanism other than a government or parliamentary budgetary allocation. The French Radio Expression Support Fund (RESF), for example, gathers significant funding from a special tax levied on commercial radio and television advertising—a small tax on a relatively large pool—and redirects it toward "associative" radio, attaching certain conditions that include the capacity to attract local support and the production of quality programs of interest locally. These RESF resources are targeted to those stations that cannot mobilize more than 25% of their total resource needs from commercial advertising. Alternative public funding mechanisms are discussed in Chapter 12.

Capacity Building for Broadcasting Reform and Development

These policy and institutional steps should be complemented with the development of both regulators' and broadcasters' capacities.

As new systems are put in place to simplify and accelerate licensing and frequency assignment to community nonprofits, the staff responsible for implementing these systems will need concerted training. Representatives of community broadcasters should participate in the same training since it is likely that the dialogue that will emerge from this shared experience will enable the procedures to be better tailored to realities, and both applicants and regulators get a clear sense of how the procedures are supposed to be implemented.

Capacity building for broadcasters is also an important factor in enabling the sector to deliver on the public interest goals of cultivating active, constructive, social engagement. A key shortcoming at present is the lack of capacity of those who work in the broadcasting industry to maximize its potential for enhancing accountability, dialogue, and interaction. Such programs should of course include training in program production, moderating, and reporting. But they should also include training in how to structure roundtable discussions and clarify and enforce ground rules, how to encourage a diversity of views and a practice of acknowledging and building on each others' contributions, how to demonstrate critical analyses and deliberative pursuit of issues, how to maintain and encourage calmness and respect for all.

For community nonprofit broadcasting, this extends to training of community reporters and producers, and stimulating people at the grass roots—even the very poor and marginalized—to raise questions that concern them, to critically evaluate the information they get, and to identify sources of information and local professional experts—the local nurse, the agricultural extension officer—to give regular programs and answer questions on the air. This mode of thinking and doing is one way of nurturing people's capacities for collective leadership.

Successfully implementing steps toward a public interest approach to broadcasting demands leadership—at the political level in the early stages and, as progress is made, at every level within the sectors, in public service, private and community nonprofit sectors. Moreover, the very purpose of a broadcasting sector that encourages informed engagement is that it builds leadership capacities and practices throughout society.

As experts pointed out consistently at a "Leadership Matters" conference in April 2007,[16] leadership is not an individual responsibility or

---

[16]World Bank Capacity Day 2007: "Leadership Matters—Vision, Effectiveness, and Accountability," Washington, DC, April 19, 2007.

ability—it is a collective process. Building capacity for leadership needs to be experiential, iterative, and continuous. It is about building collaborative capacities, abilities to respect diversity and work together despite differences, developing capacities to deliberate, analyze, propose and cocreate the future.

A public interest approach to broadcasting development has the same goals.

Bibliographical Annex

This Bibliographical Annex is a collection of core documents and reference materials designed to provide readers with summaries and links to the original text of source materials referred to in the guide, as well as other tools and materials that readers might find useful. These materials are organized into the following categories:

1. Media and Development   (267–279)
2. Community Media   (280–289)
3. Communication and Development   (290–294)
4. Financing Broadcast Media   (295–297)
5. Targeting an Audience for Broadcast Media   (298–299)
6. Sustaining Broadcast Media   (300–301)
7. Tool Kits and Handbooks on Community Media   (302–309)
8. Mass Media: Gender, Race, and Youth Issues   (310–311)
9. Information Communication Technology (ICTs)   (312–316)
10. Assessing and Measuring the Impact of Information Communication Technology (ICTs)   (317–319)
11. Impact Assessments, Monitoring, and Evaluation (General)   (320–323)
12. International Declarations on Development and Freedoms of Expression, Communication, and the Press   (324–326)
13. International Conventions and Covenants   (327)
14. Responsibilities of Special Rapporteurs on Freedom of Expression   (328–329)
15. Legal and Regulatory Development Frameworks for Broadcast Media   (330–332)
16. Freedom of Expression, Access to Information, and Press Freedom   (333–353)
17. Laws Evincing Good Practice on Freedoms of Information, Communication, and the Press   (354–360)
18. Mass Media and Governance   (361–365)

This annex is designed to be used by government officials, media practitioners, civil society groups, and members of the general public who are interested in good practices in broadcasting policy, law, and regulation. While this annex is not exhaustive, it does provide an introduction to important broadcasting issues; key international standards and good practice standard documents; useful materials that focus on evaluating communication, participatory projects, and experiences; impact assessment methodologies; useful instructional material to create and sustain broadcasting outlets (including community radio stations), salient cases, and comments on freedoms of expression, communication, and the press; guidance on creation of locally specific policies, legislation, regulation, and institutions; and much more.

TABLE 1 Media and Development

Coverage	Year	Topic	Source	Summary	Website
Global	2006	Country Profiles	BBC Monitoring	Webpage provides interactive drop menus, which allows users to access full profiles of every country and territory in the world. Each profile includes information on history, politics, economics, and background on key institutions. The webpage additionally allows users to access audio and video clips from BBC archives.	http://news.bbc.co.uk/1/hi/country_profiles/default.stm
Global	2006	Media Bias and Reputation	Matthew Gentzkow and Jesse M. Shapiro	Article examines how and why an uninformed consumer generally infers that the quality of an information source is higher quality when its content (or reporting) conforms to that consumer's prior expectations. It uses evidence to build a model of media bias in which firms slant their reports toward the prior beliefs of their target customers to build a reputation for quality. The article concludes, as the model indicates, that bias will be less severe when consumers receive independent evidence on the true state of the world and that competition between independently owned news outlets can reduce bias.	http://faculty.chicagogsb.edu/matthew.gentzkow/research/BiasReputation.pdf
Global	2006	Learning for Social Change: Exploring Concepts, Methods and Practice	Peter Taylor, Andrew Deak, Jethro Pettit, and Isabel Vogel Institute of Development Studies (IDS)	Report examines perspectives on how to facilitate learning to bring about social change. It summarizes these perspectives from dialogue that occurred through e-forums and an international workshop in 2006.	http://www.pnet.ids.ac.uk/docs/FLASC.pdf

Coverage	Year	Topic	Source	Summary	Website
Global	2005	Public Service Broadcasting—Cultural and Educational Dimensions	UNESCO	The report examines and proposes strategies to strengthen the cultural and educational functions of public service broadcasting, in light of new technological and communication environments throughout the world. Chapter 1 examines how the idea of public service broadcasting has evolved and how it is linked to the idea of citizenship, which requires that it be de-linked from the political authority of the state and the economic leverage of the market. Chapter 2 suggests that a strictly commercial approach to television (even in large, rich markets) is not reconcilable with cultural goals. Rather, it argues that broadcasting policy should provide for the maintenance, development, and support of strong, politically independent public institutions. Chapter 3 provides an overview and analysis of satellite broadcasting services in Asia. Chapter 4 examines the cultural and educational functions of public service broadcasting in Western Europe. Chapter 5 assesses the status of culture and education in electronic media programs in Eastern and Central Europe. Chapter 6 examines the educational and cultural functions of broadcasting liberalization in Sub-Saharan Africa. Finally, Chapter 7 explores the public service functions of community radio and television in Latin America.	http://portal.unesco.org/ci/en/ev.php-URL_ID=19141&URL_DO=DO_TOPIC&URL_SECTION=201.html (available in English and French)
Global	2004	Read All About It! Understanding the Role of Media in Economic Development	Christopher Coyne and Peter Leeson	Article suggests that media is integral to economic reform, because of its consensus-building potential. It uses game theory to demonstrate how a free-media sector supports economic development by transforming potential conflict into coordination. A free-media sector that operates in a favorable legal environment and provides quality information is also	http://www.blackwellsynergy.com/doi/pdf/10.1111/j.0023-5962.2004.00241.x

				a mechanism for coordinating the activities of politicians with the demands of the populace. The article also examines case studies to illustrate successful instances of this type of coordination (Poland, Hungary), continued prevalence of conflict (Ukraine), and coordination not in the public interest (Bulgaria).	ftp://ftp.fao.org/docrep/fao/008/y5983e/y5983e00.pdf
Global	2004	Communication for Development Roundtable Report: Focus on Sustainable Development	Food and Agriculture Organization of the United Nations 9th United Nations Communication for Development Roundtable	Report provides an overview of the role of communication in development. It introduces concepts associated with the phenomenon of the "information society" and sets out reasons why the rapid expansion of ICTs has not bridged the gap between knowledge and information, a result of which is limited participation by many populations in the developing world in the development process. It additionally offers recommendations on how to scale up communication for development, build a communication component into development projects from inception, and to encourage national frameworks to support free and pluralistic information systems and community media. It additionally calls for improvements in research and training for communication for development practitioners; the development of new tools and skills for evaluation and impact assessments; the building of alliances; and the fostering of local, national, and regional communication for development processes.	
Global	2004	Supporting Public Service Broadcasting: Learning from Bosnia and Herzegovina's Experience	Alexandra Wilde, with Elizabeth McCall United Nations Development Program	Report examines broadcast media sector reform, with particular regard to public service broadcasting, with a view to meeting democratic governance and poverty reduction objectives. The report is primarily informed by a case study on broadcasting restructuring in Bosnia and Herzegovina.	http://www.undp.org/governance/docs/A2I_Pub_PublicServiceBroadcasting.pdf

Coverage	Year	Topic	Source	Summary	Website
Global	2003	A Module for Media Intervention: Content Regulation in Post-Conflict Zones	Peter Krug and Monroe Price	Report examines how management in post-conflict countries of legislative and executive functions by international governmental organizations affects media regulation. It analyzes the standards used by the international community relating to media regulation, the mechanisms used to enforce its rules, and how the resulting mechanisms compare to universal standards and good practice.	http://papers.ssrn.com/sol3/papers.cfm?abstract_id=368661
Global	2003	The Diffusion of Innovations	Everett Rogers	Book sets out a theory that analyzes the adaptation of a new innovation. The theory is comprised of the following four elements: 1) the innovation; 2) communication channels; 3) time; and 4) the social system.	
Global	2003	Broadcasting and Development: Options for the World Bank	Carter Eltzroth and Charles Kenny	Working paper argues that broadcasting can be an important source of economic growth and poverty reduction in developing countries. The working paper cites research that indicates that at least 75% of the population of the world is within "easy access" of some form of broadcast technology, particularly radios. This access is beneficial because information exchange proliferates valuable social, economic, and political information, as well as educational and practical information that encourages people in rural areas of the developing world to become more fiscally efficient and aware of employment, investment, and trade opportunities. Innovations in ICT development increase the appeal of broadcasting, which broadens the reach of broadcasting, which enables more people in the developing world to have access to information, which encourages greater fiscal responsibility as well as social and political participation. The working paper provides examples of how this process has culminated in cognizable instances of economic growth and poverty reduction.	http://iris37.worldbank.org/domdoc/PRD/Other/PRDDContainer.nsf/WB_View Attachments?ReadForm&ID=85256D2400766CC78525709E005988CF&

Region	Year	Title	Author / Publisher	Description	URL
Global	2003	Use and Abuse of Media in Vulnerable Societies	Mark Frohardt and Jonathan Temin United States Institute of Peace	Report provides an overview of ways in which media might be manipulated to instigate violent conflict. It develops structural and content indicators to evaluate whether media sectors in certain countries are susceptible to this manner of manipulation. The structural indicators include: media variety and plurality, the degree of journalist isolation, and the legal environment for media. The content indicators include content designed to create fear or resignation. The report supports efforts to monitor these indicators in media sectors, and sets out methods for intervention to combat the manipulation of the media.	http://www.usip.org/pubs/specialreports/sr110.html
Global	2002	The Right to Tell: The Role of Mass Media in Economic Development	Roumeen Islam (Editor) The World Bank (WBI Development Studies)	Book compiles a series of articles from nineteen contributors, which collectively argue that an independent press is essential to sound and equitable economic development because it helps to give a voice to the poor and the disenfranchised. In nineteen articles, the book explores the watch-dog role of the media, with particular emphasis on the power of the media to increase government and corporate accountability. It also explores policies throughout the developing world that prevent the media from exercising this watch-dog role. The book further assesses the way in which the media function, to transmit new ideas and information. Some contributors present case studies of challenges faced by the media in specific countries, including Bangladesh, Egypt, the former Soviet Union, Thailand, and Zimbabwe.	http://publications.worldbank.org/ecommerce/catalog/product?context=drilldown&item%5fid=1575968 (for purchase)
Global	2002	Empowerment and Poverty Reduction: A Sourcebook	Deepa Narayan The World Bank	Book provides an overview of empowerment from an institutional perspective and discusses the relationship between individual and collective assets and capabilities, including collective action. It provides key elements of an empowering	http://siteresources.worldbank.org/INTEMPOWERMENT/Resources/486312109509 49545 94/draft.pdf

Coverage	Year	Topic	Source	Summary	Website
				approach, identifies conditions that help determine what kind of approach is feasible in different contexts, and summarizes lessons learned (from World Bank experience) to implement a systematic approach to empowerment. It includes references to the importance of free and pluralistic media, as well as the fundamental importance of access to information, community media, and more.	
Global	2002	Media and the Empowerment of Communities for Social Change	Chido E.F. Matewa (A thesis submitted to the University of Manchester for the degree of PhD in the Faculty of Education)	Thesis paper examines the extent to which participatory radio production contributes to the empowerment and advancement of women and marginalized communities. It additionally examines how community needs interests are served by participatory radio production. The paper's methodology included interviews; observations of radio listeners clubs; research mobilization of related articles, documents, annual and general reports; and more.	http://www.comminit.com/evaluations/idmatewa/sld-2241.html
Global	2002	Strengthening Partnerships among Local FM Radio Networks and Reproductive Health Agencies on HIV/AIDS–A Review of the Effectiveness of Local FM Radio in Promoting Reproductive Health, HIV/AIDS Prevention, and Gender Equity	United Nations Population Fund (UNPF) and Population Media Center (PMC)	Paper provides an overview of how local FM radio has been used in countries throughout the world to promote health and development goals. It was created to inform United Nations Population Fund country representatives of the potential use of local and community radio to achieve health objectives.	http://www.unfpa.org/upload/lib_pub_file/486_filename_157_filename_commmunityradio.pdf

Global	2002	Distributing News and Political Influence	David Strömberg Institute for International Economic Studies, Stockholm University, and Centre for Economic Policy Research	Chapter examines the effect of mass media on the recipients of the political information it transmits, as well as what information is actually received. It states that this process influences policy formation because politicians generally target informed members of the public and refer to well-covered issues because informed people are more likely to vote than uniformed people, and are also more likely to vote for the candidate who furthers their interest. The chapter additionally demonstrates that voters are more responsive to favorable policies that are thoroughly exposed by the media.	http://www.iies.su.se/~stromber/wbbook.pdf
Global	2002	Mass Media Competition, Political Competition, and Public Policy	David Strömberg Institute for International Economic Studies, Stockholm University, and Centre for Economic Policy Research	Article examines the incentives had by the media to deliver news to different groups and argues that the mass media affects policy because it provides most of the information people use to ascertain their voting preferences and offers a model that maps this phenomenon.	http://www.iies.su.se/~stromber/MediaComp.pdf (see also) http://www.iies.su.se/~stromber/Radio.pdf
Global	2002	World Development Report 2002: Building Institutions for Markets	The World Bank	Chapter 10 of the report focuses on the development implications of the media (which the report defines to include broadcasting technologies, such as radio, television, and the Internet). Specifically, the report examines the role of the media as a beneficial academic instrument, as a mechanism to improve public health, and as a mechanism to affect politics and culture. It goes on to state that to be effective, the media must: 1) be independent/accountable; 2) be characterized by high quality reporting; and 3) enjoy a broad reach (to as much of the public as possible).	http://www.worldbank.org/wdr/2001/fulltext/fulltext2002.htm

Coverage	Year	Topic	Source	Summary	Website
Global	2001	World Development Report 2000/2001: Attacking Poverty	The World Bank	Report examines the various dimensions of poverty, including the lack of adequate food, shelter, education, health, and other deprivations, as well as vulnerabilities to health problems, economic dislocation, and natural disasters. It goes on to show how poverty yields powerlessness, with particular regard to key social, political, and economic decisions. The report specifically identifies the lack of a freely flowing information exchange as a key barrier to economic development throughout the developing world, and remarks on the importance of ICTs.	http://web.worldbank.org/WBSITE/EXTERNAL/TOPICS/EXTPOVERTY/0,,contentMDK:20195989~piPK:216618~theSitePK:336992,00.html
Global	2001	A Passion for Radio: Radio Waves and Community	Bruce Girard (editor)	Book provides twenty-one alternative radio experiences, written by people from various countries who are actively involved in the medium.	http://www.comunica.org/passion/pdf/passion4radio.pdf
Global	2001	Who Owns the Media?	Simeon Djankov, Caralee McLiesh, Tatiana Nenova, and Andrei Shleifer World Bank Policy Research Working Paper No. 2620 and Harvard Institute of Economic Research Paper No. 1919	Working paper examines the patterns of media ownership in ninety-seven countries throughout the world. It concludes that in almost every country, the largest media firms are owned by either the government or by private families. It states that government ownership is more pervasive in broadcasting than in printed media, and is generally associated with less press freedom; few, if any, political and economic rights; and inferior social outcomes, particularly in health and education. It further states that these negative aspects of government control are not restricted to government monopolies of the media.	http://papers.ssrn.com/sol3/papers.cfm?abstract_id=267386#PaperDownload

| Global | 1999 | Development as Freedom | Amartya Sen | Book states that development has been reconceived by the promotion of human freedom and that open dialogue, civil freedoms, and political liberties are requisite to achieve sustainable development. The book tests this argument using several case studies, including countries in Africa, the Far East, and the former Soviet bloc. It focuses on the individual, in terms of agency and as a participant in economic, social, and political actions. The book states that there are five distinct types of instrumental freedom: 1) Political Freedoms: opportunities to determine who should govern and on what principles, including the freedom of political expression and an uncensored press; 2) Economic Freedoms: opportunities to use economic resources for consumption, production, or exchange; 3) Social Opportunities: societal approaches to education, health care, etc., which influence both individuals' substantive freedom to live better and their effective participation in economic and political activities; 4) Transparency Guarantees: the need for openness and the freedom to deal with one another under guarantees of disclosure and lucidity; and 5) Protective Security: the need for a social safety net to prevent public misery, or even starvation and death. The book further demonstrates that development requires the removal of major sources of "unfreedom" (poverty, tyranny, poor economic opportunities, systematic social deprivation, neglect of public facilities, intolerance, and over-activity of repressive states) and that the market is generally able to contribute to high economic growth and to overall economic progress. The book warns that the importance of the market must be secondary to the direct significance of the freedom to interchange (words, goods, gifts, etc.). |

Coverage	Year	Topic	Source	Summary	Website
Global	1999	Radio and HIV/AIDS: Making a Difference—The Essential Handbook UNAIDS Media Action International	Gordon Adam and Nicola Harford	Handbook examines the role of broadcasting in HIV/AIDS prevention. It focuses primarily on commercial and public service broadcasting.	http://data.unaids.org/Publications/IRC-pub05/JC429-Radio_en.pdf
Global	1995	Our Creative Diversity: Report of the World Commission on Culture and Development	UNESCO	Report provides a reevaluation of development processes, to attend to the needs of various cultural groups; generally addresses the role of media in development, including the imbalance of media control, which prevents many cultural voices from being heard. It concludes with a list of ten action items designed to sustain a continuing public forum on culture and development.	http://unesdoc.unesco.org/images/0010/001055/105586fo.pdf
Asia	2001	Media versus Globalization and Localization	Jan Servaes and Rico Lie	Article examines the contemporary disagreement regarding how to conceptualize globalization in terms of its structural, socioeconomic consequences, and which implications it has on state power and governance. It notes that this debate is essentially comprised of three separate theses on globalization: 1) the (hyper)globalist perspective, 2) the skeptical or traditionalist perspective, and 3) the transformationalist perspective. The article examines these different approaches to globalization in light of Asian media and culture.	http://www.wacc.org.uk/wacc/content/pdf/1144

Region	Year	Title	Author	Description	URL
Chile	2005	América Latina y las Fortalezas de la Radiodifusión Diario electrónico: "Radio Universidad de Chile"	Juan Pablo Cárdenas	Web page provides information on and a detailed electronic diary about the influence and importance of radio in Chile, and in Latin America in general (including community radio).	http://www.radio.uchile.cl/notas.aspx?idNota=18169 (in Spanish)
East-Central Europe	1999	Using the Principle of Publicity to Create Public Service Media	Slavko Splichal The World Association for Christian Communication	Article provides an overview of how mass media might be made accessible to citizens and used as a public instrument for the benefit of citizens, rather than as a vehicle for reaching and persuading potential consumers and voters, and/or for generating profit and power. It states that public service broadcasting should receive public funding and not be controlled by the state or commercial interests.	http://www.wacc.org.uk/wacc/publications/media_development/archive/1999_3/using_the_principle_of_publicity_to_create_public_service_media
Ghana	2001	Regional Radio: A Response by the Ghana Broadcasting Corporation to Democratization and Competition	Carla Heath	Working paper examines the reaction of the state-owned Ghana Broadcasting Corporation to the legalization of private broadcasting in Ghana: the opening of regional FM radio stations. It provides an overview of the political and economic context in which the stations were established, their structures, and examines their programming. The paper concludes that with these new stations, the Ghana Broadcasting Corporation is expanding and enhancing its public service mandate, though institutional structures and scarce financial resources have combined to prevent the GBC from becoming independent of vested interests from government, commerce, and nongovernmental organizations.	http://www.cjc-online.ca/viewarticle.php?id=620

Coverage	Year	Topic	Source	Summary	Website
India	2001	Enlightened Regulation: The Future Indian Way?	William Crawley and David Page	Article provides an overview of the Indian broadcasting experience, which serves as a case study of how democracies should carefully balance the needs of the market with the interests of civil society. The article states India's broadcasting media has been driven by advertising and international business and is characterized by a relatively new sense of diversity, which has resulted in fewer public broadcasters.	http://www.opendemocracy.net/ecology-publicservice/article_42.jsp
Mexico	1995	Social Uses and Radio Practices: The Use of Participatory Radio by Ethnic Minorities in Mexico	Lucila Vargas International Communication and Popular Culture—Westview Press	Book examines how and why race, ethnicity, class, and gender affect the extent and quality of people's participation in development efforts in Mexico. The book (Chapter 2) sets out a methodology for examining the social and cultural implications of participatory radio.	http://www.comminit.com/materials/materials/materials-1146.html (for purchase)
Nepal	2004	Come Gather around Together—An Examination of Radio Listening Groups in Fulbari, Nepal *Gazette: The International Journal For Communication Studies,* Vol. 66(1): 63–86	Suruchi Sood, Manisha SenGupta, Pius Raj Mishra, and Caroline Jacoby Johns Hopkins Bloomberg School of Public Health Center for Communication Programs, Baltimore, MD	Study explores the extent to which listening groups—or those groups exposed to broadcast media—have higher levels of correct knowledge about family planning, including intent to practice, and personal advocacy compared to nonlistening group members. The study concludes that listening groups' exposure to radio programs was positively related to correct knowledge about family planning.	http://gaz.sagepub.com/cgi/reprint/66/1/63

Peru	2006	Voces y Movidas Radiociudadanas –Experiencias, Itinerarios, y Reflexiones desde la Coordinadora Nacional de Radio	Jorge Acevedo (editor) Coordinadora Nacional de Radio	Book describes radio as a tool for democratic participation and human development in Peru, using case studies and firsthand accounts on the experience of those that have been involved in radio (including community radio).	http://www.cnr.org.pe/voces.pdf
Sub-Saharan Africa	2006	Africa Media Development Initiative Research Reports	BBC World Service Trust	Website surveys how donors, investors, media, and media development organizations might collaborate to support and strengthen Africa's media sector. It provides a series of seventeen reports on the state of the media in Angola, Botswana, Cameroon, Democratic Republic of Congo, Ethiopia, Ghana, Kenya, Mozambique, Nigeria, Senegal, Sierra Leone, Somalia, South Africa, Tanzania, Uganda, Zambia, and Zimbabwe. Each report includes information about one of these Sub-Saharan African countries and examines media sector developments and emerging challenges to be faced by future media development activities. Each report also offers a specific case study that demonstrates good practices in media development in that country.	http://www.bbc.co.uk/worldservice/trust/researchlearning/story/2006/12/061212_amdi_index.shtml
United States	1998	Public Television in America Project: Public Television and New Technologies	Monroe Price	Article discusses the challenges and missed opportunities associated with the role of public television in the United States.	http://www.iiclp.org/1_1998/iiclp_webdoc_2_1_1998.html

TABLE 2 Community Media

Coverage	Year	Topic	Source	Summary	Website
Global	n/a	Civic Voice: Empowering the Poor through Community Radio	The World Bank	Provides an overview of how public interest radio programming, including by community radio stations, can play a vital role in empowering poor people, accelerating community and local level problem-solving, and introducing more demand for accountability. It additionally provides background information on the World Bank's support to community radio in the context of several operational projects.	http://siteresources.worldbank.org/INTCEERD/Resources/RADIObrief.pdf (see also) http://siteresources.worldbank.org/INTCEERD/Resources/RADIO_EACreport.pdf
Global	2005	Community-based Networks and Innovative Technologies: New Models to Serve and Empower the Poor	Seán Ó Siochrú and Bruce Girard, United Nations Development Program	Report examines how community-based networks and technology, including community radio and related technologies, might facilitate economic and social development, particularly strengthening the voice of communities. It states that despite ever-increasing access to information communication technology, many areas—particularly rural and poor urban—continue to be underserved. It suggests that community-owned infrastructure and networks might effectively combat this trend. It will allow previously underserved people to draw on community resources and labor, which will promote sustainability, and expand in contexts previously characterized by market instability. The report argues in favor of community-owned networks because they have a stake in the continued development of the community.	http://www.propoor-ictl.net/content/pdfs/00_UNDP_Report_p.1-58.pdf
Global	2005	Public Service Broadcasting: A Best Practices Source Book	Indrajit Banerjee and Kalinga Seneviratne, AMIC (editors) UNESCO	Sourcebook provides an overview of best practices concerning public service broadcasting, designed for media professionals, decision makers, students, and the general public. The sourcebook examines legal, regulatory, financial, and other	http://portal.unesco.org/ci/en.php-URL_ID=20469&URL_DO=DO_TOPIC&URL_SECTION=201.html

Region	Year	Title	Author	Description	URL
				significant issues, such as editorial independence, universality, secured funding free of all pressures, distinctiveness, diversity, representativeness, unbiased information, education and enlightenment, social cohesion, citizenship, public accountability, and credibility.	
Global	2005	Evaluation of UNESCO's Community Multimedia Centers: Final Report	Heather Creech, et al. UNESCO International Institute for Sustainable Development	Report examines the pilot phase of UNESCO's Community Multimedia Center model	http://portal.unesco.org/ci/en/files/22129/11477736959CMC_Evaluation_Final.pdf/CMC+Evaluation_Final.pdf
Global	2005	Community Radio Licensing and Policy: An Overview	Kate Coyer	Working paper provides a general overview of the purposes and impacts of community radio, including its gradual emergence in national policies throughout the globe, as well as an examination of regulation trends, community radio legislation, and licensing issues. It additionally provides a series of examples of community radio in various cultural and geographic contexts.	http://www.lse.ac.uk/Depts/global/EventsPDFs/GCSWorkshop_Annenberg/Coyer.pdf
Global	2003	Social Accountability and Public Voice through Community Radio Programming	World Bank	Note examines how and why public interest and community broadcasting is a sustainable, interactive asset for broad-based, participatory development. It shows that community media are particularly important for people in the developing world to provide them with access to information and enable them to articulate their concerns, give feedback to government, and marshal information and local expertise to combat local problems and grasp local opportunities. The note also states that community broadcasting allows populations in developing countries to be heard, become informed, shape knowledgeable opinions, learn	http://siteresources.worldbank.org/INTCEERD/Resources/RADIO_sdn76.pdf (see also) http://siteresources.worldbank.org/INTCEERD/Resources/RADIOtranscript_part1.pdf (see also) http://siteresources.worldbank.org/INTCEERD/Resources/RADIOtranscript_part2.pdf Global

283

Coverage	Year	Topic	Source	Summary	Website
				the give-and-take of informed dialogue, and to become more decisive agents in their own development, which might yield social accountability, decentralization, democratization, and poverty reduction.	
Global	2003	Community Media and the Information Society	Steve Buckley UNESCO	Report examines the so-called digital divide and recharacterizes it as a "communications divide" in light of the unequal access of poor people to the global communications environment and the absence of structural measures and commitments to redress past imbalances. The report states that these people are thus deprived of the freedoms of information and of expression. To counteract this lack of access, the report suggests that community media are a vital means to enable public participation, strengthen cultural and linguistic diversity, and to promote gender equitable information society that includes the voices of the poor and the marginalized.	http://ifex.org/en/content/view/full/67461/
Global	2001	Community Radio—The New Tree of Speech	Steve Buckley Imfundo Knowledge Bank and the United Kingdom Department for International Development	Report provides an overview of the concept of the "digital divide" and examines the need for investment in the information infrastructure of developing countries, particularly community media. It further examines potential challenges to information infrastructure development, such as continuing mistrust among some communities in the developing world of advanced communication systems.	http://imfundo.digitalbrain.com/imfundo/web/tech/documents/kb19/kb19.pdf
Global	2001	Making Waves: Stories of Participatory Communication for Social Change	Alfonso Gumucio-Dagron The Rockefeller Foundation	Book contains fifty case studies (in story form), half of which detail community radio experiences in Africa, Asia, and Latin America. It further examines the impact of community radio on social change and community development.	http://www.comminit.com/making-waves.html

Region	Year	Title / Author / Publisher	Description	URL
Global	2000	Promoting Community Media in Africa S. T. Kwame Boafo (editor) UNESCO	Book provides case studies to present challenges faced by community media in African countries, such as insufficient economic, technical, and human resources.	http://www.unesco.org/ webworld/publications/ community_media/
Global	1991	Les Mille et un Mondes– Manuel de Radio Rurale François Querre FAO	Handbook examines several types of programming that might be used by community radio stations. It also provides guidance for community radio practitioners, in terms of south-south participation and creating programming that respects local cultures.	(available in French and English)
Afghanistan	2002	The Potential for Community Radio in Afghanistan Bruce Girard and Jo van der Spek Communication Assistance Foundation	Study examines the potential of and provides recommendations for the establishment of community-based radio in Afghanistan. It additionally provides examples of how community radio is able to support community development. It was designed to provide agencies and organizations considering supporting radio, media, or communication activities in the Afghanistan.	http://comunica.org/ afghanistan/cr_afghan.pdf
Australia, Canada, France, Holland, Ireland, and South Africa	2001	Community Radio in a Global Context: A Comparative Analysis in Six Countries Eryl Price-Davies and Jo Tacchi Community Media Association	Report provides an overview and comparison of community radio in Australia, Canada, France, Holland, Ireland, and South Africa to formulate specific recommendations related to the development and implementation of the "Access Radio" scheme in the United Kingdom.	http://www.commedia.org.uk/ about-community-media/ publications/publication-items/ community-radio-in-a-global-context/ (for purchase)
Bolivia	2004	Community Radio in Bolivia: The Miners' Radio Stations Alan O'Connor (editor) The Edwin Mellen Press	Paper examines the history and development of miners' radio stations in Bolivia and presents valuable lessons for community radio in general.	

Coverage	Year	Topic	Source	Summary	Website
Bolivia	2001	Las Radios Populares en la Construcción de la Ciudadanía—Enseñanzas de la Experiencia de ERBOL en Bolivia	Carlos A. Camacho Azurduy Universidad Andina Simón Bolívar (UASB)	Book examines community radio stations affiliated with ERBOL (the main network of community radios in Bolivia), in terms of whether their programming content promoted democratic participation. It additionally explores the impact of some of these community radios on public opinion (see Chapter IX) and provides its methodology in an annex.	
Eastern Democratic Republic of the Congo	2003	Radio Maendeleo and the Regional Peace Process in Eastern Congo—A political analysis prepared for International Media Support based on an assessment mission to South Kivu	Bjørn Willum	Report examines the role of Radio Maendeleo, a local community radio station based in Bukavu (Eastern Democratic Republic of the Congo) in the regional peace process in South Kivu. The report concludes that Radio Maendeleo played a positive role in informing the local population in and around Bukavu about development issues and local politics as well as coordinating NGO work. It went on that the station's limited broadcasting range prevented it from playing a larger, more constructive role in the regional peace process.	http://www.i-m-s.dk/media/pdf/Radio%20Maendeleo%20and%20the%20regional%20peace%20process%20in%20Eastern%20Congo%20by%20Bjrn%20Willum%202014%20October%202003.pdf
Europe	1998	Radio Pública Local	Manuel Chaparro Escudero Fragua Editorial	Report examines local and community radio in Europe, with a focus on Spain and local public radio stations in the Andalucia region. It provides an overview of how municipal radio stations brought about community-level telecommunications democratization and media decentralization.	

Country	Year	Title	Author/Organization	Description	URL
Ghana	n/a	Radios Communautaire: Apprendre a Participer—Un Manuel de Formation	Wilna W. Quarmyne Panos Afrique de l'Ouest	Training manual for community radio staff includes chapters on community radio programming and participatory acting research, as well as how to engage community actors and facilitate community participation.	http://www.panos-ao.org/spip.php?article3385
Ghana	2003	Enhancing Community over the Airwaves: Community Radio in a Ghanaian Fishing Village	Blythe McKay	Study analyzes the role of Radio Ada in the livelihood of fishermen in southeast Ghana. Following in-depth interviews, Participatory Rural Appraisal (PRA) activities, participant observation, and document analysis, the study concludes that fishermen in southeast Ghana rely on Radio Ada (among other media) for information to sustain their livelihoods, because it provides useful information related to fishing; promotes culture, identity, and community; provides access to news; creates opportunities for voice/dialogue; and establishes trust on local and regional levels.	http://www.comminit.com/evaluations/eval2005/thinking-1408.html
India	2005	Community Radio in India: A Study	Kanchan Kumar S N School of Communication, University of Hyderabad	Paper provides four case studies of grassroots projects using community radio for development. These case studies evaluate community radio initiatives through interviews with project managers and NGO personnel, as well as focus group discussions on the benefits of community radio. The publication provides a list of questions that were used during focus group discussions.	http://www.comminit.com/evaluations/eval2005/evaluations-110.html
India	2002	Community Radio Programs—India	Population Foundation of India	Paper provides overview of the processes by which the Population Foundation of India created two community radio programs to teach listening groups about customs and practices of the tribal community.	http://www.comminit.com/experiences/pdskdv42002/experiences-1279.html (see also) http://www.comminit.com/evaluations/idkdv2002/sld-2364.html

Coverage	Year	Topic	Source	Summary	Website
Latin America	2001	La Radio Popular Frente al Nuevo Siglo: Estudio de Vigencia e Incidencia	Andrés Geerts y Victor van Oeyen (editors) ALER	Book examines the impact of community radio in Latin America. The methodology included fieldwork and interviews with staff and audiences of seventy-four community radio stations in twelve Latin American countries. The Annex 2 provides a list of the instruments used to mobilize research.	http://www.comminit.com/ evaluations/idmay15/ sld-2298.html
Latin America	2001	Siguen Vigentes las Radios Populares?	Hernán Gutierrez and María Cristina Matta (editors) ALER	Book surveys the opinions of thirty communication specialists working in Latin America, and provides an overview of popular community radio broadcasting in the region. The book includes information on the impact of community radio on social change in Latin America in recent history.	
Mali	2001	Impact Data—Radio Douentza	Mary Myers	Project description provides information on Radio Douentza, one of the first independent community radio stations in Mali. Impact data indicates that the station has positively impacted local communities despite a relatively small operational budget, and was widely regarded as a primary source of information. For example, those exposed to the radio were better informed about AIDS than other regions.	
Mexico	2002	La Radio Indigenista en Mexico	Ines Cornejo Portugal Fundación Manuel Buendia	Book analyzes the development of indigenous radio in Mexico, with focus on the Yucatán region and assesses the impact of indigenous radio on social change. It provides the methodology used, which includes questionnaires, field interviews, and observation.	http://www.mexicanadecomuni cacion.com.mx/Tables/ FMB/fondoeditorial/radioind .html

Country	Year	Title	Author	Description	URL
Mozambique	2005	Assessing Community Change: Development of a "Bare Foot" Impact Assessment Methodology	Birgitte Jallov	Paper provides impact assessment of eight community radios in Mozambique. The methodology of the impact assessment focused on the extent to which broadcasting responds to the public interest, including the quality of research, the use of culturally relevant formats, and how public feedback informs subject matter; the rights and responsibilities of community radio volunteers; and whether the radio station stimulated desired development and social change.	http://www.comminit.com/pdf/ImpactAssessment FinalRadioJournalVersion.pdf
Senegal, Guinea-Bissau, and Sierra Leone	2006	INFORMO-TRAC Program—Joint Review Mission Report: A Review of the INFORMO (TRAC (Initiative for Mobile Training of Community Radio) Program.	Roy Kessler and Martin Faye	Program report demonstrates that community radio stations are an important part of south-south social engagement, which facilitates poverty alleviation. The report focuses on achievements of the INFORMOTRAC Program.	http://www.informotrac.org/downloads/informotrac_mission_report.pdf
South Africa	2005	Community Radio as Participatory Communication in Post-Apartheid South Africa	Anthony A. Olorunnisola	Paper provides an overview of the evolution of community radio in post-apartheid South Africa, in which a three-part broadcasting infrastructure (public, commercial, and community) replaced the State-run broadcasting monopoly (South African Broadcasting Corporation).	http://www.personal.psu.edu/faculty/a/x/axo8/Joburg/manuscript.htm
South Africa	2004	When the Broadcast Ends, the Program Is Not Over:	Adele Mostert and Prof. John van Zyl	Paper provides a case study of ABC Ulwazi, which created educational and development-related radio programs for community radio stations in South Africa. The paper remarks on the importance of holistic approaches to community radio	http://www.ee4.org/Papers/EE4_Mostert.pdf

289

Coverage	Year	Topic	Source	Summary	Website
		Maximising the Effectiveness of EE Programs at Community Radio Level		programming, to make community radio programming accessible to consumers of different social, economic, cultural, and psychological experiences.	
South Africa, Mali, Senegal, and Zambia	2004	Media for Sustainable Development Content Survey—A Baseline Study Report on Sustainable Development Content/ Themes for Community Radio Stations in Africa and Central America	AMARC Africa, Panos Southern Africa, Pronatura-Chiapas-Mexico, and Open Society Foundation, South Africa	Report assesses the amount of African community radio programming content that deals with sustainable development. The report also highlights the importance of community media in terms of facilitating community and national ownership of development agendas, particularly when programming content is broadcast in local languages. The report concludes that "Community radio stations [on the African continent] are not doing enough to ensure that local communities participate in the selection and production of programs regarding sustainable development issues, especially in deciding what themes or topics to cover."	http://www.id21.org/insights/insights58/art08.html (see also) http://africa.amarc.org/files/M4SDStudy May04l.pdf
Uganda	1999	Impact Data—Capital Doctor		Project description provides information on "Capital Doctor," a call-in radio show that began in 1994. Local Ugandans call in to the show and experts answer questions on health issues.	http://www.comminit.com/experiences/pds07-11-99/experiences-244.html

Country	Year	Title	Author	Description	URL
United Kingdom	2003	New Voices: An Evaluation of 15 Access Radio Projects	Anthony Everitt	Report evaluates different approaches to the concept of community radio (for the specific purpose of informing a regulatory agency how a station, "Access Radio," might be organized, funded, licensed, promoted, and regulated). The methodology of the report included broad scale community questionnaires.	http://www.comminit.com/evaluations/steval/sld-2165.html (see also) http://www.comminit.com/experiences/pdskdv112003/experiences-957.html
Zambia	2001	Development through Radio (DTR) Radio Listening Clubs, Zambia Impact Evaluation Report, Panos Southern Africa	Kitty Warnock Panos	Paper assesses the development impact of the Development through Radio project at the local, community, and national levels in Zambia.	http://www.comminit.com/pdf/zambiaDTR.pdf

TABLE 3 Communication and Development

Coverage	Year	Topic	Source	Summary	Website
Global	2006	Communication for Social Change	Alfonso Gumucio-Dagron and Thomas Tufte (editors)	Anthology offers a series of contributions, including Asian, African, and Latin American authors, on how the thinking and practice of communication might bring about social change.	http://www.communication forsocialchange.org/publications-resources.php?id=269 (for purchase)
		Anthology: Historical and Contemporary Readings	Communication for Social Change Consortium		
Global	2005	With the Support of Multitudes: Using Strategic Communication to Fight Poverty Through PRSPs	Masud Mozammel and Sina Odugbemi (editors) DFID and The World Bank	Report offers suggestions to improve the chances of success of development agencies' Poverty Reduction Strategies (PRSs) by showing policy makers how strategic communication can help them to achieve some of their objectives in formulating and executing effective Poverty Reduction Strategies, and giving technocrats and other officials who are actively engaged in the execution of Poverty Reduction Strategy Papers (PRSPs) guidance on good practice as well as lessons from a community of practice spread around the world.	http://www.dfid.gov.uk/pubs/files/strat-comm-prsp.pdf
Global	2005	The State of Communications in International Development and Its Relevance to the Work of the United Nations	Adam Rogers	Study provides an overview on the impact of communication on international development at the theory, research, and policy levels. It examines the development of various theoretical frameworks that define the practice of development communication, and interpreted survey results to examine whether an assumption that development communication is not sufficiently appreciated by decision and policy makers in development organizations is correct, and if it is, the possible	http://www.uncdf.org/english/local_development/documents_and_reports/thematic_papers/devcom/200503_state/ARogers_DevCom2005-b.pdf

Region	Year	Title	Author	Organization	Description	URL
					reasons for it. The study concludes that where this assumption is correct, possible reasons for it include: a) a deficiency of empirical indicators on which policy makers can base their budgeting decisions; and/or b) a lack of effective communication between those that advocate for development communication and those at the top of the organizational hierarchies.	
Global	2004	Will the Real WSIS Please Stand Up? The Historic Encounter of the "Information Society" and the "Communication Society"	Seán Ó Siochrú		Article examines parallel debates within the World Summits on the Information Society (WSIS): 1) the "information society" debate, taking in the role of information, the Internet, and the "digital divide"; and 2) the "communication debate," encompassing broader issues of knowledge ownership and use, media diversity, and communication. It analyzes how they individually developed and remarks on their intersection at the WSIS and the resultant implications.	http://sos.comunica.org
Global	2004	Cultural Diversity and Communication Rights	Steve Buckley	Social Science Research Council	Working paper examines communication rights and the development, within the framework of UNESCO, of proposals for an international convention on the diversity of cultural contents and artistic expressions, in light of the need to defend cultural, which has resulted from the emergence of new information and communication technologies. It sets out issues of concern and provides recommendations for civil society advocacy.	http://programs.ssrc.org/itic/publications/knowledge_report/memos/buckleymemo4.pdf
Global	2004	Communication for Isolated and Marginalized Groups: Blending the Old and the New	Silvia Balit		Paper argues that the concept of communication must respond to the effects of globalization, new social actors, and the opportunities offered by new information and communication technologies, to enhance participatory communication processes in programs to alleviate poverty and improve the livelihoods of vulnerable groups. The paper proposes approaches to overcome constraints and improve the effectiveness of communication with isolated and marginalized groups.	http://www.fao.org/sd/dim_kn1/docs/kn1_040701a2_en.pdf

293

Coverage	Year	Topic	Source	Summary	Website
Global	2004	Actor Network Theory and Media: Do They Connect and on What Terms?	Nick Couldry	Chapter provides an overview of actor network theory, which seeks to explain social order through the networks of connections between human agents, technologies, and objects. The chapter examines the possible development of a theory of the role(s) of media and communication technologies in contemporary societies, in an attempt to understand the substance and limits of actor network theory.	http://www.lse.ac.uk/collections/media@lse/pdf/Couldry/Couldry_ActorNetworkTheoryMedia.pdf
Global	2004	La Communication au Coeur de la Gouvernance Globale (Communication at the Heart of Global Governance)	Marc Raboy and Normand Landry University of Montreal	Report examines the global governance environment in communication in terms of the interaction and interdependence of various actors and policy venues.	http://www.lrpc.umontreal.ca/smsirapport.pdf (in French)
Global	2004	Communication and Global Governance	Marc Raboy World Association for Christian Communication	Working paper examines the impact of the World Summit on the Information Society on global communication governance, with particular regard to its establishment of a new paradigm in global governance in which information and communication issues are central, and in which new actors, particularly rooted in civil society, will be increasingly involved. The paper also examines the impact of this paradigm on the promotion of democratic principles.	http://www.wacc.org.uk/wacc/programmes/recognising_communication_rights/wsis_communication_and_global_governance

TABLE 4 Financing Broadcast Media

Coverage	Year	Topic	Source	Summary	Website
Global	n/a	Guide for Writing a Funding Proposal	Net-NGO.com	Webpage provides instructions on how to write a funding proposal and includes examples of a completed proposal.	http://www.net-ngo.com/funding.cfm
Global	n/a	Online Fundraising Handbook	Groundspring .org	Handbook is a detailed guide on how to raise funds online, with suggestions on how to identify donors.	http://www.groundspring.org/learningcenter/handbook.cfm
Global	n/a	CIVICUS and MDGs Campaigning Toolkit for Civil Society Organizations Engaged in the Millennium Development Goals	CIVICUS (World Alliance for Citizen Participation)	Webpage offers a series of toolkits to enable civil society organizations to raise funds and otherwise improve their capacity in various communication and management areas. Tool kits include: 1) Developing a Financing Strategy; 2) Financial Controls and Accountability; 3) Writing a Funding Proposal; 4) Budgeting; 5) Writing Effectively & Powerfully; 6) Writings Within Your Organization; 7) Producing Your Own Media; 8) Handling the Media; 9) Promoting Your Organization; 10) Planning Overview: 11) Action planning; 12) Monitoring and Evaluation; and 13) Strategic Planning	http://www.civicus.org/new/civicus_toolkit_project.asp?c=036FB9 (available in English, Spanish, French, and Russian)
Global	n/a	Nonprofit Guides: Grant-writing Tools for Nonprofit Organizations	SeaCoast Web Design	Webpage offers grant-writing instructions for nonprofit organizations and other community-minded or public groups.	http://www.npguides.org/index.html

Coverage	Year	Topic	Source	Summary	Website
Global	n/a	Small Grants Program	World Bank	Webpage provides information on the World Bank's Small Grants Program, the purpose of which is to strengthen the voice and influence of poor and marginalized groups in the development processes. The program specifically supports activities of civil society organizations whose primary objective is civic engagement of the poor and marginalized populations, to facilitate ownership of development initiatives by a broader sector of society.	http://web.worldbank.org/ WEBSITE/EXTERNAL/ TOPICS/EXTSOCIALDEVELOP MENT/EXTSMALLGRANTS/0,, menuPK:952550~pagePK:64168 427~piPK:64168435~theSitePK: 952535,00.html
Global	n/a	Proposal Writing Short Course	The Foundation Center	Webpage provides instructions on how to write a funding proposal.	http://foundationcenter.org/ getstarted/tutorials/shortcourse/ index.html
Global	2007	Mass Media and Special Interest Groups	Maria Petrova Program in Political Economy and Government, Harvard University.	Working paper argues that media revenues are an important determinant of media behavior. It states that news coverage, for example, depends on the preferences of advertisers or subsidizing groups. The working paper thus develops a theoretical model that maps how media revenues affect media behavior by examining the interaction between advertisers, special interest groups, and media outlets.	http://www.people.fas.harvard .edu/%7Empetrova/mv21. pdf Global
2007	Basic Fund-Raising	for Small NGOs/Civil Society In the Developing World	Jayne Cravens Coyote Web Design	Guidebook sets out basic fund-raising guidelines for small NGOs in the developing world.	http://www.coyotecommuni cations.com/outreach/grants.html (free, on request)

| Global | 2006 | A Guide to Fundraising | Ernest Hayes, Fadumo Alin, and Lia van Ginneken

network learning.org | Guide provides fundraising instructions in a three-part process: 1) the process of professionalism; 2) the planning of a project; and 3) finding money for the project. | http://www.networklearning.org/books/fundraising.html |
| India and Sri Lanka | 2006 | Telecom Use on a Shoestring: Expenditure and Perceptions of Costs Amongst the Financially Constrained | Avanti Moonesinghe, Harsha de Silva, Neluka Silva, and Ayoma Abeysuriya

LIRNEasia | Report examines perceptions of affordability among low-income telecommunication users in India and Sri Lanka and the effects of changes in service costs on their usage patterns. | http://www.regulateonline.org/content/view/713/31/ |

TABLE 5 Targeting an Audience for Broadcast Media

Coverage	Year	Topic	Source	Summary	Website
Global	n/a	Guidelines for Sustainable Audience Research	AMARC Africa	Webpage provides a brief description of methods of audience research for broadcast media, including a "Seven-Day Diary," samples, random sampling, different audience measures, and more. These guidelines are intended for broadcast media practitioners to conduct audience research in order to increase community participation in the broadcasting station, inform and improve programming, enhance the station's development agenda, and to develop successful marketing strategies.	http://africa.amarc.org/page.php?topic=Audience+Research+Guide
Global	2006	Quick Guide to Audience Research	Dennis List	Guide provides an overview on how to conduct audience research, with detailed guidance of conducting preliminary research, qualitative research, such as media impact assessments, and various forms of surveys (face-to-face, telephone, questionnaires, and more). It is designed for media practitioners, including radio and television broadcasters.	http://www.audiencedialogue.org/dox/qgar.pdf
Global	2002	Know Your Audience: A Practical Guide to Media Research	Dennis List	Book provides several approaches in a series of chapters on how to conduct audience research, with particular regard to estimating the size of an audience and discovering audience preferences. It is specifically designed for media practitioners, including radio and television broadcasters.	http://www.audiencedialogue.org/kya.html

| Global | 1999 | Handbook on Radio and Television Audience Research | Graham Mytton BBC World Service Training Trust, UNESCO, and UNICEF | Handbook sets out audience research methodology, including quantitative audience measurement, measurement of audience opinions and reactions, qualitative research, data analysis, and more. | http://unesdoc.unesco.org/ images/0012/001242/124231Eo .pdf |
| Global | 1993 | Handbook on Radio and Television Audience Research | Graham Mytton UNESCO, UNICEF, and the BBC | Handbook provides audience research methodology, including quantitative audience measurement, measurement of audience opinions and reactions, qualitative research, data analysis, and more. | http://unesdoc.unesco.org/ images/0012/001242/124231Eo .pdf |

TABLE 6 Sustaining Broadcast Media

Coverage	Year	Topic	Source	Summary	Website
Global	n/a	Step by Step: A Guide to Radio Browsing	UNESCO	Webpage provides information about "Radio Browsing of the Internet," which is where on-air presenters actively gather information from reliable sites on the Internet (or other digital resources) during broadcasts, in order to respond to listeners' needs and queries. The webpage states that "Radio Browsing" is currently in use throughout Asia, Africa, and the Caribbean.	http://portal.unesco.org/ci/en/ev.php-URL_ID=5590&URL_DO=DO_TOPIC&URL_SECTION=201.html (RealPlayer file)
Global	n/a	Radio Browsing	Branislava Milosevic OneWorld Radio	Webpage provides step-by-step instructions on how to produce a radio program that uses the "Radio Browsing" format.	http://www.itrainonline.org/itrainonline/mmtk/radiobrowsing.shtml
Global	n/a	Leadership and Management for Change	Fahamu (Networks for Social Justice) and University of Oxford	Webpage provides a course on developing effective leadership skills. It is particularly geared toward potential civil society leaders, and for public interest organizations.	http://www.fahamu.org/leadership.php
Global	2005	Developing Radio Partners: A Guidebook on Sustainability	Bill Siemering and Jean Fairbairn	Guidebook provides six case studies of local, independent radio stations in Africa to derive lessons on sustainability. It examines factors that contribute to the overall sustainability of stations, including context, leadership, management, partnerships, programming, human and technical capacity, will, community support, audience research, and more.	http://www.developingradiopartners.org/programsProjects/crsp.html
Global	2003	The One to Watch—Radio, New ICTs, and Interactivity	Bruce Girard	Book provides approaches to sustain radio and ICTs (including community radio), particularly community participation, to achieve social impact.	http://www.comunica.org/1-2-watch/

302

Region	Year	Title	Author	Description	URL
Global	2003	Participative Marketing for Local Radio	Dennis List	Book provides participative marketing strategies to support and sustain local radio. It is designed to be used by any type of local radio station (particularly community-owned stations), and is particularly useful for people who are new to local radio. The book also provides an overview of participative marketing, and how it extends the idea of relationship marketing to cover various types of communications and social networks.	http://www.audiencedialogue.org/pmlr.html
Africa	n/a	Africa Program Training Workshops	African Women's Media Centre	Webpage offers a list of resources on where journalists may obtain specific skill-building, reporting, and management training in the following areas: 1) leadership development; 2) media management; 3) computer training in new media technologies; 4) journalism ethics; 5) specialized journalism skills; 6) balancing work and family; 7) coalition building; and 8) reporting on HIV/AIDS.	http://www.iwmf.org/africa/
Canada	n/a	Workbook Series: Board Development Program	Government of Alberta, Canada	Workbook series provides guidance on how to recruit, train, and appraise the performance of members of a board of directors for a nonprofit organization (which might be applied to broadcast media). Specifically, the workbook series includes instructions on: 1) developing job descriptions for board members of a nonprofit organization; 2) drafting and revising bylaws; 3) recruiting and developing effective board members for a nonprofit organization; 4) hiring and conducting performance appraisals of an executive director; and 5) financial responsibilities of nonprofit boards.	http://www.cd.gov.ab.ca/building_communities/volunteer_community/programs/bdp/services/resources/workbooks/index.asp
Latin America	2004	La Práctica Inspira: La Radio Popular y Comunitaria frente al Nuevo Siglo	Andrés Geerts, Victor van Oeyen, Claudia Villamayor; ALER-AMARC	Book offers comprehensive analysis of the sustainability of community radio in Latin America. It examines thirty-two community radio stations in terms of social, institutional, and financial sustainability. It details the methodology used for each community radio study, which included community-level fieldwork, journalist and staff interviews at each radio station, audience interviews, and analyses and reviews of programming.	

TABLE 7 Tool Kits and Handbooks: Community Media

Coverage	Year	Topic	Source	Summary	Website
Global	n/a	Internet Broadcasting (also known as "Web streaming")	AMARC	Webpage provides simple instructions on how to broadcast live over the Internet, and offers software for free download to facilitate broadcasts. It states that in addition to the free software, the only requirements include: a computer plugged in to the console; a good Internet connection; and an account on an Internet server.	http://amarcwiki.amarc.org/wiiki.cgi?Internet_broadcastin
Global	n/a	Producing Content for Radio	AMARC	Webpage provides the following seven educational units designed to help community radio practitioners train volunteers and staff: 1) Scripting; 2) Interviewing; 3) Presentation; 4) Editing; 5) Radio formats; 6) Audience participation; and 7) Content for exchange.	http://www.itrainonline.org/itrainonline/mmtk/radiocontent.shtml
Global	n/a	Interviewing for Radio	BBC Training and Development	Guide provides instructions on how to prepare for radio interviews, including live studio interviews and vox pops.	http://www.bbctraining.com/onlineCourse.asp?tID=2555&cat=2772
Global	n/a	Newswriting for Radio	Michael Meckler	Webpage provides information designed to assist radio journalists improve their skills as writers and anchors.	http://www.newscript.com
Global	2005	Assessing Communication Rights: A Handbook	Seán Ó Siochrú (CRAFT Project (Communication Rights Assessment Framework and Toolkit) of the CRIS Campaign.	Handbook offers a practicable checklist for assessing communication rights in particular national contexts—what exists and what is missing—both in terms of the general enabling environment and the particulars of broadcasting. The handbook might be useful for civil society pressure groups in consultations with (or lobbying) governments for expanded communication rights.	http://www.crisinfo.org/pdf/ggpen.pdf

Region	Year	Title	Author/Organization	Description	URL
Global	2005	Successful Communication: A Toolkit for Researchers and Civil Society Organization	Ingie Hovland Research and Policy in Development Programme Overseas Development Institute (ODI)	Tool kit provides methodology that describes how to evaluate the social impact of communication programs. The toolkit might be applied to evaluating the social impact of community radio (though community radio is not specifically addressed in the toolkit).	http://www.odi.org.uk/publications/rapid/tools2.pdf
Global	2004	How to Do Community Radio: A Primer for Community Radio Operators	Louie Tabing UNESCO	Manual provides a step-by-step introduction to the concept of community radio, and how to establish a community radio station, including overviews of necessary equipment, a general code of conduct, and programming content.	http://portal.unesco.org/ci/en/files/16162/10884073091How_to_do_Com.radio.pdf/How%2Bto%2Bdo%2BCom.radio.pdf
Global	2004	Involving the Community: A Guide to Participatory Development Communication	Guy Bessette International Development Research Center and Southbound	Guide introduces participatory development communication concepts, including effective two-way communication approaches, and presents a methodology to plan, develop, and evaluate communication strategies. This methodology is designed to help researchers and practitioners improve communication with local communities and other stakeholders, enhance community participation in research and development initiatives, and improve the capacity of communities to participate in the management of their natural resources.	http://www.idrc.ca/openebooks/066-7/
Global	2001	Public Service Broadcasting in Transition: A Documentary Reader	Monroe Price and Marc Raboy (editors) European Institute for the Media	Book is comprised of documents, comments, and cases that are designed for use by government officials and citizens interested in strengthening public service broadcasting in transition societies.	http://www.global.asc.upenn.edu/docs/Reports/PSB_in_Transition.pdf

Coverage	Year	Topic	Source	Summary	Website
Global	2001	Community Radio Handbook (UNESCO)	Colin Fraser and Sonia Restrepo Estrada	Handbook introduces issues relevant to emerging community radio stations in developing countries, with particular regard to the purpose of community radio, legal and regulatory implications, technical requirements, programming, and acceptable codes of conduct. The handbook also provides several informative case studies.	http://www.unesco.org/ webworld/publications/ community_radio_handbook.pdf
Global	2001	Using Community Radio for Non-Formal Education	John Thomas The Commonwealth of Learning	Booklet provides an introduction and tips on how to use community radio as a medium for nonformal education. It also includes a brief examination of the strengths and weaknesses of this approach to education.	http://www.col.org/colweb/ webdav/site/myjahiasite/shared/ docs/KS2001-02_radio.pdf
Global	1997	Radio Drama: Directing, Acting, Technical, Learning and Teaching, Researching, Styles, Genres— A Step by Step Instruction	Alan Beck	Webpage offers instructions on how to produce a radio drama, including equipment use, research and content creation, and more.	http://www.savoyhill.co.uk/ technique/
Global	1997	Reporting Human Rights and Humanitarian Stories: A	Jo-Anne Velin, with Human Rights Internet and the International	Handbook provides guidance to journalists (particularly those with limited time, few resources, and no Internet or email access) on reporting stories with human rights or humanitarian components. It provides a glossary on international human rights law and international humanitarian law, as well as a	http://www.hri.ca/doccentre/ docs/handbook97/

Region	Year	Title	Author/Organization	Description	URL
Global		Journalist's Handbook	Center for Humanitarian Reporting	collection of country profiles to provide journalists with in-country contacts and statistics, and an address book with the contact particulars of the handbook's own contributors.	http://www.jhuccp.org/pubs/fg/3/3.pdf
Global	1996	How to Write a Radio Serial Drama for Social Development: A Script Writer's Manual	Esta de Fossard / Johns Hopkins Center for Communication Programs and USAID (under the Population Communication Services Project)	Manual provides guidance for novice and experienced scriptwriters to prepare a radio serial drama that educates and entertains, as part of a social development project.	
Global	1991	Communication in Development	Fred Casmir	Book provides a series of case studies of development communication experiences from around the world. It further introduces: 1) conceptual bases for the use of communication in development; 2) communication in the development of contemporary states; regional development and communication policies; and 3) dealing with the need of cultural minorities in terms of communication and development.	http://doi.contentdirections.com/mr/greenwood.jsp?doi=10.1336/0893916412 (for purchase)
Global	1977	Radio Management in the Small Community	Asia-Pacific Institute for Broadcasting Development	Manual demonstrates how managers of small, rural community radio stations contribute to development. It offers a series of statements from effective community radio managers on how best to manage community broadcasting stations.	http://www.aibd.org.my/publications/abstract.cgi/10.html (for purchase)
Africa	n/a	Community Radio Case Studies	UNESCO/ BREDA and The Commonwealth of Learning	Webpage provides case studies as examples of good practices in community radio in Africa. The case studies highlight challenges and demonstrate how community-based broadcasting is a way to achieve development targets.	http://www.dakar.unesco.org/education_en/sup_public_com_rad.shtml (available in English, French, and Portuguese)

Coverage	Year	Topic	Source	Summary	Website
Africa	n/a	Radio Talk Shows for Peace-Building: A Guide	Search for Common Ground	Guide offer instructions for community radio practitioners to develop content for talk shows in a manner that helps to reduce conflict (rather than stimulate or exacerbate it).	http://www.radiopeaceafrica.org/index.cfm?lang=en (register for free to access the Guide)
Africa	2006	Broadcasting Pluralism and Diversity: A Training Manual for African Regulators	Article 19	Manual clarifies the role of African broadcasting regulators and demonstrates how interests might be balanced to achieve equitable frequency allocations to public, private, and community operators. It also provides guidance on securing the public's right to receive information, as well as providing the socially and geographically diverse public with high-quality, relevant programming. The manual is designed to contribute to the harmonization of operational methods throughout the African continent, and is aimed at members and staff of African broadcasting regulatory bodies, as well as journalists, broadcasters, and civil society groups.	http://www.article19.org/pdfs/tools/broadcasting-manual.pdf Africa
	2006	Citoyens et Media: Guide Pratique pour un Dialogue entre Citoyens et Media	Jamal Eddine Naji UNESCO	Guide provides recommendations on how dialogue between citizens (civil society groups) and media (particularly broadcasters) might be fostered. It specifically describes the context of French-speaking African and Maghreb countries and proposes some good practices correlated with their identities and specific conditions including several approaches, guidance, and possible models based on experiences of other regions.	http://unesdoc.unesco.org/images/0014/001465/146533f.pdf (in French)
Africa	2000	The African Community Radio Manual for Managers: A Guide to Sustainable Radio	Ishmael Perkins AMARC Africa and the Institute for the Advancement of Journalism	Manual describes the process of managing and sustaining a community radio station on the African continent. It further provides suggestions to promote community participation to sustain community radio.	http://www.apc.org/apps/img_upload/29f744030369f46ae6e48c35512ccf2/AMARC_manual_for_managers.doc

Region	Year	Title	Author/Organization	Description	URL
Africa	1998	What Is Community Radio? A Resource Guide	Lumko Mtimde, Marie-Helene Bonin, Nikopane Maphiri, and Kodjo Nyamaku / AMARC Africa Panos Southern Africa	Resource guide details how community radio stations can be established in Africa, and provides guidance on troubleshooting problems encountered by community radio stations. It further examines the role of community radio stations in building participatory democracy and development in Africa.	http://www.comminit.com/redirect.cgi?r=http://africa.amarc.org/files/english.doc
Asia	2001	Manual for Media Trainers—A Learner-Centered Approach / Asia-Pacific Institute for Broadcasting Development (AIBD)	UNESCO	Manual provides media trainers and practitioners strategies to facilitate adult learning. It also provides guidance on how to evaluate training programs and impact evaluations, such as creating effective questionnaires and interviews for evaluation purposes.	http://www.unesco.org/webworld/publications/media_trainers/manual.pdf
Australia	n/a	Community Broadcasting Association of Australia Handbook	Community Broadcasting Association of Australia	Handbook provides operational overview of community radio stations in Australia, from legislation and regulation to program development. Chapters include information on access fees; how to establish community broadcasting (a guide for aspirants); censorship; complaints handling; the Community Radio Network; conflict resolution; digital radio; ethnic broadcasting; financial management; incorporation; insurance; management; marketing; media law; music; outside broadcasts; program evaluation questionnaire; promotions; sponsorship; staffing; technical resources; women on the air; and youth broadcasting.	http://www.cbaa.org.au/content.php/12.html?pubid=14

Coverage	Year	Topic	Source	Summary	Website
East and Southern Africa	2000	Media and HIV/AIDS in East and Southern Africa: A Resource Book	S. T. Kwame Boafo, with Carlos A. Arnaldo (editors)	Resource book provides practical guidelines and strategies for the effective reporting of HIV/AIDS issues.	http://www.unesco.org/web world/publications/media_ aids/index.html
Europe	1992	The Media in Western Europe: The Euromedia Handbook	Bernt Stubbe Østergaard (editor) Euromedia Research Group	Handbook provides an overview of national press, broadcasting, and electronic media in Western Europe. Each chapter focuses on a European country, and summarizes geographical and demographic features, the political situation, and government typology. It then summarizes the development of print and electronic media in the country (since 1945), followed by an analysis of important press issues, pertinent legislation, salient issues and policy problems, and an examination of media channels, new owners, and their media strategies.	http://www.euromediagroup.org/ publications.htm (for purchase)
Ireland	n/a	NEAR FM (Community Radio) Station Handbook, Dublin, Ireland	NEAR FM, Dublin, Ireland	Webpage provides a full community radio station handbook from NEAR FM, a leading community radio station in Dublin, Ireland.	http://www.nearfm.ie/hand book.html
South Africa	2003	Community Radio: The People's Voice	John van Zyl (editor) ABC Ulwazi	Handbook provides guidelines and strategies covering the entire process of setting up, managing, and sustaining community radio, with an analysis of the role of community radio in South African society.	http://www.abculwazi.org.za/ jsp/published_cr.jsp?pg= published_cr

| South Africa | 1999 | Community Radio Manual | Jean Fairbairn

Open Society Foundation for South Africa (OSF-SA) | Handbook details how to face challenges associated with establishing a community radio in South Africa (and with broader implications) and provides instructions that show how to set up a new community radio station. Handbook examines the legal and regulatory environment, encouraging community participation, licensing, programming, equipment, marketing, fund-raising, formats, and more. | http://www.osf.org.za/File_Uploads/pdf/CRM-1-prelims.pdf#search=%22manuals%20on%20community%20radio%20evaluation%22 |

TABLE 8 Mass Media: Gender, Race, and Youth Issues

Coverage	Year	Topic	Source	Summary	Website
Global	2007	Pioneering Women's Voices: A Celebration of Women's Journalism across the Globe	Article 19	Report offers profiles and personal testimonials from female journalists from Guatemala, Iraq, Malaysia, and Sudan.	http://www.article19.org/pdfs/publications/2007-womens-day.pdf
Global	2005	Internet Governance and Gender Issues	Interview with Mavic Cabrera-Balleza	Interview provides several insights into the gender implications of information communication technology, particularly the Internet and Internet governance.	http://www.awid.org/go.php?stid=1514 (see also) http://www.genderit.org/en/index.shtml?apc=a—e91324-1&x=91324
Global	1997	MediaWise/PressWise articles on Children and Media	MediaWise/PressWise	Webpage offers a series of articles that examine various issues associated with media coverage of children and children's engagement with the media. These articles include the creation and delivery of training materials in various country contexts.	http://www.presswise.org.uk/display_page.php?id=71
Global	1995	Mujer y Radio Popular	María Cristina Mata, coordinadora ALER	Book examines the role of women in community radio. It further examines how gender issues are represented in community radio.	
Europe	2006	Committee of Experts on Issues Relating to the	Tom Moring Secretariat of the Framework Convention for	Study is designed to inform the debate on how to promote the access of national minorities to media in a changing media environment. The study explores the phenomenon that despite the rapid emergence of new types of media and media usage,	http://www.ivir.nl/publications/mcgonagle/Access_natmin_to_media_eng.pdf

312

		Protection of National Minorities	the Protection of National Minorities and the Committee of Experts on Issues Relating to the Protection of National Minorities	existing instruments to secure access for national minorities to these media have, with only a few exceptions, remained unchanged. It also provides recommendations on how to combat this phenomenon.	
Europe	2004	Commentary: Access of Persons Belonging to National Minorities to the Media	Tarlach McGonagle	Commentary examines issues that influence the access of persons belonging to national minorities to the media, and focuses on the desire to highlight the existence of a diverse gamut of possible influences and the responses they have elicited in practice.	http://www.ivir.nl/publications/mcgonagle/Fillingtheframe-commentary.pdf

TABLE 9 Information Communication Technology (ICTs)

Coverage	Year	Topic	Source	Summary	Website
Global	2005	Experiencing Technical Difficulties: The Urgent Need to Rewire and Reboot the ICT-Development Machine	Amy West and John Barker Article 19	Report examines the dangers of assuming that information and communication technologies bring development, critical information, and participation to all sectors of society. It seeks to inform the international debate on realistic, meaningful action to sustain development and development reform.	http://www.article19.org/pdfs/publications/ict-wsis-report-on-development.pdf
Global	2004	Intervening in Global ICT Governance	Steve Buckley Social Science Research Council	Working paper examines the hypothesis that global governance structures constrain ICT-enabled networking by global civil society.	http://programs.ssrc.org/itic/publications/knowledge_report/memos/buckleymemo.pdf
Global	2004	Information and Communication Technologies and Broad-Based Development: A Partial Review of the Evidence	Jeremy Grace, Charles Kenny, Christine Zhen-Wei Qiang (with Jia Liu and Taylor Reynolds)	Working paper states that ICTs offer developing areas opportunities to raise individual income levels, improve regional and national economic growth rates, improve regional and large-scale environmental conditions, spread regional educational programs, improve health care, and improve the efficacy of governmental regimes. It seeks to demonstrate that ICTs are important to the process of development by: 1) Sharing knowledge; 2) Increasing Productivity; 3) Overcoming Geography; and 4) Contributing to Openness, such as increased governmental, corporate, and other institutional transparency. The working paper concedes that these four areas generally gloss over complex analyses, and stresses that compiling data on how ICTs precisely contribute to national	http://www.wds.worldbank.org/servlet/WDSContentServer/WDSP/IB/2004/03/02/000090341_20040302090454/Rendered/PDF/279490PAPER0WBWP0no1012.pdf

314

Region	Year	Title	Author	Description	URL
				development, government, and resource donors should ensure that ICT access simultaneously reaches as much of the target group as possible (including even the most marginalized members of that group) and that the ICT projects meet the needs and demands of the target group.	http://europeandcis.undp.org/?menu=p_cms/show&content_id=62D51851-F203-1EE9-B05EB064C88A32FA
Global	2004	How to Build Open Information Societies: A Collection of Best Practices and Know-How	Amy Mahan (editor) United Nations Development Program	Report is comprised of nineteen case studies of knowledge-based best practices in Europe and the Commonwealth of Independent States, which demonstrate how information communication technology can promote socioeconomic development and good governance. These case studies detail various e-governance programs and applications, such as policy formulation, customs reform, youth sexual education, rural deployment of ICTs and training, country database building, and more. They illustrate the development potential and transformative power of ICTs when they are deployed effectively. The report is designed to promote intercountry exchanges of best practices and innovative knowledge related to ICTs and development.	
Global	2003	Information and Communication Technologies (ICTs) for Poverty Reduction?	Richard Gerster and Sonja Zimmerman	Discussion paper provides an overview of how ICT applications, including radio, the Internet, and more, figure into economic growth strategies in developing countries. It discusses the impact of particular ICTs on poverty, as well as limitations and challenges.	http://162.23.39.120/dezaweb/ressources/resource_en_24102.pdf

Coverage	Year	Topic	Source	Summary	Website
Global	2003	Ethnographic Action Research: A User's Handbook Developed to Innovate and Research ICT Applications for Poverty Eradication	Jo Tacchi, Don Slater, Greg Hearn UNESCO	Handbook demonstrates how ethnographic action research may be used to study the impact of information and communication technologies (ICTs) on poverty alleviation. It features a detailed methodology, which might be applied to community radio, as well as to ICTs.	http://unescodelhi.nic.in/publications/ear.pdf
Global	2003	World Telecommunication Development Report 2003: Access Indicators for the Information Society	International Telecommunication Union	Report examines issues associated with measuring access to information and communication technologies and provides a snapshot of the global state of readiness (as of 2003) for an information society, such as overcoming the digital divide, the affordability and usability of ICTs, and more. The report additionally evaluates how indicators and statistical methodologies measure access to the information society, understanding of country-level and global developments, and how they help policy makers make certain decisions.	http://www.itu.int/ITU-D/ict/publications/wtdr_03/index.html (for purchase)
Global	2002	The Significance of Information and Communication Technologies for Reducing Poverty	Phil Marker, Kerry McNamara, and Lindsay Wallace Department for International Development (DFID)	Study provides an overview of principles underlying a proposed approach to information and communication technologies (ICTs) and development, and provides recommendations to DFID, to assist in prioritizing approaches to the role of ICTs in combating poverty and fostering sustainable development. The study concludes that addressing the information and communication needs of the poor and creating information-rich societies are essential parts of efforts to tackle poverty. It warns	http://www.dfid.gov.uk/pubs/files/ictpoverty.pdf

				that access to ICTs should not be seen as an end in itself and that success should be measured in terms of remaining progress toward reaching the International Development Targets, rather than bridging the digital divide.	
Global	1982	Toward a New World Information Order	M. D. Marris (editor)	Journal presents the following perspectives on the international information order: 1) Polish perspectives on the new information order; 2) the media-government relationship in Pakistan from the colonial period to the 1980s to analyze the problem of mass media development in developing countries; 3) suggestions on how to enhance journalism in the United States relating to reporting international issues; 4) perspectives on government control of the press and restrictions on the free flow of information; 5) the role of UNESCO in the international information order debate; 6) an examination of measurable indices of imbalances in the flow of news and reliability of international information; and 7) an examination of the role of Western news agencies in the international community.	
Africa	2005	Toward an African E-Index: Household and Individual ICT Access and Usage Across 10 African Countries	Alison Gillwald (editor) The Canadian International Research and Development Centre, with Wits University School of Public and Development Management	Report compiles data designed to inform ICT policy and regulatory research capacity in Africa to enhance governance and to promote African opportunities presented by the information age.	http://www.researchictafrica.net/images/upload/Toward2.pdf

Coverage	Year	Topic	Source	Summary	Website
Egypt	2005	Taking the E-Train: The Development of the Internet in Egypt	R. A. Abdulla	Article examines the development of broadcast media technologies, particularly the Internet, in Egypt and provides an overview of online connectivity, content, and their Arabization in the country. It suggests that Egypt has the potential to use ICTs to become a leader in the democratization of communication and strengthening of civil society in the Arab world.	http://gmc.sagepub.com/cgi/content/abstract/1/2/149 (for purchase)

TABLE 10 Assessing and Measuring the Impact of Information Communication Technology (ICTs)

Coverage	Year	Topic	Source	Summary	Website
Global	2005	Innovation and Investment: Information and Communication Technologies and the Millennium Development Goals Report Prepared for the United Nations ICT Task Force in Support of the Science, Technology & Innovation Task Force of the United Nations Millennium Project	United Nations ICT Task Force	Report explores ways in which ICTs might positively foster development goals. It specifically suggests that five areas must be addressed for the full and effective mainstreaming of ICTs in meeting the MDGs: 1) Evidence of Impact; 2) Policy Development; 3) Resource Mobilization; 4) Global Alliance for ICT and Development; and 5) Global Campaign and Initiatives. The report further suggest that ICTs should promote development impacts; integration and prioritization within national development, and poverty reduction programs and strategies; policy realignment on basic infrastructure deployment; improved government and donor coordination and cooperation; increased private sector engagement; and, enhanced mechanisms for resource mobilization.	http://www.unicttaskforce.org/perl/documents.pl?id=1519
Global	2005	Framework for the Assessment of ICT Pilot Projects: Beyond Monitoring and Evaluation to	S. Batchelor and P. Norrish (editors) InfoDev	Handbook reviews the experiences of *infoDev* in supporting and assessing the effectiveness of information and communication technology (ICT) pilot projects in developing countries. It provides guidance on designing effective monitoring and evaluation (M&E) components of ICT pilot projects, and explains how to go beyond traditional M&E to	http://www.infodev.org/en/Document.4.aspx

Coverage	Year	Topic	Source	Summary	Website
		Applied Research		develop more forward-looking evidence of the potential broader impact of pilot projects on a larger scale. The approaches in the handbook might be used to assess impacts of community radio stations.	
Global	2005	Gender Evaluation Methodology for Internet and ICTs: A Learning Tool for Change and Empowerment	Chat Garcia Ramilo and Cheekay Cinco Association for Progressive Communications (APC)	Evaluation model examines the relationship between ICT initiatives and the concept of the "self" and how it might facilitate social change, including the way in which individuals, organizations, and communities operate. The model has implications beyond gender evaluation in the ICT context.	www.apcwomen.org/gem/
Global	2005	Monitoring and Evaluation of ICT in Education Projects: Handbook for Developing Countries	Daniel A. Wagner, Bob Day, Tina James, Robert B. Kozma, Jonathan Miller, and Tim Unwin *InfoDev*	Handbook (designed for policy makers) examines how to measure the impact of information and communication technologies (ICTs) on student achievement in developing countries. It also provides general information about why ICTs are useful mechanisms to introduce and sustain education reform.	http://www.infodev.org/en/Document.9.aspx
Global	2003	Developing and Using Indicators of ICT Use in Education	UNESCO, Asia, and Pacific Regional Bureau for Education	Booklet explains how to identify indicators to assess impacts of information communication technology (ICTs) on education. The methodology pinpoints useful approaches to identifying indicators.	http://portal.unesco.org/ci/en/ev.php-URL_ID=12438&URL_DO=DO_TOPIC&URL_SECTION=201.html
Global	2002	Assessing the Impact of Technology in	Jerome Johnston, and Linda Toms Barker (editors)	Sourcebook provides an overview of how the impact of technology on education might be measured. It specifically examines learner outcomes, teacher outcomes, and technology	http://www.rcgd.isr.umich.edu/tlt/TechSbk.pdf

	Year	Title	Author	Description	URL
		Teaching and Learning: A Sourcebook for Evaluators	Institute for Social Research at the University of Michigan	integration. This sourcebook is valuable because it might be applied to evaluate impacts of community radio stations.	
Global	1994	La Vida Cotidiana: Fuente de Producción Radiofónica UNDA-AL	Daniel Prieto Castillo	Handbook examines the impact of distance education through radio. It provides a valuable analysis of the effect of south-south cooperation and empowerment, as well as the importance of strengthening community voices.	
Global	1993	Measuring the Impact of Information on Development	Michel J. Menou, (editor) International Development Research Centre (IDRC)	Book examines how information services impact community empowerment and governance. It provides a useful methodology for creating indicators and devising assessment methods.	http://www.idrc.ca/openebooks/708-6/
Mozambique	2005	Assessing Community Change: Development of a "Bare Foot" Impact Assessment Methodology	Birgitte Jallov UNESCO/ UNDP Mozambique Media Development Project	Working paper provides an impact assessment methodology that was designed, tested, and implemented with eight community-owned stations in Mozambique between 2000 and 2005. It examines how the methodology promoted active involvement of communities, and to ensure that volunteer community radio producers would be able to sustain assessments following the conclusion of the project. The methodology includes the following components: 1) an internal assessment of how community radio functioned in each station; 2) an assessment of the station producers' program capacity to meet the needs and desires of the community; and 3) an assessment of the impact of the community radio on positive development changes within each community.	http://www.comminit.com/pdf/ImpactAssessment-Final RadioJournalVersion.pdf

TABLE 11 Impact Assessments, Monitoring, and Evaluation (General)

Coverage	Year	Topic	Source	Summary	Website
Global	2006	Perceptions and Practice: An Anthology of Impact Assessment Experiences Technical Centre for Agricultural and Rural Cooperation (ACP–EU)	Kay Sayce with Patricia Norrish	Anthology provides eleven case studies (in story form) on impact assessment from Asia, South Pacific, Africa, and Latin American countries. The anthology's methodology is included in the annexes.	http://www.anancy.net/uploads/file_en/impact%20assessment.pdf
Global	2006	Monitoring & Evaluation Capacity.org, Issue 29, Sept. 2006	Zenda Ofir (editor)	Online magazine (Capacity.org) provides an overview of results-based monitoring and participatory evaluation, including the observation of changes over long periods of time, and recommendations on how to innovate in monitoring and evaluation, with particular regard to contributing to capacity building. The online magazine includes articles by practitioners who have developed innovative, effective monitoring and evaluation methods and explains how they have used them in practice.	http://www.capacity.org/en/content/download/5769/97948/file/EBR+07-29_ENGLISH-opmaaK+FINAL_11_Septlowres.pdf
Global	2005	Monitoring and Indicators for Communication for Development	Danish International Development Assistance (DANIDA)	Report examines how strategic communication (such as cross-cultural dialogue and knowledge sharing) promotes development. It additionally provides general guidelines to create indicators to measure the role of strategic communication for development.	http://webzone.k3.mah.se/projects/comdev/_comdev_PDF_doc/Danida_ComDevt.pdf
Global	2005	Who Measures Change?	Will Parks (editor)	Report provides a step-by-step overview of how to establish a participatory monitoring and evaluation (PM&E) process to measure process and outcomes of community-based	http://www.cfsc.org/pdf/who_measures_change.pdf http://www.cfsc.org/pdf/

			Communication for Social Change Consortium	communication programs. The methodology may be applied to community radio evaluations of impact.	measuring_change.pdf http://www.cfsc.org/pdf/communities_measure_change.pdf
Global	2003	Advocacy Impact Assessment Guidelines	Megan Lloyd Laney / Communications and Information Management Resource Center	Paper provides guidelines to NGOs to assess the impact of measurable advocacy objectives on poverty alleviation. This includes creating and adhering to "milestones," or indicators that measure when and how objectives are achieved. The paper also discusses different types of advocacy impacts, such as participatory planning, monitoring, and evaluation.	http://www.cimrc.info/pdf/news/Impactassess.pdf
Global	2003	Evaluating Capacity Development—Experiences from Research and Development Organizations around the World	Douglas Horton, et al. / International Service for National Agricultural Research (ISNAR), the Netherlands; International Development Research Centre (IDRC), Canada; and ACP-EU Technical Centre for Agricultural and Rural Cooperation (CTA)	Book outlines approaches and methods for evaluating organizational capacity development efforts. It is written for managers and evaluators in research and development organizations (including government or international agencies that support them), international development agencies, management development institutes, and educational institutions.	http://www.idrc.ca/openebooks/111-6/

Coverage	Year	Topic	Source	Summary	Website
Global	2002	Participation, Relationships and Dynamic Change: New Thinking on Evaluating the Work of International Networks	Madeline Church (editor) et al. Development Planning Unit, University College, London	Report examines challenges faced by international networks, with particular regard to monitoring and evaluation. The report's methodology is provided in Section One, and Section Four examines participation, monitoring, and evaluation. The report's analysis might provide guidance on evaluating the impact of community radio networks.	http://networkedlearning. ncsl.org.uk/knowledge-base/research-papers/participation-relationships-and-dynamic-change-madeline-church-2002.pdf
Global	1998	Knowledge Shared: Participatory Evaluation in Development Cooperation	Edward T. Jackson and Yusuf Kassam (editors) IDRC Kumarian Press	Book provides several articles that explore critical themes in knowledge sharing in development cooperation, including ethics, development strategies, case studies, and more.	http://www.idrc.ca/openebooks/ 868-6/
Global	1998	Development Research Impact: REACH	Cerstin Sander IDRC	Paper assesses accountability and the impact of outreach in development research. The paper also introduces "reach" (including factors that facilitate or inhibit it) as an impact of development research. "Reach" provides performance feedback to stakeholders, which demonstrates a realistic appraisal of circumstances on the ground, and can help to identify possible solutions.	http://www.idrc.ca/uploads/user-S/10504282450reach_e.pdf

| Global | 1981 | Poverty and Famines: An Essay on Entitlement and Deprivation | Amartya Sen | Book examines causation concerning starvation in general, and of famines in particular. It demonstrates that traditional famine analyses, which focus on food supply, are theoretically defective and misleading, and develops an alternative analysis that focuses on ownership and exchange, which he designates the "entitlement approach." The book applies the "entitlement approach" to a series of case studies of relatively recent famines, including the Great Bengal Famine (1943), Ethiopian famines (1973 and 1974), Bangladesh famine (1974), and famines in the Sahel countries in Africa (during the 1970s). The book additionally analyzes the characterization and measurement of poverty using economics, sociology, and political theory. | http://www.questia.com/PM.qst?a=o&d=85190755 |

TABLE 12 International Declarations on Development and Freedoms of Expressions, Communications, and the Press

Coverage	Year	Topic	Source	Summary	Website
Global	2000	Millennium Development Goals	United Nations	Eight goals detailed in the United Nations Millennium Declaration, in which 191 United Nations member states commit to the following by 2015: 1) Eradication of extreme hunger and poverty (halve numbers of people who suffer from hunger and increase food available to the hungry); 2) Achieve universal primary education (universal full courses of primary schooling); 3) Promotion of gender equality and empowerment of women (by eliminating gender disparities in primary and secondary education); 4) Reduction of child mortality (of children under 5) by two-thirds; 5) Improve maternal health (reduce the maternal mortality ratio by three-quarters); 6) Combat HIV/AIDS, malaria, and other diseases (halt and begin to reverse the spread of HIV/AIDS and other diseases); 7) Ensure environmental sustainability (integrate sustainable development provisions into national policies and programs, halve the number of people without sustainable access to safe drinking water, and achieve significant improvement in lives of at least 100 million slum dwellers); and 8) Develop a global partnership for development (includes the cancellation of debts incurred by certain developing countries, offering more generous official development assistance, the development of work for youth, promote access by developing countries to affordable essential drugs, and increase the availability of the benefits of new technologies, particularly ICTs with the developing world).	http://www.un.org/millenniumgoals/

Region	Year	Title	Organization	Description	URL
Global	2000	Declaration of Principles on Freedom of Expression	Organization of American States	Declaration adopted by the Inter-American Commission on Human Rights, which details the human right to freedom of expression, including the right to access information held by the state (subject to certain constraints), which will ensure greater transparency and accountability of governmental activities and the strengthening of democratic institutions.	http://www.cidh.oas.org/declaration.htm
Global	1993	Vienna Declaration and Program of Action	United Nations	Declaration of human rights, adopted by the World Conference on Human Rights on June 25, 1993, in Vienna, Austria. It includes a provision (Article 39) concerning the right to a free and independent media.	http://www.unhchr.ch/huridocda/huridoca.nsf/(Symbol)/A.CONF.157.23.En
Global	1991	UNESCO Declaration of Windhoek	UNESCO	Declaration is a collection of press freedom principles assembled by African newspaper journalists. It follows an analysis of problems associated with African print media, including instances of intimidation, imprisonment, and censorship across Africa. The document was produced at a UNESCO seminar entitled "Promoting an Independent and Pluralistic African Press," held in Windhoek, Namibia, in 1991 and was thereafter endorsed by the UNESCO General Conference. The declaration calls for free, independent, and pluralistic media throughout the world and states that a correlation exists between a fully independent press and a successful participatory democracy. It further states that a free press is a fundamental human right.	http://www.unesco.org/webworld/fed/temp/communication_democracy/windhoek.htm
Global	1948	Universal Declaration on Human Rights	United Nations General Assembly	Declaration adopted by the United Nations General Assembly on December 10, 1948, which is comprised of thirty articles that outline the UN view of human rights guaranteed to all people. It includes a provision (Article 19) concerning the human right to freedom of expression and opinion through any media.	http://www.un.org/Overview/rights.html

Coverage	Year	Topic	Source	Summary	Website
Global	1948	American Declaration of the Rights and Duties of Man	Conference of American States	Declaration was adopted by the nations of the Americas at the Ninth International Conference of American States in Bogotá, Colombia, in 1948. The Declaration details civil, political, economic, social, and cultural rights enjoyed by the citizens of signatory nations, as well as duties assumed by individuals. It includes a provision (Article 4) concerning the human right to freedom of expression and opinion through any media.	http://www.cidh.oas.org/Basicos/basic2.htm
Global	1789	La Déclaration des Droits de l'Homme et du Citoyen [Declaration of the Rights of Man and of the Citizen]	Assemblée Nationale Constituante (France)	Declaration is a fundamental document of the French Revolution, and defines individual and collective universal rights. The declaration states that these rights are valid at all times and places, and pertain to human nature. It includes a provision (Article 11) concerning the human freedom of communication of ideas through spoken word or print media.	http://www.hrcr.org/docs/frenchdec.html

TABLE 13 International Conventions and Covenants

Coverage	Year	Topic	Source	Summary	Website
Americas	1978 (Entry into Force)	The American Convention on Human Rights (the Pact of San José)	Nations of the Americas	Convention is an international human rights instrument adopted by the nations of the Americas in San José, Costa Rica, in 1969, and subsequently came into force, following the Grenada ratification, on July 18, 1978. The convention seeks to consolidate a system of personal liberties and social justice, "based on respect for the essential rights of man." It includes a provision (Article 13) concerning the right to freedom of thought and expression through any media.	http://www.cidh.oas.org/Basicos/basic3.htm
Global	1976 (Entry into force)	The International Covenant on Civil and Political Rights	United Nations	Covenant is based on the Universal Declaration of Human Rights, and was created in 1966 and subsequently entered into force on March 23, 1976. It is comprised of fifty-three articles that outline the UN view of civil and political rights guaranteed to all people. It includes a provision (Article 19) concerning the human right to freedom of expression and opinion through any media.	http://www.unhchr.ch/html/menu3/b/a_ccpr.htm
Europe	1950	The Convention for the Protection of Human Rights and Fundamental Freedoms (The European Convention on Human Rights)	Council of Europe	Convention was adopted under the auspices of the Council of Europe in 1950 to protect human rights and fundamental freedoms. It includes a provision (Article 10) concerning the right to freedom of expression.	http://www.hri.org/docs/ECHR50.html

TABLE 14 Responsibilities of Special Rapporteurs on Freedom of Expression

Coverage	Year	Topic	Source	Summary	Website
Global	1993 – Current	Special Rapporteur on the Promotion and Protection of the Right to Freedom of Opinion and Expression	United Nations (The United Nations Commission on Human Rights)	Special Rapporteur gathers information concerning discrimination and/or threats against persons seeking to exercise or promoting the exercise of the right to freedom of opinion and expression. The Special Rapporteur is charged with undertaking fact-finding country visits and transmitting appeals and communications to States to encourage the alleviation of constraints on the right to freedom of opinion and expression. The Rapporteur issues an annual report to the United Nations Commission on Human Rights, which details the state of press freedom and freedom of expression.	http://www.ohchr.org/english/ issues/opinion/index.htm
Africa	2004	Special Rapporteur on Freedom of Expression in Africa	African Union (African Commission on Human and Peoples' Rights)	Special Rapporteur undertakes investigative missions to African Union member states and other analyses of member State compliance with the Declaration of Principles on Freedom of Expression in Africa, as well as freedom of expression standards in general, and to advise member States or make public interventions accordingly, or to otherwise inform the African Commission of gross violations of the right to freedom of expression. The Special Rapporteur additionally submits reports at each Ordinary Session of the African Commission on the status of the enjoyment of the right to freedom of expression in Africa.	http://www.achpr.org/english/ _info/index_free_exp_en.html

States	1997	Special Rapporteur on Freedom of Expression of the Organization of American States	Organization of American States (Inter-American Commission on Human Rights)	Special Rapporteur monitors Organization of American States member State compliance with the American Convention on Human Rights with specific regard to freedom of expression. The Special Rapporteur conducts fact-finding missions to investigate reports of abuses in OAS member states and analyzes complaints of free expression violations received by the Inter-American Commission on Human Rights. It advises the commission on cases, issues press releases, conducts training, and expresses concerns to member state authorities to protect against violations of freedom of expression, among other responsibilities. The Special Rapporteur issues an annual report, which details the state of press freedom and freedom of expression in each country in the Americas.	http://www.cidh.oas.org/relatoria/index.asp?lID=1

TABLE 15 Legal and Regulatory Development Frameworks for Broadcast Media

Coverage	Year	Topic	Source	Summary	Website
Global	2003	Freedom of Information: A Comparative Legal Survey	Toby Mendel UNESCO	Study surveys the right to freedom of information (which is treated as the right to access information held by public bodies) by providing an overview of international basis for this right, good practice standards, an analysis of laws from ten case study countries, and a comparative analysis of additional relevant laws and policies.	http://portal.unesco.org/ci/en/files/19697/11232335331freedom_info_en.pdf/freedom_info_en.pdf
Global	2002	Global Media Governance: A Beginner's Guide	Seán Ó Siochrú and Bruce Girard, with Amy Mahan United Nations Research Institute for Social Development	Book examines media and communication governance at the global level and its key influencing forces, elements, and organizations, such as ITU, WTO, UNESCO, WIPO, and ICANN. It provides an overview of why media is regulated, the major forms of global regulation (and how they function), the participants and beneficiaries of media governance structures, and existing and emerging trends.	http://www.comunica.org/gmg/index.htm (for purchase)
Global	2002	The Enabling Environment for Free and Independent Media: Contribution to Transparent and Accountable Governance	Monroe Price and Peter Krug United States Agency for International Development	Report examines main components of the legal environment that enable media to advance democratic goals, including the legal, media, and other sectors that affect the professional independence enjoyed by print and broadcast media. It provides an overview of how even a basic understanding of pertinent laws, enforcement and judicial practices, administrative processes, ownership structures, and other aspects of the enabling environment might facilitate the development of effective strategies to establish free media, which promote government accountability and transparency.	http://www.global.asc.upenn.edu/docs/ENABLING_ENV.pdf (available in Russian, Spanish, French, Albanian, and Serbian)

Region	Year	Title	Author	Description	URL
Global	1998	Global Media Policy: A Symposium on Issues and Strategies	Marc Raboy (editor)	Report states that communication policy is created in a global environment, which necessitates the creation of new, transnational policy approaches aimed at enabling media and communication to better serve the global public interest. The report also provides recommendations for such a global regulatory framework.	http://www.javnost-thepublic.org/media/datoteke/1998-4-symposium-raboy.pdf
Africa	2004	African Charter on Broadcasting	The Media Institute of Southern Africa	Charter was designed to be a modern blueprint for broadcasting and information technology policies and laws in Africa.	http://www.misa.org/broadcasting/acb.html
Africa	2003	Broadcasting Policy and Practice in Africa	Tawana Kupe (editor) Article 19	Book provides different models on how to create a pluralistic and diverse broadcasting landscape in Africa. It stresses and provides guidance on various aspects of broadcasting policy and practice, including accessibility, funding, and management, and ensuring that broadcasting content is responsive to the needs and wants of citizens.	http://www.article19.org/pdfs/publications/africa-broadcasting-policy.pdf
Africa (Southern Africa)	2002	Legislation and Community Media for Southern Africa: A Guide	Nick Ishmael-Perkins, with Rebecca Cassidy (editors)	Guide seeks to provide guidance to new or aspiring community media initiatives on managing the regulatory frameworks in Lesotho, Malawi, Mozambique, Namibia, South Africa, Swaziland, Zambia, and Zimbabwe. It includes country-specific guidelines for community radio licensing procedures in each country.	http://www.catia.ws/Documents/Indexpage/Southern%20Africa%20booklet.pdf
China	2005	Research Note—Red Net over China: China's New Online Media Order and Its Implications	Xu Wu	Research note examines China's media order, which is comprised of the fundamental structure, management strategy, and operational pattern of all the media organizations within the country. The note analyzes China's online media development from the mid-1990s and, using interviews with online media practitioners in China, it provides an overview of China's online media order and its major characteristics and their future and international implications.	http://advanced.jhu.edu/media/files/Wu-Red_Net_over_China.pdf

Coverage	Year	Topic	Source	Summary	Website
Europe	1998	The Digital Age: European Audiovisual Policy—Report from the High Level Group on Audiovisual Policy	Marcelino Oreja (chairman) European Commission	Report summarizes key elements of a European audiovisual policy: 1) an examination of the role of audiovisual media in public policy initiatives; 2) the establishment of digital broadcasting (in its many forms) to prepare for the information age; 3) development of European distribution and rights management; 4) support broadcasters, in terms of distributing and financing audiovisual productions; 5) adapt existing support measures for film/audiovisual content to current needs; 6) implement measures to support the funding of public service broadcasting; 7) develop regulatory regimes for audiovisual content; and 8) develop copyright safeguards for audiovisual production content.	http://ec.europa.eu/avpolicy/docs/library/studies/finalised/hlg/hlg_en.pdf
India	2004	Media Reform in India: Legitimizing Community Media	Ashish Sen The World Association for Christian Communication	Article provides an overview of the direction of media reform in India and examines mainstream and community media in India to ascertain whether the course of media reforms conform to a larger and cogent media policy, or if they are symptomatic of a crisis management and reactive culture.	http://www.wacglobal.org/wacc/publications/media_development/archive/2004_1/media_reform_in_india_legitimising_community_media
United Kingdom	1997	Libel and the Media: The Chilling Effect	Eric Barendt, Laurence Lustgarten, Kenneth Norrie, and Hugh Stephenson	Book studies the impact of defamation law on several forms of mass media in the United Kingdom and any resultant chilling effect on free expression by the media, with particular regard to libel law. It further examines how the media handles libel risks, the extent to which sources of media rely on outside legal advice, and the use of insurance protection.	http://www.questia.com/PM.qst?a=o&d=14370720

TABLE 16 Freedom of Expression, Access to Information, and Press Freedom

Coverage	Year	Topic	Source	Summary	Website
Global	n/a	A Model Freedom of Information Law	Article 19	Model law is a completed template, which might be adapted for use by government officials. It includes the following provisions: Definitions and Purpose; The Right to Access Information Held by Public Bodies; Measures to Promote Openness; Exceptions; The Information Commissioner; Enforcement by the Commissioner; Whistleblowers; Criminal and Civil Responsibility; and Miscellaneous Provisions.	http://www.article19.org/pdfs/standards/modelfoilaw.pdf
Global	2006	The Role of the Free Press in Promoting Democratization, Good Governance, and Human Development	Pippa Norris (Meeting on World Press Freedom Day: Media, Development, and Poverty Eradication)	Background paper examines the impact of press freedom on several indicators of democracy and good governance and details the distribution of press freedom and regional trends. It concludes that a free press is significant for a range of good governance indicators, and it is an important part of the process of democratization. It additionally interprets this conclusion in terms of strengthening political and human development to alleviate poverty.	http://portal.unesco.org/ci/en/ev.php-URL_ID=21899&URL_DO=DO_TOPIC&URL_SECTION=201.html
Global	2006	Map of Press Freedom	Freedom House	Webpage offers an interactive map that displays the overall level of press freedom in countries all over the world. It provides users with detailed, country-by-country analyses of the state (or lack) of independent media and citizens' access to unbiased information. As of 2006, the overall global average score of press freedom, as well as the global average scores for the legal and political environment for press freedom, worsened.	http://www.freedomhouse.org/template.cfm?page=251&year=2006

Coverage	Year	Topic	Source	Summary	Website
Global	2006	Freedom of Expression and Press Freedom: Protecting and Respecting Human Security	Agnes Callamard Article 19	Speech notes increasing instances throughout the world of restrictions on freedom of expression, or attempted restrictions, justified on the grounds of national security. It provides examples of laws that restrict press freedoms, with particular regard to antiterrorism efforts, in the name of national security. The speech argues that these restrictions are not an appropriate response to security threats. It provides an overview of the approach set out by the Johannesburg Principles, which are twenty-five principles that detail a limited scope of restrictions, which might be imposed upon freedom of expression, press freedom, and access to information in the interest of national security.	http://www.article19.org/ pdfs/conferences/ human-security-speech.pdf
Global	2005	Freedom and Accountability: Safeguarding Free Expression through Media Self-Regulation	Sara Buchanan, Luitgard Hammerer, and Oliver Money-Kyrle (editors) Article 19	Report provides an overview of how countries in Western Europe, particularly Sweden, Germany, and the United Kingdom, have developed press councils or complaints commissions to achieve media self-regulation, which promotes freedom of expression and of media, as well as regulatory accountability. It further examines initiatives in five countries in Southeast Europe (Albania, Bulgaria, Bosnia and Herzegovina, Romania, and Slovenia) designed to improve journalistic standards and establish media self-regulation, using testimonials from key stakeholders in the process, such as media owners, editors, journalists, and nongovernmental organizations.	http://www.article19.org/pdfs/ publications/self-regulation-south-east-europe.pdf
Global	2005	Freedom of Information: Training Manual for Public Officials	Richard Carver, et al. Article 19	Manual is designed to provide lay persons—primarily public officials—with an introduction to principles underlying freedom of information. It describes how public bodies might provide public access to information, communicate with requesters who are entitled to information, and details the processes by which requests for information are handled.	http://www.article19.org/pdfs/ tools/foitrainersmanual.pdf

Global	2004	What's the Point of Press Freedom?	Amartya Sen World Association of Newspapers	Article argues that an independent media provides a voice to the neglected and disadvantaged, while simultaneously preventing governments from insulating themselves from public criticism. It further reiterates Sen's famous observation that no substantial famine has occurred in any independent country with a democratic form of government and a relatively free press.	http://www.wan-press.org/article.php3?id_article=3881
Global	2002	Press Freedom, Human Capital, and Corruption	Rudiger Ahrend	Working paper provides an overview of how a key function of a watchdog press is to expose corruption, and the related development implications. It states that there is an inverse correlation between the extent of corruption in a country and variables that indicate its development level. It also points to empirical evidence that demonstrate that countries with high levels of press freedom have lower levels of government corruption.	http://papers.ssrn.com/sol3/papers.cfm?abstract_id=620102
Global	2002	Access to the Airwaves: Principles on Freedom of Expression and Broadcast Regulation	Toby Mendel Article 19	Document sets out principles, or standards, on how to promote and protect independent broadcasting and simultaneously ensure that broadcasting serves the public interest as a whole. They include broad standards on how to regulate in the public interest, as well as how to prevent this regulation from becoming a means of government control. They additionally provide guidance on how to address the need for regulators to prevent commercial interests from becoming excessively dominant.	http://www.article19.org/pdfs/standards/accessairwaves.pdf
Global	2000	Voices of the Poor: Crying out for Change	Deepa Narayan, Robert Chambers, Meera K. Shah, and Patti Petesch The World Bank	Book draws on research conducted in 1999 involving over 20,000 poor women and men from twenty-three countries to highlight the common theme of powerlessness. The book examines ten dimensions of powerlessness that emerge from the study and presents the methodology and the challenges faced in conducting the study. The book includes remarks on the importance of access to information as a way to counteract	http://www.-wds.worldbank.org/external/default/WDSContentServer/WDSP/IB/2001/04/07/0000949 46_01032805491162/Rendered/PDF/multi0page.pdf

337

Coverage	Year	Topic	Source	Summary	Website
				powerlessness, as well as how media are important awareness-raising tools in the developing world.	
Global	1999	The Public's Right to Know: Principles on Freedom of Information Legislation	Article 19	Report details a step-by-step analysis of international principles to assist readers to measure whether domestic laws (in the reader's country) genuinely permits access to official information, and for governments to achieve maximum transparency. The report generally refers to broadcast media, under the rubric of the freedom of expression through any media.	http://www.article19.org/pdfs/standards/righttoknow.pdf
Global	1996	The Johannesburg Principles on National Security, Freedom of Expression, and Access to Information	Article 19	Johannesburg Principles comprise twenty-five principles suggested by a group of experts in international law, national security, and human rights, based on international and regional law, and international standards relating to freedom of expression and access to information. The principles are divided into four sections: General Principles, Restrictions on Freedom of Expression, Restrictions on Freedom of Information, and Rule of Law and Other Matters.	http://www.article19.org/pdfs/standards/joburgprinciples.pdf
Global	1994	Guidelines for Election Broadcasting in Transitional Democracies	Patrick Merloe, with Sandra Coliver Article 19	Study examines the role of election campaign broadcasting in transitional democracies and the relationship between free and fair elections and access to television and radio, and stresses that respect for freedom of expression, particularly during campaign periods, increases the likelihood of success for a democratic transition. It additionally draws from the experiences of both transitional and more mature democracies, as well as from principles of international law, to provide a set of guidelines concerning broadcast coverage of election campaigns based on international law and practice.	http://www.article19.org/pdfs/standards/election-broadcasting-in-transitional-democracies.pdf

Region	Year	Title	Author / Organization	Description	URL
Global	1993	The Article 19 Freedom of Expression Handbook: International and Comparative Law, Standards and Procedures	Sandra Coliver / Article 19	Handbook provides summaries of decisions from courts around the world that establish precedents that protect the rights to freedom of expression, assembly, association, and access to information. It additionally provides summaries of relevant international case-law (those that both protect and restrict freedoms), and basic information about human rights treaties and procedures for filing complaints with intergovernmental bodies. The handbook is designed for use by lawyers, researchers, and human rights campaigners.	http://www.article19.org/pdfs/publications/1993-handbook.pdf
Global	1964	Mass Media and National Development: The Role of Information in the Developing Countries.	Wilbur Schramm / UNESCO	Study provides an overview of the role of mass media in development. It argues that development agents might use powerful media outlets to communicate messages about technological innovations in the course of development initiatives.	http://ann.sagepub.com/cgi/content/citation/360/1/204 (for purchase)
Afghanistan	2007	Presentation to the Religious and Cultural Affairs Commission of the Afghan National Assembly	Toby Mendel / Article 19	Presentation to the Religious and Cultural Affairs Commission of the Afghan National Assembly on the development of freedom of expression principles and the draft media law.	http://www.article19.org/pdfs/conferences/afghanistan-media-presentation.pdf
Africa	2003	"Our Culture" vs "Foreign Culture"—An Essay on Ontological and	Keyan Tomaselli	Article examines perspectives on freedom of the press in Africa, with regard to professionalism, essentialism, and citizenship, and critiques the insistence by some African media academics that the media must exhibit "African values." It also examines the role of authority in determining the way	http://gaz.sagepub.com/cgi/content/abstract/65/6/427 (for purchase)

Coverage	Year	Topic	Source	Summary	Website
		Professional Issues in African Journalism		that the media are understood by communication students in some African countries, and argues for a greater integration of cultural and media studies into journalism education to broaden cultural perspectives among journalists. The article additionally provides suggestions on how to address these issues in course curricula.	
Africa	1999	The Right to Communicate: The Internet in Africa	Sally Burnheim Article 19	Report examines a comparatively subtle form of censorship: some African governments are moving to control the provision of Internet services through monopolies of existing telecommunications services. It details examples where some governments have assumed total control of new technology, to retain sole access to the revenue, and in some cases to exert control over users. The report further presents the dangers associated with the lack of adequate telecommunications, and thus, the society's ability to develop depends on lack of access to information and constraints on the freedom of expression in Africa.	http://www.article19.org/pdfs/publications/africa-internet.pdf
Armenia, Azerbaijan, and Georgia	2005	Under Lock and Key: Freedom of Information and the Media in Armenia, Azerbaijan, and Georgia	Iryna Smolina Article 19	Report provides an overview of the extent of the implementation of freedom of information legislation in Armenia, Azerbaijan, and Georgia, and the impact of this legislation on the media in these three countries. It additionally provides summaries of the evolving media landscapes in each of the three countries.	http://www.article19.org/pdfs/publications/under-lock-and-key.pdf

The Balkans	2005	Conference Report on Freedom and Accountability Conference on Media Self-Regulation in Southeast Europe	Article 19	Conference report provides an overview of the importance of media self-regulation in the context of Southeastern Europe to safeguard media independence, enhance media professionalism, and reduce judicial action against the industry.	http://www.article19.org/pdfs/conferences/sarajevo-conference-report.pdf
Bulgaria	2003	Memorandum on the Draft Law on Radio and Television of the Republic of Bulgaria	Article 19	Memorandum analyzes the draft law and finds that while it provides guarantees for the independence of the agencies responsible for regulating the Bulgarian broadcast sector (including an explicit though general provision concerning the independence of the principal regulatory agency), these provisions do not go far enough, particularly regarding appointing members to these bodies. It additionally praises the law's treatment of sources of funding for the national broadcasters, increased advertising quotas, and the creation of new governing bodies for the national broadcasters, and states that the criteria for the grant of broadcasting licenses and frequencies should be more specific.	http://www.article19.org/pdfs/analysis/bulgaria-broadcasting-law-2003.pdf
Cambodia	2006	Freedom of Expression and the Media in Cambodia	The Community Legal Education Center, with Article 19 and the Human Rights and Development Association	Study analyzes Cambodia's Press Law, which contains provisions that are intended or might be construed to regulate or control the press. It additionally generally examines the status of the media in Cambodia, with particular regard to media ownership and the laws regulating its functioning, with reference to international standards. It further provides recommendations aimed at the media and the government, to promote the development of a diverse and free media environment that promotes and protects the freedom of expression.	http://www.article19.org/pdfs/publications/cambodia-baseline-study.pdf

Coverage	Year	Topic	Source	Summary	Website
Cambodia, Timor Leste, Indonesia, Malaysia Philippines, Singapore, and Thailand	2006	Freedom of Expression and the Media in the Philippines, Singapore, Thailand, Indonesia, and Timor Leste	Article 19 and the Center for Media Freedom and Responsibility	Series of 7 reports that examine the freedom of expression and the media in the Philippines, Singapore, Thailand, Indonesia, and Timor Leste in light of continuing violence and challenges to providing citizens with balanced and objective information. The reports also provide a series of recommendations, including institutionalizing measures to prevent violence against journalists, legislation and constitutional amendments to permit foreign investment in the media sector, and other strategies to bring the media policy and regulatory environment in these countries in line with international standards and good practices.	http://www.article19.org/pdfs/publications/malaysia-baseline-study.pdf http://www.article19.org/pdfs/publications/singapore-baseline-study.pdf http://www.article19.org/pdfs/publications/philippines-baseline-study.pdf http://www.article19.org/pdfs/publications/thailand-baseline-study.pdf http://www.article19.org/pdfs/publications/indonesia-baseline-study.pdf http://www.article19.org/pdfs/publications/timor-leste-baseline-study.pdf
Cook Islands	2007	Memorandum on the Draft Media Act of the Cook Islands	Article 19	Memorandum analyzes the 2006 Cook Islands "Act to Establish the Media Commission," in light of international standards on the right to freedom of expression. It focuses the functions of the national commission, established by the act, which would be granted broad regulatory powers over radio, television, print, and Internet media content in the Cook Islands. It would additionally not only license broadcast media, but also monitor the extent to which all media comply with "community standards and expectations" and hear and decide complaints brought by members of the public, as well as levy fines. The memorandum expresses concerns over these expansive powers.	http://www.article19.org/pdfs/analysis/cook-islands-media-law-06.pdf

	Year	Author	Title	Description	URL
Ethiopia	2003	Article 19	Briefing Note on the Draft Ethiopian Proclamation Concerning Press Freedom	This briefing note provides an overview of the concerns relating to the draft Ethiopian Proclamation Concerning Press Freedom. It concludes that draft proclamation is overbroad in terms of its scope, includes problematic restrictions on who may practice journalism, and provides for a government-controlled licensing system for media outlets. Also, the draft law provides for restrictions on access to information held by public authorities and broadcasting and publication content restrictions. It further provides for the establishment of a government-controlled Press Council with powers to prepare and enforce a code of ethics, powers vested in the prosecutor to suspend media outlets, and a harsh sanctions regime.	http://www.article19.org/pdfs/analysis/ethiopia-media-law.pdf
Europe	2001	Risto Kunelius and Colin Sparks	Problems with a European Public Sphere: An Introduction	Article discusses problems associated with the application of the concept of the public sphere to the current situation in the European Union. It states that the mass media in the European Union remain predominantly organized along the lines of the constituent states of the union rather than on any genuinely transnational basis, which creates tension between ways issues are discussed: European issues versus issues of national interest.	http://www.javnost-thepublic.org/media/datoteke/ 2001-1-kunelius.pdf
Fiji	2006	Article 19	Submission on the 2006 Broadcast Licensing Bill of Fiji	Memorandum analyzes the proposed 2006 Fijian Broadcast Licensing Bill and provides recommendations to promote independent regulation of broadcasting, particularly regarding the manner in which members of the Broadcast Licensing Authority are appointed. It suggests that the bill establish a balance between providing the broadcast regulatory body with powers over broadcasting to achieve public interest purposes, and safeguarding the body's independence from potential governmental or commercial interference.	http://www.article19.org/pdfs/analysis/fiji-broadcasting-law.pdf

Coverage	Year	Topic	Source	Summary	Website
Georgia	2006	Comments on the Draft Georgian Broadcasting Code of Conduct	Article 19	Comment provides recommendations on the format and structure of Georgia's Broadcasting Code of Conduct, to improve its user-friendliness for broadcasters and its suitability for enforcement by the Georgian National Communications Commission.	http://www.article19.org/pdfs/analysis/georgia-broadcasting-coc.pdf
Hong Kong	2006	Submission to the Committee on the Review of Public Service Broadcasting in Hong Kong	Article 19	Report examines the role and justification of public service broadcasting in Hong Kong in light of public financial and other resources required, and provides an overview of Radio Television Hong Kong's accountability, with regard to broadcasting regulation. The report recommends that Radio Television Hong Kong be re-established as an independent broadcaster, governed by a board that represents the people of Hong Kong. It further recommends ways in which the broadcasting administration might evaluate the effectiveness of public service broadcasting, and how to engage the public in such a process.	http://www.article19.org/pdfs/analysis/hong-kong-psb.pdf
Iran	2006	Memorandum on Media Regulation in the Islamic Republic of Iran	Article 19	Memorandum examines the legal framework regulating the media in Iran (including the Constitution, the Press Law, and the Penal Code) in light of international standards governing the right to freedom of expression. It details constraints to freedom of expression under this legal framework, with particular regard to broadcasting content restrictions (television and radio broadcasting are controlled by a State broadcasting monopoly under the Constitution) and harsh penalties for violations of the Press Law.	http://www.article19.org/pdfs/analysis/iran-press-law.pdf

Iraq	2006	A Media Policy for Iraq	Article 19 and UNESCO	Proposal outlines a draft policy for the development of a free and independent Iraqi media. It includes safeguards that balance State intervention in certain areas with nonintervention in other areas. It further promotes the right to freedom of expression of the media, and provides for the public's right to receive information on matters of public interest from a variety of sources.	http://www.article19.org/pdfs/analysis/iraq-media-policy.pdf
Israel	2007	Memorandum on the Broadcasting Authority Law of the State of Israel	Article 19	Memorandum analyzes Israel's 1965 Broadcasting Authority Law in light of international standards on freedom of expression and public service broadcasting and provides recommendations on how the Israel Broadcasting Authority might improve its governing bodies, structure of governance, financial arrangements, and accountability to the public.	http://www.article19.org/pdfs/analysis/israel-psb-07.pdf
Jordan	2006	Memorandum of the Audio-Visual Media Law of the Kingdom of Jordan	Article 19	Memorandum provides an analysis of the Audiovisual Media Law of the Kingdom of Jordan and its accompanying bylaws in light of international standards, comparative constitutional law and good practices in countries around the world. It further outlines Jordan's international and constitutional obligations to ensure freedom of expression.	http://www.article19.org/pdfs/analysis/jordan-audiovisual-media-law.pdf
Kazakhstan	2007	Memorandum on the Draft Law of the Republic of Kazakhstan "On Publishing"	Article 19	Memorandum analyzes the 2006 draft Law of Kazakhstan "On Publishing," in light of international standards on the right to freedom of expression and details concerns regarding the licensing scheme and the publishing restrictions proposed in the draft law.	http://www.article19.org/pdfs/analysis/kazakhstan-publishing-06.pdf
Kazakhstan	2007	Memorandum on Kazakhstan's Law on Mass Media	Article 19 Representative on Freedom of the Media of the Organisation for	Memorandum analyzes Kazakhstan's Law on Mass Media in light of international standards on the right to freedom of expression, and details concerns regarding restrictions on the development of a free, independent, and pluralistic media in Kazakhstan and the public's right to receive information on	http://www.article19.org/pdfs/analysis/kazakhstan-media-la.pdf

Coverage	Year	Topic	Source	Summary	Website
			Security and Cooperation in Europe	matters of public interest. The memorandum provides recommendations on strengthening the law's provisions related to regulatory authorities; the right to publish and registration; content and language restrictions; journalists' rights and obligations; the right to freedom of information; the right of reply; the duty to deposit copies of all publications with central agencies; and the accreditation regime.	
Kenya	2006	Statement on the Draft Media Council of Kenya Bill	Article 19	Statement details concerns regarding the proposal of statutory regulation of the media in Kenya, which risks endangering the independence of the media and impinging on the free flow of information. The statement emphasizes the importance of media self-regulation.	http://www.article19.org/pdfs/analysis/kenya-media-council-bill.pdf
Korea	2003	Media, the Public, and Freedom of the Press	Hun Shik Kim	Article examines the diversification of the news media in Korea from the 1990s, as a result of deregulation and democratization. It additionally examines the impact of media diversity on the public's use patterns and its trust in the media and evaluates the current state of freedom of the press in Korea. The study concludes that the Korean press still faces a variety of restraints, despite improvements in certain areas.	http://www.springerlink.com/content/k14n7237267t4855/ (for purchase)
Kosovo	2003	Memorandum on the Law of Broadcasting through the establishment of the Independent Media Commission	Article 19	Memorandum outlines Kosovo's international and constitutional obligations, with an emphasis on freedom of expression and its implications regarding broadcast regulation, and also examines the draft law in light of these obligations, and provides suggestions for improvement.	http://www.article19.org/pdfs/analysis/kosovo-broadcast-comm.pdf

Kyrgyzstan	2005	Memorandum on the Kyrgyz Mass Media Law and the Law on Journalists' Activities	Representative on Freedom of the Media of the Organization for Security and Cooperation in Europe and Article 19	Memorandum analyzes the Law of the Kyrgyz Republic on Mass Media and the the Law of the Kyrgyz Republic on the Professional Activity of the Journalists in light of international standards on the right to freedom of expression. It sets out concerns regarding provisions within these laws that grant the regulatory authority broad power to restrict content, suspend media outlets on broad grounds, and impose a registration regime that might be abused for political purposes. Both laws additionally impose "journalistic duties" that would be unnecessary if the laws included self-regulation provisions.	http://www.article19.org/pdfs/analysis/kyrgyzstan-media.pdf
Latvia	2005	Memorandum on a Proposal for a Draft Law on Public Service Broadcasting Organizations and a Draft Law on Radio and Television in Latvia	Representative on Freedom of the Media of the Organization for Security and Cooperation in Europe and Article 19	Memorandum examines both draft laws in light of international standards on freedom of expression and broadcasting regulation, with particular attention to the proposed funding structure of public service broadcasting organizations, as well as the proposed safeguards for their independence. This memorandum further examines the proposed new regulatory plan for the broadcasting sector in general, and analyzes provisions concerning content restrictions and the proposed structure for the right of reply.	http://www.article19.org/pdfs/analysis/latvia-psb.pdf
Liberia	2005	Comments on the Liberian Draft Law and Policy Providing for the Establishment of the National Public Broadcasting Service	Article 19	Comment provides an overview and suggestions to improve the Liberian draft Law and Policy Providing for the Establishment of the National Public Broadcasting Service. It details how the draft law ensures the effective independence of the new broadcaster from government and commercial forces, as well as its accountability to the people in terms of finances and program content. It additionally examines the draft law's treatment of programming objectives.	http://www.article19.org/pdfs/analysis/liberia-psb.pdf

347

Coverage	Year	Topic	Source	Summary	Website
Macedonia	2003	Memorandum on the Draft Broadcasting Law of Macedonia	Article 19	Memorandum provides an overview of how the draft law, which proposes an overhaul of the legislative regulatory framework for broadcasting in Macedonia, is generally based on international law and good comparative practice, and would thus enhance the right to freedom of expression in broadcasting in the country. Specifically, the law proposes the establishment of a new broadcast regulator, as well as a new legislative framework for the establishment of a Macedonian public service broadcaster. It additionally introduces a set of program standards for all broadcasters—public and private—and it includes protections relating to the confidentiality of journalists' sources. It also requires public authorities to release information on matters of public interest. The memorandum additionally offers some recommendations to bring other aspects of the law in line with international standards and good practices.	http://www.article19.org/pdfs/analysis/macedonia-bro.03.pdf
Malawi	2004	Memorandum on the Malawi Communications Act of 1998	Article 19	Memorandum examines the way in which the 1998 Malawi Communications Act regulates the country's broadcasting sector in light of international standards on freedom of expression. It also generally explores the constraints and regulations that the act imposes on broadcasters.	http://www.article19.org/pdfs/analysis/malawi.bro.03.pdf
Malaysia	2006	Memorandum on Malaysia's 2006 Press Council Bill	Article 19	Memorandum provides drafting assistance on Malaysia's 2006 Press Council Bill, to encourage the establishment of an independent, self-regulating Press Council that promotes press freedom and professional and ethical journalism. It focuses on strengthening the Press Council's independence and structure using international standards governing the right of freedom of expression and freedom of the press.	http://www.article19.org/pdfs/analysis/malaysia.prs.06.pdf

The Maldives	2007	Note on the Draft Broadcasting Bill of the Maldives	Article 19	Note critiques the draft Broadcasting Bill of the Maldives, using international standards relating to broadcast regulation and democratic governance.	http://www.article19.org/pdfs/analysis/maldives-broadcasting-analysis.pdf
Mongolia	2002	Memorandum on the Law of Mongolia on Public Radio and Television	Article 19	Memorandum offers an overview of key international standards and provides recommendations on how concerns with Mongolia's Law on Public Radio and Television might be addressed. These recommendations relate to the process of appointing the Representative Governing Board, which is largely under the control of government and all of the shares of the broadcaster are vested in the government; the draft law's treatment of the role and mission of the public broadcaster; and the lack of guaranteed access to particular public sources of funding (or any detail regarding how public funding would operate).	http://www.article19.org/pdfs/analysis/mongolia.psb.02.pdf
Namibia	2006	Memorandum on the Draft Communications Bill of Namibia	Article 19	Memorandum analyzes Namibia's draft communications bill using international standards on freedom of expression and broadcast regulation, and provides recommendations on the nature and functions of the proposed regulatory body, and on the regulation of broadcasting services, with particular regard to the independence of the body. It states that without sufficient guarantees of independence, the regulatory body might be subject to ministerial influence or control.	http://www.article19.org/pdfs/analysis/namibia-broadcasting-law.pdf
Nepal	2006	Submission to the High Level Media Council (Nepal)	International Press Freedom and Freedom of Expression Mission to Nepal	Submission provides observations and recommendations to promote media freedom in Nepal, which are consistent with international standards. It specifically provides recommendations on amending Nepal's Interim Constitution to provide for greater protection for freedom of expression and of the media; reforming the State media to guarantee structural independence; promulgating legislation providing for	http://www.article19.org/pdfs/analysis/nepal-media-submission.pdf

349

Coverage	Year	Topic	Source	Summary	Website
				governmental transparency and giving full effect to the right to know; amending the Working Journalists Act of 1995 to improve protection for journalists; and encouraging comprehensive reforms of media law and regulation in Nepal.	
Palestine	2006	The Legal Framework for Media in Palestine and under International Law	Toby Mendel and Ali Khashan	Provides a general legal framework for media in Palestine using international standards and good practices.	http://www.article19.org/pdfs/analysis/palestine-media-framework.pdf
Republic of Moldova	2006	Memorandum on the Draft Audiovisual Code of the Republic of Moldova	Article 19	Memorandum analyzes the draft Audiovisual Code of the Republic of Moldova in light of international standards on freedom of expression. It remarks that the draft code seeks to regulate the country's entire broadcast sector, including the awarding of licenses to privately owned channels and the management of the country's public service broadcaster. It additionally details concerns regarding the proposed centralization of responsibilities within the new regulator, which will additionally act as the supervisory body for the public service broadcaster. The memorandum also details concerns regarding the absence of provisions that provide for community radio in the draft code.	http://www.article19.org/pdfs/analysis/moldova-audiovisual-code.pdf
Republic of Montenegro	2005	Key Recommendations on the Law on Free Access to Information of the Republic of Montenegro	Article 19	Report provides a series of recommendations designed to bring the Republic of Montenegro's draft Law on Free Access to Information in line with international standards and good practices.	http://www.article19.org/pdfs/analysis/montenegro-recs-may-2005.pdf

Country	Year	Title	Author/Organization	Description	URL
Romania	1997	Romania: An Analysis of Media Law and Practice	Monica Macovei, with Ed Rekosh Article 19	Report examines the framework of media law and policy in Romania, and offers recommendations on how Romanian law (related to freedom of expression) might be brought in line with international standards, particularly those of the European Convention on Human Rights. It is intended to be a resource for Romanian journalists and legislators.	http://www.article19.org/pdfs/analysis/romania-media-law-and-practice.pdf
Russia	2003	Memorandum on Russian Federal Draft Law "On Mass Media"	Article 19	Memorandum provides a provision-by-provision analysis of the Russian federal government's Law "On Mass Media," as well as its compliance with international standards. It praises the law for including a clear prohibition against State censorship, protecting confidential sources, and establishing a system to allocate licenses to private broadcasters. However it concludes that the law lacks provisions that ensure independence of the regulatory bodies, regulates journalists' rights and duties, and imposes content requirements.	http://www.article19.org/pdfs/analysis/russia.med.03.pdf
Sierra Leone	2004	Sierra Leone—Key Findings from 2004 External Evaluation	Search for Common Ground (SFCG)	Study evaluated the role of information in social change in Sierra Leone, as well as the effectiveness and impact of Search for Common Ground's efforts in the country. Evaluators conducted interviews with stakeholders (including individuals, focus groups, and representatives from certain organizations). The evaluation includes feedback from historically disadvantaged groups.	http://www.sfcg.org/sfcg/evaluations/summary_sl.pdf#search=%22Community%20radio%20evaluation%22
Solomon Islands	2003	Memorandum on the Broadcasting 1976 Ordinance of the Solomon Islands	Article 19	Memorandum analyzes the Broadcasting 1976 Ordinance of the Solomon Islands which established the public service broadcaster (the Solomon Islands Broadcasting Corporation) in light of international standards and offers recommendations on how to enhance its independence.	http://www.article19.org/pdfs/analysis/solomon-island.bro.03.pdf

Coverage	Year	Topic	Source	Summary	Website
South Africa	2004	Changing Media Policies in South Africa	William Bird World Association for Christian Communication	Webpage provides information on the Media Monitoring Project, an independent, nongovernmental organization that monitors the media within a human rights framework, which has examined the race and racism, gender issues, youth issues, and HIV/AIDS issues in the media.	http://www.wacc.org.uk/wacc/publications/media_development/archive/2004_1/changing_media_policy_in_south_africa
Sri Lanka	2007	Press Freedom and Freedom of Expression in Sri Lanka: Struggle for Survival	International Press Freedom and Freedom of Expression Mission	Report examines the current situation of the Sinhala, Tamil, and English language media in Sri Lanka, with particular regard to effects of restrictions on the free flow of information through Tamil language media outlets. It offers findings related to safety, informal censorship, and media policy reforms.	http://www.article19.org/pdfs/publications/sri-lanka-mission-rpt.pdf
Sudan	2006	Draft Public Service Broadcasting Bill	Article 19	Draft Public Service Broadcasting Bill for Southern Sudan, presented to the southern Minister of Information, to be considered for promulgation.	http://www.article19.org/pdfs/analysis/southern-sudan-public-service-broadcasting-bil.pdf
Sudan	2006	Draft Bill to Promote Media Self-Regulation	Article 19	Draft Bill to allow the establishment of self-regulatory mechanisms for the media for Southern Sudan, presented to the southern Minister of Information, to be considered for promulgation.	http://www.article19.org/pdfs/analysis/southern-sudan-promotion-of-self-regulation-bi.pdf
Sudan	2006	Draft Media Policy Framework	Article 19	Draft Media Policy Framework for Southern Sudan, presented to the southern Minister of Information, to be considered for promulgation.	http://www.article19.org/pdfs/analysis/southern-sudan-media-policy-framework.pdf
Sudan	2006	Draft Broadcasting Bill	Article 19	Draft Bill to provide for the regulation of independent, pluralistic broadcasting in the public interest in Sudan.	http://www.article19.org/pdfs/analysis/southern-sudan-broadcasting-bill.pdf

Country	Year	Title	Author	Description	URL
Tajikistan	2002	Memorandum on the Laws in Tajikistan Regulating Mass Media	Article 19	Memorandum notes that the laws in Tajikistan that regulate mass media provide for guarantees for media freedom, a system for allocating licenses to private broadcasters, a system for accessing information held by public bodies, and legal requirements that domestic laws comply with international law. It also outlines the obligations of Tajikistan to promote and protect freedom of expression under international law, and offers recommendations for how the laws might be brought in line with international standards relating the laws' provisions on: the registration of the media; the regulation of journalists; the regulatory regime for broadcasting; content issues; defamation; privacy; protection of sources; penalties; and freedom of information.	http://www.article19.org/pdfs/analysis/tajikistan.med.02.pdf
Tanzania	2007	Memorandum on the Tanzanian Media Services Bill 2007	Article 19	Analysis of Tanzania's draft Media Services Bill of 2007, which proposes to regulate print and broadcast media in Tanzania by creating a registration mechanism for individual journalists and print media outlets. It further provides for a Media Standards Board and a licensing regime for broadcasters, which will impose certain content restrictions on broadcasting for the purpose of protecting confidential sources of information. The draft bill additionally establishes a new defamation regime for Tanzania.	http://www.article19.org/pdfs/analysis/tanzania-media-services-bill.pdf
Uganda	1990	Mass Media as Agencies of Socialization in Uganda	Jacob Matovu	Article assesses mass media (print and broadcasting) in Uganda in terms of its contributions to socialization. It concludes that mass media in Uganda has been an ineffective agent of national socialization because few have access to television, and print media is underutilized because of low national literacy levels (particularly in rural areas, where the majority of the Ugandan population is concentrated), and the lack of an effective distribution system.	http://jbs.sagepub.com/cgi/content/citation/20/3/342

353

Coverage	Year	Topic	Source	Summary	Website
Ukraine	2005	Memorandum on the Draft Public Service Broadcasting Law for Ukraine	Article 19	Memorandum examines the draft law in light of international standards on freedom of expression and broadcasting regulation, with particular regard to its proposed structure of the supervisory and managerial bodies of Public Television and Radio Broadcasting. It further suggests that the independence of these entities should be explicit, and a statement that Public Television and Radio Broadcasting will not be required to carry state-mandated programming should be added to the language of the law.	http://www.article19.org/pdfs/analysis/ukraine.psb.05.pdf
Ukraine	2004	Press Freedom During the 1994 and 1999 Presidential Elections in Ukraine: A Reverse Wave?	Olena Nikolayenko	Article analyzes postcommunist media development in Ukraine, focusing on the 1994 and 1999 presidential elections. It provides an overview of the political, economic, and legal contexts for media development in postcommunist Ukraine and shows that press freedom declined between the early and late 1990s as a result of intensified government pressure, media owners' authority over editorial content, and the persistence of Soviet rhetoric in state-owned news media.	http://www.informaworld.com/smpp/content~content=a713618949~db=all (for purchase)
Uzbekistan	2004	Memorandum on the Law of the Republic of Uzbekistan on Mass Media	Representative on Freedom of the Media of the Organization for Security and Cooperation in Europe and Article 19	Memorandum examines the 1997 law in light of international standards on freedom of expression and broadcasting regulation, with particular regard to the law's broad treatment of media regulation. Specifically, the law regulates all aspects and fields of mass media (broadcast media, print media, and otherwise) in a single set of broad provisions. The memorandum recommends that different regimes be used to regulate different media. It further expresses concerns about provisions in the law which call for content restrictions on the publication of materials, broad registration requirements, obligations for the mass media to publish corrections or responses, and language that gives the government and courts	http://www.article19.org/pdfs/analysis/uzbekistan-mass-media-law-06-2004.pdf

				the power to command publication of certain materials. The memorandum details corrective language to bring the law in line with international standards and good practices.	
Yemen	2005	Memorandum on the Draft Law on Press and Publications of the Republic of Yemen	Article 19	Memorandum seeks to contribute to the drafting process of the Law on Press and Publication by suggesting ways in which it might be brought into line with international law and standards on freedom of expression. It specifically provides recommendations on how to promote freedom of expression and of the media by encouraging changes to the several provisions that seem intended to regulate, or to control, the press.	http://www.article19.org/pdfs/analysis/draft-yemen-press-and-publications-law.pdf
Zimbabwe	2002	Memorandum on the Zimbabwean Access to Information and Privacy Bill	Article 19	Memorandum analyzes Zimbabwe's Access to Information and Privacy Bill and determines that, while it does formally establish a right to access information held by public bodies and impose limits on the collection of personal information by public bodies and the uses to which such bodies may put this information, the bill contains provisions that restrict freedom of expression. Specifically, the memorandum reports that the bill's provisions on freedom of information include extensive exclusions and exceptions; require all media outlets to obtain a registration certificate from the commission, which has broad regulatory powers and is subject to influence (or the control) of the minister responsible for information; place conditions on who may practice journalism; require all journalists to obtain accreditation from the commission; and impose broad restrictions on media content.	http://www.article19.org/pdfs/analysis/zimbabwe.foi.1.02.pdf

355

TABLE 17 Law Evincing Good Practice on Freedoms of Information, Communication, and the Press

Coverage	Year	Topic	Source	Summary	Website
Australia	1992	Radiocommu-nications Act 1992	Government of Australia	Act provides for the management of the radio-frequency spectrum. It is designed to ensure the efficient allocation and use of the spectrum to maximize the public benefit and provide an efficient, equitable, and transparent system of charging for the use of spectrum, which accounts for both commercial and noncommercial uses of the spectrum.	http://www.austlii.edu.au/au/legis/cth/consol_act/ra1992218/
Australia	1982	Freedom of Information Act 1982	Government of Australia	Act grants the right to access information in the possession of the Government of the Commonwealth, including operational documents of departments, public authorities, and documents in the possession of ministers (with certain limitations). It also vests the public with the right to seek amendments to records containing personal information that is incomplete, incorrect, out of date, or misleading. Similar legislation has been promulgated in all Australian states and territories: Australian Capital Territory (1989); New South Wales (1989); Northern Territory (2003); Queensland (1992); South Australia (1991); Tasmania (1991); Victoria (1982); and Western Australia (1992).	http://www.comlaw.gov.au/comlaw/Legislation/ActCompilation1.nsf/0/92C0277C49A2F348CA2571A8001205D0?OpenDocument
Bulgaria	2000	Access to Public Information Act	Government of Bulgaria	Act regulates and details the general right of access to public information, including administrative public information, and other forms of official information. It includes provisions to ensure administrative transparency, and includes public interest rules governing proactive disclosures.	http://www.legislationline.org/legislation.php?tid=219&lid=6453&less=false

Country	Year	Act	Government	Description	URL
Canada	1991	Broadcasting Act 1991, c. 11 (B-9.01)	Government of Canada	Act sets out a broadcasting policy for Canada and the operating procedures and policies for the Canadian Broadcasting Corporation, and also establishes a regulatory body (the Canadian Radio-television and Telecommunications Commission, or Conseil de la radiodiffusion et des télécommunications canadiennes). The act imposes a Canadian-owned and controlled system of broadcasting, and includes provisions requiring Canadian content in programming and production. The regulatory body, the Canadian Radio-television and Telecommunications Commission, regulates all Canadian broadcasting and telecommunications and enforces the rules it creates. These responsibilities include the regulation of broadcast distributors, such as regulating which channels broadcast distributors must or may offer (the body gives priority to Canadian signals), and of certain content communicated over the Internet, including audio and video, but excluding content that is primarily alphanumeric, such as emails and most webpages.	http://laws.justice.gc.ca/en/showtdm/cs/B-9.01
Canada	1985	Access to Information Act (R.S., 1985, c. A-1)	Government of Canada	Act allows Canadian citizens to request records from federal bodies, which is enforced by the Information Commissioner of Canada. Canada's various provinces and territories also have legislation that governs access to government information.	http://laws.justice.gc.ca/en/A-1/
France	1986	Freedom of Communication Act No. 86-1067 of September 30, 1986	Government of France	Act states that the Conseil supérieur de l'audiovisuel, an independent regulatory authority, guarantees the free exercise of audiovisual communication (in accordance with the terms provided for in the act).	http://www.csa.fr/upload/dossier/loi_86_english.pdf

Coverage	Year	Topic	Source	Summary	Website
India	2005	Freedom of Information Bill, 2002 (Bill No. 98-C of 2000)	Government of India	Bill grants the fundamental right of access to official information. The bill requires all government bodies or government-funded agencies to maintain all records, and to publish all relevant facts concerning important decisions and policies that affect the public, announce decisions and policies, give reasons for its decisions to those affected by these decisions, and more.	http://www.aip-bg.org/pdf/foi_india.pdf
Ireland	2003	Broadcasting Funding Act (Number 43 of 2003)	Government of Ireland	Act provides for the development of a funding scheme to support certain broadcast programs (radio and television) for the purpose of developing programs in the Irish language based on Irish culture, heritage, and experience and to develop local and community broadcasting. To accomplish these objectives, the act provides that 5 percent of the receiver set license fee paid by television viewers should be allocated to the Sound and Vision Broadcasting Funding Scheme.	http://www.bci.ie/documents/2003fundingact.pdf
Japan	2001	Law Concerning Access to Information Held by Administrative Organs	Government of Japan	Law provides for greater disclosure of information held by administrative bodies to promote accountability and civic engagement. These bodies must respond to information requests within 30 days, or otherwise request an extension. It further provides citizens with the right to appeal refusals to information requests.	http://www.crnjapan.com/japan_law/laws/en/ freeinfo.html
Lithuania	2000	Law on the Provision of Information to the Public (1996 No. I – 1418, amended 2000. No. VIII – 1595)	Government of Lithuania	Law details the rights and responsibilities of public information producers, disseminators, holders of this information, and journalists. It further sets out the procedures relating to obtaining, processing, and disseminating public information.	http://www3.lrs.lt/pls/inter2/dokpaieska.showdoc_e? p_id=101596 (see also) http://www. rtk.lt/en/

Mexico	2001	Federal Law of Transparency and Access to Public Government Information	Government of Mexico	Law grants the right to access information from state bodies, including information on agency performance, the use of public resources, and more. The law is designed to improve governmental accountability and transparency, and to combat corruption.	http://www.ifai.org.mx/publicaciones/taia.pdf
Mozambique	1992	Telecommunications Act (LAW 22/92)	Government of Mozambique	Act sets out fundamental principles relating to the establishment and management of telecommunications infrastructures and services in Mozambique. It contains provisions requiring the state to guarantee the existence and availability of a basic telecommunications service for public use, for the communications needs of citizens, and of economic and social activities.	http://www.itu.int/ITU-D/treg/Legislation/Mozambique/law.htm
Pakistan	2002	Freedom of Information Ordinance 2002 (Ordinance No. XCVI OF 2002)	Government of Pakistan	Ordinance grants improved access to public records in the interests of transparency, freedom of information, and increase the accountability of the federal government. The law specifically grants citizens the right of access to public records held by ministries, departments, boards, councils, courts, and tribunals. These bodies are obligated to respond to requests within twenty-one days, and requestors have the right to appeal refusals to information requests.	http://www.crcp.sdnpk.org/ordinance_of_2002.htm
Poland	1992	Broadcasting Act of December 29, 1992	Government of Poland	Acts sets out that the purposes of radio and television broadcasting in Poland include: providing information; ensuring access to culture and art; facilitating access to learning and scientific achievements; disseminating civil education; providing entertainment; and promoting domestic production of audiovisual works.	http://www.krrit.gov.pl/angielska/act.pdf

Coverage	Year	Topic	Source	Summary	Website
South Africa	2000	Independent Communication Authority of South Africa Act, 2000 (Act No. 13 of 2000)	Government of South Africa	Act provides for the establishment of the Independent Communications Authority of South Africa, an independent regulatory authority, dissolves the prior national broadcasting authority, and amends applicable laws to provide for the new regulatory authority. It is designed to regulate broadcasting and telecommunications in the public interest and to ensure fairness and a diversity of views broadly representing South African society.	http://www.icasa.org.za/manager/clientfiles/documents/icasa_act.pdf
South Africa	1999	Broadcasting Act (No. 4 of 1999)	Government of South Africa	Act seeks to redevelop the national broadcasting system so it might reflect the identity and diverse nature of South Africa. It establishes a broadcasting policy in the public interest for reasons that include: contributing to democracy, developing society, gender equality, nation building, and providing for education; strengthening the cultural, political, social, and economic fabric of South Africa; encouraging ownership and control of broadcasting services among historically disadvantaged groups; ensuring plurality of broadcasting content; developing human resources, training, and capacity building within the broadcasting sector, particularly among historically disadvantaged groups; ensuring fair competition in the broadcasting sector and ensuring efficient use of the broadcasting frequency spectrum; providing for a three-tier system of public, commercial, and community broadcasting services.	http://www.info.gov.za/gazette/acts/1999/a4-99.pdf
Sweden	1980	The Secrecy Act (Sekretesslagen), SFS 1980:100	Government of Sweden	Act sets out what information must be kept secret in state and municipal activities and therefore is not subject to dissemination under the Freedom of Press Act. It additionally contains provisions relating to registration, marking as secret, the authorities' obligation to provide information to the public and to each other, appeals against decisions of authorities, and more.	http://www.notisum.se/rnp/SLS/LAG/19800100.HTM (in Swedish)

Sweden	1766	The Freedom of the Press Act (Offentlighetspri ncipen) (SFS nr: 1949:105)	Government of Sweden	Act granted public access to government documents and subsequently became a key provision of the Swedish constitution. It is the first piece of freedom of information legislation in the modern sense and remains in effect. It establishes the guarantee that the general public have an unimpeded view of activities pursued by the government and local authorities and applies to all documents handled by the authorities, subject to certain explicit restrictions in subsequent legislation. Refusals to provide information, even those that fall within these restrictions, must be handled individually, and any refusal is subject to appeal.	http://www.riksdagen.se/ templates/R_Page_ 6313.aspx
Thailand	1997	Official Information Act of B.E. 2540 (1997)	Government of Thailand	Act grants the right to request official information from any state body including central, provincial, and local administrations, State enterprises, the courts, professional supervisory organizations, independent state agencies, and more (though certain independent bodies, including the Anti-corruption Commission, are not subject to the act). It requires state bodies to respond to a request for information within a "reasonable time," and certain restrictions apply.	http://www.coe.int/t/e/legal_ affairs/legal_co-operation/ data_protection/documents/ national_laws/THAI_Infoact_ BE_2540.pdf
United Kingdom	2003	Communications Act of 2003	Government of the United Kingdom	Act provides for the establishment of the Office of Communications (or "Ofcom"), an independent regulatory body. It further provides legal recognition of community radio and introduces full-time community radio services in the United Kingdom. It additionally removes certain restrictions on cross-media ownership.	http://www.opsi.gov.uk/acts/acts 2003/20030021.htm (see also) http://www. communicationsact .gov.uk/

Coverage	Year	Topic	Source	Summary	Website
United Kingdom	2000	Freedom of Information Act of 2000	Government of the United Kingdom	Act sets out the general right of access to information held by public authorities. It further requires each public body to develop and implement a publication scheme (subject to the approval of the information commissioner), which details the classes of information it will publish, applicable fees, and the manner in which it will publish this information.	http://www.opsi.gov.uk/Acts/acts2000/20000036.htm
United States	2002	The Freedom of Information Act (5 U.S.C. § 552)	Government of the United States of America	Act requires federal agencies to disclose official records requested in writing by any person (subject to nine exemptions and three exclusions contained in the act). The act applies exclusively to federal agencies and does not create a right of access to records held by Congress, by the courts, or by state or local government agencies. Each state has developed its own public access laws governing access to state and local records.	http://www.usdoj.gov/oip/foiastat.htm (see also) http://www.usdoj.gov/oip/foia_updates/Vol_XVII_4/page2.htm

TABLE 18 Mass Media and Governance

Coverage	Year	Topic	Source	Summary	Website
Global	2006	Perspectives on Advancing Governance & Development from the Global Forum for Media Development	Mark Harvey (editor) Internews Europe and the Global Forum on Media Development	Report examines the role of the media in effective development and sets out the following five core messages to the international development community: 1) Independent media are integral to good governance, and support should be mainstreamed across both policy and practice; 2) Research on the impact of media and communications on the poor needs to be strengthened; 3) Independent media systems that are inclusive and responsive to diversity play a key role in preventing the exclusion of voices that breed extremism; 4) The lack of local media coverage of the external driving forces of change on poor countries, including international trade, climate change, and global health, is generating deficits in governance through continued public disengagement in these issues; and 5) development agencies should engage the global media assistance community to contribute to the Millennium Development Goals, such as supporting media policy and legislation, the development of journalism associations, the provision of affordable capital, professional training, and the capacity-building of indigenous media assistance organizations.	http://70.87.64.34/~intint/gfmd_info/pdf/MEDIAMATTERS.pdf
Global	2004	Governance Redux: The Empirical Challenge	Daniel Kaufmann	Chapter argues that the "governance policy gap" (i.e., the underperformance of governance) persists throughout the world, despite progress made in many countries in improving the content of macroeconomic policies. It gives examples of and seeks to quantify "governance deficits," or the phenomenon in certain countries where levels of governance are insufficient to support income levels and/or growth path. It further states that firms from emerging economies identify	http://www.worldbank.org/wbi/governance/pdf/govredux.pdf

Coverage	Year	Topic	Source	Summary	Website
				corruption and excessive bureaucracy as primary constraints to business operations. Respondent firms from the OECD identify excessive bureaucracy and tax regime as top constraints. Inflation and exchange rate regimes are not rated as significant constraints to business operations.	
Global	2003	Do More Transparent Governments Govern Better? Policy Research Working Paper 3077	Roumeen Islam The World Bank	Working paper explores the link between information flows and governance (i.e., institutional quality). It states that information is crucial in economic theory, either directly, such as its effect on prices and quantities, or more indirectly, such as its effect on other factors like institutions and the quality of governance. The paper includes evidence that countries with better information flows benefit from better governance and relies on two indicators to assess these better information flows: 1) an index based on the existence of freedom of information laws; and 2) an index called the "transparency" index, which measures the frequency with which economic data are published in countries around the world.	http://www.worldbank.org/wbi/righttotelloverview.html
Global	2003	Global Corruption Report 2003	Transparency International	Report demonstrates how access to information is an effective way to combat corruption using authoritative commentary and a series of regional reports which examine how civil society, the public and private sectors, and the media might use and control information.	http://www.transparency.org/publications/gcr/download_gcr/download_gcr_2003#download (available in English, Spanish, French, Russian, Portuguese, German, and Japanese)
Global	2003	The Media's Role: Covering or Covering Up Corruption?	Bettina Peters Transparency International	Working paper examines the phenomenon of political manipulation of news and public debate, media ownership concentration, the role of advertising and corrupt journalistic practices, and challenges faced by the media sector, including	http://unpan1.un.org/intradoc/groups/public/documents/APCITY/UNPAN008437.pdf

Region	Year	Title	Author	Description	URL
				censorship, blocked access to official information, defamation laws and other legal restriction, abuse of media services such as printing presses, lack of training, and lack of investment in investigative reporting. It notes that political and private manipulation of the media is more pronounced in countries where democratic culture is not well established.	http://www.nber.org/papers/w9309
Global	2002	The Corporate Governance Role of the Media	Alexander Dyck and Luigi Zingales	Working paper examines the role of the media in pressuring corporate managers and directors to adopt socially acceptable behavior. It provides anecdotal and systematic evidence of mass media's effect on companies' policy toward the environment and the amount of corporate resources that are diverted to the advantage of controlling shareholders. The paper's conclusions are designed to inform the corporate governance debate and to guide reforms aimed at improving corporate governance around the world.	
Global	2002	Peace Journalism: Negotiating Global Media Ethics	Majid Tehranian	Article provides an overview of the importance of ethically responsible journalism, which, it argues, has been driven by individual journalists. It states that in light of globalization, media ethics should be negotiated professionally, as well as institutionally, nationally, and internationally, based on international agreements that establish the right to communicate as a human right. It further calls for a pluralism of media structures at the local, national, and international levels. The article concludes with proposals to promote peace journalism through greater freedom, balance, and diversity in media representations.	http://hij.sagepub.com/cgi/content/abstract/7/2/58 (for purchase)

Coverage	Year	Topic	Source	Summary	Website
Global	2000	The Media's Role in Curbing Corruption	Rick Stapenhurst, The World Bank	Working paper examines how the media have exposed corrupt officials, prompted investigations by official bodies, reinforced the work and legitimacy of both parliaments and their anticorruption bodies, and pressured for change to laws and regulations that create a climate favorable to corruption. It additionally explores how the media might be strengthened, highlighting private versus public ownership, the need for improved protection of journalists who investigate corruption, press freedom, and media accountability.	http://siteresources.worldbank.org/WBI/Resources/wbi37158.pdf
Central America	2002	The Politics of Coercion: Advertising, Media and State Power in Central America	Rick Rockwell and Noreene Janus	Article reviews the type of media controls used by various countries in Central America during a transition from decades of war to a period of democratization. It traces the strong role of central governments in Guatemala, El Salvador, and Nicaragua in checking media that sought a more independent role, and shows how advertising and other constraints of the market system have been used to restrict free speech, which has impeded movement toward real democracy in each of these nations, despite trends elsewhere for more open media systems.	http://jou.sagepub.com/content/abstract/3/3/331 (for purchase)
Eastern Europe	1998	Communism, Capitalism, and the Mass Media	Colin Sparks	Book examines the impact of the collapse of communism on the media systems of Eastern Europe, with specific regard to the changes themselves and their implications for exposing flaws in accounts of the end of communism. It argues that the collapse of communist systems demonstrates how limited and frequently incorrect the main ways of discussing the mass media actually are. It concludes with an examination of the ways in which current thinking should be modified in light of these developments.	http://www.sagepub.com/booksProdDesc.nav?prodId=Book205374 (for purchase)

Region	Year	Author	Description	URL
Europe	2001	N.J. Thogersen, with B. Caremier and J. Wyles	White Paper on European Governance Work Area No. 1: Broadening and Enriching the Public Debate on European Matters. White paper examines barriers to participation in public dialogue, discussion, and debate among European countries and offers recommendations on improving the quality of exchanges of information, thought, and opinion among the EU. The paper was designed to provide recommendations on how to transform the citizens of the European Union into actors in a cooperative European political process, and it thus analyzes barriers to the flow and accessibility of information on European matters. The recommendations include strategies to combat linguistic, cultural, political, and institutional barriers; the establishment of partnership networks, cooperation between civil society and institutions; and developing a professional proactive communications strategy.	http://ec.europa.eu/governance/areas/group1/report_en.pdf
India	2000	Timothy Besley and Robin Burgess	The Political Economy of Government Responsiveness: Theory and Evidence from India. Working paper provides an overview of the types of institutions that might enhance government responsiveness to citizens' needs, using India as a case study. It concludes that information flows relating to policy actions are necessary to increase government responsiveness, and that the mass media in particular can create incentives for governments to respond to citizens' needs.	http://econ.lse.ac.uk/~tbesley/papers/media.pdf
Sierra Leone	2001	Developing Radio Partners	Sierra Leone: Using Radio to Fight Corruption. Webpage provides a case study of how independent radio stations in Sierra Leone combat corruption, help to civically engage listeners, and help to increase their self-determination.	http://www.developingradiopartners.org/caseStudies/sierraLeone.html
United Kingdom	2005	Toby Mendel The World Bank and The Commonwealth Parliamentary Association	Parliament and Access to Information: Working for Transparent Governance. Report recommends ways in which parliamentarians in all Commonwealth jurisdictions might contribute to transparent governance.	http://siteresources.worldbank.org/WBI/Resources/Parliament_and_Access_to_Information_with_cover.pdf

TABLE 19 Mass Media and Democratization

Coverage	Year	Topic	Source	Summary	Website
Global	2005	The Internet and Democracy: Global Catalyst or Democratic Dud? (Research Publication No. 2005)	Michael Best and Keegan Wade The Berkman Center for Internet & Society (Harvard Law School)	Study examines the global effect of the Internet on democracy from 1992 to 2002, by observing the relationships between measures related to democracy and Internet prevalence. It concludes that a correlation exists between Internet penetration and a nation's level of democratization, and demonstrates that this correlation is consistent even where contributing elements, such as a nation's geographic region, economic level, and social development, are variable.	http://cyber.law.harvard.edu/home/uploads/503/12-InternetDemocracy.pdf
Global	2004	Critical Social Movements and Media Reform	Robert A. Hackett and William K. Carroll The World Association for Christian Communication	Article examines the relationship between critical social movements, specifically those relating to the empowerment of the marginalized and challenging the hegemonies of dominant groups and institutions, and media reform to promote democratic principles. It recommends that critical social movements use media to gain standing in the public domain, become mobilized to attract support, and to achieve some measure of validation within mainstream news discourse.	http://www.wacc.org.uk/wacc/publications/media_development/archive/2004_1/critical_social_movements_and_media_reform
Global	2003	Media, Democratization, and Regulation	Marc Raboy	Excerpt examines perspectives on media and democratization in terms of democratizing media and fostering a role for media in the democratization of societies. It states that media democratization is possible where the following five types of intervention are present and led by five sets of actors: 1) ongoing critical analysis of media issues (researchers); 2) media literacy efforts (educators); 3) building and operating of autonomous media (alternative media practitioners);	http://media.mcgill.ca/files/Raboy_CFSC.pdf

Global	2002	Human Development Report 2002: Deepening Democracy in a Fragmented World	Sakiko Fukuda-Parr et al. United Nations Development Programme (UNDP)	4) progressive practices within mainstream media (journalists, editors, publishers, etc.); and 5) policy intervention (media policy activists). The excerpt further examines the following four formal attempts to influence media development: 1) the libertarian approach; 2) self-regulation; 3) the closed club, or top-down institutional model; and 4) the institutional approach.	http://hdr.undp.org/reports/global/2002/en/pdf/complete.pdf
				Report provides a broad assessment of poverty reduction efforts and the promotion of equitable growth against United Nations development objectives, including the Millennium Development Goals, with particular regard to building strong forms of democratic governance at all levels of society in the developing world. The report includes remarks on the importance of free, independent media as crucial pillars of democracy.	
Global	2001	Media Reform: Democratizing Media, Democratizing the State	Monroe Price, Beata Rozumilowicz, and Stefaan Verhulst	Book examines how changes in the political and institutional structures in countries that are undergoing a transition toward democracy affect the relationships between the domestic media and the public, the state, and their counterparts abroad. It examines the impact of media on democratization in a series of countries emerging from extended periods of authoritarian rule.	
Global	1999	The Role of Media in Democracy: A Strategic Approach	Center for Democracy and Governance United States Agency for International Development	Working paper provides an overview to rationales used by USAID to determine support for media freedom around the world. Specifically, USAID uses five approaches to media support activities: 1) reforming media law; 2) strengthening constituencies for reform; 3) removing barriers to access; 4) training; and 5) supporting the capitalization of media. Using these approaches, USAID seeks to move media sectors in	http://www.usaid.gov/our_work/democracy_and_governance/publications/pdfs/pnace630.pdf

Coverage	Year	Topic	Source	Summary	Website
				developing countries away from government or private control, toward serving the public interest, which is characterized by editorial independence.	http://gaz.sagepub.com/cgi/content/abstract/60/2/167 (for purchase)
Global	1998	Public Broadcasting and the Global Framework of Media Democrati-zation	Marc Raboy	Article provides an overview of how and why public broadcasting is a key institution of democratization in the context of globalization, where media power and activity increasingly shifts from the national to the transnational. It argues that public broadcasting is essential to the promotion of pluralism in the public sphere, particularly in light of the increasing commercialization of media. It additionally examines challenges faced by public broadcasting, including multilateral politics.	
Global	1963	Communications and Political Development	Lucian Pye (editor)	Book examines the relationship between communication, modernization, and globalization.	
Africa	2001	The Media and Democrati-zation in Africa: Contributions, Constraints, and Concerns of the Private Press	Wisdom Tettey	Article provides an overview on how private media in Africa contribute toward democratic governance and accountability on the part of state officials, as well as of challenges associated with this process. It suggests the private media reform aspects of its operation to better promote the development of an informed and responsible citizenry, which will promote the democratic discourse.	http://mcs.sagepub.com/cgi/content/abstract/23/1/5 (for purchase) Asia

2001	Beyo nd Orie ntalist Discourses: Media and Democracy in Asia	Chin-Chuan Lee	Article examines media and democracy in Asia, which are discussed in light of the variety of the experience of Asia and ostensible shortcomings of democratization in some Asian countries. It also analyzes barriers to effective relationships between the state and media outlets, relating to market conditions, globalization, and democratic principles.	http://www.javnost-thepublic.org/ media/datoteke/ 2001-2-lee.pdf Asia
1999	Asian NICs´ Broadcast Media in the Era of Globalization: The Trend of Commercializa- tion and Its Impact, Implications, and Limits	Junhao Hong and Yu-Chiung Hsu	Study examines the trend, impact, and implications of commercialization in the broadcast media in Asia's four newly industrialized countries: Taiwan, South Korea, Singapore, and Hong Kong. It specifically examines the "Asian characteristics" of media commercialization and their significance and limits. The report concludes that: 1) the trend of media liberalization and deregulation in Asia's four newly industrialized countries has been primarily manifested through media commercialization; and 2) media commercialization in the Asian political and social context is particularly significant because that media commercialization is an alternative or indirect way to achieve media democratization, which, the report states, is the first step toward political and social democratization.	http://gaz.sagepub.com/cgi/ content/abstract/61/3-4/225 (for purchase)
Chile 2003	The Media and the Neoliberal Transition in Chile: Democratic Promise Unfulfilled	Rosalind Bresnahan Latin American Perspectives, Inc.	Report draws on 1998–2002 interviews with media professionals, grassroots activists, and policy makers to compare the Chilean *Concertación de partidos por la Democracia*'s market- based idea of media democratization with democratic media theorists' public sphere model. It examines the changing legal framework for the Chilean media, trends in media ownership, and the development of grassroots and community-based media sectors. It also argues that since *Concertación* pursued a free market model approach to the role of the media (rather	http://lap.sagepub.com/cgi/ reprint/30/6/39.pdf

Coverage	Year	Topic	Source	Summary	Website
				than a public sphere approach), Chile's media sector currently caters to international investors and internal political interests, which has restricted media outlets from providing human rights advocates, opponents of neoliberalism, and other progressives with the opportunity to express themselves, which has been a barrier to further effective democratization in Chile. The report concludes that democracy in Chile would be best served by government support for an independent media sector and cultivation of the emerging community media sector.	
China	2001	Media and Elusive Democracy in China	Yuezhi Zhao	Study examines media and democratization in China from historical and contemporary perspectives, with specific regard to how the concept of democracy underwent several transformations during the last half of the 20th century in China. It additionally assesses China's current state-controlled and commercialized media, which, it states, is embedded in the established market authoritarian social order.	http://www.javnost-thepublic.org/media/datoteke/2001-2-zhao.pdf
Eastern Europe	2004	Between Reality and Dream: Eastern European Media Transition, Transformation, Consolidation, and Integration	Peter Gross American Council of Learned Societies	Article examines progress made in the transition and transformation of Eastern Europe's news media and the potential for its integration into the Western European media scene.	http://eep.sagepub.com/cgi/reprint/18/1/110.pdf

	Year	Title	Author	Description	URL
Ghana and Nigeria	2004	Democratization and the Media in West Africa: An Analysis of Recent Constitutional and Legislative Reforms for Press Freedom in Ghana and Nigeria	Chris Ogbondah	Article provides an overview of the democratization movement throughout Africa, with particular regard to efforts in Ghana and Nigeria to establish democratic institutions, and examines constitutional and legislative initiatives that have augmented media development and freedom in both countries. It additionally provides a series of recommendations for creating even greater press freedoms in both countries.	http://www.africaresource.com/war/issue6/ogbondah.html
Mexico	2003	From the Inside Out: How Institutional Entrepreneurs Transformed Mexican Journalism	Sallie Hughes	Article provides an overview of how to create democratic news media that foster participatory citizenship and government accountability, using the case study of Mexico. The media and journalism sectors in Mexico underwent a series of disparate transformations which resulted in the dissolution of a previously authoritarian institution into three competing models of news production with different sociopolitical implications.	http://hij.sagepub.com/cgi/content/abstract/8/3/87 (for purchase)
Middle East	2001	Mediated Culture in the Middle East: Diffusion, Democracy, Difficulties	Annabelle Sreberny	Article provides an overview of the recent developments in media in the Middle East and focuses on the dynamics of democratization, gender participation, and Internet access in the Middle East.	http://gaz.sagepub.com/cgi/content/abstract/63/2-3/101 (for purchase)

Coverage	Year	Topic	Source	Summary	Website
Middle East and North Africa	1958	The Passing of Traditional Society: Modernizing the Middle East	Daniel Lerner	Book introduces the concept of development communication. It traces correlations between expanded economic activity and a series of modernization variables, including urbanization, high literacy levels, media consumption, and political development. The book concludes that the media might serve as a great multiplier of development by communicating development messages to the undeveloped.	http://gaz.sagepub.com/cgi/content/abstract/64/1/21 (for purchase)
Southern Africa	2002	Theorizing the Media—Democracy Relationship in Southern Africa	Guy Berger	Article examines and seeks to provide a theoretical foundation for the role of media in African democratization, with particular regard to the functions of the public sphere and civil society. It provides perspectives on contemporary issues regarding media freedom, the growth of private media, the contests around government-controlled media, and broadcast deregulation in Africa.	http://iipor.oxfordjournals.org/cgi/content/abstract/13/4/355 (for purchase)
South Africa	2001	Serving a New Democracy: Must the Media "Speak Softly"? Learning from South Africa	Andrew Kuper and Jocelyn Kuper	Article examines the need of populations in democratizing environments, using South Africa as a primary case study, for an independent media sector. It maps the perspectives of populations in democratizing environments with specific regard to notions of protective rights, personal autonomy, and civic belonging, and identifies the forms of media that inform these perspectives. The article also provides an overview of how media outlets enhance personal freedom and political effectiveness and thus promote democratic constructiveness and commercial success.	

South Africa	1999	The Limits of Media Democratization in South Africa: Politics, Privatization, and Regulation	Clive Barnett	Article provides an overview of processes that have limited the development of a democratic media system in post-apartheid South Africa. It analyzes how the privatization of radio stations in 1996 yielded to the political tensions that shape media reform, and argues that the progress of democratic broadcasting reform in the country is increasingly being dictated by the state's program for restructuring the telecommunications sector.	http://mcs.sagepub.com/cgi/content/abstract/21/5/649 (for purchase)
Thailand	2001	Regulation, Reform, and the Question of Democratizing the Broadcast Media in Thailand	Ubonrat Siriyuvasak	Study examines the struggle for the democratization of the broadcast media in the context of the social and political reform in Thailand during 1997 to 2000. It demonstrates that Thailand has been cautious in its proposal to liberalize political and cultural expressions, which has constrained citizens' right to communicate.	http://www.javnost-thepublic.org/media/datoteke/2001-2-siriyuvasak.pdf

TABLE 20 Cases and Comments on Freedoms of Expression, Communication, and the Press

Coverage	Year	Source	Website
Argentina	1998	*Petric v. Página 12*, Fallos 315:1492 (April 16, 1998) (CSJN)	http://www.abogarte.com.ar/csjncidh.htm (in Spanish)
Argentina	1992	*Ekmekdjian v. Sofovich*, Fallos 315:1492 (July 7, 1992) (CSJN)	http://www.todoelderecho.com/Apuntes/Fallos/Fallos%20Nacionales/Apuntes/EKMEKDJIANsofovich.htm (in Spanish)
Australia	1997	*David Russell Lange v Australian Broadcasting Corporation* [1997] HCA 25 (July 8, 1997)	http://www.austlii.edu.au/au/cases/cth/HCA/1997/25.html
Canada	1992	*Her Majesty The Queen v. Butler* [1992] 1 S.C.R. 452	http://scc.lexum.umontreal.ca/en/1992/1992rcs1-452/1992rcs1-452.pdf
Canada	1990	*Her Majesty The Queen v. James Keegstra* [1990] 3 S.C.R.	http://hatemonitor.csusb.edu/other_countries_cases/R_v_Keegstra_1990_3SCR.html
Costa Rica	2004	*Herrera-Ulloa vs. Costa Rica* (July 2, 2004) Series C, No. 107	http://www.cpj.org/news/2004/seriec_107_esp.pdf (in Spanish) (see also) http://www.justiceinitiative.org/db/resource2?res_id=102157
European Court of Human Rights	2003	*Refah Partisi and others v. Turkey* (February 13, 2003) Application Nos. 41340/98, 41342/98, 41343/98 and 41344/98 (European Court of Human Rights)	http://www.echr.coe.int/eng/Press/2003/feb/RefahPartisiGCjudgmenteng.htm
European Court of Human Rights	2002	*Nikula v. Finland* (March 21, 2002) Application No. 31611/96 (European Court of Human Rights)	http://www.echr.coe.int/eng/Press/2002/mar/Nikulajudepress.htm
European Court of Human Rights	2002	*Dichand and others v. Austria*, Application No. 29271/95 (European Court of Human Rights)	http://www.echr.coe.int/eng/Press/2002/feb/Austrianjudsepress.htm

European Court of Human Rights	1998	*Incal v Turkey*, Application No. 22678/93 (European Court of Human Rights)	http://www.bailii.org/eu/cases/ECHR/1998/48.html
European Court of Human Rights	1996	*Goodwin v. the United Kingdom* (March 27, 1996) Application No. 17488/90 (European Court of Human Rights)	http://hei.unige.ch/~clapham/hrdoc/docs/echrgoodwincase.txt
European Court of Human Rights	1993	*Informationsverein Lentia and Others v Austria* - 13914/88;15041/89; 15717/89 (European Court of Human Rights)	http://www.bailii.org/eu/cases/ECHR/1993/57.html
European Court of Human Rights	1991	*Observer and Guardian v United Kingdom*, Application No. 13585/88 (European Court of Human Rights)	http://www.bailii.org/eu/cases/ECHR/1991/49.html
European Court of Human Rights	1986	*Lingens v. Austria*, (July 8, 1986) Application No. 9815/82 (European Court of Human Rights)	http://www.legislationline.org/legislation.php?tid=219&tid=7137&less=false
India	1985	*Samaresh Bose & Another v. Amal Mitra & Another* [1985] INSC 205 (September 24, 1985)	http://www.worldlii.org/in/cases/INSC/1985/205.html
India	1970	*K. A. Abbas v. Union of India & Another* [1970] INSC 202; [1971] 2 SCR 446; [1970] 2 SCC 780; AIR 1971 SC 481 (September 24, 1970)	http://www.austlii.edu.au/~andrew/CommonLII/INSC/1970/202.html
Inter-American Court of Human Rights	2003	*Yatama v Nicaragua* (June 23, 2003) (Inter-American Court of Human Rights)	http://www.corteidh.or.cr/docs/casos/articulos/seriec_127_esp.pdf (in Spanish)
International Criminal Tribunal for the Former Yugoslavia	2002	*Prosecutor v. Radoslav Brdjanin & Momir Talic* ("Randal Case"), The Hague (December 11, 2002) IL / P.I.S / 715-e (International Criminal Tribunal for the Former Yugoslavia)	http://www.un.org/icty/pressreal/p715-e.htm

Coverage	Year	Source	Website
Italy	2000	Cassazione Sezione Quinta Penale n. 2144 del 25 febbraio 2000	http://www.legge-e-giustizia.it/2000%20DOCUMENTI/11maggio.htm (in Italian)
Malawi	1999	*Kafumba and others v. The Electoral Commission and Malawi Broadcasting Corporation*, Miscellaneous Cause Number 35 of 1999.	http://ifex.org/da/layout/set/print/content/view/full/8002/
New Zealand	2000	*D. R. Lange v J. B. Atkinson & Another* [2000] NZCA 95 (June 21, 2000)	http://www.nzlii.org/nz/cases/NZCA/2000/95.html
South Africa	1946	*Die Spoorbond v. South African Railways*, 1946 (2) SALR 999 (S. Afr.)	http://www.article19.org/pdfs/analysis/defamation-standards.pdf
Sri Lanka	1992	*Sirisena v. Ginige* [1992] LKCA 12; (1992) 1 Sri L.R. 320 (June 6, 1992)	http://www.asianlii.org/cgi-asianlii/ disp.pl/lk/cases/LKCA/1992/12.html?query=320
Uganda	2004	*Onyango-Obbo and Muenda v. AG*, Constitutional Appeal No. 2, 2002, February 11, 2004	http://www.article19.org/pdfs/cases/uganda-onyango-obbo-v-uganda.%20Uganda (see also) http://www.ifex.org/alerts/ layout/set/print/content/view/full/5676/
United Kingdom	1969	*Vine Products Ltd v Mackenzie & Co Ltd* [1967] FSR 402, [1969] RPC 1	http://www.lawteacher.net/cases/comp3.htm/file-14.html
United Nations Human Rights Committee	2000	*Vladimir Petrovich Laptsevich v. Belarus*, Communication No. 780/1997, U.N. Doc. CCPR/C/68/D/780/1997 (2000)	http://www1.umn.edu/humanrts/undocs/session68/view780.htm
United States	1990	*Milkovich v. Lorain Journal*, 497 US 1 (1990)	http://supreme.justia.com/us/497/1/case.html
United States	1978	*Houchins v. KQED, Inc.*, 438 US 1 (1978)	http://supreme.justia.com/us/438/1/

United States	1974	*Miami Herald Publishing Co. v. Tornillo*, 418 U.S. 241 (1974)	http://caselaw.lp.findlaw.com/scripts/getcase.pl?court=US&vol=418&invol=241
United States	1971	*Monitor Patriot Co. v. Roy*, 401 US 265 (1971)	http://supreme.justia.com/us/401/265/case.html
United States	1969	*Red Lion Broadcasting Co. v. FCC*, 395 U.S. 367 (1969)	http://caselaw.lp.findlaw.com/scripts/getcase.pl?navby=case&court=US&vol=395&page=367
United States	1967	*Curtis Publishing Co. v. Butts*, 388 US 130 (1967)	http://supreme.justia.com/us/388/130/case.html
United States	1964	*New York Times Co. v. Sullivan*, 376 U.S. 254 (1964)	http://caselaw.lp.findlaw.com/scripts/getcase.pl?court=US&vol=376&invol=254
Zimbabwe	1996	*Retrofit (PVT) LTD v Posts and Telecommunications Corporation* 1996 (1) SA 847	http://www.hrcr.org/safrica/expression/retrofit_telecomm.html
Zimbabwe	1997	*Posts and Telecommunications Co. v. Modus Publications (Private) Ltd.*, November 25, 1997, No. SC 199/97	http://www.article19.org/pdfs/analysis/defamation-standards.pdf
Zimbabwe	2001	*Capital Radio (Pvt) Ltd v. Broadcasting Authority of Zimbabwe*, Judgment No. SC 162/2001	http://www.article19.org/pdfs/cases/zimbabwe-capital-radio-v-broadcasting-authori.pdf
Zimbabwe	2000	*Chavunduka and Choto v. Minister of Home Affairs and Attorney-General*, May 22, 2000, Judgment No. S.C. 36/2000	http://www.article19.org/pdfs/cases/zimbabwe-chavunduka-and-choto-v.-zimbabwe.pdf

379

Index

381

About the Authors

Steve Buckley is Managing Director of CM Solutions, a media enterprise support agency, and President, since 2003, of the World Association of Community Radio Broadcasters. He is a communications policy expert and media development adviser who has worked with governments, UN agencies, and nongovernmental organizations.

Kreszentia Duer is the New Business Development Leader in the World Bank Institute and manager of its technical assistance program to strengthen policies, institutions, and capacities for Civic Engagement, Empowerment, and Respect for Diversity (CEERD) in developing countries (worldbank.org/ceerd). She has been innovating and has developed and managed World Bank country assistance programs in diverse sectors and regions for thirty years: in community driven development and broader rural and urban development, environment, social development, cultural industries, and intellectual property rights; and through CEERD, has advised and contributed to developments in education, governance and accountability, broadcasting policy and telecommunications, in Africa, Asia, Latin America, and Eastern Europe. She is a member of the Editorial Board of the journal *Policy Sciences.*

Toby Mendel is the Law/Asia Programmes Director, Article 19, Global Campaign for Free Expression. He is the author of numerous books and articles on issues such as broadcasting, the right to information, defamation, and other freedom of expression issues.

Seán Ó Siochrú is Director of NEXUS Research in Dublin, Ireland; Chair of Dublin Community Television; and a spokesperson for the campaign for Communication Rights in the Information Society (CRIS). He has published many books, chapters, and articles on media and communication issues and works with international agencies and nongovernmental organizations across the world.

Monroe E. Price is Director of the Center for Global Communication Studies at the Annenberg School for Communication at the University of Pennsylvania, Professor of Law at Cardozo School of Law, and Director of the Stanhope Centre for Communications Policy Research in London.

Marc Raboy is the Beaverbrook Chair in Ethics, Media and Communications and is a Professor in the Department of Art History and Communication Studies at McGill University, Montreal, Canada. He has been a consultant to various international organizations, including the World Bank, UNESCO, the Council of Europe, and the European Broadcasting Union, and is the author and editor of numerous books and articles on media and communication policy.